The Struggle for Peace
in the Middle East

Mahmoud Riád with Gamal Abdel Nasser

MAHMOUD RIAD

The Struggle for Peace
in the Middle East

Quartet Books
London   Melbourne   New York

First published in Great Britain
by Quartet Books Ltd, 1981
A member of the Namara Group
27 Goodge Street, London W1P 1FD

ISBN 0 7043 2297 8

Typeset, printed and bound in Great Britain by
Mackays of Chatham Ltd,
Lordswood, Chatham, Kent ME5 8TD

TO SAWSAN, who has had to put up with the hectic life being a diplomat's wife entails, who has faced living out of a suitcase with equanimity, who has been shuttled round the world at my side with scarcely a pause for breath and certainly without a proper holiday, I dedicate this book with my love and my thanks.

Contents

Foreword

This foreword serves to introduce the book and its author to the reader. In it, I do not attempt to record all the events of which I have been a contemporary and in which I have been involved with varying degrees of responsibility from 1948 until 1979 – a period which witnessed four wars between Israel and the Arab countries, and during which I was closely involved in the Palestine question in all its political and human aspects.

Also during that period, I was a close witness of the struggle waged by the Arab countries to rid themselves of imperialist rule and foreign domination. I was able to observe the struggle amongst the major powers to acquire influence in the Arab region. I was a contemporary also of inter-Arab differences which occasionally boiled over into armed hostility. To put all those events on record would need more than a single volume and many years of sustained work.

The tragedy of Palestine, which I have watched closely since 1948, has however been my main concern and thinking throughout that period. I saw Palestine when its people were struggling for independence, then when Zionism succeeded in seizing part of its territory, and finally when it gained control of the whole of it. I therefore decided that this book should concentrate on the Arab–Israeli conflict that was caused by the Palestine issue. I have refrained from giving a historical study of the issue, which has been the subject of detailed dissertations in a number of languages, and have concentrated on the stages of the conflict and the many attempts at establishing peace which have been forfeited. Such attempts are still being tried without success in spite of the lapse of thirty years. I saw also the importance of explaining the role of the major powers who inflamed the problem and nourished the Arab–Israeli conflict, and the leading role played by the United States in the continuation of this strife until the present day.

I began considering the writing of this book in response to repeated suggestions by some friends, among whom were a number of Arab Foreign Ministers, to put on record the events I was a witness to during the last thirty years. At the time I used to explain that I could not do that while I occupied the post of Secretary-General of the League of Arab States.

After I resigned I came to London to spend my first holiday since I began my political career, when I met with some friends who reminded me of my promise. Other British friends, some of whom were established writers, urged me to commence and offered valuable suggestions. I began to consider the matter seriously and finally decided to begin when I recalled the story of the Arab scholar who was invited by an American university to lecture on the Arab–Israeli conflict, expounding each party's point of view. He consulted the university's library, to discover a multitude of books written on the issue by Israeli statesmen but none by any Arab attempting to give his version of the events so elaborately dealt with in the Israeli accounts.

When I began working on the book I had to face another problem. Whereas Arab friends advised that I should not limit myself to any specific number of pages, my British publishers felt that the English version had to be more concentrated; events which had no interest to the non-Arab reader had to be expunged while the main theme and general tone of the book should be maintained.

The work has imposed an effort and time that surpassed all my expectations. However, I have striven all along to explain, in the light of personal experience, the dangers to Arab security that can only be met with unified, concerted and organized inter-Arab activity.

I am hopeful that the English version of this book will give its English-speaking readers some insight into the hopes, the wishes and the aspirations, perhaps into the workings of the mind, of one Egyptian diplomat who was fortunate enough to be present, and to have some influence, during a period of shattering importance to all Middle Eastern countries. If all I have done is to have redressed the balance a little, then I shall be satisfied.

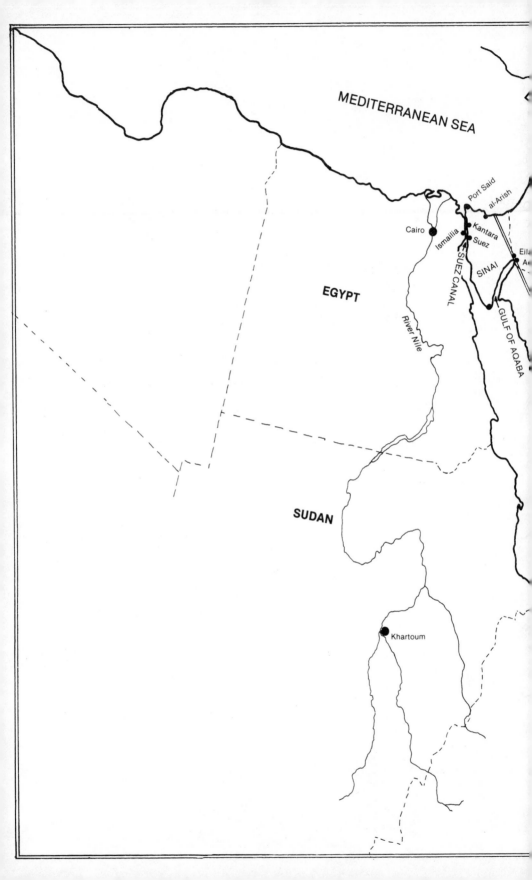

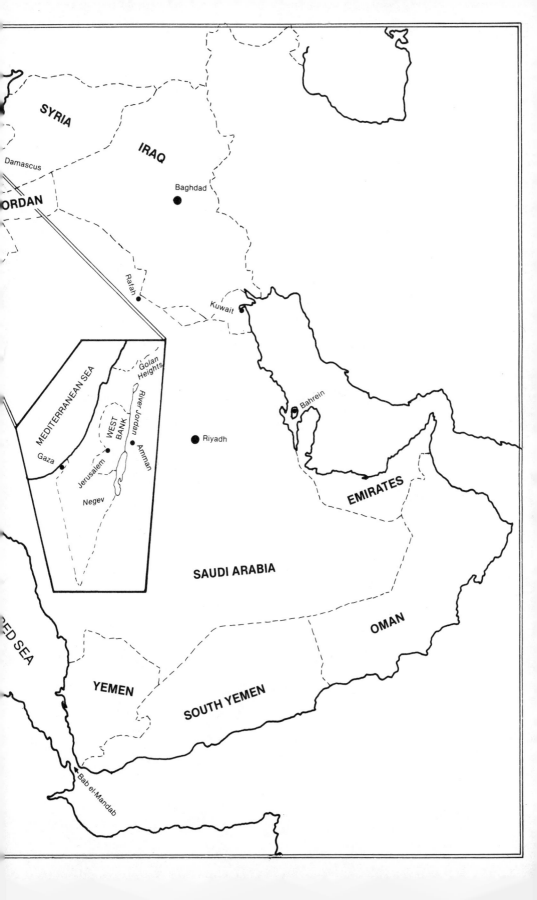

The Struggle for Peace
in the Middle East

1

Towards 1967

I was appointed head of the military intelligence office in Gaza in August 1948. This was not my first exposure to the Palestinian situation. I had been there twice before, in 1943 as a member of a study group of the Military Staff College, and in 1945 as a teacher at the Military College to supervise the military manoeuvres that cadets had to undertake before graduation. On both occasions I had been aware of a façade of peace and tranquillity imposed by the war conditions behind which lurked a gathering storm.

Since the early years of the twentieth century the Arabs had joined other nationalists in seeking their independence, and lent their total support to the Sherif of Mecca, Hussein, the great-grandfather of the present King of Jordan, in his revolt during the First World War on the side of the Allies, for promises made to the Sherif by Britain that not only would their independence be achieved but equally the long-aspired-for dream of Arab unity. The people of Palestine threw their weight behind the Arab Revolution, to discover, once the War was over, that together with the British promise for Arab independence and unity, Britain had also concluded a secret agreement with France, the Sykes–Picot, for the partitioning with France of Arab countries under Ottoman rule and a third pledge, the Balfour Declaration, promising the Jews a homeland in Palestine.

Palestinian revolutions for independence continued in the 1920s and 1930s. In 1936, when the menacing dimensions of the Balfour Declaration became apparent, with Jewish immigration reaching 400,000 persons, a nationwide armed revolution broke out to reiterate the demand for independence and an end to Jewish immigration. It was of such proportions that the British government felt forced to call upon Arab kings and Heads of State to intercede for a restoration of stability, in exchange for a promise to send a Royal Commission to satisfy the Palestinian demands.

In July 1937, the Royal Commission to Palestine proposed (the underlying cause of the revolution continuing to be the desire for national independence and fear of the Jewish National Home) the partition of the country into separate Jewish and Arab States. The Palestinian Arabs objected strongly to the idea of partition, intensifying their attacks against the British. The reaction of the mandatory authorities was violent: the Arab Higher Committee which led the Palestinian independence movement was declared unlawful, its leaders were arrested, deported or forced to flee the country, and the death penalty was imposed on any Arab carrying weapons. Arab leaders were dispersed and Arabs stripped of their weapons, at a time when the British mandate was helping to build the Jewish Agency into a quasi-government and training and arming the military arm of the Jewish Agency.

With the clouds of the Second World War looming over the skies of Europe and Britain anxious to bring about a degree of stability to a turbulent Palestine, Britain's Prime Minister Chamberlain in February 1939 invited delegations representing the Arab people of Palestine and Arab States to a round-table conference. In the course of the debates Chamberlain declared that he was inclined to grant Palestine independence after a period of transition. In May 1939, Britain issued the White Paper which expounded its policy in Palestine: the establishment of an independent Palestinian State in which both Arabs and Jews would participate after a ten-year transitional period, the restriction of Jewish immigration over a five-year period, and stringent restrictions to be placed on land sales to Jews in certain areas and complete prohibition in others.

My first two visits to Palestine were during a period when most of the Arabs had come to consider the 1939 White Paper as a British policy pledge and there were no disturbances to speak of, which left me with the impression that perhaps peace would prevail and the Jews and the Arabs would eventually come to terms and would co-exist in an independent unified State.

When I arrived in 1948, it was a different picture altogether. The Palestinian leaders I met were filled with a deep sense of bitterness and rancour over the policy of the British government that had led to the establishment of the Jewish State and their dispersal and the loss of their lands.

The Mayor of Gaza drove me in his car to an elevated spot on the outskirts of Gaza where he stopped the car and, pointing to the lands and villages that extended some kilometres east of Gaza, he said: 'These are our fields that sustained us, these are our villages where we lived, now all seized by Israel.' He accompanied me then to a huge camp which contained tens of thousands of refugees living in tents; he said that their number in the Gaza Strip alone exceeded a quarter of a million out of a total of a million refugees dispersed everywhere.

The two sights illustrated to me in a poignant manner the dimension of the problem that the Palestinians were living in and the extent of the injustice that had been inflicted on them.

The United Nations' partition resolution of 29 November 1947 was the green light for unleashing the Haganah, the military arm of the Jewish Agency, which began a series of attacks on Arab villages to force their inhabitants to flee the country. This soon escalated into massacres by the Irgun, led by Menachem Begin, among which was the Deir Yassin massacre in April 1948, where 254 of the inhabitants of the village, men, women and children, were slaughtered and their bodies thrown into the village well. The British authorities did not attempt to stop the carnage which forced the Palestinians to flee to the neighbouring Arab countries; Palestinian appeals to Arab countries to come to their help continued.

The Egyptian government had decided previously not to engage in military operations outside Egyptian territories and Nokrashi Pasha, then Prime Minister of Egypt, informed an Arab League meeting in October 1947 accordingly. King Abdel Aziz of Saudi Arabia, aware of the weakness of Arab armies at the time, was of the same opinion, maintaining instead that Arab countries should confine their support to extending all possible help to the Palestinians to enable them to resist with their own strength the attacks of Jewish military forces.

When the situation grew more serious, Egypt moved a brigade group of 3,000 soldiers to al-Arish in a military demonstration. In the meantime the Egyptian government tried to dissuade the British authorities from withdrawing their forces before providing for the safety of the Arab inhabitants; but Britain insisted on its position. The Egyptian government was unable to close its ears to the appeals for help of the Palestinians against the Jewish massacres and had to respond to a resolution by the Arab countries to dispatch her brigade group stationed at al-Arish into Palestine to restore peace and safeguard Arab lives, in the absence of any authority responsible for law and order. Thus began the armed conflict between Israel and the Arab countries.

The Arab forces restricted their operations mostly to the area allotted to the Palestinian Arabs in the Partition resolution while Ben Gurion was striving to enlarge the Jewish area. At the same time he was refusing to define the borders of Israel, which made her the only country in the United Nations even today without defined borders, while from the international point of view her borders are those defined by the Partition resolution.

The British government undoubtedly bears the responsibility for the Jewish–Palestinian/Arab conflict, forfeiting all opportunities for achieving peace; this has caused irreparable harm to the people in the area and has resulted in impairing British interests, especially economic interests, in the area, not to speak of the damage to the economic interests of a number of countries of the world as a result of the wars in the Middle East.

The Security Council's repeated resolutions led to the halting of hostilities on all fronts, and an Israeli delegation and an Egyptian delegation met at Rhodes to negotiate an armistice; this marked the first instance of an official negotiation between Israel and an Arab country.

When we left for Rhodes to negotiate the Armistice agreement, the military engagements had ended, with Israel in possession of territories beyond the borders delineated by the Partition resolution and with its expulsion of over one million Palestinians from their towns, villages and lands, to be replaced by Jewish immigrants.

The talks began on 13 January 1949 under the supervision of Dr Ralph Bunche, the UN respresentative. The first encounter between the two delegations almost resulted in the break-up of negotiations, as a result of each party holding stubbornly to its position. Bunche resorted thereafter to indirect negotiations, moving from one party to another in an attempt to conciliate between the different points of view. After forty days the two parties reached a draft agreement, which was I charged with submitting to the Commander in Chief, General Fouad Sadek Pasha, for his views. I travelled to Rafah where the Army Command was located. The major issue that he had to judge upon was the size of Egyptian forces to be stationed in Gaza. His answer was that he could not pass judgement until he was acquainted with the political decision as to whether there was a possibility of a resumption of hostilities (in which case three brigades should be stationed in Gaza) or a permanent cessation of hostilities – when one brigade would be sufficient.

I returned the same day to Cairo and called on the Minister of War, Heidar Pasha, who suggested that we ask the Prime Minister for his views on the subject. I explained the articles of the draft agreement to the Prime Minister and referred to the remarks made by the Commander General. A discussion ensued; then the Prime Minister said that, since the agreement stipulated that the two parties refrain from a resumption of hostilities, one brigade would be enough.

I returned to Rhodes and the agreement was signed, followed by a celebratory dinner party for members of the two delegations given by Dr Bunche. The Israeli members could not conceal their joy at the results they had achieved and their expectation that the greater part of their forces could now be disbanded to return to their jobs or resume their university studies. When they learnt that Cairo had appointed me head of the Egyptian delegation to the Mixed Armistice Commission, the conversation turned to the future of peace in the area. General Yadin, who later became Deputy Prime Minister in Begin's government, talked of the Armistice Agreement as a substantial step in achieving permanent peace.

I personally left with a strong impression that armed struggle between Israel and the Arab countries was over. This impression increased when I learnt that Jordan, Lebanon and Syria had signed identical agreements.

In fact the agreements signed could be considered as a substantial step towards peace. They had stipulated the cessation of armed conflict and the restoration of peace in Palestine, that no aggressive action by armed forces be undertaken, planned or threatened against the people or the armed forces of the other party. These articles were not subject to amendment, alteration or cancellation. The agreement, in fact, was termed in its last article an attempt to 'facilitate the transition from the present truce to permanent peace in Palestine'.

In the early weeks of my new post, when the Egyptian and

Israeli delegations used to meet once a week at al-Oga under the chairmanship of a UN observer, to supervise the implementation of the Armistice Agreement, I also had an impression that Israel was desirous of respecting the articles of the agreement and maintaining peace in spite of minor Israeli violations.

Before the Armistice Commission began its activities, the UN moved to establish a Conciliation Commission composed of the United States, France and Turkey in December 1948 to supervise the implementation of the resolution relating to the refugees which stipulated their repatriation and the compensation of those who had no wish to return. The Conciliation Commission proposed a meeting in Lausanne in 1949 to be attended by the countries that had concluded armistice agreements with Israel. After a few months of negotiations, the Arab countries and Israel signed a Protocol which embodied the resolution for the partition of Palestine and the map delineating the boundaries of the two States. The act of signature amounted to a recognition of the State of Israel and an acceptance of the Partition resolution which the Arab countries had objected to in 1947. Conversely, it was an expression by Israel of its commitment to implement the UN resolutions, namely the Partition resolution and the one relating to Palestinian refugees.

This was a vital step along the road to peace which made the UN pass a resolution accepting Israel as a member of the UN on the basis of Israel's undertaking to put into effect the Partition resolution and the resolution relating to the refugees.

The Tripartite Declaration issued by the US, Britain and France in May 1950 was of even greater significance in this direction. The three powers declared their unalterable opposition to the use of force between any of the States of the area, and to take immediate action both within the UN and outside it to prevent any of these States violating frontiers or armistice lines. This declaration was tantamount to a guarantee of peace issued by three major powers, which further confirmed my conviction that we were steadily moving towards peace.

With the revolution in Egypt in July 1952, I returned to Cairo and was put in charge of the Palestine Department in the Military General Command, responsible for all aspects of the Palestinian question. From the reports reaching me I became aware of a steady build-up in Israeli military power and repeated statements by Ben Gurion over Israel's need for further territories and water resources for the settlement of more Jewish immigrants whose number, during the years 1948–53, reached the staggering total of 700,000. He also declared his rejection of UN resolutions, and thereby rendered the Conciliation Commission impotent to implement the resolution relating to the refugees.

I became disturbed at the obdurate and extremist position adopted by Ben Gurion at a time when the revolution in Egypt had concentrated all its efforts on domestic reconstruction and development.

I talked to Gamal Abdel Nasser and Abdel Hakim Amer more than once, urging the extreme need to consolidate our armed forces in order to prevent a military adventure by Ben Gurion, but Nasser was adamant that priority in expenditure should be given to development projects. He was equally convinced that the Armistice Agreements offered a guarantee for peace.

He adhered to this position until, on 28 February 1955, Israel launched an attack on Gaza that led to the killing of thirty-eight Egyptian officers and men. Nasser had always referred to this attack, which was completely unprovoked, as the turning point. He was taken unawares and began to give serious consideration to the dangers posed to Egyptian security by the Israeli compulsion for expansion and aggression; henceforth, Nasser gave an equal priority to arming and consolidating the Egyptian armed forces.

Christian Pineau, then French Foreign Minister, tells that when he met Ben Gurion before the Tripartite Aggression he said he had good news for him: he had met Nasser who told him that problems with Israel would be resolved in time and that he was mainly concerned with internal development and raising the living standards in Egypt. Ben Gurion answered: 'No, this is bad news.'

Nasser had asked the US for the purchase of arms, but Dulles turned down that request for reasons relating to Britain's opposition at the time and his desire to contain Egypt in the Western sphere of influence. Nasser was left with no other choice but to turn to the Eastern bloc. He mentioned his dilemma to Chou En-lai during the Bandung Conference in 1955; the latter immediately approached the Soviet Union with the resultant Czechoslovak arms deal. Dulles considered the deal to be an insult directed at him personally. He had considered the Middle East as a Western zone of influence, and concluded that this deal, together with Nasser's adoption of a non-aligned policy, posed a threat of great strategic importance to Western influence in this area. At the same time, relations with Britain began to deteriorate in view of Nasser's rejection of the Baghdad Pact, which was patronized by Britain. The British equally felt irked and disturbed at Nasser's demand that Britain terminate her occupation of the Gulf area and close down her military bases in it. Relations with France were passing through the same straits. Egypt was lending strong support to the countries of the Arab Maghreb in their struggle for independence and had thrown all her weight behind the Algerian revolution, which made Guy Mollet consider Nasser the main instigator behind the Algerian revolution.

Nasser moved to strengthen his position by the establishment of an Arab Unified Front. He invited the heads of Arab States to a meeting in Cairo in January 1955, to adopt a unified position over the Baghdad Pact. The meeting did not lead to concrete results, but the debates revealed a concordance of views between Egypt and Saudi Arabia, represented by Prince Faisal, in rejecting the Baghdad Pact, while Iraq stood alone in defending it.

Nasser was becoming increasingly aware of the important role that could be played by Syria in the formation of joint Arab policies and decided to consolidate relations with her. He appointed me Ambassador to Syria in the spring of 1955 and gave me a free hand to achieve this end. It did not take me long to establish close relations with all Syrian parties and with the commanders of the army. I became aware of deep Syrian commitment to the concept of Arab unity and a ready willingness of the Syrian masses to support the Arab struggle for independence and freedom in any Arab country. When the Syrians became aware of the leading role played by Nasser in his struggle to remove foreign tutelage from all the Arab countries, an association between the two countries became inevitable.

In July 1955 I proposed to Nasser that we conclude a pact with Syria and establish a unified military command which Jordan could join at a later date. I felt that the success of the three countries in establishing a military unity might deter Israel from attempting any military ventures against the Arab countries.

Nasser was reluctant at first, in view of his apprehension that differences between the Syrian parties might lead to obstructing the successful conclusion of such an agreement, and this would reflect on the Egyptian political position. I assured him, however, that such an agreement enjoyed the support of all military commanders and party leaders.

The Agreement was signed in Damascus on 20 October 1955, and Jordan joined it in October 1956.

However, the events of 1956 brought radical changes to the area, injecting new factors in the Arab–Israeli conflict. The East–West confrontation was introduced in the Middle East scene: the campaign conducted by Guy Mollet reached hysterical dimensions at the beginning of the year, and Dulles was considering various means to punish Nasser for his independent posture. Dulles consequently announced on 18 July 1956 the withdrawal of the US offer to participate in financing the construction of the High Dam, to be followed in the same policy by Britain and the International Bank. Nasser's response in a speech in Alexandria on 26 July was to declare the nationalization of the Suez Canal in order to finance with its revenues the building of the High Dam. He was aware of the seriousness of such a measure and his speech was consequently of a fiery nature in order to mobilize the masses behind his decision. I was in Damascus at the time and could feel the spontaneous responsiveness of the masses and the feeling among leaders that Nasser had become a symbol of Arab struggle and hope and that his leadership had extended beyond his country.

Information began to reach us concerning the arrival of British military units in Cyprus and Malta and expectation of an imminent Anglo–French attack on Egypt grew. There was, however, almost an Arab consensus that Britain would not dare involve Israel in her attack, in view of her immense interests in the Arab world that would be completely undermined if she took such a precipitate step.

The Israeli attack on Egypt on 29 October came as a total surprise. When the Anglo–French attack started the following day, the collusion became obvious, and a wave of anger swept the Arab world. Both Syria and Jordan offered to attack Israel to divert part of its attacking forces, but Nasser refused in order to spare them from the wrath of Britain and France.

I was invited by President Kuwatly to attend a stormy meeting of the Syrian Cabinet of Ministers who insisted that Syria was under a national and historical obligation to enter the war on the side of Egypt, whatever the consequences, to convince them that it was Egypt that declined this offer. The following day I was visited by a number of army commanders including Abdel Hamid Sarraj, the head of intelligence, and we decided that the pipelines owned by a British oil company passing through Syria should be blown up.

Both Britain and France used the nationalization of the Suez Canal as a pretext for their aggression while Israel, which had absolutely no pretext, had to reveal its true expansionist intentions when it declared that it considered Sinai as part of Israel. Ben Gurion said at the time: 'Our forces did not infringe upon the territory of the land of Egypt and did not even attempt to do so. Our operations were restricted to the area of the Sinai Peninsula alone.' He later declared that Sinai 'has been liberated by the Israeli army'. Since such a claim was in contradiction to the Armistice Agreement which Israel had signed with Egypt, he proceeded to declare that 'the Armistice Agreement with Egypt is dead and buried and will never be resurrected'.

His next step was to expel the UN truce supervision organization with the claim that he would not allow the presence of foreign forces on territories occupied by Israel. He was even more explicit in a later broadcast when he said: 'Israel's aim in the Sinai operation was the liberation of that part of the homeland which was occupied by the invader . . . In the 1948 War we did not attain all that we desired. Only a short-sighted people would not use the great things which we attained this time, although the struggle is not yet ended.'

The aggressive parties did not anticipate the firm stand adopted by Eisenhower who forced the British and French forces to withdraw from Port Said and the Israeli forces to withdraw from Sinai and the Gaza Strip. His role had a tremendous impact in enhancing the image of the US in the area and projecting it as a power that was, in the last analysis, genuinely concerned for the safety of smaller nations.

The US had a golden chance to capitalize on that popularity to achieve permanent peace in the area, which would have cost less effort than when it pressured the three invading countries to withdraw their forces. In fact, no sooner did the US attain this glorious achievement than it resorted to measures that could hardly be defined as friendly. It froze Eygptian assets in US banks which Egypt needed urgently for the purchase of foodstuffs and medicaments. Egypt had, therefore, to resort once again to the Soviet Union which supplied its needs without delay. In consequence, both Syria and Egypt began to lean more on the Soviet Union for both military and economic assistance. The Soviet Union had successfully proclaimed its political support for the Arab countries when Bulganin threatened to use Soviet long-range missiles against the aggressive countries in the Tripartite War and when he declared the willingness of the Soviet Union to send volunteers to help in fighting the occupation.

The US, which had forfeited its chance earlier to terminate the armed conflict between Israel and the Arabs, could now see only the increasing Soviet influence. Eisenhower therefore came up with his bombshell of a 'doctrine' in January 1957, which proposed signing a number of agreements with the countries of the Middle East to confront armed aggression from any country ruled by international communism, without any reference to the immediate and recurring threat of Israeli aggression. The Eisenhower doctrine illustrated the tragic incapacity of US diplomacy to come to grips with the real situation in the Arab countries and the refusal of the Arab masses to accept foreign military bases in their territories or to enter into military pacts.

Meanwhile, relations between Syria and Egypt developed to the extent of a merger, announced on 22 February 1958 in an atmosphere of great jubilation and excitement. The US did not welcome the merger which meant the accentuation of the Arabs' refusal of the US policy for the establishment of military pacts in the whole of the Arab area.

The Soviets were equally wry at this measure for it resulted in the disbanding of the Syrian Communist Party, the only legally acknowledged party of its kind in the Arab World.

Israel was equally disconcerted, for it meant an obstacle to its expansionist schemes: the two merging States stood on both its western and eastern borders.

In fact, some other Arab countries felt disturbed by the national appeal the new united country projected among their peoples; they feared that they might attempt to join it.

Eventually the merger fell through in September 1961 when a number of Syrian army officers staged a *coup d'état*.

In the meantime a 'Waters War' was declared by Israel when it began to divert the waters of the River Jordan into the Negev. Nasser issued invitations to an Arab Summit Meeting in January 1964 to consider a counter-project for the exploitation of the waters of the Jordan. I had supervised the drafting of the counter-project with a number of Arab engineers and had discussed it at some length with Eric Johnstone who arrived, in his capacity as representative of the US government, to effect a distribution of the waters of the River Jordan between Israel and the Arab countries; but this fell through in view of Israel's insistence on acquiring the greater part of the waters. I was therefore called by Nasser from New York where I was appointed head of the Egyptian delegation to the United Nations, to attend the Arab Summit.

The meeting decided to establish a unified Arab military command to defend territories against any threat by Israel and earmarked £154 million for the purpose. It also established an authority for the implementation of the Arab project for the exploitation of the Jordan waters, and called for the establishment of a Palestinian organization, namely the Palestine Liberation Organization.

I was in Cairo again in April to take over the post of Foreign Minister. Israel had meanwhile attacked the Syrian work sites on the Jordan river as well as making raids on towns in the West Bank.

When I became Foreign Minister, the situation was as follows: there was a heightening of Israeli threats and an increase in arms reaching Israel from various European countries; Israel had declared that it would begin diverting waters of the River Jordan by 1964. Lyndon B. Johnson, who was known for his unequivocal support for Israel, assumed the presidency of the United States and lent his support to Israel in a more effective way, and there was an intensification of US–Soviet confrontation in the area in spite of the fact that the Cold War which reached its peak in the 1960s had ended.

To meet these threats we had to: continue arming our fighting forces and developing our industries; develop our relations with the Soviet Union to ensure the continued flow of arms;

strengthen Arab solidarity, especially with Syria and Jordan; adhere more tenaciously to the concept of non-alignment to the US–Soviet confrontation; consolidate our relationships with the other non-aligned countries and the African countries; and support the PLO.

In Cairo the year 1964 was one of unparalleled international diplomatic activity. Two Arab summit meetings were convened, in January and September, an African summit in July, and a non-aligned countries' summit in October. By the end of the year the Arab Unified Command had finalized its defensive plan against possible Israeli aggression. General Aly Amr, the Commander General, explained to the Arab Heads of State in September that the Eastern Front comprising Syria, Jordan and Lebanon could not, in its present condition, stand up to an Israeli attack and should be furnished with arms and other facilities. The build-up of that front, it was estimated, needed a period of at least three years.

It was obvious that until Arab countries could complete their defensive capacities they would continue to be subject to Israeli incursions and attacks, especially now that all peace guarantees had been nullified. Israel had declared the Armistice Agreements null and void, and the Tripartite declaration for safeguarding peace in the Middle East was a hollow vessel after both Britain and France, two of its signatories, attacked Egypt in 1956.

The road was open to Israel to initiate her aggression in 1967.

2

The June War

While the Western–Arab confrontation which ended in the occupation by a few European powers of most of the Arab countries has deep-seated historical motives, it should be borne in mind that the United States in the nineteenth century and up to the end of the First World War possessed no significant military or economic interest. It was a dynamic society, mainly occupied with the development of its own identity, the build-up of its unity and the conquest of its vast, rich territory.

Consequently, in the early years of the Revolution of 1952, Nasser was more inclined to cooperate with the US than with the Soviet Union. For its part, the US accepted the validity of the Revolution and recognized it, helped in concluding the Agreement for the evacuation of the British forces from Egypt in 1954 and later, with President Eisenhower, adopted an unequivocal stand against the joint British–French–Israeli invasion of Egypt in 1956.

After the Second World War, however, US policy in the Middle East revolved round two focal points: the first was to encircle the Soviet Union with a network of military bases. The Arab World constituted one of the main arenas of confrontation with the Soviet Union by virtue of its geopolitical strategic importance and its vast resources of oil whose assured flow was necessary for the continual growth of the Western industrial system and its concomitant affluence. The Arab countries' main concern was with liberation from foreign domination and influence and to build a solid economic base on which true national independence could rest. As early as 1951 the US, jointly with Britain, France and Turkey, approached Mustafa al-Nahas, then Prime Minister of Egypt and leader of the Wafd party, proposing the participation of Egypt in a joint defence scheme for the Middle East. The depth of Egyptian apprehension for such schemes was illustrated by its emphatic rejection within a mere forty-eight hours. US Secretary of State John Foster Dulles, with his adage 'who is not with us is against us', was equally baffled and incensed when Nasser rejected a similar scheme in 1953.

The second part of US foreign policy in the Middle East lay in its proclaimed, manifest and unconditional support for Israel in the face of Arab protests and Palestinian dispossession and suffering, and remains the main cause of the highly aggravated Arab–American relations. While support for Israel remained a central policy of all administrations from the time of Harry Truman on, it took a turn for the worse with Johnson who, by an unexpected turn of events, assumed the presidency of the US in 1963, with a high-handed policy and limited experience in international affairs.

One has to recall at this juncture, however, that with the deterioration in US–Egyptian relations caused by the arbitrary and abusive manner in which Dulles withdrew the offer to finance the High Dam and the earlier arms sales to Egypt, relations between Egypt and the Soviet Union were gradually improving with the arms sale in 1955 and its ready agreement to finance the building of the High Dam in 1958. In spite of Soviet cooperation, Nasser publicly attacked Nikita Khrushchev in 1959 and denounced Communist control over the Abdel Karim Kassem regime in Iraq; and he made the disbanding of the Syrian Communist Party a precondition for its merger with Egypt in 1958. Nasser, as one of the leading figures of the non-aligned movement, adhered faithfully to its principles – a policy which was accepted by the Soviet Union but highly resented by Johnson. (The US Ambassador in Cairo came to see me in the wake of the UN plenary session of 1965, with instructions from Washington to tackle us on our voting record at the UN. He claimed that Egypt had voted on the side of the Soviet Union twelve times, but only twice on the side of the United States. Patiently I explained to him that it was the Soviet Union, for political reasons of its own, which had voted on our side and that the twelve instances he mentioned were independence issues to which we had pledged our support at the second non-aligned summit conference held in Cairo in 1964.)

Johnson, however, initiated his high-handed policy towards Nasser in 1965 by withdrawing American aid to Egypt which at the time did not exceed £E50 million (less than $100 million) which went mainly to pay for surplus American wheat at easy-payment terms. His objective was obviously to pressure Egypt into conforming to US policies, particularly at that time in Congo and Vietnam.

Nasser's comment was: 'Johnson should be aware that neither I nor Egypt are the cause of America's troubles in the world. These are caused by the American administration itself. American society is a strong dynamic society yet it has been manipulated to bring to power an imprudent president who is inclined to flex the US muscles towards the smaller nations.'

Johnson then moved to conclude an unprecedented arms deal with Israel that included Hawk missiles. He accompanied this with a message to Nasser informing him of the deal, justifying it on the grounds that Egypt was in possession of Soviet bombers, and warning that any attempt to make capital out of this issue would bring about a polarization in the Middle East situation – 'a matter which the US was energetically trying to avoid'. It was this flagrant American position (previous arms supplies to Israel were channelled through Britain, France and Germany) that was to accelerate the process of polarization in the region towards a situation that Israel had long and arduously tried to realize.

And so the year 1966 began with all the lines of communication established by Presidents Dwight Eisenhower and John Kennedy between the US and Egypt crumbling one by one. Nasser had given up all hope of ever improving relations with Johnson. He also felt that the timing of the deal reflected a new dimension in US–Israeli relations, coming as it did at a time marked by the singular absence of tensions along the Arab–Israeli borders. In his determination not to be drawn into an armed conflict with Israel and with the pressing demands of Egyptian development, Nasser had brought pressure to bear on the Palestinians to refrain from commando raids, whether from across the Egyptian borders or the armistice lines in the Gaza sector.

Thus the situation in the early months of 1966 could be summed up as follows: accelerating US military, economic and political support for Israel; deteriorating Egyptian–US relations; a unified Arab command in its embryonic stage, constricted by Arab political differences and a lack of necessary funds; the engagement of part of the Egyptian army in Yemen; and inter-

Arab differences which had negatively affected the Eastern Front.

In addition, Israel was at the time going through a dire crisis, economic and political. The quiet that prevailed along the borders was conducive to a slackening in diaspora Jews' interest and fund-raising activities. A country whose *raison d'être* was the gathering of the Jews into Israel was undergoing a reverse movement: the migration of Israelis to more prosperous countries.

Israel needed war, not only in fulfilment of its central dream of expansion but, more so, to maintain the integrity and cohesiveness of the young State and the continued loyalty and support of the diaspora Jews. Once again the image of beleaguered Israel, fighting for its survival as a haven for persecuted Jews, had to be projected; a favourable world public opinion had to be created. The chain of events that led to the closure of the Gulf of Aqaba to Israeli navigation offered Israel an opportunity which she hastened to seize and exploit to the full.

On 13 November 1966, Israel began by an unprovoked fullscale attack on the Jordanian village of As-Samou. The Israeli force was composed of 4,000 men transported in armoured cars and tanks and supported by a number of air squadrons. The pounding of the village continued for four hours and left it in shambles. (The pretext was that it was in reprisal for Palestinian commando operations from across the Syrian borderline!) Again, on 7 April 1967, Israel launched an aerial attack on Syria, destroying six of its MiGs.

Yitzhak Rabin, Israeli Chief of Staff, lent credence to Syrian apprehensions when he declared on 12 May 1967 that 'we will carry out a lightning attack on Syria, occupy Damascus, overthrow the regime there and come back'; and two days earlier, Abba Eban, Foreign Minister of Israel, had instructed his ambassadors abroad to reiterate that Israel might be obliged to employ force against Syria. Reports received in Cairo confirmed Israeli concentrations on the Syrian borders. An Egyptian parliamentary delegation headed by Anwar el-Sadat, on a visit at the time to Moscow, received information to that effect.

On 16 May, to off-set this Israeli escalation on the Syrian borders, Abdel Hakim Amer, Commander General of the Egyptian armed forces, undertook an indiscreet and uncalculated measure. He instructed General Mohammed Fawzi, Egyptian armed forces Chief of Staff, to write to General Rijke, Commander of the UN emergency forces, that the 'Egyptian armed forces have been alerted for any action against Israel the moment it [Israel] undertakes any hostile action against any Arab country . . . our forces are [consequently] amassing in Sinai and along the eastern borders. To ensure the safety of the international force . . . I request that you give orders to pull them back from *these positions*.'

The moment I read this letter, a copy of which was sent to me by General Fawzi, I became aware that we were heading for a head-on political confrontation which could lead, with the mood prevailing in Israel at the time, to a military confrontation. I assumed, however, that no such step would have been adopted unless we had the military power to back it up and carry it through.

UN Secretary-General U Thant informed Rijke that such a communication should be addressed directly to him by the Ministry of Foreign Affairs, whereupon in my letter to him I did not ask for the withdrawal of UN troops from Gaza and Sharm el-Sheikh; my request was restricted to a withdrawal from our international borders.

When U Thant refused to effect a partial withdrawal, Egypt could not back down on its demand and had to accept a complete withdrawal, to move its troops to take their positions, and to face once more the problem of Israeli navigation in the Gulf of Aqaba.

Israel, of course, jumped at this opportunity, caused by the temerity of Amer and the inflexibility of U Thant, to transform the issue from one of open threats of the military invasion of Syria into a totally different issue, namely freedom of navigation in the Gulf of Aqaba. In fact, the roots of this latter problem go back to the time when Israel occupied Om Rashrash (Eilat) on the Gulf of Aqaba on 10 March 1949 after signing the Armistice Agreement with Egypt in 1949 and in defiance of the Security Council resolution that all parties cease their military operations. We became aware of the dangers of the Israeli step since for Israel to reach the Gulf of Aqaba put her in a position to pose a threat to Egyptian and Saudi shores on the Red Sea. As a countermeasure, a law was promulgated banning the passage of Israeli ships in this waterway which lies 1,500 yards from the Egyptian shore. The law also banned the passage of strategic material.

On 23 May, US Ambassdor to Cairo Richard Nolte, who had not as yet presented his credentials, came to see me, carrying a message from Johnson to Nasser and a *note-verbale*. The message denied that the US harboured any hostility towards Egypt. It lauded Nasser's efforts to 'develop and raise' Egypt, stressed the vital importance of avoiding war, underlined that 'the grave disputes of our age must never be resolved by the illegal crossing of borders by arms or men', and finally suggested that Vice-President Hubert Humphrey visit the Middle East for talks.

The *note-verbale* was more explicit. It expressed concern over the rising tensions and confidence that none of the parties to the strife had the intention of committing any aggression, yet there was the risk that 'those in authority in the area misapprehend or misinterpret the intention of the others'. After reviewing the areas of US concern over recent developments (incursions by 'terrorists' from Syrian borders, the withdrawal of UN forces which would make maintaining peace along the Egyptian–Israeli border more difficult, and the troop build-up which must be arrested and reversed), it maintained that any interference with this international right (navigation in the Gulf of Aqaba) could have the gravest international consequences. The note, however, concluded with this clear, emphatic pledge: 'We believe general armistice agreements remain the best basis for maintenance of peaceful conditions along the borders . . . The government of the United States maintains firm opposition to aggression in the area in any form, overt or clandestine, carried out by regular military forces or irregular groups . . . [this] has been the policy of this government under four successive administrations, a record of our actions over the past two decades, within and outside the United Nations, is clear on this point.'

For the previous ten days Nasser had been questioning me closely over US intentions and so I promptly delivered the two communications to him. He pondered them for a time and then asked for my opinion. I said I felt sure that an outbreak of hostilities was out of the question. Johnson was calling on all parties to respect the Armistice Agreement (a request Egypt had already relayed to the UN Security Council). He pledged his country to oppose aggression in the area. I said, further, that navigation in the Gulf of Aqaba was a matter to which a solution could be secured, either through the International Court of

Justice as was proposed at the time by Senator Fulbright, Chairman of the US Senate's Foreign Affairs Committee, or through the redeployment of UN forces at Sharm el-Sheikh, once Israeli threats were eliminated.

Nasser asked me if I was confident that this reflected a sincere and genuine position by Johnson. I said that I did not think the President of the United States of America would put his seal to an official document to beguile and deceive us.

Yet Nasser was not to be reassured. After a moment's silence he said: 'I doubt gravely the sincerity of Johnson. For a man who has always sided with Israel it is inconceivable that, all of a sudden, he would become even-handed.'

My assessment was soon to be proven wrong.

The Egyptian political concept at the time, as demonstrated by Nasser, was to put an end to Israeli threats to Syria and its marauding incursions into Arab lands. Consequently he welcomed the forthcoming visit of US Vice-President Hubert Humphrey in order to reach a solution that would exclude war. U Thant arrived in Cairo; in spite of his outward calm he was gravely worried. His proposals which, we assumed, must have been underwritten by the US boiled down to the following: to call on Israel to refrain from sending any of its vessels through the Gulf of Aqaba; to call on countries whose vessels call at the port of Eilat to refrain from carrying strategic material to Israel; and to call on Egypt to refrain from exercising its right to inspect vessels sailing through the Straits of Tiran (Aqaba).

Nasser promptly accepted the proposals. U Thant then posed the question: 'Mr President, the Israelis fear that you might carry out a military attack on them. Will you give me your word that this is not going to take place?'

Nasser replied: 'We have never at any time intimated that we will attack Israel. It was Israel who has formally threatened to invade Syria. What we are attempting now is a defensive measure to prevent such a threat from materializing. You may have my word therefore that we will never begin the attack.'

U Thant left Cairo on 25 May, elated at the success of his mission. The ready acceptance of his proposals together with the assurances he received from Nasser should, he felt, be enough to defuse the crisis.

Nasser's formal reply to Johnson's message was another move

aimed at containing the crisis. Nasser commended a direct dialogue that would dispel the assumption that portrays 'the exercising of right as sinful, and the right of self-determination as aggression'. He recapitulated the measures adopted by Egypt in an attempt to off-set Israeli military escalation against Syria, and as a reaction to threats of invasion levelled in public pronouncements by the Israeli leaders. He went on to pin-point two essential factors in the present Arab–Israeli complex: the expulsion of the Palestinians from their homes and the trampling of their rights, including the right of repatriation, repeatedly upheld by the UN; and Israel declaring the Armistice Agreements null and void. He went on to assert that not only was Egypt committed to the cause of peace; he further pledged that Egypt would never initiate an act of aggression. He reiterated that the crux of the strife and its root was the Palestinian right to repatriation and the responsibility of the international community to guarantee the exercise of this right. He concluded by welcoming the visit of Hubert Humphrey and suggested an immediate visit to Washington by Vice-President Zakaria Moheiddine.

On 1 June I reassured Charles Yost, Johnson's envoy, saying: 'For our part we shall never begin an armed attack. We have, at your request, confirmed this. Should Israel, on the other hand, initiate aggression, then I would caution you, as a friend of long standing, that both the prestige and the interests of the United States in the area will be seriously damaged and Soviet gains will be further consolidated.'

Disconcerting signals were continually coming. A report from Washington mentioned a conference between Abba Eban, Johnson, his Defence Secretary and the CIA Director, after which Johnson was quoted as saying to his aides: 'Israel will hit them.' We were also informed that Johnson was failing to show any interest in U Thant's mission: he had probably been counting on our turning his proposals down, and when we did not they became superfluous.

Upon my asking US Ambassador to Cairo Richard Nolte about the chances of an Israeli attack on us, he answered gloomily: 'I would say around fifty-fifty.' I was greatly disturbed by this answer. Here we had two US envoys, Yost and Anderson, assuring us of US concern for peace, while Nolte, even in his personal capacity, expressed apprehension of an Israeli attack.

On the following day Yost came to see me to say that President Johnson welcomed the visit of Moheiddine and would like to be notified of the date of his arrival. I relayed the message to Nasser who suggested 5 June, that is, in less than forty-eight hours' time. I informed Yost accordingly. I then told him that we would accept a US commitment to support and protect Israel in return for an equal commitment to us that Israel would refrain from aggression.

Nasser was becoming increasingly aware that a confrontation with Israel would inevitably lead to an overt and direct clash with the US, which he was anxious to avoid. He was also aware that, with a substantial part of his armed forces engaged in Yemen, he did not have at his disposal the military power to attack Israel. I have equally no doubt that, whatever the risks, had he decided to launch the first strike, immediately after Israel announced general mobilization, he would have a scored a marked advantage over his adversary and probably have avoided the disaster that ensued: a supposition which highlights the role played by Johnson in misleading us and his success in involving the Soviet Union in this scenario.

Yet, in those days, I kept telling myself and Nasser, whose anxiety was mounting daily, that if the figures and data conveyed by Amer and Badran, the Minister of War, about our military preparations were authentic, Israel, which had a clear picture of the deployment of our forces, would think twice before attacking. Even if Israel was foolhardy enough to attack, our troops and arms would certainly be able to repel the initial thrust and then the outcome of war would depend, in the final analysis, on able command and the level of training and alertness. I was soon, however, to be disillusioned.

On 28 May, at a luncheon party at Nasser's residence, Amer, who had arrived a little late, took his seat and laughingly announced that Israel had panicked at noon that day. He had ordered two MiG-21 fighters to carry out a reconnaissance mission over Beersheba, and the pilots had picked up frantic Israeli signals indicating their fright at the presence of two Egyptian aircraft. I was gravely disturbed by this piece of news. However, Beersheba was only forty miles from the Egyptian border, which meant that Egyptian planes had only stayed for a few minutes in Israel's air space, which made the action of little or no significance.

On 29 May, I was visiting Nasser at his residence. It was an exceptionally warm day for the time of year and he suggested we take a stroll in the garden. I brought up the subject of our air force. If Israel was to attack, I said, the efficacy of our air force would be decisive. I inquired how far this had been accomplished. Nasser answered that Amer had assured him of our preparedness.

A few days later, after a meeting at the Qubba palace, Amer drew me aside and said: 'You look very tired . . . What is worrying you?' I answered that the situation was becoming increasingly tense and I lacked information on our military preparedness. Amer chuckled, saying: 'Listen. If Israel actually carried out any military action against us I could, with only one third of our forces, reach Beersheba. If you want to put your mind at ease, why not come to headquarters where we could explain the military position to you.'

I promised to do so but thought better of it, knowing that I would be deluged with plans, maps and figures which might not mean anything, and so I did not go.

At a Cabinet meeting, one of the Ministers asked the Minsiter of War, Shams Badran, if any thought had been given to the possibility of intervention by the US Sixth Fleet which Israeli Prime Minister Eshkol described, in a public announcement, as Israel's strategic reserve. Badran said that the Egyptian armed forces were capable of handling such an eventuality!

Some of the Ministers believed that Badran, who had just returned from the Soviet Union, must have received either arms or assurances for him to speak so valiantly and confidently about confronting the US Sixth Fleet.

I woke up on the morning of 5 June to the reverberating sound of a shattering explosion that seemed to be coming from the west of Cairo; I realized that Israel had begun its attack. I hastened to my office in the Ministry of Foreign Affairs and was soon to receive the shock of my life.

Nasser telephoned to inform me that all Egyptian military airfields had been hit and that our air force had been paralysed.

This was indeed a colossal setback but one that should not have led to the total collapse that ensued, had there been sound command and planning. The military command, meanwhile, was broadcasting communiqués claiming the shooting down of dozens of Israeli aeroplanes. It was, of course, discovered later that jettisoned reserve fuel-tanks were being counted as falling Israeli aircraft.

I tried several times to get to Amer at headquarters, where utter confusion seemed to rule, but I could not reach him. I finally got through to one of the senior officers and suggested that a liaison officer be appointed to supply the Ministry of Foreign Affairs with accurate information on which we could base our political moves. However, this request went unheeded.

Coming as it did on 5 June, the Israeli air strike should not have taken the commanding officers by surprise. Nasser had conferred with them on 2 June and informed them in explicit terms that the Israeli attack would probably be launched on 5 June, and that the first strike would be directed against our air force. Had this advice been heeded and an air cover maintained over the airfields on that day, losses could have been minimized so as not to exceed twenty per cent. What was even more staggering was the knowledge that such air cover had been maintained for several days and was withdrawn *that very day*. Marshal Amer, together with several of his senior officers who should have been at headquarters, was, instead, on that very day on an air inspection of a base in Sinai. Field commanders were at the base to welcome him. To ensure the safe passage of the Marshal's plane, the air-defence system was instructed not to engage in action and was, therefore, shut down! Two early warnings of the impending air attack went unheeded because there was nobody at headquarters in a position to act upon them. One warning came from an Egyptian border position, Om Besseiss, which was attacked one hour before the general onslaught. The other was dispatched by Egyptian General Abdel Moneim Riad from Ajloun in Jordan, stating that Jordanian radar had spotted large numbers of Israeli warplanes taking off from military airfields and heading towards Egypt. This latter message was not even decoded, as the code was changed that very same day. Had our forces been alerted, they could have intercepted the raiding planes before they reached their target . . . and the course of the war might have taken a different turn.

Panic and confusion ruled supreme. Six Tu. bombers which were already airborne were instructed to land at Luxor airport and not to proceed to Sudan (as was logical in the circumstances); they were destroyed, a few minutes later, on the ground with another eight Antonovs.

In the early hours of 6 June, after a sleepless night, I received a call from Nasser; he repeated that the air force was totally paralysed and added that he had no doubt in his mind that there had been US collusion and he had, therefore, decided to sever diplomatic relations with the United States.

I argued that such a decision was not beneficial to us, although I was equally convinced that collusion had taken place.

Nasser said: 'The US must be made to feel the brunt of its collusion with Israel. We must bring the weight of mobilized Arab anger to bear on her. The severing of relations is imperative.'

I said: 'Granted, but we shall need to deal politically with the US within the near future.'

Nasser retorted: 'Never. Collusion between the US and Israel at this level means that the US has something up its sleeve, a price we have to pay for Israeli withdrawal. The problem now is that while the US objective is to pressure us to minimize our dealings with the Soviet Union, it will drive us in the opposite direction altogether. The US leaves us no choice.' (A statement made that day by Dean Rusk, to the effect that the US could not decide who was the aggressor, lent credence to Nasser's impressions of, if not outright collusion, complete coordination.)

I immediately went to my office and summoned US Ambassador Richard Nolte to convey to him Egypt's decision to sever relations with the US. (A few minutes earlier I had communicated the same message to all Arab Heads of State.) The Ambassador, who was appreciative of Arab demands and the tragedy of the Palestinians, suggested that we keep our doors with the US open, and that Zakaria Moheiddine proceed to Washington as originally scheduled. For his part, he affirmed that no US or British planes had taken part in the fighting. (This was later confirmed.)

I said that both the proposed visit of Moheiddine and the suspected participation of US warplanes were of secondary importance. The crux of the problem was that we had received, in an official communication, assurances from President Johnson that Israel would not initiate hostilities if we refrained, which we had. He had pledged that the US would maintain firm opposition to aggression in the area. Now that Israel had started the war by attacking us, the least we could expect, in the light of these assurances, was that President Johnson would demand the immediate withdrawal of Israeli forces to their original positions; then perhaps we could move to a debate of the Palestine question in all its aspects to defuse the basic causes of strife in the area. I added that Dean Rusk's statement that the US was not aware who had started hostilities did not augur well and might well have a disastrous effect on the US position.

Nolte was an honest and sincere man and sympathized with our case. Yet he was in no position to influence events that were being manipulated by interest groups and a reckless double-dealing leadership that lulled us by false assurances while abetting Israeli aggression, and then moved to erase political truth in favour of widely accepted domestic fiction.

In the afternoon of 5 June I managed to get through to General Fawzi who informed me that Gaza was still fighting off intensive Israeli attacks but that Israel had managed to break through the defensive perimeter, south of Rafah, with the intention of cutting off Gaza. General Fawzi added that the General Command was planning a counter-attack the following day, 6 June. When I inquired how he would fare without air cover, he answered that this factor had been taken into consideration and that naturally we would sustain losses. Prior to the war, Egypt had deployed some of its paratroops in Jordan. Fawzi told me that they were instructed to move that night into Israel to carry out harassing operations. The Iraqis, he added, had raided airfields in north Israel.

I suspected that Fawzi's fighting spirit and determination to stand firm would not take him very far. I knew that Marshal Amer had already restricted his powers and that he had little authority to direct operations during the battle.

All through that morning, 6 June, I was busy consulting with Arab and foreign ambassadors to notify their respective governments of the necessity for calling for a Security Council resolution ordering the withdrawal of Israeli forces. I also informed them of Egypt's decision to suspend navigation in the

Suez Canal as a result of Israeli aggression. I cabled Syria, requesting that they close the oil pipeline at its Mediterranean terminal. Iraq, which had decided on 4 June to join the Egyptian-Jordanian Defence Agreement, informed us that it had stopped oil operations.

At 7.30 p.m. on 6 June, our UN Permanent Delegate, Ambassador el-Kony, telephoned me from New York to tell me about the Security Council resolution. The procedure at the UN in similar cases was to adopt a resolution underlining two principles: the first called for an immediate ceasefire and the second for the withdrawal of the aggressor's forces. This was the case following the Tripartite Aggression on Egypt in 1956. This time, however, I was told, the US administration was employing every trick in the book to block a resolution calling for Israeli withdrawal. On the contrary, France's President de Gaulle who, prior to the outbreak of fighting, had declared that France would firmly oppose the aggressive party now stood fast by his pledge. Together with India, France sponsored a draft resolution calling for an immediate ceasefire and the withdrawal of Israeli forces to 4 June positions. The Soviet Union and a group of other countries, members of the Security Council, supported the resolution. The US stood alone in opposing any reference to Israeli withdrawal, and employing all the pressure and delaying tactics at its disposal to secure this end.

In the meantime, the US delegate at the Security Council, Arthur Goldberg, presented a draft counter-resolution which made no reference to Israeli withdrawal but confined itself to expressing concern over the outbreak of fighting and calling upon the governments concerned, as a first step, to take forthwith all measures for an immediate ceasefire and for a cessation of all military activities in the area.

By submitting this draft, Johnson sought to prevent the adoption of a resolution similar to the one drafted by Eisenhower in 1956.

This was unacceptable to us and posed a dangerous precedent because it excluded any reference to the necessity of an Israeli withdrawal. Furthermore, it could never be implemented in its present wording as the Israeli forces in Sinai had become intermingled with Egyptian troops and there were no UN emergency forces to determine or identify the positions of either party.

The following day, 7 June, I contacted Ambassador el-Kony

and all the ambassadors whose countries were represented in the Security Council to inform them that a resolution calling for a ceasefire must, by necessity, order a cessation of Israeli hostilities and a withdrawal to the armistice lines. I referred to Jordan which had accepted the ceasefire and yet Israel proceeded with its military operations as evidence of the necessity.

The Security Council convened on the same day to adopt a new resolution which reiterated the contents of the US draft with the addition of the words 'all military operations must cease by 20 hours GMT on 7 June'.

On the same day, Algerian Foreign Minister Abdel Aziz Bouteflika arrived to inform me and, later, President Nasser that Algeria was placing all it had in military equipment at the disposal of Egypt and that Algerian President Houari Boumedienne had decided to send all available planes to Egypt. Bouteflika requested that a number of Egyptian pilots accompany him on his return to Algeria to fly back the Algerian warplanes.

Nasser began to explain to Bouteflika the main features of the war with the aid of a map of Sinai. He pointed to the passes, a series of rough hills about thirty to forty miles east of the Suez Canal, and said that our forces would pull back and hold that line so as to stem an Israeli advance.

I was at the airport to see Bouteflika off when I met the Egyptian pilots who were to accompany him. They were seething with anger and told me that since we had anticipated an Israeli attack we should have struck first and not left our planes a sitting duck for Israelis to destroy. They gave me firsthand information on the Israeli air strike, describing how Israeli aircraft had flown at low altitude to avoid detection by our radar and how some of their squadrons had flown across the Mediterranean then turned south to attack targets inside Egypt and how all our airfields were hit simultaneously. Their wrath was caused by the fact that although a political decision restrained a pre-emptive strike, at least air cover should have been operative over our airfields.

When I returned to my office that evening I felt slightly more comforted: there was the grim determination of our pilots to continue the fight; there were also Nasser's words about holding fast to the passes. I could not, however, suppress a nagging doubt: Nasser was at his residence and not at the headquarters when he was making these plans. How could he keep abreast of developments and carry out decisions? My apprehensions were later confirmed for while Nasser was speaking on 6 June about holding the passes, Amer had already issued orders for the general retreat of our forces from Sinai to positions west of the Suez Canal. What was even more staggering was the knowledge I gleaned through my telephone calls to the Supreme Head-quarters that no Egyptian contingents had been left to impede the Israeli advance along the northern coastal road running parallel to the Mediterranean, a fact that contributed to the rapid advance of the Israeli troops to seize Kantara on the Suez Canal.

Very late that evening the Chinese Ambassador came to inform me that Chinese leader Mao Tse-tung had ordered the immediate dispatch to Egypt of half a million tons of foodstuffs as a gesture of solidarity and a contribution to our struggle.

Ambassador el-Kony telephoned me to say that agreement had been reached on a ceasefire between Jordan and Israel that would come into effect at 20 hours GMT that evening.

The following day the Under-Secretary of the Ministry of Economy informed me that the First Secretary of the US Embassy had informed him that the whole of the West Bank of the Jordan had fallen into Israeli hands, that the Egyptian army in Sinai had been destroyed and that it would be best for Egypt to accept the ceasefire without further delay. This information was later verified by our embassies abroad.

Yet the same day I was to receive from the Military Command a communication to the effect that Israeli air sorties had decreased, that our anti-aircraft fire was highly effective and had downed a large number of Israeli planes, and finally that an Israeli paratroop unit had been wiped out at Mitla Pass, while the advance of an Israeli armoured column had been arrested at Rommana, close to the east bank of the Suez Canal.

The previous evening we had received a message from the Central Committee of the Soviet Communist Party urging us to accept the ceasefire. Nasser asked me to formulate a reply that would convey our concern over the Soviet position and which would contain the following points: that the amassing of Egyptian troops in Sinai had occurred on the basis of information received from the Soviet Union relating to Israel's intention to attack Syria; that Soviet overtures for refraining from attack had coincided with similar pressures exerted by the US (once again with this request for accepting a ceasefire without provision for Israeli withdrawal there seemed to be a distinct similarity in approach between the two powers); how could we terminate our military operations when enemy forces continued to launch ground and air attacks against us; and finally that we were determined to continue the fight until Israeli withdrawal was achieved, and we expected the serious and instant support of the Soviet Union in this venture. I was also to inform President Atassi of Syria and President Boumedienne of Algeria of our determination to continue the fight.

At 4 p.m. the Algerian Ambassador called to inform me that nineteen planes had already arrived from Algeria and that another fifteen were on the way, and that his President had just contacted him to request another batch of Egyptian pilots to fly more planes.

That evening the Soviet Ambassador requested an urgent meeting with me. I immediately received him, anticipating a vital decision by the Soviet government. Instead, he took out a piece of paper which turned out to be a copy of a letter from Johnson to Kosygin and proceeded to read it slowly and carefully. The message claimed that a US intelligence ship, *Liberty* by name, had been attacked inadvertently by Israeli warplanes near Port Said and the US aircraft carrier *Saratoga* had been ordered to send a plane to investigate the incident. The US government was making it clear to the Soviet government that the mission of this aircraft was purely investigative in nature and was hopeful that the Soviet government would take the necessary measures to acquaint all parties with this action . . . The inanity of the situation left me speechless.

At nine that evening President Nasser telephoned me. In a voice choking with grief and bitterness he told me that the collapse of the armed forces had been total, far beyond anything he had imagined, and that we were no longer capable of continuing the fight . . . and would I instruct el-Kony to inform the Security Council that we agreed to terminate military operations.

When I finally got through to el-Kony in New York it was already 10 p.m. in Cairo. I conveyed Nasser's message to him and it shook him to the very core. During the past few days, I had been feeding him the exuberant military reports I had received, which he accepted, discrediting the accounts of the collapse of the army conveyed to him by his fellow ambassadors as malicious and inaccurate. For several moments we were silent. In one dismal moment the great illusion we were living crumbled.

El-Kony communicated to the Security Council our unconditional acceptance of the ceasefire, but Israel continued its military operation through 9 June with air strikes on Suez and the port of Adabeya.

With both Egypt and Jordan out of the war, Israel concentrated on Syria, occupying Kuneitra and the rest of Golan, and continued its operations, despite the ceasefire resolution, until it had secured all its objectives on the Syrian front on the night of 10 June.

On 9 June President Nasser announced in Cairo that he would make a statement to the people of Egypt. I had no foreknowledge of what he would say and sat in my office, my eyes glued to the TV. With a sombre face and choking voice he declared that he alone was responsible for what had taken place, and consequently had decided to resign in favour of Zakaria Moheiddine.

I drove hurriedly to Nasser's residence. All of a sudden I found myself wading through multitudes of people, hundreds of thousands of them, who had taken to the streets, all heading in the same direction. Angry people and highly incensed, clamouring that Nasser must stay. At Nasser's residence were a number of cabinet ministers and top officials. We tried vainly to persuade him to reverse his decision. Outside his house the multitudes were growing into millions, fulminating and vehement, insisting that Nasser stay, and honour and dignity be avenged. It was a spectacle I have never witnessed before and was extremely moving in its spontaneity and sincerity. The same spectacle was to be seen in different Arab capitals.

Nasser had to bow down to this universal Arab demand and on 10 June withdrew his resignation. He felt that he had erred when he had taken Amer's assurance about the combat readiness of the Egyptian army at its face value; that when the first signs of incompetence became obvious later, on 5 June, he should have removed Amer as Chief of Command and himself assumed military command of the armed forces. He could then have implemented the only logical plan, namely holding fast to the passes. Had he done so, he could have spared Egypt a total defeat. Nasser, however, did not expect Amer would order a general retreat on the evening of 6 June, a mere thirty-six hours after the outbreak of fighting.

I later asked General Fawzi why we failed to hold the passes, which were considered our best defence line east of the Suez Canal. He said that Amer had called him on the afternoon of 6 June and asked him to prepare a plan for total retreat from Sinai. Fawzi and other commanding officers drew up a plan for the withdrawal of our forces in three days. Amer waved it aside and said that he had already given his instructions to the Egyptian forces to pull back west of the Suez Canal before daybreak, in other words, to abandon the whole of Sinai in only twelve hours. It was a frantic and irrational move. It meant moving thousands of tanks, trucks and guns as well as huge quantities of military equipment along a few narrow roads in a scorching desert. The retreat began.

The few roads traversing Sinai were soon jammed with hundreds of tanks and trucks. Many broke down, blocking the roads, and traffic was brought to a standstill. It was one colossal traffic bottleneck which Israeli warplanes found an easy target and, at low altitude, strafed the stranded vehicles and men. All tanks, trucks, guns and equipment east of the passes were demolished, and 10,000 men lost their lives on that day alone. Thousands returned on foot and in desperate condition. Many others died of hunger and thirst and, in the days after the war, Red Cross planes and helicopters worked overtime to rescue the stragglers.

Later still, on 25 July, Nasser told me that he had gone on the morning of 5 June to Military Command Headquarters and explained that the success of Israel's air strike was not the end of the battle. The Israeli ground attack, he expected, would be directed towards the northern sector of Sinai (the al-Arish zone) and he advised the consolidation of the defensive line there. Instead, Amer had pulled out the Egyptian forces from al-Arish, leaving its defence to one brigade. Israel's main thrust came, as Nasser had predicted, through the northern sector to al-Arish. Nasser did not go to headquarters on either Tuesday or Wednesday (6 and 7 June). On Thursday he received an urgent telephone call from Shams Badran requesting that he come immediately to headquarters, as Amer wanted to commit suicide by taking poison.

Nasser went and confided to Amer that he would be making a public statement the following day announcing his resignation. Amer retorted that he too could not remain to command the army.

On 10 June, Amer relinquished all his responsibilities while Badran resigned from his post as Minister of War, but maintained, according to what Nasser told me, his contacts with the secret organization of the army which had been set up years earlier to off-set any attempt at a military coup and to defend the regime. Badran was originally responsible for this organization and its secret nature; he knew the names of the officers involved, while Nasser was familiar with only some of them. Nasser became aware that some of them were in the habit of visiting Amer's and Badran's houses, where they would indulge in attacks on Nasser and the regime. Amer, meanwhile, had reprinted the text of a resignation he had submitted in 1964, demanding the introduction of democratic procedures in the system of government, and was distributing them on a wide scale.

Nasser informed me that he had no other choice but to arrest a large number of officers, including all those who belonged to the same graduation year as Badran (1948).

He got together with Amer, he continued, on 29 June and reproved him for his behaviour, his attacks on the regime made in the presence of army officers, and the contacts he was trying to establish with some members of the National Assembly.

In his talks with me, Nasser did not conceal what he was trying to convey: that what was happening was not a mere personality conflict but a struggle for power between the President and his Deputy, which resulted in the complete paralysis of the armed forces. I recall that I was with Nasser in the *Liberty* on our way to Casablanca in December 1961, when the two escort destroyers supplied by the navy were forced to withdraw because of malfunction. Nasser ordered the dismissal of the Navy Commander, but Amer refused to implement the order. This was neither the first nor the last incident of this nature which placed Nasser's control of the army in some doubt.

Had this confrontation between Nasser and Amer taken place

some years before 1967, events would definitely have taken a different course and, most likely, the catastrophe of 1967 could have been avoided.

Amer was escorted to Nasser's residence on 25 August where a number of the Revolutionary Council members were present. A heated discussion over Amer's behaviour ensued and continued until after midnight when Nasser left the meeting. Amer went to the washroom and, after a while, came out of it screaming that he had committed suicide. A doctor was called and it became obvious that Amer was only attempting to pressure Nasser by an imposture. Nasser decided the same day to place Amer under detention in his house in Giza.

General Fawzi told me that at the same time he was instructed to go to Amer's residence and place under arrest all the officers and men he found there; they numbered three hundred. Another three hundred civilians from Amer's village in Minia were also placed under arrest. The same day, Shams Badran was arrested for his increasing anti-Nasser activities.

Amer continued to get in touch with some of his supporters so Nasser ordered him to be moved to a house outside Cairo. Generals Fawzi and Abdel Moneim Riad, Chief of Staff, were instructed to escort him there. When he was finally prevailed upon by Riad to accept this decision, his daughter was heard screaming that her father had taken poison and Riad noticed that Amer was actually chewing something. He hurriedly moved him to Maadi Hospital where, after a few hours of treatment, he was declared fit to be moved to his new place of detention.

The following day he died. An autopsy was performed and the Prosecutor General, after an exhaustive investigation, issued a report which intimated that Amer had died by poisoning with the intention of committing suicide. He established that he had found capsules of Oktien taped to the lower part of his belly.

Thus ended tragically a long association of two comrades-in-arms and close friends. The role of Amer does not vindicate faulty political assessments that led us into a losing war. They were, however, political errors which had been contributed to by the Soviet Union with its extravagant promises and by the US with its duplicity. The Soviet Union had been extravagant in extending promises of support to both Egypt and Syria. This created an impression in Cairo and Damascus that the Soviet

Union would side with us militarily, should Israel initiate aggression. In addition to the messages that were exchanged, the Kremlin issued an official communiqué on 23 May in which it said: 'Any aggression in the Middle East will be met not only with the united strength of the Arab countries but also with strong opposition to aggression from the Soviet Union.' This term 'strong opposition' was interpreted by the Arabs as a pledge of military support to meet Israel's threat of invading Damascus.

When Minister of War Shams Badran visited Moscow at the time, he was asked by Soviet leaders not to escalate the situation. However, Marshal Grechko told Badran at the airport: 'We shall be by your side always.' Shams Badran interpreted those words as a pledge of Soviet support, lest Israel start a war. Nasser, for his part, announced this promise. He declared: 'When I met Shams Badran yesterday after he returned from Moscow, he handed me a message from Mr Kosygin saying that the Soviet Union is standing by our side in this battle and will not allow any country to interfere.' This statement was disseminated by the radio and press on the widest possible scale. If, hypothetically, we presume that Shams Badran had misread the Soviet pledge, then the Soviet Union should have been quick to rectify and correct the matter to Nasser, after such a public statement. But the Soviets refrained from taking any action. As a result, these pledges – imbued with more than a single meaning – were aimed solely at securing political advantages.

From the beginning this trend was a factor that encouraged Syrian officials to carry out some military operations against Israel at the time without any consideration as to the consequences, prompting Israel to exercise an unpecedented military escalation, and utter open threats to occupy Damascus, especially now that the opportunity for which Israel had been preparing itself for many years was at hand, and especially now that information had reached Cairo from Moscow of Israeli troop concentrations along the Syrian borders, which prompted Nasser to push Egyptian troops across the Suez Canal into Sinai.

Moscow had long been convinced that Israel was preparing for an all-out attack on the Arab countries, especially Egypt and Syria. Still, it was the Soviet Ambassador in Cairo who got Nasser out of bed, at dawn on 27 May, to relay an urgent message from the Soviet leaders requesting Egypt to refrain from firing first. It was also that morning that the Soviet Ambassador said that US President Johnson had informed the Kremlin that Egypt would attack Israel at dawn that very same day.

What was really startling, however, was that the Soviet Ambassador should request 'Egypt to refrain from firing first'. The role of the Soviet Union seemed then not to go beyond relaying Johnson's message (albeit with more civility); the Soviet Union was well aware of Israel's military superiority, and our deployment of large contingents in the Yemen, as well as the inadequate training of the remaining forces. The Soviets must have been equally aware that should Israel carry out a first strike – when Egypt had pledged not to initiate war, this would endanger Egypt, and consequently Syria and Jordan. It was incumbent upon the Soviets, besides acting as couriers between the US and Egypt, to secure a clearly defined commitment from the US that Israel would not carry out any aggression and, as a superpower, guarantee that this would be implemented.

Now we come to the role of the US itself. In a meeting with Lucius Battle, the US Ambassador in Cairo, prior to his departure from Egypt, I brought up the matter of US–Israeli collusion. The Ambassador vehemently denied it, saying: 'The very moment I learn of such collusion I shall tender my resignation from the US diplomatic corps!' Sincere as he was, I could not help but reiterate my firm belief that the days to come would witness the unveiling of more evidence of this collusion.

Now, after many years and reading the works of top officials in the US and Israel, I am in a better position to assess the extent of US duplicity.

Levi Eshkol, fully aware of the lessons of the Tripartite Aggression, was not only anxious to consult with the US before any major hostility but equally to acquire its prior approval. One of the more significant messages that Eshkol received from Johnson, dated 17 May, stated: 'I am sure you will understand that I cannot accept any responsibility on behalf of the United States for situations which arise as the result of actions on which we are not consulted.'

Eshkol replied: 'Request that the United States reaffirms its commitment to Israeli security and informs the Soviet Union, in particular, of this commitment'. (Johnson did dispatch a message to Kosygin, conveying the requested pledge). So while Israel enjoyed the protection of the US, Egypt did not receive an equal Soviet commitment.

On 23 May, in a letter to Kosygin, Johnson proposed the cooperation of the two countries to confront the problem. The Soviet Union actually played the role demanded of it by Johnson, and requested Egypt to refrain from any military action. The Soviet Union, however, did not ask for a similar commitment by the US that Israel would not undertake any military action. Johnson further requested Israel to refrain from any military action for a period of forty-eight hours. Israel abided and unleashed its attack after the lapse of fifty-eight hours. It is evident that Johnson's manoeuvres aimed at freezing an Egyptian initiative as well as Soviet support.

We came to know later that Dean Rusk had submitted two alternatives to President Johnson: either (1) that the Israelis decide how best to protect their own national interest, in the light of the advice we have given them, i.e. to 'unleash them'; or (2) to take a positive position but not a final commitment on the British proposal (a multinational naval force from maritime countries to supervise navigation in the Gulf of Aqaba).

It was obvious that Dean Rusk favoured the second proposal. The choice, nevertheless, rested with Johnson who opted for the first alternative, to unleash Israel's military action.

The CIA also played a major role in opting for war; it assured Johnson that Egypt lacked any plans or preparations to attack Israel, and confirmed that Israeli forces could win the war. Abba Eban elaborated on this theme in his meeting with the CIA Chief at the Pentagon on 26 May.

At a meeting with Israel's Foreign Minister, Abba Eban, Johnson made his well-known statement: 'Israel will not be alone unless it decided to go it alone'. When Eban left the White House, Johnson was sure that Israel would attack, and he communicated the fact to his advisers.

3

Rebuilding from Scratch

The 1967 June War ended with Israel occupying all Palestine (including the West Bank of Jordan and the Gaza Strip), the Sinai Peninsula in Egypt and the Golan Heights in Syria.

The possibility of peace between the Arabs and Israel consequently became more tenuous. While before there had been only one problem, the Palestinian problem, the implementation of the UN 1947 resolution for the partition of Palestine between Jews and Arabs and the subsequent resolutions for the repatriation of the Palestinians, there was now an added problem: the occupation by Israel of the remaining part of Palestine, as well as of parts of Egypt and Syria. The hopes we had entertained of realizing peace after the Armistice Agreements in 1949 were now completely shattered.

Egypt was going through dire economic straits after the loss of its revenues from the Suez Canal and the oil wells in Sinai; while Israel, with undreamed-of military success and with its unconditional support becoming an established tenet of US domestic and foreign policies, was now more determined than ever to repudiate the Palestine question and block the resolution of the consequences of its 1967 aggression.

In like manner the United States which prior to the war, had pledged to support the political independence and territorial integrity of all countries in the area and had denounced any party that would initiate hostilities, now trampled over all these precepts, once Israel had won its war. At the Security Council it rejected any condemnation of Israeli aggression, obstructed a call for its withdrawal and went further, to deny the validity of the Armistice Agreements to which it had committed itself less than two weeks before the war.

On 18 July 1967, US representative to the UN Arthur Goldberg reached an agreement with Soviet Ambassador Dobrynin on a draft resolution affirming the principle of the inadmissibility of the invasion of territory in accordance with the Charter and calling on all parties to the dispute to immediately withdraw their forces from the territories they occupied after 4 June 1967. The US withdrew its support for this draft resolution only forty-eight hours later.

Judging by the US position, I became aware that the US–Israeli drive would concentrate on forcing Egypt to accept the *fait accompli* in the hope that the Arab area would surrender to US hegemony and to Israeli demands.

To counter this drive, these factors had to be established: to maintain the unity of the internal front in Egypt which had been established on 10 June when the Egyptian populace demanded that Nasser remain at the helm; and the expeditious operational build-up of Egypt's military power to liberate the occupied territory.

Moreover, with the total alignment of the US to Israel we were left no other choice but to turn totally to the Soviet Union. Consequently one of the main upshots of the June War was escalating US–Soviet rivalry in the Middle East area in a manner that further complicated the quest for peace.

After the defeat I would constantly try to recall to memory the whole panorama of events since I arrived in Palestine in 1948 and would ponder, with anguish and solicitude, on where we had gone wrong. The military blunders were of course monstrous, yet this could not absolve the political leadership of its responsibility for appointing an able military command that could shoulder its duties effectively.

The fault was with the regime itself, a fact which Nasser did admit. I felt I could not continue in my post as Foreign Minister, but I was prevailed upon to reconsider. Only concerted, determined effort could bring us out of the dismal situation we were in. I felt that, just as we shared in the victories, so we should share equally the responsibility in the hard days to come. I was inspired by Nasser's grim determination at the time to off-set the outcome of defeat, to rebuild the army and then liberate the occupied territories, a plan which, he estimated, could be carried out by the end of 1970 or, at the latest, early 1971.

At a meeting of the Executive Committee of the Socialist Union on 3–4 August 1967, Nasser underwent self-criticism in which he expressed serious misgivings over the system that had allowed the mistakes that led to defeat, that had permitted struggle over authority, concluding that the one-party system had failed; and he suggested a new system based on a democratic foundation which would allow an opposition party side by side with the ruling Socialist Union, with a newspaper of its own; and that the people in general should be released from the feelings of fear that inhibited full expression of their views. He said that the new system would safeguard the country from the rule of a dictatorship. He proposed that elections for the candidates of the two parties could begin the following December. He said further that a continuation of the present system would lead Egypt to an unknown future, a dark future. After lengthy debate the majority ruled that no such venture could be undertaken before the resolution of the consequences of aggression.

In fact, it was Nasser, more than anybody else, who bore the brunt of those pitiless days. He realized that he was, in the final analysis, historically responsible for the defeat.

At a cabinet meeting, Nasser explained himself in these terms: 'I can never forget the first few days immediately after 5 June 1967. I felt great bitterness, an indescribable bitterness. There is no doubt that what happened in June has affected us all, morally and psychologically. Yet, more than anybody, I was responsible for the home front and the external contacts.

'On 11 June, when I resumed office, I was in such a disturbed state that I sent my family away from Cairo and I kept my gun next to me, to use it at the last minute. On that day I asked about the number of tanks still in Cairo and was told that there were only seven. I used to speak to General Fawzi every night before going to bed and called him at six in the morning to review the position of the armed forces.'

With determination and patience, Nasser began to rebuild and reorganize the army. He had lost his contacts with the armed forces years ago and was not aware which elements could be entrusted with professional military leadership. He was anxious at the time to elicit all views, then sift them and draw from them his own conclusions.

There was equally a dire need to address himself to the deteriorating economic situation caused by the defeat. Numerous foreign circles had predicted that the Egyptian economy could not survive beyond six months.

On the foreign front there were the urgent objectives of achieving Arab solidarity and the greatest possible support of the Soviet Union and the Socialist countries, attempting to reduce US support to Israel and gaining the support of Europe and the Third World.

National unity was preserved by Nasser's remarkable ability to relate to the masses, his empathy with them and his ability, in the darkest hours, to imbue them with confidence and hope.

After the removal of the military command responsible for defeat, Nasser assumed personal responsibility for the armed forces and appointed General Fawzi Minister of War. While Marshal Amer was in command, his primary objective was that the army should safeguard the regime—now, however, it was established that the duty of the armed forces was exclusively the liberation of the occupied territories and Nasser made an appeal for Arab solidarity, by-passing ideological distinctions.

From my side, I began political contacts the minute the cease-fire was effected. I received the Soviet Ambassador on 10 June; he informed me of the results of the extraordinary meeting of the Socialist countries held in Moscow to study the Middle East situation; their unanimous decision, with the sole exception of Romania, was to sever relations with Israel, to provide emergency aid to the Arab States and assist them in reversing the consequences of the Israeli aggression. At this meeting I raised, for the first time, the possibility that Egypt might need Soviet experts in addition to its need for arms.

Other ambassadors of the Socialist countries began calling on me. Democratic Germany extended to us an emergency aid of fifty MiG-17s, and a substantial number of tanks and artillery. The Polish Ambassador was actively offering ideas which, in many cases, sounded like Soviet feelers. At his meeting with me he indicated that Israel was adjacent to a number of US military bases which allowed her quick access to military assistance. He asked whether it was feasible to consider granting Socialist countries military facilities in Egypt, thus enabling them to render a similar service. I replied that the most urgent matter now was the prompt delivery of arms to rebuild the army. He went on, however, to propose a military agreement with the Soviet Union in order to expedite arms shipments.

On Friday 16 June, a Soviet military delegation arrived in

Cairo to study our military needs and to invite Nasser to visit Moscow for further talks. Nasser directed me to inform the Soviet Ambassador that he did not contemplate visiting Moscow at present and that he felt it would be more appropriate in the circumstances if one of the Soviet leaders was to come to Cairo.

Thus Podgorny arrived in Cairo on 21 June and met with Nasser the same evening at a dinner banquet. Podgorny spoke of the Soviet Union's and the Socialist countries' commitment to help Egypt overcome the consequences of the aggression and indicated the importance of realizing this through a peaceful settlement. Nasser answered that reaching military parity with Israel would be more conducive to achieving this end.

Official talks began the following day at Qubba palace. Podgorny was accompanied by Marshal Zakharov, Soviet Army Chief of Staff, and the Soviet Ambassador in Cairo. At Nasser's side were Zakaria Moheiddine, Ali Sabry, General Fawzi and myself.

Podgorny began by saying that he was keen that this visit should take place before Kosygin's visit to Johnson for talks on the Middle East, the Vietnam war, the ICBMs and anti-missile systems. The Soviet leaders expected Johnson to urge certain concessions from the Arab side, as a way out of the present impasse, and the Soviet Union would not agree to proposals unacceptable to the Arabs. Podgorny added that he had sent a message to Moscow the preceding night relating to Egypt's air-defence system and that our needs were currently being studied in Moscow, also to Egypt's wish for a Soviet naval presence in the Mediterranean to balance the US Sixth Fleet—which Israel considered a strategic reserve. It would be better, however, if the military on both sides studied the details pertaining to this proposed presence, such as supplies and the joint measures needed to confront any air attack on the fleet.

Nasser responded: 'We in Egypt have been the victims of aggression both in 1956 and in 1967 because the US and the West considered us in both instances as aligned to the Soviet bloc, inasmuch as we rejected colonialist stances and policies. Our policies were, in fact, based on our national interests and the principles of non-alignment which allow for friendship with the Soviet Union. Now we have seen Israel attack us and occupy our territories, with the consent of the United States. With the growing US support to Israel we feel it is not logical to maintain neutrality between those who strike us and those who help us. We wish to deepen and strengthen Egyptian–Soviet relations with the aim of eliminating the consequences of Israeli aggression.

'There are two alternatives before us: either to submit to the United States which would then help us in the same way it helps some of the Asian countries, imposing the condition that we submit to its colonial hegemony. The other is to struggle and fight for our freedom. Since the struggle to free our territories will depend on the deployment of armed force, we have to conclude an agreement with the Soviet Union. We are ready to extend facilities to your fleet in the Mediterranean. Naturally we will hear people in this country say "you drove the British from the door to let in the Soviets through the window". Yet we can take such talk in our stride for the sake of liberating our land, and as long as this is pursued by a serious and effective military support from your side. I know that our people are resilient and understanding enough to accept it.

'The building of our armed forces should come within the framework of a joint effort, a Soviet–Egyptian venture, which would offer our officers and soldiers the experience and training of your cadres . . . if we cannot drive the Israelis from Sinai peacefully we shall resort to war, yet this is not your responsibility, it is exclusively ours. We would, however, ask you to help in the air defence of Egyptian territory. Israel may attempt to cross the Suez Canal and penetrate deep into Egypt. Confronting such an attack should be the responsibility of our joint defence systems. For if an attack of this nature happens it will be at the behest of the United States and primarily because we would have concluded an agreement with you and opened our ports to your fleet.'

Podgorny said that he had received a cable from Moscow agreeing to Soviet participation in strengthening Egyptian air-defence systems. However, the presence of foreign troops in the territory of any sovereign country was a highly sensitive issue and he would, therefore, suggest that the control of air defence remain in Egyptian hands, while receiving Soviet support and training.

When asked by Podgorny about China's approach, Nasser said

that the Chinese had offered to supply us with small arms. They resented our acceptance of the ceasefire and believed we should have continued resistance in every village and hamlet in the Delta, avoiding large concentrations around Cairo and other larger cities. (They were, of course, unaware of the nature of our terrain and our local conditions.) Podgorny referred to Chinese attempts to vilify the Soviet Union, by claiming that the Soviets had betrayed the Arabs as well as the Vietnamese. Nasser intimated that this was a point of no great concern. Podgorny expressed interest in the role that could be played by Arab oil-producing countries which had declared at the time the suspension of oil production. He then referred to talks between General Fawzi and Marshal Zakharov, and affirmed that all needed weapons and equipment would be shipped immediately upon his return. Arms for stockpiling could be discussed by specialized military commissions.

In the second round of talks on 23 June Nasser stated: 'It is imperative that you promptly replace the arms we have lost – this will boost the morale of our officers and men. Immediately after the battle we received from you twenty-five MiG-21s and ninety-three MiG-17s. I learned from our military delegation today that agreement had been reached for a further forty MiG-21s. I would like to raise a technical point in the presence of Marshal Zakharov. The MiGs have a short range when compared with the Mystères and Mirages that Israel owns. [This was before Israel received from the US the more sophisticated and longer-ranging Phantoms.] Therefore we are in need of a new type of aircraft, a long-range fighter-bomber. Otherwise Israel will maintain its air superiority and strike us at will. You must immediately send us – by air – a number of MiG-21s. We have more pilots at present than planes. We also have a shortage of infantry equipment . . . I would like to remind you of your cable and that of Prime Minister Kosygin which I received after I resigned, confirming that the Soviet Union would undertake the immediate re-arming of our forces. I anticipate that Israel will attack us as soon as the UN meetings are concluded. What, in such a case, would be the aid you could offer us, so that the country does not fall into Israel's hands? I heard from General Fawzi that his talks with you this morning did not include your participation in our air-defence systems . . .'

Podgorny said: 'I would like to put on record that we in the Soviet Union are committed to our promise to re-arm the Egyptian forces and, despite the huge distance between us, we shall expedite your needs by land, sea and all other possible means.'

Nasser then proceeded to elaborate on his expectations for the future. 'Yesterday, one of the US delegates at the UN told our representative [Ambassador el-Kony] "You are now trying to correct your mistake by another mistake" – meaning, of course, cooperation with you. Yet we have no faith in American promises for an Israeli withdrawal. In fact I believe that Israel will probably resume her attacks on us after 27 June, for the simple reason that both the US and Israel have failed so far to achieve their objectives. No peace agreement has been concluded with the Arabs and the kind of stability sought by Israel has not materialized. They are beginning to realize that no military defeat will deter the Arabs from taking action once they recover from the shock. To them the results of the battle have been para-doxical. The military defeat, instead of subjugating the Arabs to the will of the United States and Israel, has driven both Egypt and Syria into closer alignment with the Soviet Union, an alignment that will grow in proportion to the increasing US support to Israel. I would therefore reiterate that it is imperative that you supply us immediately with our requirements in MiG-21s, and with a long-range type of aircraft which we at present lack. One final question: in what way are you going to help us should Israel attack within the next few days? You must bear in mind that we cannot retreat from our present positions. We will hold to them to the last breath. You had the Volga to retreat to, we don't have a similar line to retreat to. Cairo is only 100 kilometres from the Canal.'

Marshal Zakharov itemized the arms shipments for immediate delivery: forty-three MiG-21s with their technicians, two train-ing planes, thirty-eight Sukhois, 100 tanks.

In the ensuing discussion Nasser stated that Egypt would agree on a form of association with the Soviet Union that would not infringe on 'our reputation and leading role in the Third World', to which Podgorny readily agreed. Nasser and Podgorny agreed that Podgorny would stop over in the Yugoslav capital to acquaint Marshal Tito with Egypt's new ideas with respect to the policy of non-alignment.

Podgorny left, leaving behind Marshal Zakharov to conclude the details of the military talks. On 29 June Nasser received Zakharov, who informed him that the Soviet Command welcomed greater military cooperation, including the sending of military advisers and air–defence experts.

Having disposed of the issue of rebuilding the Egyptian armed forces, Nasser directed his attention to the Arab situation. The Arab world was seething with anger and resentment against both the US and the West in general for perpetrating the military defeat. A number of Arab countries severed their relations with the US. Nasser was impressed by General de Gaulle's firm stand against Israeli intransigence and was hoping that perhaps more Western countries would adopt a similar policy; at the same time, Nasser was anxious to steer away Arab resentment from the West and channel it exclusively towards the United States.

Kuwait called for a meeting of the Arab Foreign Ministers on 18 June to be resumed in New York during the UN General Assembly meeting. My contribution was to explore means of further consolidating Arab solidarity, while Sheikh Sabah al-Ahmed, the Kuwaiti Foreign Minister, announced that the Arab oil-producing countries still held fast to their decision on suspending oil production.

Nasser was deeply impressed by how King Hussein of Jordan had stood shoulder to shoulder with him during the war which, with his limited forces and lack of aerial cover, had cost him the whole of the West Bank; he wrote to Hussein on 22 June, paying tribute to his heroic struggle and offering 'to put all we have in the service of the common destiny of our two peoples'. He later received the King in Cairo while on his way to the United Nations to tell him that Egypt was ready to share everything it had with Jordan, even if it meant sharing the last loaf of bread between them. 'We have entered this war together, lost it together and we must win it together,' he said. Nasser also felt that the United States might feel more inclined to better accommodate King Hussein, an old friend of theirs, and so urged him to negotiate with the Americans in any way he wanted to and for as long as he wanted to for a peaceful settlement in the West Bank which would lead to total Israeli withdrawal, as long as he refrained from signing a separate peace treaty, going so far as to end officially the state of belligerency with Israel, and even, if he wanted, concluding a joint defence agreement with the United States. Nasser warned him that the price would be high and he should not expect the US to force Israel into a complete withdrawal from the West Bank, the annexation of which is central in the Zionist programme . . . but perhaps he was wrong. (King Hussein had a chance to tell us later that Johnson, while extremely bitter towards Egypt, offered Hussein nothing beyond vague general promises.)

On 30 June, a group of Latin American States submitted to the General Assembly a draft resolution which failed to elicit unanimous Arab support because it was felt by the Arab States that to subscribe to the draft resolution which contained the recognition of Israel and the opening up of international waterways to its navigation was in fact giving it a prize for its aggression, and they refused to vote in its favour, which led eventually to the defeat of the Latin American draft resolution.

The Soviet Ambassador came to see me during that period with a message from the Central Committee of the Soviet Communist Party advising that we vote in favour of the Latin American draft, on the grounds that while it called for a termination of the state of belligerency, which did not include either a formal recognition of Israel or holding direct negotiations with her, it did stipulate the complete withdrawal of Israeli forces from all the occupied Arab territories. I informed the Soviet Ambassador that while we approved the draft resolution, we were bound by the principle of Arab unanimity. The Arab countries felt strongly that Israel should not be rewarded for its aggression and its withdrawal should consequently be unconditional.

The defeat of the draft resolution predictably delighted Israel and the United States. Goldberg, who had all along tried to obstruct and derail the draft resolution, could not hide his elation from a number of UN delegates at the result.

During the month of July a number of Arab Heads of State began arriving in Cairo without prior arrangement. Algerian President Boumedienne and King Hussein arrived in Cairo on 11 July. At a meeting which included them as well as Nasser and myself, King Hussein indicated the futility of seeking a solution at the UN not only because of US delaying tactics but equally because of widely differing stands by the Arab delegates 'who were outbidding each other'; he proposed holding an Arab Summit Meeting, and referred to his meeting with General de Gaulle who had told him: 'If Israel can claim a right to live in peace and security then Jordan, most certainly, is entitled to the same right.' The Algerian President Houari Boumedienne advocated the continuation of the struggle and building up a defensive front, strong enough militarily, economically and politically to stem any renewed Israeli attacks; while the task of rebuilding the armed forces for an eventual confrontation with the occupying Israeli forces would go on.

Nasser, while feeling that the time was not opportune for convening an Arab Summit Meeting, dwelt on the situation on the West Bank of Jordan which, with its population density, was far dissimilar to Sinai, and urged King Hussein to pursue his efforts and talks with the United States.

The following day saw the arrival of Syrian President Nouriddine al-Atassi, Iraqi President Abdel Salam Aref and the Sudanese President, Ismail al-Azhari. King Hussein had left while Boumedienne remained. Thus the five Heads of State held their first meeting on the morning of Thursday, 13 July. Atassi advocated the establishment of a unified military and political command and said that Syria was prepared to merge with Egypt. Nasser answered that the liberation of the occupied territories was at present a more crucial and immediate concern than merging separate States. Nasser proceeded to reiterate his reading of the current situation. While he would offer every chance for reaching a peaceful settlement, he personally felt that this would never materialize. What has been seized by force can only be restored by force. Egypt was in the process of rebuilding its armed forces to liberate the occupied territories; the date of the battle would depend on attaining military parity with Israel which should be within three years. In order to bring this date nearer, he suggested that the Arab States with close ties with the Soviet Union urge it into the prompt and immediate delivery of our military needs.

I proposed that, since a continuation of the suspension of oil production would harm those States with no other energy resource and the frontline States were in need of economic support to enable them to continue their resistance, production be resumed and that ten per cent of the revenues be allocated for military preparedness. I estimated that this should bring in some £150 million.

The presidents decided that Boumedienne and Aref would leave immediately for Moscow for confidential talks with the Soviet leaders and would report their results upon their return to Cairo. The two presidents held two meetings with the Soviet leaders, Brezhnev, Podgorny and Kosygin. During heated discussions between the two sides, Brezhnev made the following points: Israel maintains military superiority. With a population of two and a half million, it has an army of 350,000 soldiers, fifteen per cent of the population. The Soviets have helped with arms and diplomatic action. The Socialist countries have met twice within a short period to consider how to stop an Israeli invasion of Cairo and Damascus. They have severed relations with Israel, exerted pressure on the US, started an airlift of supplies and weapons to Egypt and Syria: 48,000 tons of military equipment delivered in 544 airlifts and fifteen transport ships. ('We were grieved to see our latest planes and rockets displayed at US research centres, and to hear Israelis speak of them as the best of their kind,' he said.) The Socialist countries have agreed to strengthen the Arab States militarily by providing them with weapons, and experts to help reorganize the army according to the requirements of modern warfare, especially aerial capacity and tank formations. In the meanwhile, the Arabs have to be more flexible and accept, in exchange for a withdrawal of Israeli forces, the termination of hostilities with Israel—which neither implies the recognition of Israel nor entering into a peace agreement with her, otherwise the alternative will be the continuation of the war, which is unrealistic. The Arabs will be well advised to consider the oil situation. In his recent talks with Kosygin Johnson was apprehensive of losing the Arab world.

Boumedienne, on the other hand, maintained the following: we will continue to explore peaceful solutions until we complete our preparations to restore our rights, and urge the Soviet Union and the Socialist countries to step up their supplies of sophisticated weapons and military equipment and meet the economic requirements. This Soviet insistence on a UN resolution in which the Arabs accept the end of belligerency would mean opening up navigation in the Suez Canal to Israeli vessels and could lead to direct negotiations with Israel for a peace treaty. A resolution by the United Nations, whatever it implies, will not solve the problem and will fail to force Israel to withdraw from the occupied territories. The problem is twofold: the consequences of the 1948 war, the Palestine question and the consequences of Israeli aggression towards the Arab countries in 1967. US policy is to suppress the Palestine question and lend permanency to Israeli occupation. Its ulterior aim is to overthrow the progressive regimes in both Egypt and Syria and eventually in Iraq.

Afterwards, upon his return to Cairo, Boumedienne commented on his meeting, saying: 'I noticed contradictions in the Soviets' political analysis due to political considerations of their own. For instance, they insisted on violently resisting reactionary forces throughout the Arab regime while at the same time calling for total Arab alliance, regardless of extreme ideological differences. They have also insisted many a time on the importance of having the UN adopt a resolution. I personally feel that they maintain this position out of a desire to spare the Soviet Union another diplomatic defeat. With regard to arms, they maintain that they have already sent us numerous consignments and will continue to meet our requirements. Personally I feel they will, although there is the possibility of some delay. They feel that we shall not be in a position to take any military action within two or three years. They therefore consider it necessary that we resort to political solutions for the time being.'

Nasser commented: 'We must work towards the armed struggle. When the Soviets realize that we are determined on an armed struggle they will find themselves obliged to proceed with us, despite their fears that an armed struggle on our front might ignite the whole region.'

Finally, President Boumedienne stated that the Soviets talked at length of our military defeat and bitterly criticized the condition of the Arab armies which withdrew, leaving behind them on the battlefield weapons and equipment.

The presidents decided that a Foreign Ministers' meeting should convene in Khartoum in August.

After the departure of the Arab presidents, I called on Nasser at his residence where he was deeply engrossed in studying a number of military reports submitted to him by General Fawzi. He asked me whether we had a field commander who could lead the army in battle.

I replied that, in modern warfare, commanders of the historical calibre of Hannibal, Napoleon and Khalid ibn el-Waleed who would be present in the field of battle to command, direct and supervise were now superfluous. What we needed, I continued, was a well-trained and well-equipped army, led by a commander who should follow the established rules of warfare.

Nasser then asked me about my proposal concerning Arab oil. I explained that we were losing £120 million annually in Suez Canal dues and as a result of the disruption of our oil production in Sinai. We should not be able to hold out economically without making up this sum and the Arab oil-producing countries should therefore resume oil production and allocate ten per cent of their oil revenues for strengthening our economic position, and also to serve their own domestic needs.

Nasser remained silent for a while, then said that it would be difficult for him to ask the Arab States for money in the name of an Egypt which used to help them financially before they discovered oil. 'Can you imagine the effects this will have,' he said, 'on the Egyptian people and on myself?'

I said that we were engaged in a battle that affected them all. Israel now posed a threat to the whole of the Arab world and we were all partners in this.

Nasser referred to Egyptian differences with some Arab countries in the past which may have left them with malice against Egypt.

I replied that I did not think so; that they were all now aware that the Israeli threat overshadowed Arab differences and rose above political or ideological strife.

I left for Khartoum to attend the Arab Foreign Ministers Conference on 1 August; the Arab climate of emotion was such that a joint working plan was quite unfeasible. The meeting therefore proposed that a summit meeting convene in Khartoum at the end of August. The Syrian government refused to participate in the summit conference because of its differences with Jordan and Saudi Arabia at that time.

The chief objective which I wished to achieve through this summit meeting was the restoration of good relations among the Arab States, specifically between Egypt and Saudi Arabia so as to resolve the Yemeni problem and withdraw the Egyptian forces stationed there, and to agree on economic support for the frontline States.

Before the Summit Meeting in Khartoum, US President Lyndon Johnson had sent a memorandum on 9 August 1967 to Yugoslav President Tito to be forwarded to us, in which he reaffirmed US determination to exert its utmost efforts towards achieving a permanent and just settlement in the Middle East. In his message, Johnson added that any settlement must be realistic and that the US agreed that the settlement should not infringe on the pride of the Arabs or force them to abandon any legitimate rights or interests. Tito arrived in Cairo on 10 August to confer with Nasser and informed him of Johnson's message. He then proceeded to elaborate on his proposal which was based on full Israeli withdrawal, since he firmly believed that it was in the interests of neither the Arabs nor the Third World countries to allow the aggressor to be rewarded for his aggression.

Once more, on 24 August (only five days before the Arab Summit Conference was to convene in Khartoum), Johnson sent a message to those Arab States which had not severed relations with the US, in which he reiterated the same message and the five principles he had previously announced for solving the conflict. Our political analysis of the Johnson move was that it aimed, through vague promises, to convince some Arab States of America's goodwill in order to dissipate Arab enthusiasm for a united front at Khartoum and thus thwart their determination to mobilize Arab power in order to confront Israeli aggression.

Nasser went to Khartoum on 28 August where he had his first meeting with the Arab leaders since the defeat. The Sudanese people marched out from Khartoum and the neighbouring areas to welcome, greet and cheer Nasser. By instinct, the people knew that Nasser had now become the symbol of Arab resistance and struggle. As soon as Nasser's plane landed at the airport, the crowds broke through the security barriers, and men were shouting 'Long live Nasser' and calling for vengeance against Israel and the US, and for Arab solidarity with Egypt to liberate the land by force. I was riding in a car behind Nasser and I felt that all the inhabitants of Khartoum had come out to welcome him. I believe that this was the first time in history that a defeated leader received a conquerer's welcome. The important factor was that this particular welcome, and Nasser's realization that they were putting their trust in him to achieve victory, raised his confidence sky high.

Before the plenary session began, I contacted members of the Saudi delegation, Prince Sultan and Omar el-Sakkaf, the Minister of State for Foreign Affairs, and mentioned that Egypt needed £120 million to make up for her losses from the Suez Canal and oil revenues. I suggested that Saudi Arabia specify the sum it was ready to contribute so that it would be possible to ask the rest of the oil-producing countries to contribute the same. I did not expect that Saudi Arabia would pay more than £30 million.

Later, Omar el-Sakkaf said he had spoken to King Faisal who, however, refused to voice an opinion before the convening of the plenary session. The King also objected to contributing on the basis of a percentage of the oil revenue resources. He refused in principle to pay any sum to the government of the Syrian Baath Party because of the differences between the two countries and their continuous attacks against him. So it was a total surprise at the plenary session when the issue of financial support came up for debate to see King Faisal raise his hand, indicating with his five fingers that Saudi Arabia would contribute £50 million; the Prince of Kuwait pledged £55 million and Libya in turn decided it would contribute £30 million.

In a separate later meeting between members of the delegations who would provide the aid and the representatives of Egypt and Jordan, the Jordanian Ministry of Economy asked that Jordan receive £40 million. I informed Nasser and proposed that we increase Jordan's share from £15 million to £20–25 million. Nasser disagreed and said: 'Let Jordan immediately take what it wants . . . King Hussein has been brave and honest with us . . . if they want £40 million, let it be so and let it be part of Egypt's share so that we don't have to ask the Arab States for more money.'

Because I understood each Arab State's position and the differences in opinion, I considered that the Conference had achieved positive results in this way, and that Nasser had succeeded in strengthening his bilateral relations with the Arab kings and presidents, especially with those with whom he had had differences in the past, such as King Faisal.

On 31 August, Nasser told the evening session in Khartoum: 'We must take into account two main factors in dealing with our political action to remove the consequences of the aggression: military preparedness and economic resistance. No doubt the resolution adopted by the previous session concerning economic aid will be a great help. We must also take into consideration the fact that there is agreement between the US and the Soviet Union to resolve the problem by political means. This has been expressed by the American–Soviet project which was based on two major points: an end to the state of war [with Israel] and withdrawal from the occupied Arab territories, in addition to other matters such as Jerusalem and navigation.

'It is thus imperative that the Arab States define their position. I hope that we all understand that when we talk of political action, it means not only taking, but giving as well. Here, we must look at what we can afford to give. The situation in the world now differs from what it was in 1956. That year, both the US and the Soviet Union agreed to oppose the Tripartite Aggression. Today, in 1967, the US and the Soviet Union have agreed that Israel has a right to exist and survive, just as they have both agreed on an end to the state of war. Despite everything, we in Egypt can wait until we complete our military preparations. Then we will carry out the only action that Israel understands perfectly – the liberation of our territories by force.

'On the other hand, I am really worried about the situation in the West Bank. Here, we must ask ourselves: Will the time factor be in our interest or not? I personally believe that it will not be in our interest at all. I am following in detail all the developments in Israel today. The three parties which represent the peak of extremism have merged into one bloc under the name of "Likud". This faction insists on retaining the whole of the West Bank, refusing to give up one inch of the land. This is why we must move quickly and exert our utmost efforts to regain Jerusalem and the West Bank through the means available to us at present, for if we delay, neither Jerusalem nor the West Bank will return to us.

'Is it possible to regain the occupied land by military means at present? I believe that the answer to this question is evident. This road is not open before us at the present time. Thus we have before us only one way by which to regain the West Bank and Jerusalem: political action.

'President Tito has informed me that he is ready to fly to Moscow to arrange with the Kremlin leaders that the Yugoslav proposal replace the American one. The Americans, however, will not accept the Yugoslav proposal because it stipulates the return of our occupied land. In my opinion, the Tito proposal will lead us to an acceptable political solution; the American proposal, on the other hand, will lead us to surrender and humiliation, and consequently it can never be acceptable. If we fail to reach agreement on a particular proposal here, I believe King Hussein should approach the Americans and agree with them on the restoration of the West Bank. I am ready to announce this publicly because America alone can order Israel to take its hands off the West Bank.'

Total silence fell upon the hall when Nasser finished his speech, and looks were directed at King Faisal of Saudi Arabia who began speaking in his calm, deep voice. 'I propose, Your Excellencies, that brother President Nasser's address be the working paper of the conference and the basis for the resolutions that will be adopted.' With this, King Faisal's speech ended, and at this point the conference was regarded as successful, for Egyptian–Saudi solidarity in these difficult times for the Arab nation was to a great extent a vital and fundamental matter.

King Hussein said: 'The situation in the West Bank is extremely serious and difficult. If we succeed in rebuilding our armed forces, we will not be able to liberate the land in the near future. At the same time, if we leave the West Bank in Israel's hands for a long time, it will be difficult for us to regain it later. The issue is not that of the West Bank alone. The future of Jerusalem does not only concern the Palestinians and Arabs, but the Muslims and Christians as well.'

Nasser proposed that King Faisal, in view of his good relations with the Americans, contact them and explain our point of view.

Ahmad Shokairi focused on the fact that, although the Palestine question was an Arab issue of destiny, only the people of Palestine had the right to determine their own destiny. He continued: 'The five principles in the Johnson proposal are a high price for restoring the West Bank to us. As an Arab citizen and as Chairman of the PLO, I refuse to pay this high price and I hereby declare that I disagree with the Yugoslav proposal which aims at achieving a permanent settlement and permanent peace in the region before finding a solution to the Palestinian question.'

Nasser said: 'At the present time, none of us can restore the West Bank by military means. Shall we bequeath it to Israel then?

What is the alternative? The West Bank is more important to me than Sinai. We must not forget that one half of Palestine was lost in 1948 and the other half in 1967. If our objective is to restore the West Bank through political action, then we must pay the price. King Hussein had good relations with the Americans. I believe that they are keen on maintaining these relations. There will certainly be a price, but it will not be the resolution of the issue. Possibly the price will be the consolidation of King Hussein's ties with the Americans and his getting closer to them . . . If we have chosen political action because of our circumstances, then I differ with Shokairi in describing the Tito proposal as a liquidation of the Palestinian issue. There is a difference between political action and the liquidation of the issue. And if we do not undertake positive action to restore the West Bank, then the land that the Israelis occupied will gradually become Israeli territory.'

It was clear that confidence was lost between King Hussein and Shokairi, the latter reflecting Palestinian fears that if King Hussein were to be delegated by the Arabs to talk with the Americans about the restoration of the West Bank, the matter would end in the termination of the Palestinian issue. Various trends and ideas had been mooted before the conference, among them severing political relations with the US by those Arab States which had not yet done so, the withdrawal of Arab stocks from the sterling and dollar zones and the continuing suspension of Arab oil production. Nasser opposed these tendencies and called for the resumption of oil production. In explanation he said that such measures as those proposed would be favourable if he were in a position to engage in immediate military operations but, since we had to concentrate at the present juncture on rebuilding our armed forces which would take a long time, the suspension of oil production would gravely harm the economies of the Arab oil States. Although Egypt had severed relations with the US and maintained this policy, Nasser did not ask the other Arab States to take the same step, especially those countries which enjoyed a traditional friendship with the US. Nasser's aim was to keep an Arab door open for dialogue with the US, not to mention the fact that he wished to give the US an opportunity to prove to the few remaining friends she had in the Arab world—if she wanted to—that she seriously intended to reduce her total alignment with Israel.

Thus, when it held its closing session to vote on the resolutions and issue a political communiqué, the Arab Summit Conference in Khartoum unanimously approved that no negotiations, no recognition and no peace treaty be concluded with Israel, that none of the rights of the Palestinian people should be relinquished and that annual aid should be provided to Egypt and Jordan.

Zionist propaganda later exploited these resolutions as reflecting an Arab hard-line policy. But we who attended the Conference had seen how the Palestinians feared that the climate of military defeat in the June War would open the door to the abandonment of their rights. Consequently many Conference members emphasized that, as long as Israel remained in occupation of Arab territories, no trafficking with Israel would be feasible.

From a purely Egyptian point of view, the Khartoum Conference was a success. The loss of our revenues from the Suez Canal dues as well as Sinai petroleum threatened our ability to find the necessary hard currency to import our requirements in wheat and foodstuffs during the coming few months and consequently this economic aid which we received was complementary to the rebuilding of our armed forces. Both military build-up and economic resistance were the key to a long struggle that we hoped would end with the liberation of our territories.

4

Resolution 242

The UN General Assembly's emergency session failed to adopt a resolution calling for an end to the Israeli occupation. Bilateral consultations between the US and the USSR during and after the session equally failed. Tito, together with a number of non-aligned leaders, was actively consulting with the Arab States, the US and the Soviet Union for the promulgation of a satisfactory resolution, which also failed.

While some expected a resumption of the issue before the General Assembly in September, I was of the opinion that the problem should be raised with the Security Council, and Nasser agreed. The reason was to relieve the Arab States who were not members of the Security Council from voting on such contro-versial issues. Moreover, any resolution adopted by the General Assembly would call on the Security Council to take the necessary measures for its implementation. So, in any case, we had to go to the Security Council. Consequently I began consultations with representatives of member States of the Security Council to inform them of my decision and pave the way for a favourable resolution.

While I did not entertain any false hopes that Israel would abide by a Security Council resolution calling upon it to withdraw, my conviction was based on the following considerations: Egypt did not as yet possess the military strength to resist an Israeli attack across the Canal – we needed time to rebuild our armed forces; we needed to negate the idea that Israel had succeeded in propagating – that we did not want peace – by reaffirming our willingness to accept a just, peaceful settlement; we wished to unmask Israel's position and force it into a position where it would have to reject the resolution publicly; we had to comply with the Soviet demand to give a peaceful solution all chances possible; and finally, we could offer the US the opportunity to lessen its conspicuous bias towards Israel – if it did not, it would lay bare its position before the Arab world.

At the time New York was seething with hatred for anything that was Arab. Israel, the occupier, enjoyed support while the Arabs, the victims of Israeli aggression, were regarded as the villains, deserving of punishment. I felt bitterness at the slanting of news; the main facts – who fired the first shot in the war, who was pursuing an expansionist policy, who was dealing savagely with the Palestinians living under the terror of military occupation – were ignored. It was ironical how the Jews of America were even more fanatic in their attitude than Jews elsewhere, including those of Israel.

I recall two incidents from this time whose significance remained with me for a long time. Once, as I was returning to my hotel, a young man stepped forward and shook my hand. He spoke Arabic with an Egyptian accent and asked me to help him return to Egypt. At first I thought he was an Egyptian student studying at one of the American universities. As he told his story, I discovered he was an Egyptian Jew who had been expelled from Egypt by the security department. He wished to return to Egypt because he was Egyptian and Gamal Abdel Nasser was his president . . . not Levi Eshkol! I was very much touched by this young man's patriotic feelings. I could only tell him that he was one of the many victims of the Arab–Israeli conflict.

The second incident – and here I was a mere spectator – occurred as I entered the hotel elevator. I found myself face to face with Arthur Goldberg, the US Permanent Delegate at the UN, and spokesman for the US at the international forum before, during and after the June War. A few seconds later, another man entered the lift. Upon seeing Goldberg, the man raised his hat and introduced himself: 'Like you, I am an American Jew living in New York. I have followed closely all your statements to the TV networks, and now I bow my head to you in thanks and gratitude . . . We shall never forget the noble services you have extended to Israel.' Goldberg smiled, though he was embarrassed at my witnessing this.

I decided to begin immediate consultations with the member States of the Security Council. There was no difficulty in diagnosing the situation and agreeing on the necessity for the complete withdrawal of Israel's forces to 4 June positions. My problem, however, was with Goldberg.

During my consultations with him, I noticed Goldberg's insistence on employing the term 'conflict' while I used 'aggression' in interpreting Israel's actions in June. This prompted me, after hearing his diagnosis of the situation, to say: 'There is no need for me to get to know Israel's position now, for the US political position conforms to that of Israel.'

Goldberg said: 'Do not forget you were the ones to start the aggression against Israel. War, from our point of view, was declared the moment you closed the Gulf of Aqaba, not with the Israeli military operations.'

I said: 'First of all, we did not begin the aggression, and the whole world knows that. The Gulf of Aqaba was closed once before, in 1951. It could be the subject of legal litigation, and we know for a fact that international law is on our side. Anyway, the Security Council did not consider the closure as an aggressive act when it debated it in 1951. Furthermore, you speak as if it were an absolute defeat for us and we must submit to Israel's terms and conditions. We were defeated, but we did not yield, and we will never surrender, although we are willing to work for a just peace.'

When Goldberg and I began discussing the draft that could be adopted by the Security Council, I said that we must first agree on a political position on which any draft could be based, and that, in my opinion, it must be clear from the start that a total Israeli withdrawal to 4 June positions was the basis for any political position.

Goldberg said: 'The draft resolution that we could submit to the Security Council must be based on the five principles declared by President Johnson [on 19 June].'

I answered that they were general political slogans, applicable to almost any issue in the world. They were deliberately ambiguous and did not contain one clear statement about Israeli withdrawal.

Thus, consultations between us and with the other Security Council parties continued for many days. It was clear that the majority of the Security Council members supported us completely, but in the end they would clash with the Israeli-based US veto. In reverse, the US position could not hope to win the support of the Council. So, from the practical point of view, the successful adoption of a resolution by the Security Council required the approval of both Goldberg and myself.

Once again, Goldberg resumed consultations with me, saying: 'What is important is that we agree as to what is suitable to be submitted to the Security Council in the form of a draft resolution.'

I said: 'First of all, I want to ask you about the content and the dimensions of the proposed draft.'

Goldberg asked: 'What do you mean exactly?'

I said: 'There are two specific issues. There is, first of all, the fundamental Palestinian issue, which is tabled on the agenda of the UN General Assembly since 1947. There were also previous resolutions on the issue which have not been implemented by Israel, and which represent the fundamental problem, resulting in the Arab–Israeli conflict. Then there is the latest issue concerning the Israeli aggression against Egypt, Syria and Jordan, on which no resolution has so far been reached. So, on which of the two bases should we carry out our consultations?'

Goldberg said he could not give me an answer before referring to Washington. A few days later, he informed me that his government was of the view that consultations on a draft resolution to the Security Council should be confined to the consequences of the June War, and not extend to the Palestine issue.

I said: 'In this case, I have one further question to ask. What is required: is it a procedural resolution to appoint another UN intermediary, another Count Bernadotte, to explore solutions to the problem; or is it to seek a comprehensive settlement? I am ready to accept either view, on condition that we are clear, from the very beginning, on the objective of the proposed draft resolution.'

Goldberg replied: 'What is required is a resolution containing a comprehensive settlement.' (This became a standard phrase later.)

Consultations with all Security Council members continued throughout October on the basis defined and approved by the US. At the beginning of November, Goldberg sent me a copy of the US draft resolution that he would submit to the Security Council. A reading of this draft showed a reversal of previous American positions at General Assembly meetings. It is enough to point to the paragraph on Israeli withdrawal; it states: 'The Security Council . . . affirms that the fulfilment of the above Charter principles requires the achievement of a state of just and lasting peace in the Middle East embracing withdrawal of armed forces from occupied territories . . .' After this extremely ambiguous reference in the text on the subject of Israeli withdrawal, we find the American draft was very decisive and binding in its commitments over the Arabs, including the termination of a state of belligerency and the recognition of Israel's boundaries, guaranteeing freedom of navigation (to Israel) through international waterways in the area.

I confronted Goldberg. 'This is nothing more than an Israeli draft under a US name. It does not even meet the limited objective which you previously stated, namely the consequences of the June War. For example, it does not restore to us Sinai, Gaza, the West Bank or the Golan.'

Goldberg said: 'There is no problem concerning Israel's complete withdrawal. Our draft seeks to achieve that goal even without a clear statement, because Sinai is a part of Egypt, the West Bank is part of Jordan, and the Golan part of Syria.'

I said: 'This is information that can be gleaned from a geography book anywhere in the world. But here at the UN we talk a political language. There is occupation of our territories as a result of Israel's aggression. We must secure a clear-cut text on its termination; furthermore, we still require clarifications – and even fundamental modifications – to the draft before accepting it.'

Goldberg replied: 'We have actually submitted this draft to the Security Council. Believe me when I say it means Israel's withdrawal.'

I said: 'Unless what you have just stated is included in the draft, I assure you I will never accept it.'

On the same day, the US draft resolution was officially tabled on the Security Council agenda. On 7 November, I called for a Security Council meeting to consider the situation. Consequently, the Council convened on 9 November, chaired by Mr Mamadou Bubaker Kante of Mali.

Since the Security Council was convened at the request of Egypt, it was only natural, according to Security Council procedure, that I would be the first speaker to address the

Council. However, the US delegate, Arthur Goldberg, raised an objection that led to a crisis and a procedural debate which lasted for five hours. The US delegate requested that the Israeli delegate should be allowed to speak directly after me, giving him priority over all the other speakers. On this point alone Goldberg argued with the Council for hours. The problem was finally put to the vote at his own request and was defeated. When the Council turned to considering the real issue, the President said that officially the Council had before it two drafts: one submitted by the US, and the other submitted jointly by India, Mali and Nigeria. (This draft was basically derived from a previous draft submitted by the Latin American group to the General Assembly emergency session stipulating the necessity of total Israeli withdrawal from all the occupied Arab territories.)

In my address, I reminded the Council that we had 'emphasized that we were seeking a peaceful and just solution . . . and that the cornerstone of that political solution was naturally the immediate and unconditional withdrawal of the aggressive forces to the positions they occupied prior to 5 June. That is a basic requirement which emanates from every essential provision of the Charter. The minimal measure requiring adoption by the Security Council would be a resolution demanding that Israel immediately withdraw its aggressive forces to the positions held on 4 June. Indeed, the Security Council cannot afford not to meet this minimal requirement.'

Statements by the other speakers followed. The Indian delegate dealt with the joint draft whose first item stressed the inadmissibility of the acquisition of territory by military conquest. The French delegate reiterated his country's condemnation of the Israeli aggression. Other speakers followed, each stating his country's position on the situation. Then it was decided to adjourn the meeting until 13 November.

International support for us within the Security Council was mounting. Actually, the US position was the only capital asset left to Israel within the Security Council. The US insistence on refusing to admit that Israel had launched an aggression against the Arab countries was the foundation on which Israel based its behaviour and actions. The US did not even attempt to condemn Israel's refusal to implement two General Assembly resolutions which the US had itself at the time endorsed, namely condemnation of Israel's measures in Jerusalem, and secondly the demand for the repatriation of the Palestinians who had left the West Bank as a result of the June War.

Abba Eban summed up the US–Israeli stance at the meeting of 13 November with the words: 'The June War ceasefire lines will not change except for secure borders and peace treaties which would terminate war with the Arab countries.' Israel, which considered itself a conqueror, wanted to impose its own conditions.

Several delegates at the meeting expressed their surprise at our determination to continue resistance, following such a heavy military defeat. Gradually, however, this surprise turned to admiration, especially when our resistance took concrete and real shape at the front. Our armed forces sank the destroyer *Eilat* and, the following day, 24 October, Israel took revenge by shelling the petroleum refinery at Suez and the civilian inhabitants of the city. Egypt decided to evacuate all the inhabitants of the Canal Zone so that they were no longer potential targets of Israeli blackmail.

On the very same day that Israel shelled Suez, the US announced its intention of supplying Israel with an additional number of bombers, which was regarded as encouragement to Israel's occupation and barbaric acts. All these actions were not without effect on the mood of the Council.

The Security Council which convened on 13 November had three draft resolutions tabled before it: the US draft, the India–Mali–Nigeria draft, and the Soviet draft. It was, in fact, imperative that the Soviet Union submit a draft so that the debate should not be restricted to the US draft resolution.

At about that time, King Hussein visited the US and met for the second time with President Johnson. When I met King Hussein in New York, he told me he had received assurances from Washington on Israel's complete withdrawal from all the Arab territories if we would accept the US draft resolution. I told King Hussein that, with all due respect to US assurances, I was firmly convinced that Johnson would never change his policy of supporting Israel's aggression, and that I could never accept a resolution that did not clearly stipulate the inadmissibility of Israel's occupation of Arab territories and the necessity of its withdrawal. Finally, I said, if Johnson was serious in his assurance, why did the US not include in its draft resolution a clear statement stipulating Israel's withdrawal from the Arab territories?

Once again King Hussein emphasized: 'But I believe all the assurances of President Johnson . . . These are assurances given at the highest American level, and we cannot take them lightly. What, then, is to be done? If we do not agree to the US draft resolution in particular, the US will exercise its right of veto to defeat any other resolution . . . and we do need a resolution.'

I said: 'Rest assured, we will ultimately secure a resolution, and it will not be the American resolution. If need be, I will take the matter up to the General Assembly where we would be more favourably received than we were in the summer.'

On the same day I learnt that Goldberg had spoken with Lord Caradon, Britain's Permanent Delegate to the UN, on the necessity for reconciling the US draft (which we did not accept) with the non-aligned draft which was now being rejected by the US, though it had previously accepted it.

Goldberg came to see me again on 12 November and inquired about my feelings as to the explanations given to King Hussein in Washington over the US project. I answered: 'In spite of the explanations you have given King Hussein, I still remember your words the first time we met when you insisted that we leave no word without a clear interpretation – which I agreed to at the time. The US draft does not speak in clear terms about the withdrawal but refers to movements of military forces. I believe that it is imperative that the line to which Israel is to withdraw should be as clearly stated as are all the obligations that you have imposed on us.'

His answer was among the strangest I ever heard. He said: 'While it is important to use clear language, at times circumstances impose the injection of a degree of ambiguity, in order to overcome obstacles. The important thing, however, is that this ambiguity should be balanced.' He then went on to say that he understood our objection to the non-mention of Israel's name in connection with withdrawal and that he was ready to correct that in the final draft. He added, in an attempt to express appreciation of our position, that he was aware of the problems that faced us in signing an agreement with Israel, and consequently the US draft avoided any reference to such a step, and confined itself to an agreement that would be reached through the United Nations' representative.

To rebuff him, I said that signing a document with Israel did not bother us since we had already signed an Armistice Agreement with it; what bothered us was that Israel did not respect its signature. I then proceeded to ask him what he meant by the phrase 'mutual recognition' that occurred in his draft. He said that it did not include diplomatic recognition, while he asserted that the US draft did not prevent Egyptian forces from returning to Gaza or Jordanian forces to the West Bank.

Lord Caradon had begun his mission of reconciliation, starting with the US draft submitted by Goldberg on 7 November, which was clearly threatened with defeat because of our opposition, and consequently failed to secure the necessary votes for adoption. Because Lord Caradon maintained good and cordial relations with everyone, and because of his previous experience in the Middle East, he, no doubt, had an easier task than anyone else.

When Lord Caradon and I met to discuss the situation, I said: 'The non-aligned draft contains a fundamental principle which must be contained in any resolution we are to accept, namely "that occupation or acquisition of territory by military conquest is inadmissible under the UN Charter". Consequently, the Israeli forces must withdraw from all the Arab territories they occupied as a result of the recent conflict. The essential matter to us is total Israeli withdrawal to 4 June positions. In the light of this principle, we are prepared to accept anything reasonable, provided it does not jeopardize the fundamental issue, the Palestinian question.'

I mentioned to Caradon that in the fifty days since my arrival in New York I could hardly believe that the US could have backed down on every commitment she had undertaken, whether in the US–Soviet draft or in relation to the Latin American draft that she had previously approved in the General Assembly, and that consequently I was not in favour of any resolution that could harm the Arab position. He hastened to say: 'Why do you object to a resolution that stipulates in clear terms the withdrawal of Israel?' I answered that I had not read his draft yet, and he asserted that he would not submit a draft that did not stipulate in clear terms the necessity for Israeli withdrawal from the Arab territories, and added that the situation relating to the West Bank was critical and in dire need of a resolution.

Kuznetsov, the Deputy Foreign Minister of the Soviet Union, came to see me to ask my view on submitting the text of the joint US–Soviet draft resolution which stipulated the inadmissibility of the acquisition of territories by force, the withdrawal of all forces from the territories occupied after 4 June 1967 and the recognition of the right of all countries of the region to live in peace and security.

I answered that Dean Rusk had assured the Moroccan Foreign Minister that no such draft resolution existed and that the matter did not go beyond an exchange of views between the two super-powers during the extraordinary session last July.

Incensed, he answered that this was an American attempt at chicanery and that he was aware that the US was trying to derail the Security Council and exert tremendous pressure to acquire a convenient resolution.

I told him that I was ready, in case Israel declared its intention to withdraw from all occupied Arab territories and from Arab Jerusalem, to accept from my side the opening up of international waterways to Israeli navigation.

He commented that this was a realistic position which would also cause embarrassment to the US, which would then bear the responsibility of refusal.

On 15 November Lord Caradon showed me the text of the draft resolution he intended to submit to the Security Council the following day. The text reads as follows:

The Security Council
Expressing its continuing concern with the grave situation in the Middle East,
Emphasizing the inadmissibility of the acquisition of territory by war and the need to work for a just and lasting peace in which every State in the area can live in security,
Emphasizing further that all member States in their acceptance of the Charter of the United Nations have undertaken a commitment to act in accordance with Article 2 of the Charter,
1. *Affirms* that the fulfilment of Charter principles requires the establishment of a just and lasting peace in the Middle East

which should include the application of both the following principles:

(i) withdrawal of Israeli armed forces from territories occupied in the recent conflict;

(ii) termination of all claims or states of belligerency and respect for and acknowledgement of the sovereignty, territorial integrity and political independence of every State in the area and their right to live in peace within secure and recognized boundaries free from threats or acts of force;

2. *Affirms* further the necessity

(a) for guaranteeing freedom of navigation through international waterways in the area;

(b) for achieving a just settlement of the refugee problem;

(c) for guaranteeing the territorial inviolability and political independence of every State in the area, through measures including the establishment of demilitarized zones;

3. *Requests* the Secretary-General to designate a Special Representative to proceed to the Middle East to establish and maintain contacts with the States concerned in order to promote agreement and assist efforts to achieve a peaceful and accepted settlement in accordance with the provisions and principles in this resolution;

4. *Requests* the Secretary-General to report to the Security Council on the progress of the efforts of the Special Representative as soon as possible.

Here I turned to Lord Caradon and said: 'I will, of course, consult with my Arab colleagues on this resolution. But I do have a few questions. For example, this word "territories" and not "the territories", in the paragraph on the withdrawal of Israeli forces, does this mean that the Israeli forces will withdraw from some, not all, territories?'

Lord Caradon replied: 'Of course not. The text means all and not some of the territories. Proof of this is that the resolution in the preamble emphasizes the inadmissibility of the acquisition of territory by war. This is *my* language, Mr Minister [addressing me], and I assure you the text conveys the meaning you want. This English text is taken from the US draft . . . Furthermore, the term "the territories" is in the text of the draft in the four other official languages [French, Russian, Spanish and Chinese]. In any case, you can check up on this with Arthur Goldberg.'

The Security Council met the following day when Lord Caradon formally submitted his draft. I immediately requested the floor to say that the duty of the Security Council in accordance with the Charter, as well as with the various decisions previously adopted by the organization, was very clear, that is, to secure the withdrawal of the Israeli forces from all the territories which they had occupied after 4 June 1967. Our position on this question was absolutely firm, emphasized throughout all the informal consultations which had taken place, and stated in no vague or ambiguous terms in the deliberations of the Security Council and the General Assembly. Under no circumstances would Egypt compromise on the point, nor, in our judgement, should the Security Council.

During all this time, our consultations with the Americans and British concerned specific points. Lord Caradon told me that, according to his consultations with Goldberg, the draft resolution that was presented would be implemented within a period not exceeding six months. He added that the exact terms employed by Goldberg were that the 'resolution is for implementation . . .', otherwise there would be no need to appoint a representative of the UN Secretary-General. Lord Caradon was firmly convinced that without a solution which aimed at the roots of the problem, total Israeli withdrawal from all the occupied Arab territories, there could never be any peace, or even the probability of peace, in the area.

When Arab consultations in New York began to consider Lord Caradon's draft resolution to the Security Council, some of the Arab delegates emphasized the importance of the term 'the territories' rather than 'territories' in the English text of the draft. I requested Lord Caradon to accompany me to a meeting of the Arab delegations, so that he could personally answer their questions and queries. However, I personally was convinced that Paragraph 1 in the draft, stipulating the inadmissibility of the acquisition of territory by war, clearly implied total Israeli withdrawal from the occupied Arab territories. Lord Caradon did actually accompany me to a meeting of the heads of Arab delegations at the Jordanian UN mission where he stated that the mere mention of Paragraph 1, both according to his consultations with Goldberg and on his own understanding, as well as the wording of the resolution itself, left no room for any doubt on this point.

At that meeting, I deliberately directed a number of questions, which were later described as provocative, to Lord Caradon.

I asked: 'According to your consultations with the Americans, and according to the meaning of the draft resolution, does it mean the withdrawal of Israel from all the West Bank?' Caradon: 'Yes.' 'Sinai and the Gaza sector?' 'Yes.' 'The Golan Heights?' 'Yes . . . In brief, the resolution means the return of Israel to the 4 June position.'

At the same time, I had to ensure that this was clear to all the main parties concerned. So I told Goldberg: 'I want to be absolutely clear . . . unless this resolution means total Israeli withdrawal from all the occupied Arab territories then we shall have arrived at nothing more than a piece of paper . . . and you yourselves would make our return to war inevitable.'

I then conferred with the Soviet Deputy Foreign Minister, Kuznetsov, who headed the USSR's delegation to Security Council meetings. He held his meeting in a room at his Permanent Mission that had been specially proofed against intelligence and bugging devices.

I said: 'We have understood from the British and Americans that the draft presented by Lord Caradon means total Israeli withdrawal from all Arab territories . . . Do you have the same understanding?'

Kuznetsov replied: 'Yes.'

I said: 'But I am still apprehensive of a last-minute manoeuvre by Goldberg, for the American draft is still formally tabled on the Security Council agenda and they could put it to the vote at any time.'

Kuznetsov paused for a while to think. He was a very stable, fair and far-sighted person who enjoyed the respect of all delegates at the UN. He said: 'I have an idea . . . We could present a new draft to the Security Council in order to contain this manoeuvre, should the Americans make such a move.'

The following day, the Soviet Ambassador – who headed his country's UN mission – visited me to deliver a message. I noticed that he did not say anything, beyond a few words of greeting. He did not read out the message, for fear of bugging devices, but just handed it to me. After I finished reading it, we spoke in a lighter vein about things of no import.

And so, on 20 November, the Soviet Union presented a new draft resolution to the Security Council, based on the Latin American draft, containing a paragraph on the limitation of arms in the area, which the US had previously demanded.

Goldberg came to see me on 20 November to acquaint himself with my position *vis-à-vis* the Caradon and the Soviet draft resolutions, and he mentioned that Johnson had already contacted Kosygin to assure him that, if Moscow did not insist that its draft be put to the vote, the US would follow suit. I said: 'You are thinking in terms of a Security Council meeting while I am thinking in terms of the future months. I therefore wish to tell you again that I would agree to a resolution and will cooperate with the UN's representative only if one condition is met, namely the complete withdrawal of Israel.'

At the session where Lord Caradon presented his draft, he expanded on the interpretation of the resolution, clarifying his government's position, and reiterating the statement made by Foreign Secretary George Brown to the General Assembly a month earlier in which he had said: 'Britain does not accept war as a means of settling disputes, nor that a State should be allowed to extend its frontiers as a result of war. This means that Israel must withdraw. But equally, Israel's neighbours must recognize its right to exist, and it must enjoy security within its frontiers.'

Caradon was followed by Arthur Goldberg, requesting the support of the Council members to the British draft resolution. He affirmed: 'On behalf of my Government I now pledge to this Council and to the parties concerned that our diplomatic and political influence will be exerted, under the United Kingdom draft, in support of the United Nations' special representative, to achieve a fair and equitable settlement so that all in the area may live in peace, security and tranquillity. As Lord Caradon has indicated, the United Kingdom draft resolution now before us is the product not only of recent discussion but, in fact, of more than five months of intensive consultations among the members of the Assembly, this Council and the parties concerned.'

Finally, it was decided to adjourn the meeting until 22 November to carry out last-minute consultations before the final vote.

At the meeting held on 22 November, after the representative of India had supported the position taken by me, Lord Caradon reaffirmed that the resolution was not exclusively a British text, but was the result of close and prolonged consultations with both sides (Israeli Foreign Minister Abba Eban was present) and with all members of the Security Council. Then the draft resolution submitted by Lord Caradon, and which was to be known as Resolution 242, was put to the vote and was unanimously adopted by the fifteen member States of the Security Council. The hall rang with warm applause, inspired by the belief that the international community had, at last, taken the first steps towards peace in the Middle East.

The representative of France, M. Bérard, then said: 'We must admit that on the point which the French delegation has always stressed as being essential – the question of withdrawal of the occupation forces – the French text of the resolution leaves no room for any ambiguity, since it speaks of withdrawal "*des territoires occupés*".'

There followed statements by the representatives of several countries, all expressing relief at the adoption of the resolution and hope for the advent of peace in the near future in the Middle East.

I also made a statement at this session following the vote, re-stating the points I had made before, both publicly and in private meetings, and placing the onus for implementing Resolution 242 firmly on the United Nations Organization.

In this chapter I have tried to show the positions of the various Security Council member States prior to their endorsement of Resolution 242, and the circumstances in which it was adopted. This will partially explain the scope of the subsequent distortions and misinterpretations perpetrated by Israel.

My stay in New York had lasted for sixty-seven days, and I returned to Cairo very exhausted. But that very same day I had to attend a Cabinet meeting, chaired by President Nasser.

The Foreign Affairs Committee of the Egyptian National Assembly requested a meeting with me to consider the issue. The Committee was headed by Anwar el-Sadat, who was then Speaker of the National Assembly. Some members asked me: 'Does the resolution mean that we have to conclude a peace treaty with Israel or establish diplomatic relations with it?' I replied: 'Of course not.'

Another member asked about frontiers; I said that according to the resolution we recognized Israel's international boundaries.

Yet another member asked: 'Does the resolution mean that we now recognize Israel?' I replied: 'We recognized Israel as a *fait accompli* when we signed the Armistice Agreements with it in 1949.'

A journalist, attending the meeting in his capacity as a member of the National Assembly, remarked: 'Then this means that all that we journalists have been repeating for years has been wrong!' I replied simply: 'Yes.' Here some members covered their ears, saying they did not wish to hear any more!

This was the emotional climate prevailing at the time of the adoption of Security Council Resolution 242. Faced with our people's anger against the US and their desire to seek revenge against Israel, I felt I was undertaking a most distasteful and unpopular role. But at the same time, I felt it was my duty to shoulder the burden of rectifying outdated concepts and adopting a more realistic position.

Israel was soon to concentrate on the use of the word 'territories' in the English version to release itself from the commitment of withdrawing from all the occupied Arab territories.

The most appropriate reply to this that I could find lay in the words of George Ball, the former US Secretary of State and head of the US mission at the UN after Arthur Goldberg; he wrote that he had never heard of a more ridiculous excuse. It would mean that we do not recognize the documents of the United Nations and the Security Council unless they are written in English, thus removing at a stroke four of the five official languages of the United Nations. It would also mean that we were eliminating the clarifications made by the representatives of different delegations, members of the Security Council who had voted on the resolution and without whose vote the draft would not have become a resolution . . . and they were all decisive clarifications, and were accepted in the presence of Israel's Foreign Minister, who had voiced no protest either before or after the vote. Finally, it would mean the elimination of a fundamental part of Resolution 242: the inadmissibility of the acquisition of territory by war. If this had been the sole text of the resolution, then this in itself would be sufficient indication of

Israel's commitment to total withdrawal from all the territories it had occupied by military conquest in the June War of 1967.

Lord Caradon himself wrote: 'We must state once more the inadmissibility of the acquisition of territory by war, and this means that the annexation by Israel of Arab regions prior to the June 1967 War can never be justifiable just because Israelis occupied them by the force of arms during that war.'

We now turn to a further misleading interpretation by Israel, saying: 'If the resolution means the withdrawal of Israel from all Arab territories what is the meaning of stating "secure and recognized borders"?'

In principle, the point in the resolution concerning the right of all these States 'to live within secure and recognized boundaries' refers to 'all countries in the region', especially since Israel was the one who threatened our security in previous years. This means that Arab countries should not be the subject of Israeli marauding raids, while the Arab countries should not permit commando operations against Israel from across their borders. It is therefore a mutual right and is one that is not confined to Israel.

Finally, we come to the greatest fallacy attributed to the Resolution. It concerns the Palestinian issue as a refugee problem. Actually, Resolution 242 did not tackle the Palestinian question. It confined itself to the consequences of the 1967 June War. For our part, we did not object to this since it would not have helped the Palestinian cause for it to be debated at a time when we had just suffered a total military defeat, and we preferred at this juncture to concentrate on the liberation of Arab territories occupied by Israel.

If Resolution 242 included a paragraph on the just solution of the question of refugees, this was quite normal, for the General Assembly every year issued a resolution concerning the Palestinian refugees, reminding Israel of the necessity for implementing the Assembly's resolution of 1948 for repatriation and the compensation of those who did not want to return. Equally, as a result of the 1967 War, Israel expelled an additional 500,000 Palestinians into Jordan, which moved the Security Council to request Israel to effect their repatriation. Israel refused to comply, and consequently it was natural for the Security Council to incorporate the Palestinian refugee problem in the resolution.

As regards the Palestinian question itself, it was the United States who had insisted in 1947 on the partition project by which two States should be established in Palestine: one Jewish and one Arab. All the current arguments about the rights of the people of Palestine to self-determination are, in fact, a reflection of Israeli military strength and Arab weakness, since the right to establish their own independent State has been laid down ever since 1967.

Consequently US attempts to force the PLO to recognize Resolution 242 are highly arbitrary, for the PLO was not party to the resolution, and the Palestinian people is not in any way involved, either in the content or in the consequences of the resolution.

At the meeting of the Egyptian Cabinet on 18 February 1968, I reviewed the developments in the political situation and said in conclusion: 'Despite the fact that Israel has pledged itself to implement Resolution 242, Israel will not do so because it is committed thereby to withdrawal, whereas it launched an aggression on 5 June 1967 to capture new Arab land. Consequently, the UN representative's mission will soon end in failure, achieving nothing. The main reason for Jarring's failure is that President Johnson has decided that the US role is not confined to safeguarding Israel but will assist Israel in continuing the occupation of Arab land.'

Nasser commented: 'We will cooperate with Jarring although we already believe he will fail in his mission. We will listen to the United States, although she wants to make us enter a dark room called "negotiations on Resolution 242". We will cooperate with the devil himself, if only to prove our good intentions! However, we know from the start that we are the ones to liberate our land by the force of arms, the only language Israel understands. Let the US assist Israel in its invasions, let them both try to bury the Palestinian issue. But they know very well that we have not been defeated in the war as long as we have not negotiated with Israel, not signed a peace treaty with her and not accepted the eradication of the Palestinian issue.'

5

The Campaign for a Separate Settlement

The June War, together with the occupation of new Arab territories almost three times the area Israel occupied before June 1967, led to a series of fundamental changes in the Middle East political set-up, which had a considerable impact on the prospects for peace in the whole area. Most prominent of these was the emergence of the Palestine resistance movement as a main party to the Arab–Israeli conflict. The defeat of the Arab countries was only second to the establishment of the State of Israel in 1948 in arousing national feeling among the Palestinians; it made them conclude that they should not depend exclusively on the Arab States for the fulfilment of their aspirations, but rather on their ability to organize their rank and file and to establish the national identity.

On the other hand, Israel's military occupation and its suppression of the Palestinians led to a change in the Arab image among the international community. Israel, which had always portrayed itself as the gentle David battling against giant Goliath, was in fact a military power superior to all the Arab States put together and occupying the whole of Palestine. It had displaced more than a million and a half Palestinians, and the rest lived under its military rule.

The new conditions, resulting from the June War, consolidated Soviet influence in the Arab region on an unprecedented scale. With the escalation of US political and military support for Israel, the Arab side (specifically Egypt and Syria) needed similar support to balance the contending forces, and this had to come from the Soviet Union.

As a result of the June War, hostility and antagonism towards the US in the Arab world intensified and, once more, Arab suspicions were confirmed: Israel was not working for itself alone, but was a tool employed by US policy to serve its own purposes and interests in the area, and to dominate the Arab world. Whereas the US had protected and shielded Israel prior to the June War, after the war, the US was virtually protecting Israel's conquests as well!

Egypt, therefore, began to need Soviet arms in huge quantities. Gradually, parallel to escalating US military aid to Israel, we made increasing demands on the Soviet Union. Thus, cooperation with the Soviet Union – which until 1967 had been restricted to the importation of arms – three years later came to be based on the participation of Soviet combat-pilots in defending the Egyptian interior.

It was this phenomenon that prompted Nasser to say to a number of Ministers: 'I am no longer able to understand the logic behind American foreign policy . . . The Americans spent thirty billion dollars in a futile attempt to combat Soviet influence in South East Asia, and they send their sons to be killed in Vietnam . . . And here in the Middle East we find them paying billions of dollars in cash and arms to Israel, opposing the minimal in Arab national demands . . . and this, practically, is leading to the strengthening of Soviet influence in the whole of our area! America is forcing us into inviting Soviet influence so as to counter America's blind support for Israel!' Nasser later termed this the element of 'self-destruction' in US policy.

Towards the end of 1967 and the beginning of 1968 – and following US support for Israeli claims, and its hostile position in the Security Council and the General Assembly, and before the adoption of Resolution 242 – the Americans requested that US–Egyptian diplomatic relations be restored, on the basis that we officially declare that the US had not participated in actual fighting during the June War! I, however, maintained that, although the American flag had not taken part in the war against us, the American political position entailed even worse results . . . there was US–Israeli collusion that had more serious consequences than actual participation in the fighting.

This condition was withdrawn but, instead of a balanced policy, Lyndon Johnson agreed in January 1968 to supply Israel with Phantom fighter-bombers.

The Phantom was a longe-range fighter-bomber, more sophisticated and lethal than any aircraft in Israel's arsenal. The sinister implication of such a move was that Israel was being abetted and encouraged to continue its occupation of the Arab countries. By contrast, de Gaulle imposed a total embargo on arms shipments, including the Mirage, to Israel until it withdrew its forces.

The US informed us that it had only agreed in principle to supply Israel with Phantoms! Although we had no doubts that they would ever back down on such a commitment, we set a condition for the restoration of diplomatic relations: that the US issue a brief statement declaring that it advocated total Israeli withdrawal from the occupied Arab territories. No such statement was issued. What really irked the Americans was the fact that unless Egypt restored diplomatic relations with the US, no other Arab State, from among those that had severed relations with America as a result of the June War, could resume those relations.

I daresay that the period following Security Council Resolution 242 was to witness the fiercest political and diplomatic struggle between us and Israel, for while we were in need of every minute we could gain to complete our defence build-up and preparations, Israel was anxious to use that same period to impose on us its own peace terms and conditions, while the US exerted great political pressure to force us into a separate settlement with Israel.

When Gunnar Jarring, the representative of the UN Secretary-General who was appointed to supervise the implementation of Resolution 242, began his mission in December 1967, I extended every facility to him to ensure his success; Israel, meanwhile, began placing obstacles in his way by demanding direct negotiations (which Resolution 242 did not stipulate) and by claiming that Resolution 242 was not for implementation, but was rather an agenda for negotiations. This meant that Israel, from the very outset, was determined to undermine the provisions of the Security Council resolution.

It must be understood that we refused to have direct negotiations with Israel not because we simply chose to ignore its existence, but rather because such negotiations would be taking place while Israel was in physical occupation of our territories. Therefore all such negotiations would necessarily be conditioned by the pressure and intimidation of actual military occupation.

During his visits to Egypt, Jordan and Israel, Gunnar Jarring exercised great patience and efficiency. I truly sympathized with him during his strenuous shuttling from one capital to another, listening to suggestions and ideas from all parties. Jarring spared no effort to achieve a break-through in this jungle. Whenever he thought he had found a way through, he would pursue it, only to arrive at a dead end.

On 27 December, Israel notified Jarring that Egypt and Israel should discuss the basis and details of the nature of peace. Thus Israel began to project a completely different interpretation of Resolution 242.

I told Jarring: 'We have, as it were, two rooms before us: one for political manoeuvring, and the other for achieving peace. Israel is seeking to contain us in the first, where we would remain for years! If, however, we moved to the second room, we could achieve a result within a matter of weeks! But moving to the second chamber depends on Israel's agreement to implement Security Council Resolution 242 to the letter and without any distortion.'

A few weeks later, Israel came up with yet another idea: that the Foreign Ministers of Egypt, Jordan and Israel should meet in Cyprus, to consider Resolution 242 as an agenda for negotiations, under the auspices of Ambassador Jarring. When Jarring conveyed this Israeli demand to me I said: 'Resolution 242 is not for negotiation but contains obligations for implementation . . . The quetion is, whether Israel is prepared to withdraw to 4 June positions.'

Jarring laughingly replied: 'The main advantage of the Israeli proposal is that it would spare me the effort expended in these shuttles! There is always a chance that my plane could meet with an accident during the shuttle between the different capitals, but if I were to remain in Cyprus, this will be safer for me.'

I said: 'If it is necessary for us to meet on an island, then let us meet on the Island of Manhattan at UN Headquarters. Why not hold your consultations there?'

Jarring thought this a very good idea.

Once again it was Israel who rejected the proposals, after we had agreed that consultations would be carried out at the level of our Permanent UN Representatives who would be in close contact with Jarring and up-date him on any new development. Thus Jarring was obliged to resume his shuttle.

I was aware of the very real difficulties confronting Jarring. I once told him that in any quarrel between two persons, any third party seeking to separate them would naturally pull the weaker one away. In the dispute with Israel, we were still the weaker party. Our problem was that if we took one step backwards, we would fall into an abyss – therefore any attempt to push us backwards would never achieve the desired peace.

Again Israel, during this period, resorted to military pressure, but this time directed at Jordan. We received information that Israel might take military action in Jordan within a few days. Nasser ordered that the information be relayed to King Hussein. He also questioned Minister of War, General Mohammed Fawzi, on the possibilities of our taking military action in case Jordan faced a large-scale military offensive. General Fawzi said that the Egyptian armed forces, stationed along the Suez Canal, could open fire on all Israeli positions in Sinai within thirty minutes of receiving the order. When Nasser consulted me on this point, I said I was not in favour of such an action as it would not really help the situation on the Jordanian front.

On 21 March 1968, Israel attacked the village of 'Karama' in Jordan, sustaining heavy losses owing to the heroic resistance of the Palestinians, side by side with Jordanian troops.

The US at this time was exercising great pressure on King Hussein not to demand condemnation of the Israeli aggression by the US Security Council, for such a condemnation would arouse wide-ranging resentment against the US support for Israel. But Jordan insisted on bringing the issue before the Security Council, and a resolution was adopted, denouncing the Israeli aggression.

King Faisal of Saudi Arabia was meanwhile maintaining contact with US President Johnson and urging him to work towards Israel's withdrawal from the occupied Arab territories. On 12 April 1968, Johnson dispatched a message to King Faisal, which he in turn relayed to President Nasser. The message said: 'Our position on withdrawal remains as expressed by Ambassador Goldberg to King Hussein in New York in November . . .' Johnson was therefore reconfirming the official US commitment, communicated to King Hussein by Arthur Goldberg, to Israeli withdrawal from all Arab territories. Nevertheless, when we examined Johnson's message, we found that in the second paragraph there was an interpretation of withdrawal to the Jordan–Israel armistice lines, in which Johnson said: 'While we could not guarantee that everything would be returned to Jordan and that some territorial adjustment will not be required in establishing permanent boundaries, we are prepared to use our influence to get the most favourable arrangement possible for Jordan. We are committed to the principle of political independence and territorial integrity. While there must be withdrawal of troops they must be withdrawn to recognized and secure frontiers for all countries, rather than necessarily to these old and inadequate armistice lines. However, there must be compensatory adjustment for changes in those lines. We believe these adjustments must be the minimum compatible with mutual security and economic needs.' Also in this message, the US President mentioned for the first time the need for a dialogue between the different parties, when he said: 'Some form of dialogue between the parties would seem essential to achieving secure and permanent arrangements, even if a peace treaty is not among the possibilities at this time.'

A few days before this message arrived, King Hussein came to Cairo for consultations with Nasser. In the first meeting on 6 April, King Hussein informed us that the Americans, twenty-four hours prior to his departure for Cairo, had asked him to conclude a peace treaty with Israel. He had replied that Security Council Resolution 242 did not demand such a measure. The Americans then claimed that Jarring's mission faced failure and that they were anxious to salvage it. The King then said that Israel was the party responsible for this failure; pressure should be exerted on Israel, not on him, to make further concessions. He added that there was an inclination in Israel to hang on to the occupied territories and, in fact, to occupy the rest of Jordan.

At that point, Nasser commented: 'We feel we have to continue political action and give the Americans the chance to prove how serious the commitments they made to you and to the Security Council members were. What I find really strange is that I had expected their attitude to you would be more accommodating than it is towards us. Our attitude – of which they are fully aware – is that we shall never bring to an end the state of war with Israel until after it has withdrawn from the Golan, the West Bank, Gaza and Sinai.'

King Hussein then complained that the Syrians had so far rejected any form of military coordination with him, though they were fully aware of the great deficit in Jordan's defence capacities. Nasser agreed and said that he had informed the Syrians that if they desired to establish joint command, it should be with Jordan and Iraq, rather than with Egypt, because the Iraqi army possessed great combat potentialities that should be exploited to reinforce the Eastern Front. In the end, Nasser told the King that so long as Israel had not succeeded in forcing the Arabs into signing a peace treaty, then Israel had not won the June War. Israel's strategy aimed at forcing us into accepting a settlement; that would never happen unless we were to lose our self-confidence. Nor should we despair, for that was exactly what Israel wanted. We also had to avoid any weakening of the Arab position.

In fact, the Arab position was one of our chief preoccupations following the Khartoum Summit. I decided therefore to make a tour of a number of Arab countries, which I began early in January 1968. The aim was to explore how far these States were ready to support an Eastern Front in order to bridge the serious gap in the defence capacities of both Syria and Jordan. The tour covered Syria, Lebanon, Jordan, Iraq, Kuwait and Saudi Arabia.

In Syria, I informed President Atassi that Egypt would not ask him to accept Security Council Resolution 242, because Syria had every right to wait and see if Israel was really serious in its commitment to total withdrawal – something that we ourselves doubted, though we had accepted the resolution. In fact, I informed all the Arab countries I visited that this was the position we maintained. Moreover, I was of the view that rejection of Resolution 242 by the Arab States would prove helpful to the Egyptian–Jordanian position, for at least it would show the Americans the scope of the concessions we had made by accepting the Security Council resolution.

During this tour, I became aware that Arab differences constituted a large obstacle to the establishment of an Eastern Front: Syria had strong reservations on King Hussein's policy, and Syrian leaders complained that Iraq had so far failed to dispatch military units to the front. For its part, Iraq complained of certain Syrian activities that were hostile to the Iraqi regime! However, in Kuwait as a result of my talks with Crown Prince Sheikh Jaber al-Sabah, Sheikh Saad and Sheikh Sabah, I felt there was genuine willingness to establish a Kuwaiti air force that could be assigned to any front.

In Saudi Arabia, King Faisal said he was ready to provide everything that was asked of him for the battle. Moreover, he was actively trying to consolidate relations with Egypt.

Iraqi President Aref came to Cairo, following an official visit to France. When he met with President Nasser on 10 February he intimated that de Gaulle had informed him that tremendous pressure was being brought by Zionist forces inside France on him. Nevertheless, de Gaulle was determined to maintain his policy of opposing Israeli aggression and demanding its total withdrawal since this was the only feasible way to genuine peace in the Middle East. It was for this reason that France was willing to meet all Iraqi requirements and extend any assistance, including arms and military equipment. He added that it was necessary that the Arabs adopt a unified position, as this might assist France in playing a major role in the Middle East question.

President Nasser told President Aref at the end of the talks: 'I regard your visit to France and your talks with General de Gaulle of extreme importance, for he was the only Western leader with the courage and farsightedness to support justice in the June War. We should spare no effort to multiply French interests in the Arab world. French dependence on Arab oil will increase and should be supplied without the need for US mediation or intervention.'

During this period, President Tito came to Egypt and met with President Nasser in Aswan on 5 February. From the very start, Tito had exerted continual efforts to mobilize world public opinion for our cause. President Nasser explained to President Tito that the US position in abetting intransigent Israeli policies was motivated by a desire to freeze the present situation, in the hope that the present regime in Egypt would fall, to be replaced by another more receptive to US interests, or alternatively to instil utter despair in us, driving us to make peace with Israel on its conditions. He referred to relations with the USSR, saying that while their military support was forthcoming Egypt still lacked a long-range fighter-bomber equal to the Mirage or the Skyhawk used by Israel.

Tito said that he was aware of a greater degree of international support for the Arab cause, in spite of US pressures. He mentioned, for instance, that Mrs Indira Gandhi, Prime Minister of India, had persistently resisted strong pressure from her parliamentary opposition to reduce her support for Egypt and the

Arab cause. He was of the view that Egypt's perseverance and military build-up would eventually restore a balance of power that might induce the US to re-assess its position.

I made a tour of Libya, Algeria and Morocco, to seek their support for the Western Front, i.e. Egypt. On my way, I stopped in Rome to meet the Italian Foreign Minister, Ementori Fanfani, who informed me that Israel was claiming I had made Israeli withdrawal a precondition for accepting the Security Council resolution. When I denied this, he proposed that we draw up a timetable for the implementation of all items on the resolution. I considered this a valid suggestion and communicated it to Jarring in a letter dated 9 May. However, Jarring did not put forward this proposal, knowing that Israel would reject it, which in turn might lead to the failure of his mission. In fact during that period he confined himself to asking questions of the parties concerned in the hope that he would find in the answers some leeway to help him evolve a solution. Thus passed the year 1968 so far as Jarring's mission was concerned, Israel flooding him with notes containing its interpretation of the Security Council resolution, in an attempt to repudiate its commitments according to the dictates of the resolution. Jarring used to pass these notes on to me for comment. I noticed that they all concentrated on the same few points. On one occasion Jarring informed me that he would be sending me a note he had received from Abba Eban, where-upon I called one of my aides to draft an immediate reply. The aide asked me how he could do this before he had received the note. I told him: all you have to do is refer to previous communications from Israel and compose your reply accordingly. He did, and when we received Eban's note, our prepared reply was quite adequate and all we had to do was to insert the date!

On 18 April I paid a visit to Moscow in an attempt to reach a joint understanding with the Soviets over future moves. In a three-hour meeting with Leonid Brezhnev he talked at length about the importance of pursuing a peaceful solution. He spoke of Soviet efforts in this direction, including continuous pressure being exerted on Washington to agree to the implementation of Security Council Resolution 242.

I replied that we had accepted the Security Council resolution, and continued to call for its implementation, as well as all the formulas that the Soviet Union proposed in this direction. We were sure, however, that the US had retracted from pledges she had agreed to, whether in connection with the Security Council resolution or with regard to the joint Soviet–US proposal, and was determined to push us into direct negotiations with Israel with the object of a separate settlement between Egypt and Israel. I referred to Lord Caradon's statement that the resolution would be put into effect within six months. The six months had now elapsed without any progress. In fact we were convinced that Israel had no intention of implementing its part of the resolution and that Johnson would not pressure Israel to this effect. Instead, he was pressuring us to surrender to Israeli dictates.

A lengthy discussion ensued. Brezhnev stated that it had become clear from this analysis that a political solution remained a remote possibility, and that military action to liberate the land had now become inevitable. This, however, necessitated re-building the Egyptian army first, a matter that would still take two years at least. It also required a unified home front that would be prepared for battle. Egypt would also need the support of the other Arab States. At this point, Brezhnev referred to the importance of using oil as a weapon to strengthen the Arab position.

I told him that we were aware of the situation and were prepared to wait another two years in order to complete re-building our armed forces. The home front was unified behind Nasser. In fact, every Egyptian was anxious to bring forward the hour of battle, to liberate the land by force. 'We do need, how-ever, increased efforts on your part to supply us with the arms necessary to rebuild our army and more experts to train and organize our forces, taking into account our economic condi-tions. We have recently received your message demanding that we pay the Soviet experts the equivalent of $20 million. I believe that an extra zero was added to the amount by mistake and that the sum requested is $2 million, not $20 million.'

Laughing, Brezhnev said: 'I agree, you can consider that the sum requested is $2 million and not $20 million.'

Brezhnev had feared that providing more Russian experts would cause a reaction within the Egyptian army, but Nasser felt that the greatest possible number of Soviet experts should be provided, in order to ensure that the Soviet Union would con-tinue its military assistance at the required rate. The meeting thus ended on the understanding that political efforts would be continued and that Moscow would provide us with the weapons and experts required to enable the Egyptian army to liberate the land.

In Cairo, Nasser had been very happy with the results of my talks with Brezhnev and upon receiving a message stating that the Soviet Union had agreed to provide Egypt with 120 Soviet pilots to be placed under Egyptian air force command.

I believe that the major factor that prompted the Soviets to take this decision after dragging their heels for ten months was that they felt the Americans had deluded them as far as the implementation of Resolution 242 was concerned. In fact, we soon received a message from the Central Committee of the Soviet Communist Party informing us that the Soviet Union had lost all hope of political cooperation with the US and admitting that the Americans had deceived them. By dangling an illusory imminent solution the United States was obviously hoping to persuade the Soviet Union to pressure us into making further concessions which would lead to friction developing between the Arabs and the Soviets, or alternatively to a decrease in its military help to us.

In June 1968, after quick visits to East Germany and Poland, I visited the Scandinavian countries. A statement I made in Copenhagen caused a furore in the Arab press, although it was welcomed with enthusiasm by the media of the West. It all happened when a journalist asked me the extent to which we were prepared to recognize Israel. I replied that the Egyptian and Israeli governments had signed the 1949 Armistice Agreement under UN supervision, and we had not signed an agreement with ghosts but with a government; therefore Israel had the *fait accompli* recognition of the four Arab States which had signed the agreements.

Later I was to join Nasser on his visit to the Soviet Union. Yasser Arafat accompanied Nasser to Moscow where he was introduced for the first time to the Soviet leaders, who promised him support and assistance.

In Moscow, the first symptoms of Nasser's health problems became manifest. On visiting him I was surprised to find him sitting in his pyjamas on the bed and complaining of an acute pain in his leg due to arteriosclerosis. Soviet doctors advised him to take the mineral water treatment at Toskhalbutu but, rejecting my efforts to persuade him to begin the treatment immediately, he insisted on finalizing the arms agreements with the Soviets first, then returning to Egypt to attend the 23 July celebrations. Only then would he return for treatment at Toskhalbutu. Nasser's ailments were to increase continuously, due to his total preoccupation with immediate matters.

On his way back from Moscow, Nasser stopped over in Yugoslavia where Tito advised him it was necessary to build huge army reserves which would enable Egypt to continue fighting for a long period, because a peaceful solution could never be achieved, due to Israel's policy of blocking every possibility for a peaceful settlement.

In Cairo, the British Ambassador was to raise once more the issue which British Foreign Secretary George Brown had previously raised towards the end of 1967: the thirteen ships which had been blockaded in the Suez Canal since its closure. Studies and operational measures for the release of the ships had been prepared, but when actual operations had begun Israeli occupying forces had opened fire from the east bank of the Canal and foiled our attempts.

In September 1968, I went to Algeria to attend the African Summit Conference which issued a resolution calling for Israel's withdrawal to the 4 June positions in accordance with Resolution 242. This was of considerable importance from our point of view. First, the resolution contained a clear interpretation, made by an important regional organization, relating to the line to which Israel should withdraw. Second, it represented a crucial setback for Israel in Africa where it had attempted to infiltrate several years before. At last the African States had come to the realization that Israel sought to seize others' lands by military conquest. Prior to the June aggression, Israel had claimed that its people had lived under the yoke of British colonialism and had fought the British colonialists until, in a great war of liberation, they had achieved their independence, but were suddenly faced with the realization that the Arab States wished to deprive them of their 'independence' and drive them into the sea. A few African leaders, such as the late Jomo Kenyatta, had realized the truth about Israel. Kenyatta told me it would have been perfectly possible for the State of Israel to exist on Ugandan and Kenyan land. At the beginning of the twentieth century, he said, a Zionist mission had come to investigate the area which the British had promised would be their national homeland. However, the British had set the Masai tribes to harass the mission every night until they had fled, refusing to establish their proposed State in Africa.

On 10 September, Johnson made a new statement, clarifying the American position. 'The Arab governments,' he said, 'should convince Israel and the international community that they have abandoned the idea of destroying Israel. Equally, Israel should convince its Arab neighbours and the international community that it has no plans or programmes of expansion within Arab territories. A return to the 4 June 1967 positions will not bring about peace. Secure and recognized boundaries must be established. The neighbours concerned should agree on those lines as part of the transition from truce to peace. At the same time, it should be equally clear that the boundaries cannot and should not reflect the weight of military conquest. One thing is for sure, the peace process will not begin until the leaders in the Middle East exchange views on the difficult issues through an acceptable process which would allow for active discussions. Without this, no progress towards peace will be achieved.'

This attitude was one of the main factors that prompted Nasser to decide at this stage to allow the Soviet Union to negotiate with the US over any proposals for a peaceful settlement. Nasser explained his view to the Cabinet: 'I think we should allow the Soviets to enter into debates and disputes with the Americans. In this way, instead of allowing disputes to break out between Egypt and the Americans, they will be between the Americans and the USSR. Naturally, when the Americans and Soviets sit at the same table, a different language will be used. Moreover, when the Soviets realize the dead end to which the Americans are finally leading them, they will become more committed to supplying the arms shipments we are asking for.'

It was with this aim that I left Cairo to attend the UN General Assembly in September, stopping over in Paris to meet with French Foreign Minister Michel Debré. Our discussion focused on Jarring's failing mission and his need for the assistance of the great powers, especially France. I also welcomed de Gaulle's proposal for a four-power meeting to consider the situation in the Middle East. On this occasion I had the opportunity to meet General de Gaulle, whose clear and frank manner deserved admiration and respect. He was against Israeli aggression and emphasized the necessity for Arab unity, which was the key to action against Israeli aggression. Referring to France's relations with Israel, he said that prior to 1956, Israel had received Mystères to participate in the Tripartite Aggression because Guy Mollet had believed that Nasser should be destroyed because of the support he had given to the Algerian Revolution. Mollet's anti-Egyptian attitude continued after the 1956 aggression and France had offered Israel the Mirage aircraft.

Later, I paid a visit to Britain, the first by an Egyptian Foreign Minister since 1953, where I met Prime Minister Harold Wilson and Michael Stewart, the Minister of State for Foreign Affairs. It became clear to me at that time that Britain was as yet unable to adopt a position independent of US foreign policy (as France had done) despite their understanding of the Arab point of view.

At a press conference in New York on 9 October, I strongly attacked the US decision to intensify its support of Israel by supplying it with an additional fifty Phantoms at a time when Israel refused to implement the Security Council resolution.

The time was now ripe for bringing pressure on Israel, in order to show the world that the failure of Jarring's mission was the responsibility of Israel. On 19 October, in a memorandum to Jarring, I requested that Israel reply to the following two questions: (1) Was Israel prepared to implement the Security Council resolution? (2) Would Israel withdraw its forces from the Arab territories occupied as a result of its aggression on 5 June 1967?

The Israeli Foreign Minister sent Jarring a note containing the bases upon which a separate agreement with Egypt could be realized. Among the points raised, the most significant were: (1) the transition from war to peace between Egypt and Israel should be part of an agreement in the form of a treaty; (2) that secure and recognized boundaries should not be the armistice lines, the 4 June position; and (3) that the correct interpretation of the resolution – from Israel's point of view – was that 'the resolution is not self-executing. It is a framework of principles to guide the parties in their efforts to reach agreement.'

In our reply, we refused to be swayed by this appeal to transform Resolution 242 into a set of principles for negotiation and thus detach itself from its only commitment, that of Israeli withdrawal from Arab territories.

In my reply I pointed out that Egypt accepts the Security Council resolution issued on 22 November 1967 and is prepared to fulfil her commitments as stipulated by Resolution 242. Further, Egypt believes that Jarring should set a timetable for the implementation of all the items in the resolution and that the resolution should be implemented under Security Council guarantees and supervision.

On the following day, Jarring explained that the Israeli Foreign Minister's point of view was that Israel had no expansionist aims in Egyptian territories, and that it was the issue of security which would determine its position in talks with Egypt. This would include the guaranteed passage of Israeli vessels through the Gulf of Aqaba and a pre-knowledge of the date when permission would be granted for Israeli ships to pass through the Suez Canal after it was re-opened to navigation.

I informed Jarring that Israel's view was based, from the outset, on the false assumption that we had accepted and were ready to conclude a separate agreement under which Israel would withdraw from Sinai. However, we had made it clear, also from the outset, that in speaking of withdrawal, we meant not Sinai only, but the Golan, the West Bank, Jerusalem and Gaza too. We were not in the least prepared to terminate the state of belligerency with Israel until it had removed itself from every inch of these Arab territories. Moreover, the question of Suez Canal navigation was tied up with Israel's implementation of the UN resolution on the refugees, while the Gulf of Aqaba issue should be settled by the International Court of Justice. As for Israel's desire to establish regional cooperation or economic relations with Egypt, there was no place for that whatsoever.

On 2 November I met US Secretary of State Dean Rusk at his office in New York. He told me that he was keen to achieve peace before leaving his post in January, and would like to present me with a seven-point proposal in an attempt to clarify US policy towards the current situation. It went as follows:

(1) Total Israeli withdrawal from Egyptian territories.
(2) Termination of the state of belligerency (between Egypt and Israel).
(3) Re-opening of the Suez Canal to Israeli navigation.
(4) Solving the problem of Palestinian refugees by asking every

refugee, secretly and on a personal basis, whether he wished to return to Israel. If not, then he would be given the right to choose any country without previous commitment by that State.

(5) The presence of an international force in Sharm el-Sheikh which would only withdraw by a Security Council or General Assembly resolution.

(6) Agreement on the level of armament in the region.

(7) The signing by Egypt and Israel of a document containing these commitments.

When he had completed his presentation of the proposal, I reminded Rusk that Resolution 242 stipulated the withdrawal of Israel from all the occupied Arab territories, not just Egyptian territory.

'I am now speaking to Egypt's Foreign Minister,' he said.

'True, but our Arab commitments do not allow us to conclude a separate agreement with Israel, leaving out Jordan and Syria.'

'We believe,' he said, 'that every Arab State should determine its position, independent of the others. In this case, we can tackle each problem separately. There would be an Egyptian–Israeli settlement, a Jordanian–Israeli, a Syrian–Israeli, and so on. When at the end we put the three together we would have reached a comprehensive settlement. I have begun by approaching you because Israel has no desire to retain Egyptian territory. Jordan can take care of itself. It could originally have avoided its current situation had it not intervened in June 1967.'

At this point, I interrupted him. 'It would be unethical on our part in Egypt to set Israeli withdrawal from Sinai as the basis for a settlement, leaving out the rest of the occupied Arab territories. I would like to remind you that Jordan and Syria joined the war after Israel actually launched its aggression against Egypt on 5 June 1967. It would therefore be unacceptable for us to seek a settlement with Israel and abandon the others. We have told King Hussein that he can detach himself from us, but at the same time we cannot absolve ourselves from our commitment to the Arab States.'

'But,' Rusk argued, 'I got you total Israeli withdrawal from Egyptian territories . . . from Sinai!'

'I do not pretend that Israeli withdrawal from Sinai is not

crucial to us,' I said, 'yet that has been imposed by the Armistice
Agreement of 1949 and the Security Council resolution of 1967.
We, however, will not agree to terminate the state of belligerency
before Israel withdraws from all the occupied Arab territories.
Moreover, in addition to the ethical considerations I just mentioned, there is a legal commitment in the joint defence agreement between Egypt and the other Arab States.'

'I could, on behalf of the US, submit a similar proposal to
Jordan,' Rusk suggested, 'but we cannot do the same for Syria as
long as it rejects the Security Council's resolution. In any case,
why not wait until you return to Cairo before you reply to my
proposal, in which case you can send me a written reply and you
can add any points to those I have mentioned.' (It appeared that
Dean Rusk, one of the American personalities whom I held in
greatest respect, imagined that my position would be altered
after presenting the proposal to Nasser. This was why he asked
me repeatedly to send him a written reply from Cairo.)

I prepared a written reply on 1 December 1968 in which I
reiterated that peace in the region demanded a comprehensive
solution that could only be achieved by Israeli withdrawal from
all Arab territories.

However, I have never forgotten Rusk's words as I was
leaving his office in November. In fact, I can still hear his words,
though many years have elapsed. He said: 'Johnson's
administration ends at the end of next month, so do not expect it
to put pressure on Israel. Moreover, do not ever believe that any
future American administration will put pressure on Israel.'

By this time we had completed our military capabilities for
defence, but continued to lack the strength required to launch an
offensive. The solution which had been offered first by Israel's
Foreign Minister and later by the US Secretary of State represented the high point of joint attempts to divert us into a
separate settlement with Israel at the expense of other Arab
countries.

During my stay in New York to attend the UN session in
October and November 1968, many delegations, motivated by
good intentions, attempted to find a solution to the crisis. For
example, one day, Romania's Deputy Foreign Minister suggested that I hold a secret meeting with Israel's Foreign Minister.
The Israelis, he said, had assured him that were such a meeting to

take place, all problems would be resolved immediately. I refused this approach of a secret meeting and suggested that if Israel had new ideas they could easily be channelled through Jarring or through the Romanians.

Romania was not the only one to propose a secret meeting. On another occasion, Yugoslavia undertook the initiative, although it was of a completely different nature. Nahoum Goldman, a personal friend of Tito, had held unorthodox views, for example, that the establishment of peace between Israel and the Arab States would be more useful than attempts to annex new Arab territories to Israel. Tito thought that establishing a contact with Goldman might prove useful so, during Tito's visit to Aswan to meet Nasser, it was suggested that I hold a secret meeting with Nahoum Goldman. Once more I refused. Nahoum Goldman, I said, did not represent Israel and could not take any decision concerning its policy. What then would be the use of such a meeting? Nasser, I may say, totally approved of my action.

Approaches were also made through my friend Ihsan Sabry from Turkey and through Dr Joseph Lunz, Holland's Foreign Minister and NATO's Secretary-General, who told me he had questioned Abba Eban on Israel's position regarding a settlement. Eban had assured him that it was 'maximum security' for Israel and minimum changes in the 4 June borders. Then Lunz asked for my opinion.

I said, 'I agree!'

Surprised, he looked at me questioningly.

Assuring him, I said: 'I agree on the question of Israeli security without any condition. But, in view of the region's history, Israel has been the one which has always threatened our security, and therefore the Arab States have the right to obtain the same guarantees Israel was demanding for itself.'

This was a fair demand, he said.

'As far as the borders are concerned,' I said, 'I hope you can provide me with a map on which the "minimum" that Israel talks about is marked.'

Holland's Foreign Minister was very happy when he left me. He was a man who did not know deceit.

Later on, I asked him whether Eban had supplied him with the map.

Embarrassed, he said the problem was that Abba Eban was a good man but his government was bad. It refused to give him the map!

I did not need to explain to Dr Lunz that no such map would be forthcoming since it would impose limits to Israel's compulsion for expansionism.

While in New York in 1968, I was invited to dinner by Elmer Bobst, a prominent American businessman. I asked him whether he expected Richard Nixon or Barry Goldwater to win the presidential election. He said that many businessmen had been working towards Nixon's election. They were expecting two things from Nixon: a tough stand with the Soviet Union and firmness with Israel, which was beginning to threaten American interests. Nixon may have tried to be tough with the Soviet Union and mildly firm with Israel at the outset, but finally he had to yield to Kissinger's policy of bolstering Israel to a degree never attempted by any previous administration, in spite of the fact that only nine per cent of the American Jews voted for Nixon. In the meantime, as an indication of his willingness to make a fresh start with the US after Johnson's departure, Nasser cabled his congratulations to the newly-elected President whom he knew personally ever since Nixon had visited Egypt a few years before, at which time Nixon realized that the US had committed a grave error by withdrawing its loan, financing the building of the High Dam in Aswan. Soon after his election Nixon dispatched his personal friend, Mr William Scranton, on a tour of the Middle East, including a meeting with Nasser. Scranton arrived with the news that the US would pursue an even-handed policy in the Middle East crisis. Scranton, however, soon disappeared from the political scene, along with his statement of an 'even-handed policy'.

Meanwhile, Andrei Gromyko arrived on 21 December with a Soviet proposal for a settlement, containing a timetable for the implementation of Resolution 242, and suggesting that I submit it to Ambassador Jarring as an Egyptian proposal. However, I was disinclined to do this since I had already made the same suggestion to Jarring but he had not relayed it to Israel for fear of a refusal. Nasser felt that the proposal should be submitted to the US by the Soviets direct, in order to maintain the dialogue between the two superpowers.

Gromyko appeared optimistic, describing the points presented by the US Secretary of State as constructive. The Americans had become convinced of the necessity of Israeli withdrawal from the Arab territories. Nasser interrupted him to say that the Americans had been talking only about an Israeli withdrawal from Sinai. Gromyko said that he was referring to Dean Rusk's statements to the Soviet Union. He added that, in this context, the Americans had been talking of Israeli withdrawal from all the Arab territories. Furthermore, he hoped that the US would pressure Israel into adopting this course. That was why it was necessary that this proposal be submitted to the Americans, in order to test their sincerity. Nasser made the point that the US had altered its position towards Egypt, as to the Soviet Union, more than once. There was no harm, of course, in continuing the search for an acceptable peaceful solution if it were possible but, from Egypt's point of view, this should not occur at the expense of building up its military forces. (Nasser's remarks were not without foundation. Lately, the Soviets had come to fear that we might lose patience and launch a huge military operation to liberate our land before completing our military preparation. To prevent this, a slow-down was effected in their supplies of vehicles, troop carriers and equipment.)

In the meantime, what we had anticipated had occurred. The Americans had rejected the Soviet proposal which stipulated that Israel pull back forty kilometres east of the Suez Canal in the first stage and withdraw its forces to 4 June positions a month later; that Israel would be committed to implementing the UN resolution on refugees; but that Egypt would be committed to guaranteeing the passage of the ships of all States, indiscriminately, through the Suez Canal; and at the same time, UN emergency forces would be stationed in Sharm el-Sheikh. Finally, according to the proposal, the concerned Arab States and Israel were to draw up the final agreement through Jarring. The US rejection of the proposal resulted in the Soviet Union taking steps to deliver the military supplies it had promised earlier.

A further development occurred in the region at that time. Israel had launched a huge raid on Beirut International Airport on 28 December 1968, inflicting on Lebanon losses exceeding £40 million.

At a special meeting of the Council of Ministers, I explained to the Cabinet that the Beirut raid was new evidence that a peaceful settlement was neither expected nor even possible. A peaceful settlement meant Israeli withdrawal from all the Arab territories. The raid showed, to the contrary, that Israel was trying to expand further at the expense of Arab territory. Despite the Beirut raid, the US remained committed to maintaining Israeli military supremacy, including carrying out the Phantom jets deal with Israel. Such continuous military reinforcements were allowing Israel to persist in its occupation and to attempt to force a settlement which would terminate the economic boycott, thereby becoming the banking capital of the East.

At this point, Nasser said that Palestinian commando activities had been causing Israel enormous trouble and now its actions were reflecting anxiety, despair and rashness, as evidenced in its raid on civilian targets at Beirut Airport. For our part, he continued, a full-scale operation against the Israeli occupation in Sinai and Gaza would be launched within weeks, though we would also be subject to counter-strikes.

By early 1969, we were as far as it was possible to be from the road to peace. It had become necessary for us to force Israel to reveal its cards and admit that the annexation of the Arab territories was its top priority. Therefore we had to continue co-operating with Jarring and make evident our readiness to implement all the clauses of Resolution 242, and rekindle the political situation in such a manner that would force Israel into declaring its position *vis-à-vis* the Resolution. This required that the Security Council move towards implementing its resolution, or that the great powers do so.

In my contacts at the UN session, I was anxious to get Western countries, especially France and Britain, to play a more active role in order to disprove the Israeli allegation of a polarization in the region between the two major powers.

The French Foreign Minister was being frank when he told me: 'Do not at present expect from Western Europe any decisive role, for Western Europe is still unqualified at present to perform a common political act of which the US would not approve.'

I told him: 'The European Community will get economically stronger during the next few years, and will conduct policies serving its own interests, not always necessarily in accordance with American policy.'

France, however, finally moved on 16 January 1969, when it sent a letter to the US, the Soviet Union and Britain, suggesting that the representatives of the four countries meet to consider the question of peace in the Middle East. This was a practical application of de Gaulle's previous idea of the necessity to reach a clear-cut agreement on peace in the Middle East among the four great powers, on the basis of which the UN's representative would act. On 6 February, Nixon declared his approval of the French proposal, to be carried out by their permanent representatives in the Security Council. Furthermore, he gave his support to Jarring's mission and added that he would also hold talks with the concerned countries in the region.

In view of the developments, I found it necessary to submit to U Thant, the UN Secretary-General, and to the member States of the UN a memorandum dated 13 February concerning the situation in the region since the adoption of the Security Council's resolution. In this memorandum, I referred to the statement of Levi Eshkol, the Prime Minister of Israel, before the Knesset on 11 November 1968, in which he stated that 'Israel would hold on to the captured Straits of Tiran as part of any Middle East settlement'. In another declaration to the American magazine *Newsweek*, dated 9 February 1969, Eshkol also stated that 'the Jordan River must become the security border for Israel with all that that implies. Our army shall be stationed only on the strip along that border.' In the same interview he said: 'As for the Golan Heights, we will, quite simply, never give them up. The same goes for Jerusalem. Here, there is no flexibility at all.'

It had become clear after such declarations exactly what Israel meant by its interpretation of a peaceful settlement based on Resolution 242. However, what was new in the matter was that Israel had begun to employ a new terminology in the international diplomatic arena. From 'internationally recognized borders' it moved to a newly-minted expression, 'security borders'. Under this new label, it would be able to occupy any territory it wished, under the pretext of protecting its security. Thus, both the Israeli Foreign and Defence Ministers made declarations, in February, on Israel's right to establish settlements in the occupied 'Arab' territories. According to the content of these declarations, Israel had summed up its goals as follows: the annexation of Arab Jerusalem; the continued occupation of the Golan Heights in

Syria; the continued occupation of the West Bank; the economic and administrative integration of the Gaza Strip into Israel; the continued occupation of Sharm el-Sheikh (in the Egyptian territories) and of the Aqaba Gulf region, as well as maintaining a military presence in parts of Sinai; and the establishment of Israeli settlements in the occupied territories.

When the four-power meetings between the representatives of France, Britain, the Soviet Union and the US began in New York in 1969, Gunnar Jarring felt that the time had come to clarify the positions of the concerned parties regarding Resolution 242. Thus, I received eleven questions from him, the same as those addressed to Israel, all of them related to the implementation of the resolution. Among these were: (1) Does Egypt accept the right of Israel to live in peace within secure and recognized boundaries, free from threats and acts of force? (2) If so, what is Egypt's conception of secure and recognized boundaries?

I consulted with Abdel Moneim al-Rifai, the Jordanian Foreign Minister, and we agreed on a single position on which I based my answer to Jarring in the following way: (1) Egypt accepts the right of every State in the area to live in peace within secure and recognized boundaries, free from threats or acts of force, provided that Israel withdraws its forces from all Arab territories occupied as a result of its aggression of 5 June 1967 and implements the Security Council's resolution of 22 November 1967. (2) When the Palestine question was brought before the United Nations in 1947, the General Assembly adopted its resolution for the partition of Palestine and defined Israel's boundaries.

At the first meeting of the representatives of the four great powers in New York, the French delegation had proposed issuing a declaration called 'The Declaration of Principles and Intentions' in which there would be a clear definition of the principle of complete Israeli withdrawal from the Arab territories which had been occupied in the June War, in exchange for the termination of the state of belligerency between the three Arab countries (Egypt, Syria and Jordan) and Israel, in implementation of Resolution 242. The American delegation, however, refused to subscribe to this declaration.

During this period, Nasser decided to send Dr Mahmoud Fawzi, Assistant President, to attend the funeral of former US President Dwight Eisenhower, in spite of the severed diplomatic relations between Egypt and the US since the June War, as an expression of our appreciation of the role he played in the Tripartite Aggression.

Dr Fawzi – in a previous meeting of the Council of Ministers held on 12 November 1968 – had inquired about our readiness to respond to the American demand to restore diplomatic relations with them. Nasser's point of view was that US bias in favour of Israel had not changed and they did not respond to our basic demand which was to declare a clear official position regarding the Israeli occupation of the Arab land. Therefore, he said, it was his opinion that we should wait and see what Nixon would do after he formed his administration. And we would continue the political dialogue with the new incumbents.

Dr Fawzi met the new American President and his Secretary of State, William Rogers, who, when asked by Dr Fawzi to present proposals that would be reasonable to the Arabs, said: 'Don't forget that you have lost the war and therefore have to pay the price.' Nixon, however, expressed a wish that diplomatic relations between the two countries be resumed, but Nasser did not see any change in the US attitude to prompt him to do so.

Meanwhile the Americans were spreading reports in diplomatic circles that they had reached an agreement with the Soviet Union over the Middle East. Reports to this effect were reaching me from different sources and so I informed Nasser accordingly. He saw fit to raise the issue in a meeting of the Council of Ministers in May, saying that the Americans were trying to persuade us they had concluded a secret agreement with the Soviets. Nasser went on: 'I have learned from the Soviets, among them the Soviet Ambassador here, that this is an utter fabrication and attempt to sow friction between us and the Soviets and so close the only door open to us for our arms supplies. This attempt has been coupled with a marked increase in CIA activity inside Egypt, including efforts to establish contact with some army officers. Anyway, since the June War the Soviets have committed themselves to not approving any solution to the conflict without our prior approval.'

During this particular period, which was linked with our fundamental rejection of any separate settlement and our growing military power, Israel intensified its air raids against us, and attacked Egypt's heartland, taking advantage of its aerial supremacy, our shortage of combat pilots, and the fact that our air-defence network to protect all vital targets inside Egypt was incomplete. It was obvious that the objective of these Israeli air attacks on civilian targets deep in Egypt was to undermine the prestige of the regime as well as cast doubt on the feasibility of our military preparations. Israel also continued its air raids on the Egyptian workers who were building the missile bases along the Canal front.

However, all these attempts failed to make the Egyptians despair. In fact, these air raids had the contrary effect, for they strengthened the people's belief in a military solution with Israel, and even made them exert pressure on the leaders to bring forward the date of the liberation of the occupied territories. Egypt actually intensified its War of Attrition against the Israeli occupation in Sinai, and the people accepted the sacrifices they had to make with high spirits and a great determination to fight.

The American position, during this period, moved along various axes: there was the Jarring mission to which the US did not extend any support and which was therefore frozen; there were also the great-power talks in New York which saw the increasing isolation of the US; and there were the bilateral US–Soviet talks during which the US sought to get the Soviet Union to agree to a separate settlement between Egypt and Israel . . . but the Soviet Union refused.

On 16 May, the US presented a 13-point project for a separate agreement between Egypt and Israel which, while it did not stipulate Israel's withdrawal to Egypt's international borders, did propose the demilitarization of Sinai. The American project contradicted the Security Council resolution in terms of Arab demands, and imposed commitments on Egypt that were not included in the Security Council resolution.

In another attempt, the US prepared a '14-point' project, which was submitted on 15 May by Joseph Sisco, Under-Secretary of State, to the Soviet Union as 'counter-proposals' to the Soviet proposals. The objective of this American project was to engage the Soviet Union in a new political manoeuvre. It was significant only because it was the worst American attempt to date in its stubborn determination to effect a separate Egyptian–Israeli settlement.

The new American project included the following main

points: direct negotiations under the auspices of Jarring; the withdrawal of Israel to boundaries agreed upon by the two parties (though it did not exclude a withdrawal to the Egyptian borders: this text gave Israel the right to modify our borders); demilitarization of all areas evacuated by Israel; the Straits of Tiran to be regarded as an international waterway; the state of belligerency between Egypt and Israel to be considered as terminated, once the documents of agreement were deposited with the UN Secretariat; Israel's withdrawal from the Gaza Sector to be the subject of negotiations between Egypt, Jordan and Israel, with consideration given to the temporary administration of the Gaza Sector by the UN; the 1948 Palestinian refugees to have the right to repatriation or settlement where they were residing, within the framework of an agreement governing the number of those repatriated annually (thus Israel would have the right to determine the number of those refugees it agreed to repatriate. Of course, this could very well be a token figure, which would be in direct contravention to the resolution on the refugees).

In his presentation of the project, Sisco explained that Sinai could be demilitarized partially in return for an Israeli military presence at Sharm el-Sheikh; in other words, the US proposed that Israel maintain its occupation of parts of Egyptian territory.

The new American project not only adopted without reservations Israeli policies; it equally imposed direct Egyptian–Israeli negotiations over a number of issues.

I turned down the project as not even fit for discussion. Nasser described this project, like the one that preceded it, as aiming at our surrender to Israeli dictates, leading us into a separate agreement by which we would leave the other Arab countries and the Palestinian issue behind. He added that we would escalate the War of Attrition and that there were two factors in our favour: the mounting US alignment to Israel would oblige the Soviet Union to agree with us on the futility of a peaceful settlement; and the arrival of the Phantoms in Israel in August would prompt the Soviet Union to deliver its arms supplies to us.

In his annual speech marking the Revolution celebrations, Nasser declared that we would be taking deterrent action against the Israeli military occupation. This escalation would have a radical impact on the whole Middle East situation, and particularly on the positions of the US and the USSR.

The Soviets had never concealed their reservations on our escalation of military action against Israel. In fact, they came very close to opposing Nasser over the issue of the War of Attrition. Nasser, however, took those reservations in his stride; and the Soviets now saw an Egypt determined to bear all sacrifices of a military confrontation with Israel regardless of the cost.

These were the most significant factors as we saw them in our review of the period. The latest American project epitomized the peak of joint US–Israeli pressure to force us into a separate settlement with Israel. In all these efforts to effect a separate settlement, the restoration of the whole of Sinai to us was never questioned by the US, in spite of talk on demilitarization of Sinai, or an international presence at Sharm el-Sheikh, or a temporary UN administration of the Gaza Strip. Despite its energetic attempts, the US failed to split us from the Soviet Union or to pressure the Soviet Union into reducing its arms shipments to us. Though the Soviet Union often delayed in the delivery of arms, because of its belief that a political negotiation with the US was possible, in the end it responded to most of our demands. With the presentation of the new American project, 'polarization' in the area began to emerge clearly: the US adopted Israel's position to impose its terms on us fully, while the Soviet Union totally aligned itself with our position on the necessity of Israeli withdrawal to 4 June positions.

Naturally, in this polarization, the US was in a stronger position, because it had only to reinforce the existing *fait accompli* – Israel's military occupation. The Soviet Union, on the other hand, was in a weaker position because it was obliged to help us change this very *fait accompli* by force of arms.

6

The Struggle for a
Comprehensive Settlement

If the two years following the June War of 1967 were characterized by extreme pressure on Egypt to conclude a separate settlement with Israel, the third year, in particular from July 1969 to July 1970, witnessed essentially a more bitter struggle for a comprehensive settlement. In the process there were times when Israel directed all its military weight against us, inflicting on us the greatest sacrifices. It was also during that very same period that the struggle between the two superpowers accelerated.

Israel's prime instrument of pressure against us was to establish the permanency of Israel's occupation of our territories. Conversely, our prime pressure lever against Israel was to change that *fait accompli*, by force of arms if necessary.

During the two years immediately following the June War, clear-cut offers were made to us for a separate settlement with Israel. This had been a standing offer ever since November 1968 when the US formally submitted it to us, calling for total Israeli withdrawal from all occupied Egyptian territories in return for Egypt ending the state of war with Israel.

All the other Arab countries were aware of our rejection, in form and content, of any separate settlement. When I turned down Rusk's offer, I conferred the following day with heads of Arab delegations and informed them of our decision. I also enclosed it in a communication sent to all Arab States upon my return to Cairo. Nasser equally kept Arab Heads of State abreast of political developments. In a meeting with King Faisal of Saudi Arabia, in Cairo in December 1969, Nasser said that were Egypt to accept a separate settlement with Israel, then that would not pose a danger to Egypt alone, but would also mean the end of the Palestine issue and the whole of the Arab cause.

Actually, that year, 1969, witnessed fundamental changes in

the region. On 25 May there was an army takeover of the government in Sudan. This was soon followed by the revolution in Libya, led by Muammar el-Gaddafy, on 1 September 1969. These two events were of great significance as regards our conflict with Israel. On the one hand, such events meant that the US had failed to correctly assess developments in the area: instead of prompting a *coup d'état* in Egypt, the aggression had actually brought about revolutions which from the outset pledged support to Egypt. Our military defeat had not led to an overthrow of the Egyptian regime; rather, it prompted greater Arab solidarity with Egypt and further isolation for the US in the region. Furthermore, militarily they represented real added depth to Egypt, so much that at one stage the Military College was moved to Sudan and the Naval College to Libya when speculation grew that Israel would launch air strikes against these two colleges in Cairo and Alexandria.

However, the most important factor resulting from the Sudanese and Libyan revolutions was the political impact on American interests in the area. There is no doubt that the role played by the US in supporting Israel was a main cause of the two revolutions and, consequently, became one of the fundamental tenets of their foreign policy. The US was in political and military control of Libya, which made it possible for the US to exert control over the Mediterranean and lend support to its Sixth Fleet. The first act of Gaddafy was to terminate the US military presence and to take over its air base. This lesson had important and fundamental consequences. It alerted those voices within the US that were genuinely concerned about American interests in the area to the dangers of continued US total alignment to Israel, not only to the huge American interests within the Arab World but also within all those regimes which, by American standards, were still regarded as 'moderate'.

During that year, Egypt managed to rebuild its army after the Soviets provided us with large quantities of arms and fighter pilots to cover the country in depth. The US thus discovered that the escalation of its military aid to Israel, instead of deterring the Soviets and consequently subjugating us to Israel's demands, had actually resulted in increasing Soviet support for us, to a level exceeding the scope of the Arab–Israeli conflict, and within the scope of US–Soviet confrontation. This was naturally no easy decision for the Soviet Union, especially as we saw how hesitant they had been, from June 1967, to escalate military support to Egypt. The long-range Israeli air strikes deep into Egypt against civilians and economic targets prompted the Soviet Union to intensify its military commitments to Egypt.

The most important factor in attempting to change this *fait accompli*, and which alerted the US to the dangers of its pro-Israeli policy, was the War of Attrition which Nasser decided to wage against the Israeli occupiers. Thus, on 10 July 1969 an Egyptian commando force stormed an Israeli fortified position in Sinai and raised the Egyptian flag over it. When it withdrew, it had inflicted losses on the Israeli forces that amounted to forty men killed and wounded, and brought back a number of prisoners. On 24 July, forty Egyptian planes bombed Israeli positions deep in Sinai. Israel, however, employed its air force as its main strike weapon in attacking Egyptian positions. During the next weeks, the Israeli air force made about 1,000 sorties over the Egyptian front. When, on 6 September 1969, Israel officially announced the arrival of the first shipment of US Phantoms, this signalled a dangerous escalation of air warfare. From 1969, Israel, with the help of the United States, was also introducing electronic warfare into the area. On many days during the year 1969–70, Israel would bombard Egypt with about 1,000 tons of bombs a day, costing about £1 million, in order to force us to halt the War of Attrition.

This, in actual fact, was the crux of the War of Attrition. Some Israelis called it 'The Three Years' War', others 'The Fourth Egyptian–Israeli War', and we had to go on waging it, at whatever price, to resist the *fait accompli* that Israel sought to impose. In February 1970, Israeli Phantoms raided a civilian factory at Abu Zaabal, at the end of a shift involving over 2,000 workers. The delayed-action bombs killed seventy men and wounded 100 others. Again in April 1970, US-built Israeli Phantoms raided an Egyptian primary school at Bahr el-Baqar, killing forty-six children and injuring forty others.

However, our people and armed forces confronted these air raids with calm and unparalleled determination. From the beginning Nasser was very honest and clear with his people about the burdens of the War of Attrition. In several public addresses he emphasized that in such a war what was important was not only our capacity to strike at the enemy, but also our capacity to absorb counter-blows. Though we restricted our own strikes to military targets of the Israeli occupation forces inside Sinai, Israel, on its part, exceeded such parameters and raided civilian inhabitants in Egypt indiscriminately.

In addition to its political objectives, the War of Attrition itself was a part of our military preparation and combat training to cross the Suez Canal and liberate all our occupied territories. The people of Egypt were equally involved in the war and were living it in a very real sense.

My first meeting with William Rogers was at the UN General Assembly session in September 1969. My first impression was that he was sincere in his efforts to understand the true nature of the conflict in the Middle East. He was serious in his desire to deal with me with an open mind, which immediately gained my confidence in his wish to promote US interests in the area. At that meeting, Rogers told me that – during the General Assembly – he had been introduced to about fifty Foreign Ministers, and had grown dizzy, never imagining that the world was beset by so many problems . . . especially as everyone expected the US to have a role in resolving all of them.

When we turned to the question of the Middle East crisis, Rogers expressed his conviction of the need to improve US relations with the Arab world. I remarked that the US would have every opportunity to do this if it were to adopt a more even-handed policy. I then explained to him the circumstances in which Security Council Resolution 242 had been adopted, pointing out that at the time the US had pledged that the resolution was for implementation, and was not a mere set of principles, as Israel claimed, and that we had pledged an end to the state of belligerency in return for Israeli withdrawal from all occupied Arab territories. I added that two years had passed since Resolution 242 had been adopted, and Israel had made no move whatsoever to implement it and was in fact supported in this posture by the US. I added that it was difficult to absolve the US from responsibility for the air raids Israel was unleashing on civilian targets with aircraft and bombs supplied by the US. I then told Rogers that unless the US undertook the same role that Eisenhower had adopted with the 1956 Tripartite Aggression, this would inevitably lead to a new full-scale war.

Rogers said: 'We cannot pressure Israel, otherwise we would have the right to pressure you also. For this reason, I am seeking to persuade the parties concerned of the importance of a peaceful settlement through negotiations.'

I said: 'If, for argument's sake, we cede that you cannot put pressure on Israel we nonetheless feel it is your duty at least to declare your position clearly. Do you agree that one country should occupy, by military invasion, the territories of three other UN member States?'

Rogers said: 'We are not Upper Volta or Gabon. We are a superpower, so if we were to declare our position on the necessity of total Israeli withdrawal from all the occupied Arab territories, we must be sure that it will be carried out.'

Rogers' frankness reminded me of what I had heard, a year earlier, from his predecessor, Dean Rusk: that no American administration would ever exercise pressure on Israel. Rogers was not content with merely admitting their inability to pressure Israel; he also added the US was unable to declare a clear-cut position on the provisions of the Security Council resolution stipulating the inadmissibility of the acquisition of territory by military force or war. The only deduction to be made from this was that the Zionist elements inside the US were now able to bring pressure on the Administration, and not vice versa.

Rogers raised the issue of holding negotiations along the lines of those that were held in Rhodes. I made it clear that Israel was seeking direct negotiations which we rejected because Israel would be negotiating while still occupying our territories. I added: 'Would you, as an American, have accepted your government negotiating with Japan after its attack on Pearl Harbor? Was de Gaulle at fault when he refused to negotiate with the Nazis while they still occupied part of France? We find ourselves in the same position now. If we were to accept negotiation with Israel while its forces still occupy even one square foot of our territory, then we would be taking a road of no return, namely the road of submission to the aggressor. What took place in Rhodes was not direct negotiation between us and Israel. Dr Ralph Bunche, the UN representative, moved between the residences of delegations. And this is what Ambassador Jarring is doing at present.' I went on to say that the issue of communications and contacts was a procedural matter raised by Israel so as to distract us from the essential, namely: how far was Israel prepared to abandon its expansionist policy and commit itself to implementing the Security Council resolution?

Rogers had heard a completely different account from Abba Eban of what had taken place in Rhodes. However, he appeared convinced by what I had said, especially as I explained that I had been a member of the Egyptian delegation to Rhodes.

At the end of my meeting with Rogers I reasserted that peace would never be realized in our area unless two things were achieved: total Israeli withdrawal from all the occupied Arab territories, and resolving the Palestine issue on the basis of UN resolutions.

Prior to my departure from New York I met with Ambassador Jarring who appeared pessimistic about the possibility of reaching a binding commitment with Israel. He informed me that he would be returning to Moscow at the end of the week to resume his office as Swedish Ambassador, awaiting results of the bilateral talks between Washington and Moscow, and the four-power meetings of the great powers.

I met Gromyko, the Soviet Foreign Minister, and referred to his last visit to Cairo when he had mentioned that the US had extended assurances to the Soviet Union that, according to Dean Rusk's project, Israel would withdraw from all Arab territories, and that the US had since retracted on this position.

Gromyko, in the meantime, had held several meetings with Rogers, but failed to report any change in the position of the US. For this reason, I met with Nasser, immediately upon my return to Cairo, to explain the situation. I added that the US position could deteriorate even further – from our point of view – since Nixon had decided to supply Israel with an additional 150 aircraft (including fifty Phantoms). Nasser decided that I inform the Egyptian National Assembly of the situation in detail, so that those Egyptian circles that still entertained hopes of reaching an understanding with the US would realize the futility of such an exercise. I explained to the National Assembly the respective positions of Israel and the US. The Assembly made a statement to the effect that the US was fundamentally responsible for the failure of all peace efforts and was equally responsible, by its total support for Israel, for pushing the region into a new war. This declaration was broadcast by all Arab States.

Thus, by the end of 1969, hostility towards the US had intensified all over the Arab world, which worried the new US administration, especially after the unexpected revolutions in Sudan and Libya and the extension of support to Nasser.

Along with Nasser's determination to proceed steadily with the War of Attrition against Israeli occupation, we began to receive large arms shipments from the Soviet Union. Actually, the arms deals we concluded with the Soviet Union in 1969 alone exceeded by far the arms we had secured in the previous twelve years (1955–67).

The arms supplies and our escalation of the War of Attrition against Israel all pointed to an increasing future Soviet presence in the area, which the US knew full well would undermine the US strategic position in the Middle East. Furthermore, the US began to feel that its West European allies were gradually moving away from the US position on the Arab–Israeli conflict. The first indication of a belated awareness of the dangers to American interest in the area came in a message I received on 9 November 1969 containing new American proposals comprising ten points.

Rogers began his message by saying: 'I know you are concerned with the manner by which we shall take into consideration the other aspects of an Arab–Israeli comprehensive settlement. I can assure you that we have no intention of separating the aspect concerning Egypt from the others. We, like yourselves, see comprehensive settlement as a package deal.' Here, Rogers was, for the first time, clearly indicating that the US had finally realized its grave error in pressuring us into a separate settlement.

The new American proposals, submitted by Rogers, were: to conclude agreement between Egypt and Israel, containing all the points previously submitted by Dean Rusk in November 1968, together with suggesting a new approach for Ambassador Jarring to carry out his tasks, namely to adopt a 'Rhodes Formula'.

I noticed, however, that Rogers had added several points which were not contained in the Rusk draft – such as Egyptian–Israeli talks on guarantees for freedom of navigation through Sharm el-Sheikh, consideration of the future of the Gaza sector, and the creation of demilitarized zones. On the question of borders, the American proposals were very clear on this point: the Egyptian–Israeli borders meant Egypt's international boundaries, implying total Israeli withdrawal from all Egyptian territory. Actually, the American position on this was very clear and definite from the start. However, the real problem had always been to secure a similar commitment by Israel towards the West Bank, Jerusalem and the Golan Heights.

The new American proposals submitted by Rogers may be summed up as follows: (1) Egypt and Israel agree on a timetable for the withdrawal of Israeli armed forces from Egyptian territories captured in the 1967 war; (2) the state of belligerency between Israel and Egypt be terminated; (3) the parties agree on the location of secure and recognized boundaries between them; the former international boundaries between Egypt and Palestinian territory (under mandate) to be the secure and recognized boundaries between Egypt and Israel; (4) the agreement to include the creation of demilitarized zones, together with adopting effective measures at Sharm el-Sheikh to ensure freedom of navigation through the Tiran Straits, as well as security arrangements for final decision on the Gaza sector; (5) Egypt to guarantee the right of freedom of passage to all ships of all countries, including those of Israel, without distinction or interference; (6) the two parties agree to the terms of a fair settlement to the refugee problem, to be agreed upon in the final agreement between Jordan and Israel; (7) the two parties recognize each other's right of sovereignty and political independence, and the right to live in peace within secure boundaries, free of any threat of force; (8) the final agreement will be contained in a document signed by the two parties and deposited with the United Nations; and (9) the two parties agree that the final agreement be deposited with the Security Council for ratification.

Though we maintained reservations on a number of points contained in the new American draft, there were equally some positive points, most important of which was Israel's total withdrawal to Egyptian international boundaries and Rogers' admission of the necessity for a comprehensive solution. My view, as communicated to Nasser, was not to reject the American project but to continue our contacts with Rogers to find out his attitude towards the other fronts.

On 16 November 1969, I sent Rogers a message in which I stated: 'I noticed in your message you say you have no intention of separating the issues pertaining to Egypt from the other components, and that the settlement must be comprehensive. This, in my opinion, is a fundamental matter.

'It may be useful, in this respect, to inform you that I had previously heard such views from Mr Dean Rusk when I received his proposals on 2 November 1968, and which aimed at achieving a partial settlement with Egypt. I made clear to him, at the same time, the necessity of formulating a comprehensive settlement wholly on the basis of the Security Council resolution of 22 November 1967. Mr Rusk agreed with me.

'However, since then, we have not heard anything of any project for the other parts occupied by Israel. What we have received are several projects, in different formulas, which ultimately seek to effect partial settlement with Egypt only.

'Therefore, I am sure you will appreciate that our final position cannot be defined until we examine the integrated formula for implementing the Security Council resolution of 22 November 1967.'

Thus, in my reply, I did not reject Rogers' proposals; rather, my acceptance depended on the position of the US on the fronts in Jordan and Syria.

When Rogers announced his proposals, on 9 December 1969, Israel rejected them the following day. Rogers had already forwarded his proposals to the Soviet Union. The issue of communications and contacts to reach a settlement had gone through several phases: following the aggression of June 1967, contacts were direct between the Soviet Union and the US; with the adoption of Resolution 242, contacts between the parties concerned were made through Ambassador Jarring. This method satisfied us since Jarring's movements were within the framework of the Security Council resolution that we had accepted, and he was not empowered to make proposals not contained in the resolution, neither could he propose a settlement that contradicted the UN Charter and resolutions. In November 1968, the US adopted a new method for contacts, when Dean Rusk submitted his proposals direct to me, thus by-passing Ambassador Jarring.

When Gromyko came to Cairo to acquaint Nasser with the Soviet draft resolution to the Security Council, he proposed that it be submitted by Egypt. Nasser, however, requested that direct contact be maintained between the Soviet Union and the US, perceiving that such a method would definitely reduce the pressure on us, as well as preventing the US from having the field to itself to submit proposals that were unsuitable to us.

France, in an effort to restore the UN as the framework for contacts, proposed a four-power meeting to help Jarring in his mission. I supported this move. I noticed, however, that the issue of contacts and communication had in several cases caused confusion and misunderstanding. The immediate reason was that, though Gromyko had previously affirmed that the USSR would not agree to any draft without first consulting with us, the Soviet representative during these four-power meetings had agreed to American proposals on peace commitments, which I had previously rejected, since they contained a vague paragraph that the parties were pledged not to interfere in each other's affairs. When I requested the Soviet Ambassador in Cairo to clarify this point, he failed to do so and said it was a paragraph that had been included in the Soviet–Japanese peace treaty. In spite of the apparent insignificance of this point, I felt that it constituted a precedent that demanded we should take a firm stand. For this reason, I reported to Nasser my views on the subject of contacts: that a dialogue between the superpowers depended on their respective bargaining power; that the Middle East problem could not be discussed in isolation from, say, Vietnam or European security; that all this would take years and jeopardize our interests. I stressed that we should keep the Middle East issue within the framework of the United Nations because, in bilateral discussions between the two superpowers, the US was in a better bargaining position since its client was in occupation of the territory and maintained military superiority. The US need do no more than maintain this superiority.

The minimal level of concessions acceptable to us were contained in the Soviet draft based on an integrated timetable to implement the Security Council resolution on all fronts. Nasser decided to send a delegation to Moscow in December 1969, headed by Vice-President Anwar Sadat, and comprising myself and Minister of War General Fawzi; he asked me to make my views clear to the Soviet Union.

At the very outset, I noticed that the Soviet leaders were very worried at the escalating military operations on both sides of the Suez Canal and were apprehensive that we would undertake a premature military action to cross the waterway. Sadat emphasized that though we were firmly convinced that political efforts had reached a dead end, we were still maintaining political contacts, determined that the settlement be comprehensive, not partial – an oblique reference to the latest American proposals which had still not crystallized into a comprehensive settlement.

Brezhnev emphasized that the Soviet Union, while assisting the Egyptian army to take the offensive and liberate Sinai, was at the same time energetically seeking a political settlement, and that there was no contradiction between the two. Referring to the Sudanese and Libyan revolutions, he said they were positive developments in the region, since they had declared unqualified support for Egypt's policy and for Nasser. However, he emphasized that we must refrain from battle until we had completed our military preparations, and we should never allow the enemy to drag us into battle prematurely – time, he said, was in this respect a factor in favour of the Arabs. Brezhnev pointed to the importance of continuing tough training and the formation of a large reserve and said that the Soviet Union was willing to receive a large number of Egyptian pilots for training. He added that the USSR had selected over sixty Soviet pilots to go to Egypt within a month, under the name of experts. Furthermore, due to the inability of the Egyptian air-force systems to cope with Israeli air strikes and the US-built ECMs (Electronic Counter-Measures), the Soviet Union had decided to dispatch a large number of SAM-3s with their crews, to train Egyptian soldiers on their operation. The Soviet Union was also prepared to train Egyptian soldiers on modern missile systems, but that training would require a period of six months. Finally, Brezhnev promised to send an additional batch of missiles to defend the main cities and towns of Egypt against Israeli air attacks. He said such missiles would be effective against low-flying aircraft, and would be accompanied by about 1,000 Soviet military personnel to operate them in the first phase of action. At the end of the talks, Sadat reiterated our demand for long-range aircraft, stressing that Egypt would not undertake any offensive action before consulting with the Soviet Union.

When I met with Gromyko, I expounded my views on Rogers' proposals. We had noticed a slight retreat in the US position following Israel's rejection of these proposals, to the extent that Rogers felt under an obligation to defend himself against these charges. In the light of such observations, and Israel's rejection of any solutions based on a comprehensive settlement, and in the absence of a clear-cut US commitment to the principle of comprehensive settlement, the USSR drafted its answer to the US proposals, which was submitted by the Soviet Ambassador in Washington on 3 January 1970. The Soviet Union rejected the proposals on the grounds that they left all the details and particulars to be negotiated by the Arabs and Israel; that they did not specify a timetable for Israel's withdrawal; that they infringed on Egypt's sovereignty over Sharm el-Sheikh; and that they ignored the Constantinople Agreement when referring to freedom of navigation through the Suez Canal.

Although our reply to Rogers on 16 November 1969 had not been negative (that we wait for a complete US position relating to other fronts) the Soviet reply to the same proposal on 3 January 1970, after consulting us, was to reject them. This was due to a number of factors that emerged from 16 November 1969 to 3 January 1970.

Israel had already officially rejected Rogers' proposals, which robbed the American initiative of any practical significance. Pro-Israeli elements in the American Congress launched a severe attack on Rogers which made us conclude, in the light of past experience, that this particular initiative represented only one American trend, that of the State Department. There was another very important reason, which did not figure among the reasons listed by the Soviet Union for rejecting the US proposals, although it was the fundamental issue in my discussion with Gromyko in Moscow. We had already observed that the US would take the initiative and submit projects and proposals from which it would invariably retreat immediately Israel rejected them. We felt that such procrastination was not worthy of our confidence.

There was, however, one positive point in Rogers' project: it did essay an attempt at a comprehensive solution. In my reply to him on 16 November, I therefore avoided rejecting it, in spite of many reservations. However, after Israel announced its rejection of the project on 10 December, I saw no point in our accepting it, for it would mean further concessions within the framework of a settlement which we were doubtful the US could get Israel to accept.

When Jordan received Rogers' proposals to it two days before the Rabat Summit Meeting, King Hussein decided to send his Foreign Minister to Cairo on 14 January for consultations with President Nasser and myself on the American proposals.

The draft submitted to Jordan contained many items identical to those in the draft submitted to Egypt. However, on the question of the borders to which Israel would withdraw, and which would become permanent boundaries, the Rogers proposals stipulated that the armistice lines (i.e. the 4 June positions) be the basis for the final boundaries, with modifications agreed upon by both parties for administrative and economic purposes. On the question of Jerusalem, the draft supported Israel's demand to unify the city, thus rejecting the Arab demand for restoration of Arab Jerusalem to Jordan, and offered Jordan only limited participation in the civic and economic administration of the city. The draft also called for Jordanian participation in the talks on the future of the Gaza sector. The solution for the problem of the Palestinian refugees depended on arriving at an agreement between Jordan and Israel on the implementation of UN resolutions.

Jordan's Foreign Minister said there were several factors influencing Jordan's position: the failure of the Rabat Summit to adopt a resolution extending material help to Jordan; Jordan's inability to purchase its arms requirements; the weakness and fragmentation of the Eastern Front (Iraq, Syria and Jordan); Israel's superiority in the air posing continuous threats to Jordanian territory.

I concurred with his assessment, and we therefore reached agreement on two points: the necessity of maintaining a dialogue with the US, and not informing the US that Jordan had rejected the project as a whole, but to hold intensive discussions with the Americans on every item rejected by the two of us.

The Rabat Conference was preceded by a meeting between King Faisal and Nasser, to consider Egyptian–Saudi relations as well as the situation in the region. US alignment to Israel had aroused King Faisal's anxiety. However, he still entertained the limp hope that the US might finally wake to its own interests in the area, and therefore the possibility of convincing the US to adopt a more even-handed position. (King Faisal never abandoned that hope.) I still recall my last meeting with him in 1975, only one month before he was assassinated. He told me he had received assurances from President Nixon that the US was committed to having Israel withdraw from all the occupied Arab territories. The same promises were made to King Hussein in 1967, but never materialized.

During that period I paid a number of visits to Arab capitals to prepare for an Arab summit meeting which would agree on a unified plan of action to be preceded by a meeting of the Arab Defence Council on 10 November.

There was a tendency among some Arab countries to announce the failure of efforts towards a peaceful solution, so that Arab countries attending the Summit would make their utmost contribution to the battle. The raising of this issue was based on doubts planted by the US that Egypt might conclude a separate agreement with Israel.

At the meeting of the Arab Defence Council I said that we, in Egypt, were quite convinced that the liberation of our territories would be achieved only through our armed forces. However, the defeat of 1967 imposed on us that we explore all peaceful avenues so that the world would become aware of the real Israel and its expansionist aims. After two years of Israel's refusal to abide by the Security Council resolutions, it would be natural if we were to announce the failure of our peaceful efforts. The Council adopted a resolution that a peaceful solution had failed as a result of Israel's obduracy and the supply by the US of military, economic and political support. The Council also studied the drafting of American citizens into the Israeli army while maintaining their citizenship, and considered this a hostile act by the United States. General Fawzi, in his capacity as commander of the Eastern and Western Fronts, submitted a report quoting the least forces needed for battle. The Council also proposed that the Summit Meeting convene on 20 December.

The declaration relating to the failure of peaceful efforts was what prompted Rogers to relay his proposals to Jordan two days before the Summit Meeting.

Before proceeding to Rabat I asked the Egyptian Minister of Economy to prepare a report of the revenue of each Arab country and its contribution in support of the confrontation States.

I showed King Faisal this study before proceeding with Nasser to Rabat on 20 December. It pointed out that Saudi Arabia was contributing twelve per cent of its national income and proposed that an increase of one to two per cent be applied to all Arab oil-producing countries. He promised to study the matter.

When the Heads of State began considering the item on economic aid to the front-line countries (Egypt, Jordan and Syria), they were unable to reconcile the many contradictory proposals. Gaddafy's emotional demands for support for Egypt and Nasser were directed towards Faisal whom he asked to raise his contribution. King Faisal turned to me to ask whether the study I had shown him mentioned that the Saudi contribution was twelve per cent of its national income while that of Libya was four per cent. I answered that it was true. King Faisal then said that the other Arab countries must first contribute the same percentage as Saudi Arabia before Saudi Arabia increased its contribution. The debate proceeded along these lines until suddenly Nasser, who had run out of patience, stood up and said he was leaving the meeting. With Nasser's exit, and his decision to leave Rabat, the Arab Summit disbanded without adopting any resolution.

The natural result of the failure of the Arab Summit Conference was that Nasser found himself with no choice but total dependence on the Soviet Union, economically and militarily. This was actually the one weak point I tried to avoid before the Arab Summit. I had my views, which I communicated to Nasser and a number of Arab Heads of State, on the vital importance of further consolidating Arab solidarity and its effect on US–Soviet confrontation in the region. I said that 'Soviet policy in the Middle East crisis was based on three tenets: to terminate the consequences of the aggression – to avoid confrontation with the US – to strengthen Soviet pressure in the area, while attempting to undermine American influence'. The ideal procedure for the Soviet Union, to end the Israeli aggression, was through a peaceful settlement; thus the Soviet Union would avoid any possibility of confrontation with the US, while at the same time maintaining its influence in the area. This is what prompted the Soviet Union to continue talks with the US and to be prepared to consider projects containing Arab concessions. I therefore deduced that the Soviet Union was faced with a dilemma: if the Arabs achieved military superiority, how would they deploy this superiority? Would they just use it as a lever for pressure, or proceed to destroy the Israeli armed forces, an eventuality which would force the US to intervene, with the risk of a US–Soviet confrontation? This was therefore the reason the Soviet Union was reluctant to provide us with the armament necessary to achieve the required military supremacy. For this reason we, for our part, must endeavour to avert all possibility of such a US–Soviet confrontation. This could be achieved through lightening the responsibilities of the Soviet Union, as far as possible, in the following ways: not having military supremacy linked totally with Soviet aid, and endeavouring to benefit from Arab potential; endeavouring to have the largest number of Arab countries participate in the battle, so that the confrontation, in case of American intervention, would be with all the Arabs; endeavouring to have contacts carried out through UN channels in future; affirming that our objective was confined to terminating the consequences of the aggression and obliging Israel to implement the Security Council resolution.

Actually, none of the objectives I raised in my memorandum (Arab solidarity and non-dependence on the Soviet Union) were achieved. Arab dispute continued, and in fact became more acute following the Conference and as a result of its failure.

Arab solidarity was demanded not only by Egypt and the Arabs themselves, but also by all our friends outside the Arab world. I heard this from de Gaulle and Pompidou in France; from General Franco in Spain; from Fanfani and Aldo Moro in Italy; from Chou En-lai in China; and Tito in Yugoslavia; from Brezhnev and Kosygin in the Soviet Union. I used to argue that it had taken Europe two devastating wars to reach their present stage of cooperation and dialogue, and I was certain that time would witness the realization of Arab solidarity.

On 7 January Israel launched a new series of concentrated air raids on the Egyptian depth, using electronic devices to jam our aerial defence. Cairo suburbs like Maadi, Helwan and Khanka received thousands of tons of bombs. These raids were accompanied by Israeli threats to the effect that if the armed forces were not yet convinced of the futility of fighting, Israel would bring that lesson home to the Egyptian people.

In September 1969 the *New York Times* wrote that the next stage would be directed at targets more sensitive to the Egyptian economy and probably at populated areas. On 18 January it wrote that Israel had given priority to psychological warfare, which had the double objective of bringing the war to the Egyptian people and creating dissent inside the Egyptian military command. On 13 January Golda Meir declared she could see no chance for peace as long as Nasser remained in power, and that therefore the downfall of Nasser and his whole regime must be realized prior to any talk of peace. Abba Eban intimated that some US circles (meaning the CIA) had asked Israel to concentrate its efforts on bringing about the downfall of Nasser. By its selection of targets, Israel was trying to achieve this end. It chose a populated residential area, Maadi, which lies ten kilometres south of Cairo, and nine other sites in areas surrounding the capital.

However, these air raids brought about the opposite results to those hoped for. The armed forces, especially the air force, were urging Nasser to allow them to undertake larger military operations against Israel. The intensity of Israel's in-depth air raids on Egypt made the people more determined to mobilize themselves for battle. The air raids also succeeded in convincing the USSR to speed up the shipments of the armaments we had contracted for, and to conclude more arms deals, especially for sophisticated equipment for our air-defence system. Though only a month had elapsed since our political and military talks in the Soviet Union, Nasser decided to go to Moscow on a visit which he kept secret, to confront Soviet leaders with this new Israeli military escalation, as part of the overall reassessment he had decided upon in that period.

Nasser left for Moscow on 22 January and returned on the 25th after securing from the Soviets a consolidation of the Egyptian defensive capabilities, most important of which was that the Soviet Union would provide Egypt with complete battalions and formations of air-defence forces, until Egyptian units had completed their training in the Soviet Union. This included SAM-3s and Soviet pilots who would, for the first time, undertake combat duties inside Egyptian territory. And it was agreed that these supplies would reach Egypt within thirty days. The number of Soviet experts would also be increased. At the request of Nasser, the task of the Soviet pilots was confined to protecting the Egyptian heartland, while actual engagement with the Israelis along the front would be exclusively entrusted to Egyptian pilots.

After our return from Moscow I expressed the view that,

instead of an overall Arab plan of action, we should concentrate on joint action with the front-line countries, and that other Arab countries should be left to contribute in accordance with their capabilities. I also felt that, for Syria and Jordan to fulfil their part adequately, Iraq's participation in the Eastern Front was to a large extent decisive. The Shah of Iran was raising difficulties for Iraq; Nasser was suspicious of the timing of these difficulties since they led to freezing large contingents of the Iraqi army on the borders with Iran. Both King Hussein and Podgorny, each in his own way, tried to dissuade the Shah from adopting this posture in order to enable Iraq to meet its commitments on the Eastern Front.

In my contacts with the countries of the Arab East during that period I was mainly concerned with the consolidation of the Eastern Front. The leaders in Damascus were aware of this factor and were insistent upon it, which led to the signing of an agreement between Egypt and Syria in August 1969 which included the creation of a joint political command and stipulated, among other things, that priority be given to the air force and air-defence systems in planning and training.

Thus, at the beginning of 1970, in the course of the meetings between Nasser, General Fawzi and myself, my view of the political and military position was as follows. Our armed forces had completed the necessary training on arms received from the Soviet Union. The US would never allow us to achieve air supremacy over Israel, or even air parity. Whenever we received an arms shipment from the Soviet Union, the US was quick to ship additional and more sophisticated aircraft to Israel. However, we were able to realize a reasonable ratio of trained combat pilots: three pilots to every two planes. If, therefore, we could consolidate our air-defence missile system along the Suez Canal, this would enhance decisively the crossing operation. The Egyptian armed forces now numbered 540,000, a large percentage of whom were secondary school and university graduates, compared with 170,000 prior to the June War, and plans were in operation to increase that number to 750,000 before the end of 1970. Egypt would not be in need of Arab infantry support. However, it could prove useful to have Libya negotiate with France to up-date the delivery of the 100 Mirages Libya had contracted for with France.

At a four-power Summit Meeting comprising Egypt, Syria, Iraq and Jordan on 1 September 1969, agreement was reached to complete the organization and consolidation of the Eastern Front by 1970.

Rogers' proposals to Egypt and Jordan constituted the first US move in the direction of a comprehensive settlement. Yet as soon as Israel announced its rejection, Rogers announced that the role of the US was 'to bring the parties together for a negotiated settlement'. Nixon went a step further when he declared in January 1970 that the US believed that peace could be established on an agreement between the parties to be arrived at only through negotiations. He later subscribed to the Israeli claim that Security Council resolutions were mere principles that should be negotiated.

In fact Washington adopted a highly provocative posture when on 22 February Bergus, the US Minister in Cairo, delivered a message from his government which intimated that the US felt anxiety at Israel's raids deep inside Egypt and regretted the victims that were falling to those Israeli raids. For this reason, the US was advising us to accept an immediate ceasefire as provided by the Security Council resolution of 1967, in which case we should not tie the ceasefire resolution to Israeli withdrawal. If we did not accept, then Israel's air raids against Egypt's heartland (and particularly against civilians) would continue, and perhaps on a more intensive and wider scale, to include targets that would fundamentally harm Egypt's economy. This constituted blackmail by the US.

At the time we received the US threat, Soviet Premier Alexei Kosygin dispatched a message to US President Richard Nixon on 31 January that was characterized by firmness, clarity and frankness. He referred to Israel's air raids on civilian targets inside Egypt and Jordan, and on the civil population in industrial areas, and on other civilian constructions. All that was happening at a time when Egypt and the other Arab countries had not taken retaliatory strikes against civilian targets in Israel. Kosygin went on to say: 'The danger exists that military actions in the near future may assume a larger scale . . . We want to tell you with all frankness that if Israel continues her adventurism and bombs the territory of Egypt – and other Arab States – the Soviet Union will be forced to see that the Arab States have in their possession the means with which it would be possible for them to repel the presumptuous aggressors.' Kosygin sent similar messages to French President Pompidou and British Prime Minister Wilson.

On 4 February, Nixon dispatched his reply to the Soviet Union, in which he refused to hold Israel responsible for what was happening, and suggested that 'we use our influence over both sides . . . for strict observance of the ceasefire'. On the warning that the Soviet Union would provide the Arab States with the means to repel the aggressor, Nixon said: 'The United States have always objected to steps which could result in a deeper involvement of the great powers in the Middle East conflict.' He went on to say that the US 'supported quick restoration of the ceasefire' and favoured 'limitation of arms delivery to this area. The United States are following attentively the relative military balance in the Middle East' and 'will not hesitate to supply friendly countries with arms if such a necessity arises. On the broader question of the peace settlement, the United States continues to have an obligation to help to achieve a peaceful settlement between sides, as the November 1967 UN resolution calls for. We note your thought that if the question of withdrawal is solved, then there will be no serious obstacles for agreement on other questions. As you know, the withdrawal cannot take place until full agreement between both sides on all elements of a peaceful settlement is achieved.' In this communication Nixon referred to the US proposals submitted to the Soviet Union on 28 October (concerning Egypt) and on 18 December (concerning Jordan), charging that 'Soviet unresponsiveness to these proposals' was delaying the peace process.

These messages show the wide gap between the US and Soviet positions. The US wanted to curb arms delivery to the area prior to effecting Israeli withdrawal. In its draft resolution to the Security Council in November 1967, the Soviet Union had agreed in principle to the arms limitation, which would be put into effect after Israel's withdrawal.

The isolation of the US can be seen, when compared with the position of other powers, as revealed by the replies of Pompidou and Wilson to Kosygin's message.

The British Prime Minister in his message said that it was 'essentially important to establish once again an effective cease-fire' (along the Suez Canal front) and emphasized that 'until a just settlement is reached there can never be any confidence that hostilities and acts of violence will stop in this area. Our support for Security Council Resolution 242 means, first of all, the support for the interrelated principles of the withdrawal of the Israeli armed forces from the territories occupied during the conflict in June 1967, and, on the other hand, the termination of all claims and states of belligerency and respect for the sovereignty, territorial integrity and political independence of every State in the area, and their right to live in peace within secure and recognized boundaries, free from threats or acts of force.'

In his message, Pompidou referred to the military situation: 'I share your anxiety in regard to the extension of the military operations in this region, which can only incandesce the atmosphere and impede the search for a peaceful solution which France has always been looking for. I believe that the present situation shows it is necessary that the mission of the UN Secretary-General's representative should be resumed in the immediate future.' Thus Britain reiterated its interpretation of Resolution 242, while France demanded that Jarring resume his mission to implement Resolution 242. Neither of them referred to the US proposals which Nixon had emphasized in his message to Kosygin.

Thus the isolation of the US at the four-power talks in New York was increasing steadily, with France exerting new efforts when, on 9 December 1969, it forwarded proposals for a settlement between Israel and Jordan which could be applied to all the other areas – stipulating Israeli withdrawal to 4 June lines on the Jordanian front, with minor border rectifications to be agreed on by both parties under the auspices of the UN, together with a timetable for Israel's withdrawal. But France later ran into a US rejection of its proposal on the basis that, while it was acceptable to the Arabs, Israel had rejected it. During the four-power meetings in January and February 1970, several debates took place on the US proposal that Arab–Israeli negotiations be carried out on the basis of the 'Rhodes Formula' . . . which the Israelis interpreted to mean direct negotiations. I told the Soviets that we rejected such a formula, and consequently the Soviet Union withdrew its approval on this point. The Soviet Union also criticized the American interpretation that the Rhodes talks had been direct negotiations.

The US administration, during that period, was increasing its patronage of Israeli claims. In February 1970, the administration informed us that the 'Rhodes Formula' was of special importance to the US, and therefore we should accept it. On the Rogers proposals to Egypt and Jordan, the US position was: 'Frankly we do not know whether we could persuade the Israelis to talk on the basis of the two US proposals relating to Egypt and Jordan.' This meant that the US, while unsure of getting Israel to agree to its proposals, was attempting first to secure our acceptance and use it as a springboard for demanding further concessions. The same message contained the news that the US considered that Egypt shared in the responsibility for the failure of Jarring's mission, and unless Egypt adopted a more positive attitude the four-power meetings would meet the same fate!

Meanwhile the War of Attrition had prompted the Soviet Union to speed up deliveries of arms – which would hardly have been the case, had the front remained calm.

The isolation of the US in the Arab world had intensified while anti–American sentiments were mounting. Rogers, to contain this wave of antagonism, toured the region and visited countries that, according to US definition, were moderate. He visited Morocco and Tunisia, only to hear scathing criticisms of US policy.

The four-power meetings continued in New York. The US could not terminate them but was anxious to undermine their work. At its meeting on 12 March each country had defined its position relative to the issue of withdrawal. Soviet delegate Malik then posed the following question to Charles Yost: 'Does the United States agree that after the final settlement no Israeli forces would be stationed in the Arab territories occupied in the June War?'

Yost, who was among the team that drew up the Brookings Report, was a man of integrity who believed that peace must rest on Israeli withdrawal and guaranteeing Israel's security. How-ever, in his answer he had to follow the line of his government. He said that with regard to Egypt, withdrawal would be to its international boundaries, while with regard to Jordan, there should be agreement on minor border rectifications. Yost went on to say that 'parties must first agree on the dispositions of Gaza and the demilitarized zones because this will clarify where Israeli troops will be stationed along the Jordan–Israel borders'.

Soviet delegate Malik, commenting on the reply given by the US delegate, said that the US would then be adopting a position that was opposed to total Israeli withdrawal, and that everything should be left to negotiations between the parties – whereas Security Council Resolution 242 stipulated Israeli withdrawal to 4 June lines, on which all Soviet and French proposals were based. So long as no agreement had been reached with the US on Israel's withdrawal, then the big-four meetings would only arrive at a dead end.

I had anticipated even graver differences between the US and its West European allies. This was evident during my visits to Western Europe, where countries were becoming convinced of the justice of the Arab position. The continuation of the problem and the escalation of the War of Attrition against Israeli occupation along the Egyptian front had a severe impact on the economic interests of the Western countries, and presaged even greater dangers to come. The West European governments were able to state their positions in a more even-handed manner than the US, because their governmental systems allowed them to face up to Zionist pressure in a more positive manner than the US. Zionist arrogance in the US reached a level that incensed Nixon himself.

French President Pompidou had begun an official visit to the US on 24 February, in a highly-charged atmosphere. Israel had mobilized Zionist organizations to undermine US–French talks, with the hope that Nixon would pressure Pompidou into abrogating the Mirages deal with Libya, and lift the French arms embargo that de Gaulle had forced on Israel in the wake of the 5 June aggression. Pompidou was met with hostile demonstrations in Chicago and New York, and the mayors of those cities refused to meet him. Pompidou denounced such action as shameful and repugnant, whereupon Nixon was obliged to fly to New York to extend personal apologies to Pompidou.

Meanwhile the Egyptian air force was insistent that Nasser allow it to participte in the battle; Nasser urged more self-control and perseverance. Israeli air raids continued on civilian and economic targets from the beginning of the year 1970 until 18 April when a number of Israeli planes flying over South Suez on their way to the Nile Valley were intercepted by a number of MiGs with Russian-speaking pilots. The Israeli planes returned to their bases and their raids on civilian targets were suspended.

For Israel the challenge of Soviet pilots represented a grave threat. It was aware that the Soviet Union could always replace a shot-down aircraft with two more. The newly arrived Soviet arms contained complete units of developed missiles operated by Soviet personnel and more Soviet pilots to reinforce the air defence of Egypt, which allowed Nasser to concentrate his forces on the battle-front after he had provided the largest possible protection to the civilians. Israel began a hysterical worldwide propaganda campaign against the new consignments of air-defence missiles reaching Egypt which, as far as I could judge during my visits abroad, had little effect on foreign capitals where the prevailing feeling was that Egypt had every right to defend her territories in any way she considered fit.

The target of the campaign was, in fact, to pressure the US into further deliveries of arms to Israel. In a statement to the press Eban said that the US should adopt practical measures to limit this imbalance in arms and should supply Israel with aircraft necessary for its security and stability. Eban's statement came in the wake of an announcement by Nixon that he had decided to postpone his decision on Israeli demands for aircraft. Although we considered this decision by Nixon a positive step, from the practical point of view the US was aware that Israel already possessed air superiority. In fact the announcement mentioned that the US would revise it if the present balance of power was affected – which meant that if the Soviet Union supplied us with arms to enhance our defensive capabilities the United States would resume supplying Israel with more aircraft – which turned the whole measure into an attempt to pressure the Soviet Union to stop its arms supplies to Egypt.

When the new air-defence missiles actually arrived, the next step was to deploy them in the Suez Canal Zone to protect our advanced position, and also to build what was later called 'The Rocket Wall' (Missile Barrier). Israel exerted every effort to prevent the construction of our network of air-defence missile systems. Once completed, such a network would give protection to our troops crossing the Canal, against Israeli air attacks, and would definitely be turned in full force against any assault of the waterway.

Thus, on 30 March, Israeli Deputy Premier Yighal Allon

declared that he intended to exert the utmost effort to prevent the enlargement of the Egyptian air-defence network, and that the presence of the SAM-3 in Egypt upset the balance of power on the Egyptian–Israeli front.

On 14 and 15 April, Israel launched intensive air attacks on Egyptian positions along the Suez Canal. On 16 April, Egyptian aircraft retaliated in a large-scale attack on Israeli positions in Sinai, to signal the beginning of a series of systematic air attacks authorized by Nasser.

It was in such a climate that the US requested that we receive Assistant Secretary of State Joseph Sisco in Cairo. He came to see me on 10 April when he repeated the US request for a resumption of diplomatic relations with Egypt, asserting that we should place our confidence in the United States now that it was about to adopt a new policy. I reported the meeting to Nasser, commenting that I failed to see any new elements worth considering, only more of the old vague promises. When he was received by Nasser, Sisco asked him: 'Why don't you initiate a diplomatic and political dialogue with us, why do you let the Soviet Union speak on your behalf?'

Nasser answered him bluntly: 'Because we do not trust you, because of your alignment with Israel. Every time you present us with a new project you ask us for new concessions.'

Sisco attempted to convince Nasser that there was going to be a radical change in US policy and that it was important that Egypt trust the good intentions of this new policy.

Nasser answered that good intentions should be clear and outspoken and based on definite behaviour, not on vague promises.

Sisco did not submit one clear-cut point of view, so talks with him were of no consequence. When he arrived in Jordan he could not land in Amman because of huge hostile demonstrations.

On 23 April, Egyptian planes raided the Israeli settlement 'Nahal Yam' in northern Sinai, 100 kilometres east of the Suez Canal. Two days later, Egyptian planes raided Israeli positions deep inside Sinai, in the vicinity of the coastal town of al-Arish. The following day, 200 Egyptian 'Saika' troops (Special Forces) attacked and destroyed an Israeli strong-point across the Canal in the southern sector. On 28 April, Egyptian planes, staging their sixth large attack in eleven days, raided Israeli positions inside

Sinai. Meanwhile, Egyptian artillery was pounding some Israeli positions in Sinai at the rate of ten shells a minute. Thus, the Egyptian army was in a state of real war with Israel.

In much the same way as Israel made public all US arms deals, to act as a political and military deterrent to the Arabs, so the Soviet combat presence in Egypt now became a political and military deterrent to Israeli attacks. It was of no small significance – especially to the US which imagined that military escalation in the Middle East would be its private monopoly!

President Nixon made a reassessment of the Middle East situation, and the State Department declared that the participation of Soviet pilots in defending Egyptian territory constituted a 'serious development with dangerous implications' in the situation, and that the US had the intention of 'raising the issue with the Soviet Union'. However, the most ironical development was the appeal made by Israel's Foreign Minister, in a press conference, for 'immediate international assistance' to counter Egypt's move of having Soviet pilots defend its air space . . . As if it were our duty to keep our skies open to the US-built warplanes as they bombarded our children and civil installations!

Our armed forces in the meantime were engaged in intensive combat training on a large scale, including the assault on the Suez Canal, as a fundamental part of the coming battle. Thus, on 1 May, Israel announced that it had thwarted a crossing or assault operation by eighty Egyptian 'Saika' troops – the third operation by our troops within three days.

All this time, while the War of Attrition against Israeli occupation escalated, tremendously heroic efforts were being exerted by General Fawzi to install the new Egyptian missile network along the Suez Canal front under intensive daily attacks by Israel which aimed at aborting the completion of the new 'Rocket Wall'. Israel, during that period, averaged 526 sorties per week.

Slowly but steadily, the new network of missiles began taking its toll of Israeli aircraft. It shot down an electronic reconnaissance plane, manned by a crew of twelve Israeli officers. On 30 June, two Phantoms and two Skyhawks were destroyed, and three pilots captured. On 2 and 3 July, three other Israeli aircraft were shot down; and on 6 July two more Phantoms were destroyed which made Eban declare that the Israeli air force was suffering a dangerous erosion.

The continued escalation of fighting along the Egyptian front was mobilizing Arab feelings and sentiments against the US. Consequently, the US was becoming seriously apprehensive about the future of American interests in the area. The US had chosen to ignore one very fundamental and vital reality: the fighting along the Suez Canal front was actually a 'national battle', in the full sense of the phrase, in which all Arabs were united together against the Israeli occupation.

The US found itself in a very awkward position, sufficient to destroy all the bases on which US policy was founded. Richard Nixon was now trying to act in a way that would remove the stigma of total alignment to Israel and, at the same time, improve relations with the Arab States in order to avoid the dangers that were beginning to surround US interests. Simultaneously, Nixon was seeking to undermine Soviet presence in the area. He found himself in the unenviable position of trying to harmonize three contradictory requirements. His main predicament was that he could find no solution to that complex equation: how to achieve a balance between Israel's expansionist ambitions and the Arab refusal of any territorial concessions. It was then that Nasser decided to intensify the critical attitude of the Arabs towards the US to the utmost; he also decided to give the US one last chance before he began all-out mobilization of Arab sentiments against the US. Thus, on 1 May 1970 (Labour Day) Nasser began by reviewing the political situation from the very beginning, and then said: 'I call on President Nixon and say the US is about to take a very dangerous step against the Arab nation [referring to the new shipments of sophisticated aircraft to Israel the US was considering at this time]. The US, by taking such a step to ensure Israel's military superiority, would be imposing on the Arab nation a position from which there can be no retreat . . . a position from which we must deduce what is necessary, and which will affect American relations with the Arab nation for years, and perhaps centuries to come. I say to him – and he knows that I mean what I say – that the Arab nation will not surrender or give in; while it wants genuine peace it is also convinced that peace can only be based on justice. If the US wants peace, then it must order Israel to withdraw from the occupied Arab territories. This is within its power for Israel depends on the US for its very existence. Anything else would never be acceptable or permissible by us. This is one solution . . . The second solution is definitely within the power of the US, namely to refrain from extending any future political, military or economic support so long as it occupies our Arab lands. If the second solution does not materialize, then the Arabs must conclude one irrefutable fact: that the US desires that Israel continue occupation of our lands until it succeeds in imposing its terms of submission on us. This will never happen. All the plots and conspiracies against the Arab nation and the Liberation Front will never succeed. I say to President Nixon there is a decisive point coming in Arab—American relations: either severance for ever, or a new, serious and clear beginning. Future developments will not only influence Arab—American relations, but will also have greater and more serious complications later on. Our insistence on liberating our lands is the fundamental and legitimate right of any nation that values its dignity.'

In the meantime, Israel was actively engaged in a political campaign, inside the US itself, in a bid to pressure the US government in a deal for an additional 125 aircraft. In fact, on 4 June, some eighty-five Senators signed a petition which they delivered to William Rogers, that called on the government to supply Israel with additional sophisticated warplanes. On 7 June, the Secretary of State said the US would shortly announce its decision on the sale of military aircraft to Israel. But he stressed that the decision would be positive 'only partially' and 'will be in a balanced and calculated manner so as not to imply to the Arabs that we support Israel regardless of what she may do'.

Nixon finally decided to make a move in response to Nasser's Labour Day appeal. The move came in the form of a message from Secretary of State Rogers, on 19 June, and was relayed to me the following day.

Rogers began his message by stating that he had 'read carefully President Nasser's statement of 1 May', and that he agreed 'that the situation [in the Middle East] is at a critical point'; that he thought it was 'in our joint interest that the United States retains and strengthens friendly ties with all the peoples and States of the area. We hope this will prove possible and are prepared to do our part.' He went on to say: 'In our view, the most effective way to agree on a settlement would be for the parties to work out under Ambassador Jarring's auspices the detailed steps necessary to carry out Security Council Resolution 242.' He concluded his message with a set of proposals for consideration by Egypt. These were: (1) that both Israel and Egypt subscribe to a restoration of the ceasefire for at least a limited period; (2) that Israel and Egypt (as well as Israel and Jordan) subscribe to the following statement which would be in the form of a report from Ambassador Jarring to the Secretary-General, U Thant:

Egypt, Jordan and Israel advise me that they agree:

(A) that having accepted and indicated their willingness to carry out Resolution 242 in all its parts, they will designate representatives to discussions to be held under my auspices, according to such procedure and at such places and times as I may recommend, taking into account as appropriate each side's preferences as to method of procedure and previous experience between the parties;

(B) that the purpose of the aforementioned discussions is to reach agreement on the establishment of a just and lasting peace between them based on (1) mutual acknowledgement by Egypt, Jordan and Israel of each other's sovereignty, territorial integrity and political independence, and (2) Israeli withdrawal from territories occupied in the 1967 conflict, both in accordance with Resolution 242;

(C) that, to facilitate my task of promoting agreement as set forth in Resolution 242, the parties will strictly observe, effective 1 July until at least 1 October, the ceasefire resolutions of the Security Council.

Finally, Rogers said he was sending similar messages to the Foreign Ministers of Jordan and Israel and was awaiting my early reply.

At the same time, we received additional clarification and assurances from the US in a memorandum submitted by Donald Bergus, stating: '(1) Ceasefire, to be effective, would have to include understanding that both sides would stop all incursions and all firing, on the ground and in the air, across ceasefire lines, and would refrain from changing military *status quo* in an agreed zone west of the Suez Canal and in a similar zone east of the Suez Canal. (2) Egyptians should bear in mind that we are asking that Israelis make what they will consider very significant political concessions in (a) agreeing to enter indirect negotiation on implementation of the resolution and to pursue these in a sincere desire to achieve results, and (b) accepting the principle of withdrawal prior to negotiations. This may seem to the Egyptians no more than what the Israelis should do. Israelis will undoubtedly feel the same way about things we are asking [Egypt] to do. (3) The US Government is prepared to remain engaged in the process, once negotiations begin. We continue to maintain there can be no withdrawal without peace and no peace without withdrawal. (4) On aircraft to Israel, the US Government is limiting itself not to go beyond the level committed in past contracts during the period in which we are pursuing our peace initiative. Our deliveries during this period will keep the Israeli total within the fifty Phantoms which will have been delivered to Israel by the end of June, three will be delivered in July, and three in August, bringing the total to fifty. As to Skyhawks, eighty-eight have been delivered and the remainder, to 100 level, will be delivered over the coming months as scheduled. We have also made contingency arrangements which will put us in a position to supply Israel with replacements of aircraft in future if situation so requires. These arrangements could be influenced by status and prospects for success of our peace efforts and whether ceasefire is in effect. (5) We hope agreement along such lines can in time help to create a favourable climate for the restoration of US-[Egyptian] relations. (6) We are explaining these proposals directly to [Egypt] in response to President Nasser's 1 May appeal and also because we want [Egypt] to hear them from us and to make certain they are understood. Nevertheless, [Egypt] should be aware that we are informing the Soviet Union, the United Kingdom, and France of these proposals and will be urging them to work with us in this initiative. We intend to pursue our bilaterals with the Soviets as well as the four-power talks and see all these efforts as complementary. (7) While we are aware of and acknowledge the fact that it has taken the US Government a period of time to formulate this present initiative, we strongly hope for an early response from the Government of [Egypt]. A decision having been taken, it is imperative that we move quickly if it is to work. (8) Assistant Secretary Sisco is prepared to fly to London or some other halfway point at any time to meet with Under-Secretary Gohar to discuss our proposals further, should the Government of [Egypt] so desire.' Thus ends the memorandum we received from the US government. I have reproduced it in full because of its great importance to subsequent events and developments.

Donald Bergus informed Egyptian Foreign Under-Secretary, Ambassador Salah Gohar, that a similar message would be delivered the same day to Jordanian Foreign Minister Abdel Moneim al-Rifai, containing US proposals for Jordan. He also said that Secretary of State William Rogers would be making a statement on the Middle East the following week, but would not deal with the contents or details of the American initiative.

On 25 June, only five days after submitting the Rogers Initiative, Donald Bergus requested a meeting with Gohar and said he had been instructed by his government to assure us that the declarations made that very same day by Secretary of State Rogers (that Washington had decided to restrict the delivery of aircraft to the numbers already contracted) did not in any way contradict what he had submitted on 20 June. He said that withholding announcement of that position should not be interpreted by Egypt as a change in US policy. His government had requested him to be very clear and precise in assuring Egypt that the position would remain unchanged.

In answer to our queries, and because many Arab capitals had queried Washington on its position on the Palestinians, the State Department had instructed him to state the US position as follows: 'The US recognizes that the Palestinians represent an important party and their concerns must be taken into account in any settlement.'

Bergus added that Rogers, both in his messages to me and in his press statement, had referred to the governments and *peoples* of the area, and that, naturally, included the Palestinians, for Rogers had said: 'To move towards a fair and lasting peace, that takes into account the aspirations and legitimate interests of all the governments and peoples of the area'.

Rogers had made several statements at a press conference in Washington that day. And though he had declared the US commitment to Israel's security, Zionist pressure over eight months had been urging the US government to commit a further hundred Skyhawks and twenty-five Phantoms to Israel. So when the US announced it would take that step, and still remain committed to delivering a hundred Skyhawks (contracted in

1966) and fifty Phantoms (contracted in 1968) to Israel, then that should be regarded as a positive American move towards peace. Furthermore, Rogers had declared that Resolution 242 contained a solution to the problem, which was further evidence of the seriousness of the move, since the US regarded the resolution 'as a solution for implementation' from the very start. The Secretary of State then pointed out that the Soviet presence in Egypt did not prevent Israel from being able to defend itself, until that very moment. He then added that the initiative by the US was in response to President Nasser's appeal of 1 May, and that the US had so far received no reply from the Soviet Union to those proposals, though the Soviets had listened to them carefully. On the method of negotiations, Rogers was very clear that they would be indirect, not direct, negotiations.

During his meeting with Gohar on 26 July, Donald Bergus said he appreciated the circumstances of the large-scale battle between Israel and Syria the day before, and that he was also aware of the fact that, in Arab thinking, withdrawal was associated with all the territories captured after 5 June. However, he expressed the hope that Egypt would not allow any Arab party (meaning Syria) to impose a veto on the proposed settlement. Gohar said Egypt never gave anyone the right to veto its policy. Our policy, however, was based on total Israeli withdrawal from all the occupied Arab territories, including the Syrian Golan Heights.

Bergus replied that Syria had not yet accepted Resolution 242. Gohar stated that Syria could not see any serious commitment on the part of Israel or the US to total withdrawal. If Syria were to find sufficient evidence of such a commitment, then the Syrian position would assuredly conform to that – until we secured such evidence, we would never demand that the Syrians accept Resolution 242.

It became clear to me that this time the American initiative was striving more seriously towards peace based on a comprehensive settlement, for the following reasons: (1) The US had at last abandoned its pursuit of an Egyptian–Israeli settlement, having exhausted all methods of bringing pressure on us. This, in itself, would be bringing us closer to genuine and fair peace. (2) What made us regard this American initiative with more seriousness than the previous Rogers proposals was the fact that the US had formally and publicly committed itself not to give in to Israel's demands for additional aircraft. (3) The US was now convinced that Egypt was determined to liberate its territories by force of arms, and that its military power was increasing day by day. The intensive air strikes by Israel during the past weeks had not prevented us from completing our air-defence network and deploying the new Soviet-built SAM-3s. Furthermore, the Soviet combat-presence in Egypt was sufficient warning to the US, for this was the first time that the Soviet Union had provided Soviet combat pilots to a non-Communist State. (4) The latest American initiative was chiefly prompted by a desire to preserve American interests in the area, which were being jeopardized as a result of the tremendous opposition caused by the total US alignment to Israel. (5) In the past we had refused to have any direct dialogue with the US because of its lack of earnestness in its pursuit of a comprehensive settlement. Now that a minimum level of earnestness was apparent, we should begin, and even encourage, such a dialogue with the US.

Nasser was due to visit Moscow after a visit to Libya, for talks on arms shipments – a matter that took up all his thoughts.

On 25 June, Nasser delivered a speech in Benghazi in which he said: 'The United States has, since 1969, delivered 150 Phantoms and Skyhawks to Israel, and has sent pilots of dual nationalities, American and Israeli, to Israel. At the same time, the United States is demanding of the Soviet Union that it refrain from arming the Arab countries, under the pretext of maintaining the present power balance in the Middle East – which means Israeli superiority. But the Soviet Union has refused to respond to America's demands. Today we are not fighting only Israel . . . we are fighting an Israel supported and reinforced by the United States of America. We in Egypt are daily subjected to air raids, carried out by eighty to 200 planes in a single day. But in spite of that, we shall never allow Israel's terms to be imposed on us or America's terms to be imposed on us.

'The Israelis are concentrating their air raids on the Canal area so as to prevent the Egyptian army from mobilizing its forces for an attack across the Canal. Once it secures the opportunity of parity in the air, then no power on earth can prevent it from crossing "the Canal". We shall soon be able to compensate for Israeli air superiority by securing a balance in air power, because we are training hundreds of pilots and receiving hundreds of aircraft.'

Nasser did not comment on the latest American initiative as we reserved our judgement until the study he had asked to have prepared on 20 June was completed.

7

The Rogers Initiative

Donald Bergus came to see me after my return from Libya to inform me that his government wished to relay to President Nasser that it would appreciate his taking into consideration the specific steps the US had adopted so as to enable him to view the initiative in a positive spirit. Foremost among these steps was that the White House had postponed a decision on the new US–Israeli arms deal, despite great pressure by Congress. In this way the US government was responding to the repeated demands by Egypt and American efforts, this time, would be more serious so as to effect a just peace. For this reason, Washington urgently awaited the Egyptian reply so that it could take the next step whereby Ambassador Jarring could resume his mission to implement the Security Council resolution.

This new American attitude was in complete contradiction to its threats made less than five months earlier of further Israeli escalation of in-depth air raids on our civilian installations. We had rejected that threat at the time and had confronted subsequent Israeli military escalation; and it had become clear to everyone that the military situation was rapidly turning against Israel.

I submitted to Nasser the studies on American initiatives undertaken by the Ministry of Foreign Affairs, concluding that the initiative did not go beyond requesting that Jarring resume his mission. Therefore, there were two probabilities: that the US was actually seeking to implement the Security Council resolution, having seen our capacity to resist and becoming aware of the dangers to which its interests in the area were being exposed, in addition to the impact of increased Soviet military presence; or that it was but another manoeuvre in favour of Israel, now that the US found itself in an awkward political position at the four-power talks in New York, or because of its unwillingness, or inability, to call on Israel to effect total withdrawal. In this latter case, the US would have made the initiative to refer the whole issue once again to Jarring, while investing a certain degree of fairness on its position by reaffirming that it would withhold the new Skyhawks and Phantoms deal. I reached the conclusion that the first assumption was closer to reality, while taking into consideration that if the issue was to be referred to Jarring, without clear-cut backing, then it would only lead to the same deadlock as in the previous two and a half years. On the other hand, we should not ignore the international efforts, embodied in the two superpowers or the four-power meetings, which lent support to Jarring's mission. I added that we could formulate our answer on the basis of accepting the American initiative as conforming to our demands. This would indicate our willingness to cooperate with the American initiative, especially since it ran counter to Israel's refusal to implement the Security Council resolution and to declare, in advance, its commitment to withdraw. In this case, there existed the probability that Israel would reject the initiative and this would definitely lead to an open dispute between Israel and the US, as well as to splits inside Israel. I said that we must therefore consult in advance with the Soviet Union on the steps to be taken in the coming phase, especially should the American initiative end in failure.

Meanwhile, President Nasser had instructed General Fawzi to review the military position, in case we accepted the initiative. He said: 'From the military aspect, all our assessments must be based on the fact that the ceasefire would expire in three months' time without Israel effecting a total withdrawal. That, of course, means that we would once again revert to military operations until we liberate our territories by force in the spring of 1971, at the latest.'

The main reason for setting that particular date was that Nasser had carefully examined with Fawzi the details of 'Operation 200', a plan to liberate Sinai. We had in our possession all the means to carry out the first phase, code-named 'Granite', whereby our armed forces would reach the passes in Sinai. However, the necessity still existed to provide the means to execute the other phases of 'Operation 200'. Nasser asked Fawzi to list the arms required from the Soviet Union.

Nasser was aware that it would be extremely hazardous, from

the military aspect, to order the army to effect a ceasefire, and then countermand that order, and order a resumption, as such a procedure could lower the combat morale of the armed forces. So while he wished to give enough opportunity to the American initiative, he was of the opinion that, once that initiative ended in failure, we must resume fighting and never cease firing.

On 29 June, the night we left for Moscow, our armed forces moved a new batch of missiles in the Canal Zone, which came as a surprise to Israel, for on the morning of 30 June, we knocked down four Israeli aircraft (two Skyhawks and two Phantoms) and captured three pilots. Within the next five days, five more Israeli planes (including two Phantoms) were shot down: the first three weeks of July would prove the effectiveness of the new missile systems!

The first session of talks in Moscow began on the afternoon of 30 June and was attended on the Soviet side by Brezhnev, Kosygin, Podgorny, Ponomaryov, Gromyko, Marshal Grechko, and Ambassador Vinogradov.

Nasser began by reviewing the results of his visit to Libya. He said the Libyan leaders were calling for complete unity between Egypt, Syria and Libya and he had agreed to consider the establishment of a Federal Union, though he was aware of the problems that would confront it. Brezhnev, at that point, inquired how we were going to prepare for such a union of the three countries. Nasser said that a committee would be created to lay down the general principles within a month; once they were approved by the three countries, they could be put to a public referendum at the beginning of 1971. Nasser went on to say: 'I was not very keen to form such a union, prior to resolving the consequences of the Israeli aggression. However, what made me agree in principle on a Federal Union was my fears of outside conspiracies against Libya.' Brezhnev wondered whether there were sufficient historical roots linking the Egyptian and Libyan peoples. Nasser replied that historical roots had always existed between the Arab peoples.

Turning to the military front, Nasser said: 'We are now being subjected to intensive air raids by the US-built Israeli Phantoms, employing the most sophisticated US electronic equipment. The objective of these air raids, as Dayan has declared, is to prevent the Egyptian army from completing its offensive preparations to liberate our occupied lands. Our losses last May amounted to about 1,000 casualties, killed or wounded. Despite these losses our officers and men have a very high morale and are fully confident that our increasing capabilities will enable us to inflict unbearable losses on Israel. The Egyptian armed forces, by the end of this year, will amount to 750,000 men, and will reach the one million mark by the first quarter of next year. The main problem here is that the US supplies Israel with the most sophisticated electronic equipment. Israel has received specially equipped planes that can pinpoint missile bases and jam their radar, so that they can then be bombarded. The problem with our air force is that the MiG can remain airborne for only twenty minutes, while the Mirage can stay up for an hour, and the Phantom even longer. Therefore, it would be wrong to say that a hundred Mirages and Phantoms could be confronted with a hundred MiGs.' Nasser elaborated on this point, emphasizing the role of electronic warfare, and saying that unless we received similar electronic devices, our air-defence system would remain weak.

The second session began the following morning, 1 July. Marshal Grechko, who had received fresh information on Israel's air raid on Egyptian missile bases the previous day (during which we shot down two Phantoms and two Skyhawks), stated that two more Phantoms had been shot down by Egypt's air-defence systems.

Brezhnev once again raised the question of the proposed Egypt–Syria–Libya union, asking if there was a coordinated plan to resolve the existing crisis peacefully or by war, or whether such a federation would lead to complicating the crisis even further. Obviously, Brezhnev, by his last query, was expressing his dissatisfaction over the proposed federation. Nasser, in reply, said: 'When we accepted the Security Council resolution, we had every intention of honouring our pledge, accepting a peaceful settlement if it would really achieve our just demands. However, no peaceful settlement will ever be fair or just unless Egypt has acquired sufficient military power to prevent Israel disregarding the Security Council resolution. Syria's rejection of the Security Council resolution is not a rejection of a peaceful settlement, but because Syria had doubts about the possibility of imposing it on Israel. If we should set up the federation between us we in Egypt will not alter our position. However, the achievement of a peaceful settlement means increasing our military power, for Israel will never give up the land unless it feels our power.' He added that we had accepted the peace commitments the US had been pushing, and that the Soviet Ambassador to Washington had relayed our approval to Rogers.

Nasser then turned to the latest initiative by Rogers, saying that it contained nothing new. It was just a readjustment of the US position which had deviated from the Security Council resolution and to which they were now returning, proposing that Jarring resume his mission. Nasser added: 'This time, there must be specific directives to Jarring, without which I expect his mission to fail.'

Kosygin asked: 'Have you had any talks with the Americans on the initiative?'

Nasser said that Bergus had informed us that the US was serious in its effort to reach a peaceful settlement, and that our acceptance of the Rogers Initiative would help the US bring pressure on Israel.

Brezhnev agreed that Gromyko would confer with me, to consider a joint position on the American initiative and to examine all its details, remarking that if Egypt objected to certain items, then the Soviets should be informed of them.

The next day Nasser went to a hospital near Moscow for medical tests which would last a few days. Meanwhile, joint meetings were to be held between Gromyko and myself to consider the political situation, and between General Fawzi and Marshal Grechko to consider the arms supplies we required. Nasser summoned Ali Sabry and me to his hospital. While in Cairo, Nasser had agreed with my views, as contained in my memorandum on the US initiative, concerning our assessment of the US position and our reply, and the necessity of our consulting with the Soviets. Nasser therefore now asked about my expectations from the Soviet leaders. I said that our acceptance of the American initiative would not be satisfactory to the Soviets, for an acceptance would give credit to the US and the settlement would then appear tied to them alone, while the Soviets would find themselves relegated to the role of spectators.

I had actually expressed that view in one of my memoranda to Nasser, prior to our departure from Cairo. Now Nasser began discussing with me the method of implementing the proposals, should Egypt declare its acceptance of them. I said I would need time to contact the Americans, in order to be assured of their intentions and to secure further assurances including, perhaps, the question of total withdrawal. Secondly, I should consult with Jarring on the supervision of the ceasefire to ensure that Israel would not violate it. It would not be acceptable for the US to interpret its own initiative and, at the same time, supervise the ceasefire. (We remembered what the former Secretary of State, Dean Rusk, had declared on 5 June 1967, that the US did not know who had fired the first shot in the war! Such a distortion could occur once again.)

Nasser was shaken by some bad news relayed by General Fawzi. Prior to his departure from Cairo, Nasser had visited one of the missile bases and talked to the officers in charge. That day the missile base had received a direct hit and all the officers had been killed. This incident affected Nasser very deeply, for he felt personally responsible for all the officers and men in the missile bases, and that they should be stationed in fortified positions underground.

Forty-eight hours after we knocked down several US-built Phantoms, Israel received very sophisticated Electronic-Counter-Measures (ECMs), which were installed on the aircraft to deflect missiles off-target. Our armed forces, however, in order to counter the ECMs, resorted to firing missiles in salvoes and this proved very effective since no plane could counter a number of missiles simultaneously! So, in the first twenty days of July, we succeeded in knocking down thirteen Israeli aircraft (incuding six Phantoms) and capturing nine pilots.

At the same time, there were other political developments that cast shadows over the US position. In a TV speech, on 2 July, President Nixon referred to Egypt and Syria as 'hostile neighbours' of Israel, and then said: 'I believe that the Middle East situation has now reached a frightening level. It is similar to the Balkan situation prior to World War I, whereby the two super-powers [the US and the Soviet Union] could be dragged into an undesired confrontation because of the sharp differences there.' He then went on to explain US policy in the Middle East, saying that it was based on 'first: peace is our interest as well as the security of every State in the area. Second: we recognize that Israel has no desire to throw any other State into the sea, while the

Arab States wish to throw Israel into the sea. Third: should the balance of power change, whereby Israel becomes weaker than its neighbours, then war will break out. Therefore it is in the interest of the US to maintain the power balance, and we shall maintain that power balance.'

Meanwhile, news agencies reported Nixon's National Security Adviser, Henry Kissinger, as saying: 'We are about to reach a settlement that would strengthen moderate [Arab] regimes, but not the radicals. We are about to expel the Soviet military presence before it really establishes a foothold.'

Such declarations confirmed Nasser's suspicions concerning the seriousness of the American initiative and he said later: 'No Arab State wishes to throw Israel into the sea, but it was Israel that threw one million Palestinians into "a sea of sand".'

At the sitting of 11 July Brezhnev took the floor, saying that the Soviet Union had decided to agree to most of General Fawzi's requests, amounting to almost $400 million. Moreover, they had decided to make a discount of fifty per cent on the price. Brezhnev emphasized that the arms would reach Egypt according to the timetable agreed upon, and therefore seventy-five per cent of the shipments would arrive before the end of 1970.

Nasser replied: 'I wish to thank the Soviet Union for its assistance to us to resist Israeli expansionist ambitions. Israel wants us to abandon Jerusalem, the West Bank and the Golan. If I agreed to that, I would have been able to regain all of Sinai, and perhaps the Gaza Sector, in 1968. We are ready to accept a peaceful settlement and to recognize Israel's existence, despite Arab objections, and permit the passage of its ships through the Suez Canal. But Israel must first withdraw from all the occupied Arab territories and implement the UN resolutions on the rights of the Palestinian people.'

Nasser then said that the American initiative called on us to accept a three-month ceasefire and the resumption of Jarring's mission in order to implement the Security Council resolution. This meant that we would return to the situation in November 1967, when the US was pledged to implement it. 'But what comes next?' Nasser wondered. 'The declarations by Nixon and Kissinger, early this month, indicate hostile US intentions towards the Arabs. Nixon's declaration means that the US will never allow Egypt to attain air supremacy over Israel, or even parity. Therefore, we shall always be in need of reinforcements for our air force, especially aircraft that could confront the US-built Phantoms Israel has secured.'

In reply Brezhnev said: 'You just said that you are ready to accept the American initiative . . . what does this mean?'

Nasser said: 'Before I came here, I met with the members of the Higher Executive Committee in Cairo, and we agreed that our reply to the American initiative would be in concordance with you. In our opinion, Israel will not agree to the American proposals, which could effect a split inside Israel itself. We believe that the US administration expects us to reject the initiative. They also believe that the Soviet Union does not wish to establish peace in the area. Therefore, if we were to reject their initiative, they would exploit our rejection to justify further arms supplies to Israel. In such a case, we would revert in three months to talking about Jarring, just as we have done in the past.'

Brezhnev remarked: 'We believe the US has reached an agreement, in advance, with Israel on the initiative; or that they expect Israel to agree to it. Therefore, Israel's rejection could be just a smokescreen.'

Podgorny then inquired: 'Are you of the view that it would not be in Israel's favour to accept a three-month ceasefire, as indicated by the latest American proposals?'

Nasser said: 'Israel is seeking a permanent ceasefire, not one of a specific or limited duration. A permanent ceasefire would enable it to establish itself in the occupied Arab territories. A ceasefire of a limited duration – say, three months – means that, upon its expiry, renewed fighting would be legitimate. Furthermore, they are aware that during that period we will reinforce our missile bases.'

Brezhnev: 'In other words, we exploit that period to reinforce our positions.'

Nasser: 'That is true . . . but it would also benefit us politically, and prove that Egypt and the Soviet Union were working for peace.'

Gromyko then presented the political report on the initiative which we had prepared together and said: 'Mr Riad and I have come to the conclusion that it is a misnomer, since there is actually no initiative. We have also concurred that if there is anything new, it is only procedural, for in the past they insisted on direct negotiations, and now they are proposing indirect talks.' Gromyko added: 'The Americans admit to us the necessity of Israeli withdrawal. However, every time we ask them to make a clear statement on withdrawal they hesitate and talk of the necessity of effecting modifications. This means that this vital issue remains undecided. Therefore, when Jarring resumes his mission, we must call for the withdrawal of Israeli forces from all the occupied Arab territories. If we announce our acceptance of the initiative, we should – and Minister Riad concurs – make it clear that this represents our previously declared position.'

Here, Brezhnev said, emotionally: 'We are your friends, in fact your brothers, and together we have participated in huge activities in the military, economic and political spheres. Now the US is trying to grab the initiative as if they deserved the credit for resolving the problem. We should think of a way which would not allow the enemy to reap the fruits of our efforts. We should never take up a position where we appear to be defending ourselves as if we were the aggressors.' In conclusion, Brezhnev said that he had spoken frankly, and perhaps emotionally, because of the shrewd and cunning way in which the American proposals had been presented.

Nasser then remarked: 'I concur with President Brezhnev that there is actually no initiative. If we are seeking a peaceful settlement that would be fair to the Arabs, then I am sure the US will never offer such a settlement; for they wish to get rid of us in Egypt and then control Egypt itself and turn it into an instrument serving their interests in the area. For this reason, we have entered into a long and tough battle against them. Hence, we wish to agree with you on the reply. We have understood from you that there would be no rejection of the initiative with respect to its content, though we know that it will have no serious results.'

Brezhnev asked: 'If we accepted the US proposal for a three-month ceasefire, what happens after that?'

Nasser: 'We will return to the previous situation.'

Podgorny here said: 'It appears that the Americans are hopeful that the three parties, Egypt, Jordan and Israel, will be able to reach a result during those three months; otherwise, such a proposal would be meaningless.'

Kosygin then asked: 'Do the Americans have any idea whether

you will accept their initiative? What would be best for the Arabs: to accept the American initiative or make an initiative yourselves?'

Nasser: 'If we are to accept the principle, then it would be better to accept the US initiative since this will put both the US and Israel in a tight corner. If we were to ignore the issue, then they would claim that we had rejected their initiative, and would exploit this, to justify the shipment of more aircraft to Israel. Anyway, assuming we accept the initiative, then we must have – from now on – a plan to confront any repercussions or developments that would arise from its failure. With regard to the Arab world, I shall be speaking on 23 July on the anniversary of the Revolution, and I shall explain the matter in detail. Therefore it would be useful to give our answer to the US on 22 July, before my address to the people. In my speech, I will say that the US initiative contains nothing new, except in procedural matters. What happens after that is the really important thing . . . Jarring will resume his mission, but we are not prepared to remain in this vicious circle once the three months are over. I feel that our friend Andrei Gromyko and our Foreign Minister Mahmoud Riad should meet once more to complete consideration of all political eventualities, especially now that we have agreed on all military issues.'

I then conferred with Gromyko and we agreed on the basic lines of our reply, which did not differ from the points I had proposed to President Nasser in Cairo on 27 June. However, Gromyko was of the view that, in our contacts with the Americans, we must emphasize the importance of maintaining the four-power meetings and and the bilateral talks.

The fourth and final meeting between us and the Soviet leaders was held on 16 July. Brezhnev began by summing up the results of the previous meetings. He then turned to the question of the Egypt–Libya–Syria union, which had been raised at our first meeting, and said: 'Our policy is still that of bringing rapprochement to the Arab countries and unifying their efforts. However, on behalf of my colleagues, I would like to express our views on the question of union. Unity is indeed a noble objective, but we must also take into consideration what we have learnt from history, especially as the new rulers in Libya are young and lack experience, and in Syria there are disputing and conflicting parties. Consequently, the union of Egypt, Libya and Syria will face problems. We, as your friends, believe that the matter requires more thinking, especially since the merger between Egypt and Syria broke up in 1961. If a unity is established now and were to break up once more, then the reputation, weight and leadership of Nasser would be affected throughout the Arab world, and this is something that must be avoided. I hope my words are not misunderstood and it is thought we are adopting a position that opposes Arab unity. What I meant was to make sure that there would be nothing to harm Egypt in the future . . . We agree with you that the war between Egypt and Israel is basically an air war. However, war in the end requires a strong and efficient army, because it is the main force, without which no planes can ever resolve the problem. We have allocated a large part of the arms consignments to reinforcing the Egyptian army to a very high level. In the new arms deal we shall be sending you a new type of rocket, "SAM-3", and the Soviet missile crews will remain at their posts to protect Egypt's depth. I know we have not met all your demands, but I want to assure you that we have given all we can. I also believe we should postpone the question of the Tu. bombers because of international repercussions.'

Brezhnev continued: 'I wish to make it clear that once the Middle East crisis is resolved, our advisers, experts and pilots will leave Egypt immediately, because we do not believe in occupying the territory of others. This is the image that hostile American propaganda has portrayed of us.'

This time it was Nasser's turn to be upset, and he retorted somewhat sharply: 'I am unhappy to hear these words . . . I would never have originally agreed to come to Moscow if I had the slightest suspicion of a so-called Soviet occupation . . . It was I who asked for experts and pilots from the Soviet Union . . . and it will be I who will ask the Soviet Union to recall them, once their mission has been completed. Those who talk of Soviet occupation of Egypt are Golda Meir, Nixon and Kissinger.

'We have agreed to accept the initiative and to effect a ceasefire for three months. But what is the next step? What if the initiative were to end in failure? The US, once we accept the ceasefire, will stir up trouble for us and will attempt to effect a split between us and the Palestinians, and among the Arab countries themselves. I daily speak of peace, while Israel daily speaks of war. I do not, however, beg or plead for peace. A militarily weak Egypt can only obtain a shameful surrender to Israel's demands. Therefore, we must be clear, now that we have become strong, that we are accepting the American initiative from a position of strength. Consequently our negotiations will be on such a basis. But there is a great possibility that the three-month period will end in absolutely nothing. In this case, we would have done everything in our power to prove to everyone that we were serious to the last minute. When Jarring resumes his mission, we shall never agree to talk for another year. We are now at the beginning of the fourth year since the aggression. I can persuade the people to stand fast, but only on condition that there is a clearly defined hope of liberating all our territories. You resisted Hitler's invasion of your lands but, at the same time, you made plans with a clear hope of ending that aggression. Last week, both Nixon and Kissinger were furious because we shot down Phantoms with our missiles; according to their concept, this changes the arms balance. From the military point of view, the war is essentially an air war. We have come to Moscow asking for arms, but we must make it clear that we have given every opportunity for a peaceful settlement.

'At present, there is no coordination between us, and this could be very hazardous in military matters. At present, General Fawzi commands the Egyptians, while General Katchyn is in command of the Soviet contingents in the Egyptian hinterland, without any apparent coordination between them. You have actually become involved in the war, and the whole world now knows of the presence of Soviet combat pilots and the Soviet-manned missile bases deep inside Egypt. What is required at present is that we work with greater efficiency.'

The talks in Moscow ended at this point. However, it was obvious on the flight back to Cairo that Nasser was very happy with the results of this visit.

Upon my return, I wrote my reply to US Secretary of State William Rogers, saying: 'I am confident that you realize that to continue to ignore the rights of the Palestinian people who were expelled by Israel from their homeland can in no way contribute to the achievement of peace in the area, and that to establish peace in the Middle East it is necessary to recognize the legitimate rights of the Palestinian people in accordance with United

Nations resolutions.' I also pointed out that for Jarring to carry out his mission, Israel should declare unequivocally its acceptance and readiness to implement Resolution 242, and that a timetable for Israeli withdrawal should be drawn up.

As soon as we declared our acceptance, Israel immediately began a series of political manoeuvres since it also had not anticipated that Egypt would accept the initiative. The initiative contained several items that contradicted what Israel had always sought, for example, there were no direct Arab–Israeli negotiations, which Israel had been demanding since 1967; neither was there a permanent ceasefire as Israel had demanded, but a ceasefire of ninety days' duration. Furthermore, the initiative spoke of a resumption of the Jarring mission to implement Security Council Resolution 242, a matter that Israel had been avoiding from the outset. Thus it was that on 26 July Nixon wrote to the Israeli Premier, urging her to 'immediately declare' acceptance of the Rogers Project.

Two days later, Israeli Defence Minister Moshe Dayan stated that Israel was not 'strong enough to lose its allies', obliquely referring to the US. Again, Israeli Deputy Premier Yighal Allon was to say that 'even if there were differences in views between the US and Israel, when the US undertakes an initiative such as this it seems to me that we should, under the circumstances, accept it though we may not be satisfied with all the details'. Thus, after several political manoeuvres, the Israeli government notified the US on 31 July of its acceptance of the Rogers Initiative.

Meanwhile, the US government had received Jordan's acceptance of the initiative. Upon our arrival in Cairo, I had coordinated our position with that of Jordan, and had informed King Hussein of the outline of our reply before delivering it officially to the US government.

On 23 July, Nasser in his address to the people dealt with the US initiative which he had tabled for discussion before the National Congress. In the deliberations that ensued at the Congress there emerged a strong trend in favour of turning down the US initiative. Nasser, however, finally managed to win their reluctant approval.

Our acceptance of the American initiative meant that Jarring should return to New York to begin consultations with the US – the party submitting the initiative – and the other great powers to

secure their support for the resumption of his mission. I had
anticipated that Jarring would consult with Secretary-General
U Thant on measures related to supervising the ceasefire, and
then begin consultations with each of Egypt, Jordan and Israel. I
also anticipated that he would require something like two or
three weeks to perform these tasks. For this reason, I accepted the
invitations that had been extended to me by the Foreign Ministers
of Hungary, Bulgaria and Turkey, with whom I had personal
friendships.

On 30 July I left for Sofia. I had spent only a few days in Varna,
on the Black Sea, when I began to receive cables from my office
in Cairo, saying that consultations were under way with Donald
Bergus, on a ceasefire along the Suez Canal front. I then travelled
directly to Istanbul and, the next day, I received a cable from my
office, saying that we had reached agreement with the US on a
ceasefire.

This came as a surprise to me and I returned to Cairo on 9
August. I was met by the Director of my office, Ambassador
Mohammed Riad, who told me that Donald Bergus had
presented a proposal from Washington concerning the date and
arrangements for a ceasefire, and that President Nasser had
agreed that the ceasefire be effective as of 01.00 hours on 8
August for a period of ninety days.

When I read the report, prepared by Mohammed Riad, on the
contacts with Donald Bergus, beginning on the evening of 6
August, proposing that the ceasefire go into effect that same
midnight, or on the morning of 7 August, I immediately realized
that if there had been a one per cent chance that the initiative
would succeed in establishing peace, then even that very slender
chance had evaporated. In fact, I even anticipated further complications between us and the US. I had two observations to make:
first, that the US was in a desperate hurry to effect a ceasefire
(Donald Bergus claimed that this urgency was motivated by the
fact that time could tempt Israel to launch a huge air strike on
Egyptian missile bases inside the 50-kilometre zone west of the
Suez Canal; time could also tempt Egypt into building more
missile posts within that very zone. At the time I failed to
understand the significance of this threat until I discovered later
that Israel had a plan to land forces by helicopter behind our
troops, to destroy the missile wall); second, this threat exposed

the impotence of the US to execute its own initiative from the outset. If we were really on the road to peace, why should Israel attack Egyptian positions? The crucial question was: why should the US allow Israel to undertake a measure that would undermine its initiative? If the US could not impose restraint over Israel, how could it force it later into implementing the Security Council resolution and agreeing to withdraw?

I also noticed that the US had appointed itself as supervisor of the ceasefire. However, instead of notifying us that it would undertake such duties as a neutral party, the US informed us that it would employ high-flying reconnaissance aircraft (at 10-kilometre altitude) to assist Israel in observing the ceasefire. The US expected the Soviet Union to perform the same tasks on behalf of Egypt! I could never comprehend such a proposal by the US, especially since we had not requested it from the Soviet Union. I would have expected the US to call on a neutral party – the UN, for example – to carry out such tasks, or that it ask us to agree to accept the US as a neutral party. But that the US should undertake to represent Israel, and expect the Soviet Union to represent Egypt, must lead inevitably to deep differences.

From the outset, Egypt refused to recognize the right of the US to deploy high-flying U-2s to spy for Israel! My suspicions of the US were further increased when I examined the details of the ceasefire agreement: both sides were to stop all incursions and all firing on the ground and in the air, across the ceasefire line; both sides were to refrain from changing the military *status quo* within zones extending 50 kilometres to the east and west of the ceasefire line. Neither side was to introduce or construct any new military installations in these zones. Activities within the zones were to be limited to the maintenance of existing installations at their present sites and positions and to the rotation and supply of forces presently within the zones. It was obvious that these items could be given any one of several interpretations and, at the same time, there did not exist a neutral body or party to supervise their implementation. For this reason, when Egypt, during the few hours before the ceasefire became effective, completed the preparation of missile bases in order to strengthen our missile-defence systems, this did not constitute a violation of the ceasefire agreement. The operation, no doubt, was carried out so rapidly and efficiently that it really surprised Israel: for the whole thing was completed in a matter of hours, just before the time the ceasefire went into effect, so, by morning, Israel found itself face to face with an integrated network of air-defence missile systems. Therefore, once the ceasefire became effective, Egypt had no need to violate any of the details. Furthermore, the ceasefire agreement did not contain any item that forbade the reinforcement of existing positions, so this was what Egypt did. In fact, the agreement allowed for the rotation of troops and this was carried out by Egypt; we had retained several dummy missile bases, and continuously rotated the forces and changed positions, within the 50-kilometre zone, so as to prevent Israel from pinpointing our missile bases.

Obviously, the US and Israeli agencies that had formulated the ceasefire in a manner serving their own schemes had not realized the numerous loopholes it contained. Furthermore, Israel never imagined Egypt could complete such a superhuman task in a few short hours before the ceasefire became effective, and so Israel turned all its anger and fury on the American initiative itself, while Secretary of State Rogers tried tenaciously at first to keep it going. For this reason, when I received the first message from Washington on 19 August, it referred to Israel's accusations, though the US could not confirm that any violation had been committed. In fact, Rogers insisted that talks begin immediately through Ambassador Jarring.

On 31 August, US Defence Secretary Melvyn Laird announced to Congress the necessity of providing Israel with the arms it required. Israel had ultimately defeated the Rogers Initiative, thanks to its supporters in the US administration. On the following day, Nixon, Kissinger and Rogers met together and decided to dispatch eighteen Phantoms to Israel, and to notify Egypt of this step. The justification was that these aircraft were to replace the losses Israel had sustained lately. The inconsistency of the US became very clear when on 3 September Donald Bergus unexpectedly submitted an official note to me in which the US government claimed Egyptian violations of the ceasefire agreement.

And to complete the scenario, on 6 September (only three days after the US note) Israel officially declared its refusal to have contacts with Jarring as stipulated by the Rogers Initiative. It was open collusion in order to sabotage the initiative Rogers had presented in the name of the US.

On 4 September I handed Bergus a note containing our reply to the US memorandum. In the note I said: 'We have been keeping a close watch, particularly as of late, on developments in Israel . . . It is now quite clear to us that Israel is seeking to find pretexts, with regard to certain allegations concerning the ceasefire arrangements, to avoid carrying out its commitments to the American initiative . . . We have also been closely watching the position of the US, notably whether it would follow an even-handed policy commensurate with the role of a mediator, or would pursue its traditional role as a protagonist of Israel. We have noted that the US is responding favourably to the Israeli viewpoint and is yielding to Israeli pressure by considering whatever occurs in the Canal Zone as a violation of the ceasefire arrangement . . . It is to be recalled that we have repeatedly assured the US that we respect these arrangements on the basis of not introducing new missiles and not establishing new sites . . . We have also considered that we are entitled to move the missiles from place to place inside the zone and to replace these missiles with others from outside the zone . . . The US has requested of the Egyptian Military Command the reasons for undertaking such procedures. The position of the Military Command is that the safety of the missile sites, as well as the personnel, required such action. The missiles, if not moved from their places, would be the target for Israeli attacks at any moment . . . Could the US provide us with a guarantee that Israel will not attack our positions, and if Israel disregards the US guarantee and launches another treacherous attack, what specific action will the US then take against Israel to honour the American guarantee?'

I next turned to the question of Israeli violations which we communicated to the US, and said: 'When the US submitted its proposals we were given assurances that the US would not supply Israel with planes, that is, not add to Israeli military superiority or to Israel's military offensive capability. However, it has been revealed that the US had supplied Israel, during the ceasefire period, with electronic devices and guided missiles. Moreover the US Secretary of Defence has disclosed that the US intends to supply Israel with Phantom jets . . . It is our considered opinion that this course of action runs contrary to the assurances given to us by the US. As for Israel, we have definite proof that it has been constructing new fortifications on the Bar-Lev Line. This clearly underlines its real objective is not to withdraw from Sinai, pursuant to the Security Council resolution. Had Israel seriously intended to carry out that resolution, there would have been no need to rebuild the Bar-Lev Line or build new fortifications; it is to be emphasized that both actions are clear violations of the ceasefire arrangements.'

Thus the Rogers Initiative ended in failure . . . in fact, it was doomed to failure even before it started! There were two factions in the US who had sponsored the initiative: Rogers and a group of State Department experts who were fully convinced of the need to establish peace in the area in order to safeguard American and Western interests. There was, however, an opposing faction led by Henry Kissinger which believed that it was in the interest of the US to support Israel totally, since Israel was America's natural ally in the area, thus ignoring the friendship of many Arab countries for the US. Kissinger was able to persuade Nixon to adopt his views under the pretext of confronting Soviet infiltration in the area. This was the real beginning of the failure of the initiative.

The only interest Israel had in the initiative was the ceasefire, for it was beginning to suffer rising losses in aircraft after the introduction of the new missile systems in Egypt's air defence. However, Israel was quite unprepared to effect total withdrawal on all three Arab fronts. We in Egypt were aware of Israel's position, and our experiences with the US indicated that it would retreat from any proposal that was not to Israel's liking.

The US immediately launched a large-scale diplomatic and propaganda campaign against us in order to cover up its own retreat. The campaign sought to distort Egypt's position and accuse it of failing to honour its commitments.

Thus I found myself in the middle of a diplomatic battle with a superpower and I was quick to seize upon the opportunity afforded by the Non-Aligned Summit that was convening in Lusaka, Zambia.

Speaking on behalf of President Nasser, I addressed the inaugural session on 8 September, and explained the circumstances of the American initiative and our acceptance, as well as the dimension of the US retreat. The news that Israel had refused even to make contact with Ambassador Jarring greatly influenced the resolutions adopted by the Non-Aligned Summit. In fact, most of the Non-Aligned leaders openly condemned the US and Israel.

I then paid a visit to Madrid, since we attached special import-ance to Spain's support of our position; it had strong relations with the US and special influence with the Latin American coun-tries. I was received by General Franco. After I had explained the falsity of US allegations, General Franco became more convinced of the rightness of our position, and said that as a military man he could only commend our efforts to strengthen our air-defence systems, because it was the duty of the Military Command to perform this task. It was impermissible to deny any country the right to safeguard the lives of its sons, and to defend its territory would never be considered a violation of a ceasefire. This deep conviction by General Franco prompted Spain to lend more support to our stand in the UN.

I next met Aldo Moro. My meetings with Moro were always important to me, because I trusted his sharp thinking and down-to-earth outlook, and he was representative of a large sector of European thinking. I remember that at our first meeting he was very reserved, and I felt that most of his information on the Middle East had come from Washington. However, after several meetings, I felt that there was more appreciation of our position, especially after he began to realize the scope of Israeli intransi-gence and tried to help us in his quiet manner and through his contacts with Washington and other European capitals. When I met him in Rome this time, I felt he was fully convinced of our viewpoint. However, I realized that he could not, in his country's name, declare a position hostile to that of the US. The practical thing, therefore, was to call on him to convince Nixon, who was about to visit Italy, of the drastic effects of the US Middle East policy. At the voting in the UN General Assembly, Italy ab-stained from voting on the US side.

While in Rome, I received a cable urgently summoning me to Cairo, and I returned to witness one of the greatest tragedies of the Arab world on the Eastern Front. But before we deal with this Arab tragedy, it is important that I outline the basic features of this vital year in the struggle for peace in the Middle East. The whole conflict, throughout 1969–70, was characterized by two prominent features: the War of Attrition and the approach to the minimal level possible for a comprehensive settlement as a sound method to realize peace. As regards the War of Attrition, Israel would not admit the huge losses it had sustained until much later. Over a whole year had passed when the Israeli newspaper *Haaretz* published an interview on 17 September 1971 with Colonel Matti Bilid who was in charge of army supplies. He said: 'Militarily, the Israeli army failed in the War of Attrition. It was the first time it was defeated in the battlefield since the creation of the State, to the extent that we [in Israel] grabbed at the first straw thrown to us, to stop the fighting.' Yitzhak Rabin and Abba Eban were both to admit at the same time that Israeli losses in lives, as well as in valuable equipment, had made the War of Attrition extremely costly. This in no way means that we did not ourselves sustain losses in the War of Attrition. War essentially depends on inflicting the greatest losses on the other party and being ready to sustain losses oneself. There is no doubt whatsoever that Egypt's military position towards the end of the War of Attrition was much better than at the beginning. On the other hand, we did not consider the war as an end in itself; rather, it was linked to political objectives that were realized by the war. Basically, the war made continuous Israeli occupation very costly, so that, by the end of the war, Israel was obliged to accept what it had rejected at the start, especially with regard to a separate settlement and the acceptance of the principle of a comprehensive settlement. Furthermore, Israel retreated from its demands of direct negotiations and accepted entering into indirect talks. Regardless of later developments, these were the conditions that were faced by Israel at the end of the War of Attrition when it accepted the ceasefire.

Despite some cruel moments during some stages of the war, no dissenting voice was heard to cast doubt on the value of our sacrifices.

The War of Attrition is directly linked with the struggle for a comprehensive settlement, which we had waged since the 1967 June War. In the previous stage, we had resisted all pressures and measures to force us into a separate settlement. Now, in 1969–70, began serious talk of a comprehensive settlement, linked with total Israeli withdrawal on all three fronts.

In actual fact, the nearest the US came to achieving genuine peace – nearer than at any time past – was in June/July 1970.

The Rogers Initiative – though falling short of our conception of a comprehensive settlement – was the first American step on the correct path. In this the US was not motivated by its friendliness to the Arabs, or by a weakening of its alignment to Israel, but rather in order to safeguard its own interests – a vital and essential matter for any foreign policy. If the US did not give its efforts the desired push, or if it succumbed to Israeli manoeuvres immediately the ceasefire became effective, then this was due to the very special circumstances of American politics at that particular stage.

In all these stages of political manoeuvres, the US was quick to make additional political and military concessions to Israel, only to discover, later, that Israel was seeking even more concessions!

I took comfort in the fact that by the end of the ninety-day ceasefire, our position, militarily and politically, would have improved more than at any other time in the past. Politically, we had proved to everyone that we were serious in our endeavours to achieve a just, peaceful settlement and, to achieve that, were even prepared to cooperate with the US. Militarily, we now had an air-defence system in which the Soviets participated by maintaining an air cover on the Egyptian hinterland. Furthermore, we had completed the 'Rocket Wall' that would cover our armed forces' crossing into Sinai. We had in fact – according to military analysts – set up 'the most sophisticated air-defence system in the world'.

With the approaching expiration of the ninety-day ceasefire – a date scheduled to be decisive – two catastrophes took place, one after the other; they were to change everything . . .

8

The Death of Nasser

The possibility of a confrontation between the Palestinian Resistance Movement and the King of Jordan had always existed. At every meeting between President Nasser and King Hussein or the Palestinian leaders in 1968 and 1970, the conversation would turn to the same subject, and Nasser would urge self-restraint and alertness to Israeli attempts to exaggerate Palestinian–Jordanian differences. Israel was anxious from the beginning of the Israeli–Arab conflict to suppress the Palestinian aspect which projected a national resistance movement striving to liberate its national territory and establish its own independent State. However, we were of the opinion that world awareness of the Palestinian issue, its centrality in the Israeli–Arab conflict, was fundamental. Consequently we had to try and contain any differences as they arose, however unavoidable they were inasmuch as the Palestinian Resistance Movement represented a people, part of whom lived under the yoke of direct military occupation and the others were dispersed in refugee camps in Lebanon, Jordan and Syria.

In both the West Bank and Gaza, the Israeli occupation resorted to every conceivable form of suppression and penalization for any sign of resistance. As regards the hundreds of thousands who lived in Lebanon and Jordan, there have always been disputes between the Palestinian Resistance Movement, which was anxious to work against Israeli occupation, and the authorities in both countries who felt that such activities could expose their citizens to acts of retaliation.

The line adopted by Egypt rested on the necessity of safeguarding the Palestinian resistance while avoiding a collision between the legitimate authorities in both Lebanon and Jordan and the Palestinians. Consequently, when in 1969 a confrontation between the resistance and the Lebanese authorities threatened to have dire consequences, the two parties asked Egypt for mediation whereupon I called upon both Yasser Arafat, President of the PLO, and General Bustani, Commander of the Lebanese army, to come to Cairo for talks to solve the problem. I was aware of the situation: on one hand I had the complaint of Lebanese President Charles Helou about the lack of coordination between the Palestinian Resistance Movement and the Lebanese army command which was permitting brutal Israeli attacks against the Lebanese people; on the other hand there was the complaint of the Resistance Movement that the Lebanese authorities were imposing restrictions on their freedom of movement in southern Lebanon.

The meeting took place in November 1969 at the Ministry of War and with the participation of General Fawzi to maintain secrecy. After a few sessions we reached an agreement, the 'Cairo Agreement', signed by the two parties, which regulated relations between the Palestinian Resistance and the Lebanese government inasmuch as it restricted Palestinian concentrations to the Arquoub area inside Lebanon and along the Lebanese–Syrian borderline, and accorded ample freedom of movement to Palestinian forces in the rest of southern Lebanon, without the right to establish permanent bases. This agreement continued to be operative for the following four years.

With the situation in Lebanon subsiding I noticed an escalation in Jordan. Reports from our Embassy in Amman in the summer of 1970 pointed to an approaching collision between the Jordanian army and the Palestinian Resistance Movement which could lead to the eradication of the resistance movement in Jordan. Nasser, who received information that the US was feeding these differences, was disturbed over the fate of the Palestinian resistance. For my part, I was aware that any Jordanian–Palestinian confrontation would affect the Eastern Front unfavourably, the consolidation of which was central in our political and military thinking.

When Egypt accepted the Rogers Initiative and the ceasefire was imposed, some Palestinian elements attacked Nasser, accusing him of working in league with the Americans. Such accusations used to be broadcast from the Voice of Palestine in Cairo. Nasser felt forced to close the station, a facility which had been extended by the Egyptian government; however, he did not permit the situation to develop into one of enmity between

Egypt and the people of Palestine, maintaining that the Palestinians had every right to criticize the Rogers Initiative.

When I went to Qubba Palace on 20 August to confer with King Hussein who was then on a visit to Egypt, I found him vexed in the extreme over what he called Palestinian transgressions. He deplored the attitude of some Palestinian elements who believed that the occupation by Israel of further Arab territories as a reaction to Palestinian commando operations would force the Arab countries into mobilizing their resources to confront Israeli aggression and eventually liberate Palestine. To accept this kind of logic, he said, was tantamount to inviting Israel to occupy more Arab territories; on the contrary, we should be working in every conceivable way to safeguard the territories we still had in our hands as a launching-off board to recapture what we had lost in the 1967 war.

While I was aware of the problem that King Hussein was facing I was equally conscious of the deep sense of bitterness that filled the Palestinians over the injustice that afflicted them and which drove them at times to desperate acts. It was equally difficult to ask the Palestinians who had been living in refugee camps since 1948 to think along the same lines as those who had been living in their own homes with hopes for their own and their children's future. I tried to explore a solution along the same lines as the Cairo Agreement of 1969, but circumstances were not propitious this time.

When King Hussein conferred with Nasser the following day in Alexandria, he raised the matter of the increasing differences between the Jordanian authorities and the Palestinian resistance and referred to their operations inside Israel from across the Jordanian borders without prior coordination with the army authorities, which led to Israeli reprisal raids on Jordanian villages.

Nasser explained to King Hussein how he had handled the PLO over the Rogers Initiative and asked the King not to work against them for, in such a case, the beneficiary would be Israel. Nasser added: 'I am aware of the existence of some radical elements among the Palestinians, but there are equally level-headed elements who fortunately are in the majority. This is the most crucial issue at the moment and I urge you to handle the situation not with police action but with political action.'

King Hussein answered: 'The presence of all the different resistance organizations in our territory has introduced into Jordan all the contradictions present in the Arab world. Resistance personnel are increasingly trying to spread confusion and doubts even within the Jordanian armed forces. Their provocations are incessant.'

Two weeks had hardly elapsed before the situation exploded again between the Resistance and the Jordanian authorities. At the same time a more perilous development took place when one of the Palestinian organizations hijacked three passenger aircraft, two of which landed in al-Mafraq airport in Jordan. The third was destroyed immediately upon landing at Cairo airport on 7 September. On 9 September, a fourth aeroplane was hijacked and the hostages exceeded 500 persons. After destroying the aeroplanes at Mafraq, most of the hostages were released on 12 September; forty passengers were kept as hostages until the release of some Palestinian commandos held in Israeli, Swiss and West German prisons. International reactions were so violent that the Executive Committee of the PLO was forced to issue a statement in which it announced the freezing of the membership of the organization responsible.

A military government was established in Jordan on 15 September, when the situation exploded as a result of Palestinians refusing to hand over their arms. On the other hand, some official US sources began on 11 September to hint at a possible American military action, which might take the form of an Israeli military operation, and the possibility of resorting to force, added to the movement of the US Sixth Fleet to the eastern Mediterranean.

President Nasser had gone to Mersa Matrouh to rest for his health's sake. He had been there only one day when he became aware of the dangerous climax to which the Palestinian–Jordanian crisis was heading. He returned to Cairo and sent General Sadek, C-in-C of the Egyptian armed forces, to King Hussein in an attempt to stop the fighting. Nasser further cabled King Hussein on 19 September, asking him to order a ceasefire. King Hussein answered the following day, intimating that he had ordered a ceasefire in Amman. However, fighting continued in Jordan, while the Syrians began moving their tanks to Jordan to support the Palestinians. This led to a serious clash with the Jordanian forces.

With the failure of the Arab League to stop hostilities and Israeli war-cries against Syria, we received a communication from Moscow referring to the seriousness of the situation as a result of Israeli military movements supported by the United States. The Soviets asked Nasser to exert his efforts to defuse the crisis. Nasser decided that the situation needed a joint concerted Arab effort to stop hostilities in Jordan, especially as US military movements pointed to a possible American military intervention which would inevitably enlist Israeli army support, the pretext for which would be the danger of Syrian involvement in the fighting in Jordan. Nasser cabled Syria, requesting it to refrain from military involvement; he also issued a general invitation for an immediate meeting of Arab Heads of State in Cairo, to which there was an immediate, positive response. Nasser initiated his consultations with them from the evening of 21 September, continuing until the early hours of the following day in an atmosphere of great tension. A delegation headed by President Numeiri left for Amman, to return on the following day without achieving anything decisive. News, however, kept coming: the US had 10,000 soldiers ready for military action in Jordan, while the USSR addressed a warning to the US against intervention. Nasser, however, did not despair of being able to contain the deteriorating situation. While the Libyan President advocated the dispatch of Arab armed forces, composed of Libyan, Iraqi and Syrian troops, to Jordan, a view that was shared by others, Nasser opposed it, claiming it was the duty of Arab countries at this moment to save the Palestinians, since Jordan was far superior militarily. King Faisal supported his views.

Nasser managed finally to convince the meeting of the necessity of continuing the dialogue with King Hussein; it was then agreed that a delegation proceed once again for Amman. The delegation returned on the following day, 25 September, after achieving a ceasefire that did not continue longer than a few hours. On its return, the delegation was accompanied by Yasser Arafat who reported to the meeting on the perilous situation in Jordan and the devastating attacks on the Palestinians there. On that day the debate became heated as the majority of the conference members demanded an immediate and universal Arab boycott of the Jordanian King. Nasser commented: 'It may be easy to boycott King Hussein but this will mean that he will take his fight with the Palestinians to extremes. There is also the possibility that Israel will avail itself of this opportunity for direct military intervention. We have to cable King Hussein now, informing him that he should cease the fighting immediately.'

Upon his receipt of the cable Hussein contacted Nasser and expressed his readiness to come to Cairo to explain his position to the Heads of State. Nasser preferred to delay his answer until he could create a more welcoming atmosphere for his presence, especially since there was a strong tendency that wished to boycott him.

The debate continued for over four hours with Nasser insisting on allowing King Hussein to attend and looking at his watch from time to time, saying: 'We must remember that every minute that passes, dozens of Palestinians are killed. Our main objective must be to stop the massacre.'

When Nasser finally managed to sway the conference to his opinion, it was after midnight. Although he was completely exhausted he did not retire to his bedroom until he had informed the Jordanian King that he was welcome in Cairo. Nasser slept for hardly two or three hours that night.

An immediate meeting was convened which was attended by both King Hussein and Yasser Arafat. It does not need much imagination to guess at the harsh words that were exchanged, the accustions and counter-accusations, so much so that both Nasser and King Faisal had to exert superhuman efforts to bring the meeting to order. After more than five hours of discussions unanimous agreement was reached which imposed an immediate ceasefire all over Jordan, the withdrawal of the Jordanian army and Palestinian resistance from all cities before sunset the same day, and the formation of an Arab commission to leave for Jordan the following day (Monday, 28 September) to supervise the implementation of the agreement.

Thus an end was brought to the biggest tragedy since the defeat of 1967 to which the Arab world was exposed, thanks to the extraordinary efforts exerted by all the Heads of State participating in the conference who had responded promptly to Nasser's invitation and, together with him, bore the brunt of lengthy hours of reflection, debate and discussion. The only respite came when Nasser would leave the conference hall every two hours to walk for a few minutes to relieve the pain of the inflamed nerves of his legs. Nasser had exerted tremendous effort and shown great courage in confronting emotional diatribes until an agreement was reached to stop the carnage in Jordan. The conference offered ample proof of the respect in which Nasser was held by Arab Heads of State, while his leadership was re-asserted and his great capacity to by-pass all irrelevancies was once again established. His great achievement was to get the two conflicting parties to reach a binding agreement.

There is no doubt that he was helped in containing the crisis by the wise decision of Syria to withdraw its forces from Jordanian territory. Another element that prevented a further deterioration of the situation was the non-involvement of the Iraqi forces stationed in Jordan, in spite of the hostile political attitude the Iraqi government adopted towards King Hussein.

After the crisis ended both Nixon and Kissinger tried to take the credit, claiming that the crisis was abated by the flexing of American muscles via the Sixth Fleet, a warning to the Soviet Union against siding with Syria, and through close cooperation with Israel. Not one of these allegations rests on viable evidence. The crisis was, briefly, a confrontation between the Jordanian authorities and the Palestinian resistance in which the Jordanian army, if fighting continued, could have overpowered the resistance. The movement of Syrian tanks across Jordanian borders was the element that was exploited by the US to change the character of the problem. The US claimed that military movements in the Mediterranean were the factor that forced Syria to withdraw its tanks. Once again this is belied by the fact that, had the US been seriously considering deploying its naval power, it would have come face to face with the Soviet fleet in the Mediterranean, with the risk of a military confrontation between the two superpowers – which Nixon would not have welcomed. In fact, US muscle-flexing did not intimidate anybody, and consequently would not have been the decisive factor in the withdrawal of the Syrian tanks.

In my assessment, the real danger was the possibility of Israel taking advantage of the opportunity to deal a military blow against Syria. Although Egypt at the time did not possess enough forces to support Syria, it would have had no choice but to immediately resume fighting on the Sinai front, which would have inevitably led to a new war.

Kissinger had tried in his book to picture the crisis as a confrontation between the United States and the Soviet Union, not between Jordan and the Resistance. He admits in his book that he continued to urge on his president that liquidation of the Resistance would be a blow to the Soviet Union, ignoring the fact that the Soviet Union had no interest in coming to their defence in Jordan. Elaborating this myth, Kissinger wrote that he considered it vital to safeguard the rule of King Hussein as it would prove that friendship with the West and adopting a 'moderate' policy would be recompensed by effective US support. It is ironic that such goodwill towards the 'moderate' King Hussein could only be projected within the context of squashing the Palestinians and ignored in the more pressing and more ominous context of wresting the West Bank from Israeli occupation.

In the same way, Kissinger admits that he strived to frustrate Nasser 'because of his dependence on the Soviets and support to radical movements'. He ignores the glaring fact that it was Nasser who tried to stop the fighting in Jordan, and that Kissinger's support for suppressing the Palestinian commandos was in real fact a support of a basic Israeli and not a Jordanian objective. He equally assumes that the entry of Syrian tanks at Jordanian frontiers on 18 September was at the behest of the Soviet Union, and consequently the US threat to Syria and the withdrawal of the tanks constituted a Soviet defeat – another wrong assumption among many on which US policy was based. The Soviet Union was among the first to advise the withdrawal of Syrian tanks. The only role played by the USSR during the events of Jordan, as proved by its communications with us in Egypt and by its contacts with the Syrians and Iraqis, was to urge the containment of the crisis rather than accelerate it.

Whatever the case, it was the conviction of a majority of Arab leaders and Ministers of Foreign Affairs that it was the United States and Israel who had a vested interest in the collapse of the Eastern Front and an aggravation of Arab differences.

At the same time as Kissinger was maintaining that the US had addressed a warning to the Soviet Union not to intervene in the events in Jordan, and that it was that warning that had a decisive effect in ending the crisis, we were informed by the Soviet Prime Minister that the Soviet Union had directed a warning to the US

against intervention and had moved more naval units of the
Soviet fleet in the Mediterranean, and that it was this action that
was the deciding factor in preventing US and Israeli military
intervention. I personally feel that neither of the two warnings
had any effect, since the two superpowers were well aware of the
risks of intervention, and each was quite convinced that the other
party would not intervene.

The Palestinian–Jordanian crisis ended with the collapse of
Arab efforts to establish a powerful and effective Eastern Front
comprising Syria, Iraq, Jordan and the PLO, a situation that
obliged us to exert exceptional new efforts to remedy the effects
of the worst setback the Arabs had undergone since their defeat in
June 1967.

The containing of the crisis was a great achievement by Nasser;
it was to be his last contribution to the Palestinian cause for which
he had continuously suffered and had to overcome all types of
obstacles.

After the termination of the extraordinary Summit meeting on
27 September, Nasser was going to Cairo airport on the morning
of the following day to say goodbye to each of his guests. That
evening, I was called unexpectedly to attend an emergency meeting of the Cabinet of Ministers at Qubba Palace, and I had a
premonitory and eerie feeling of depression. I thought of everything but what actually had happened: Nasser had died. The man
whose leadership had left its ineradicable mark on the history of
his country, nay, on the history of the whole area, had died after
steering the destiny of Egypt during some of its darkest hours,
facing up to powers greater and more menacing than any the
Arab world had faced in its modern history. It was difficult for
anybody to accept the news at first. Until the six p.m. news
bulletin the people of Egypt had been watching on their TV
screens their beloved leader standing erect, walking with his head
high and bidding farewell to his guests in Cairo.

Amidst an atmosphere of gloom, bitterness and pain the extraordinary meeting of the Cabinet of Ministers began at 9.30 p.m.
on 28 September, chaired by Anwar el-Sadat who had been
appointed by Nasser as his deputy ten months before. During the
discussions that ensued, Sadat asked me if the death of President
Nasser could result in the Soviets withdrawing their commitments to Egypt. I said that what counted was neither the Soviets

nor the Americans, but the continuation of the tenacity of our home front. Finally Sadat asked me to draft a political statement emphasizing our continued adherence to policies laid down by Nasser, including a clear-cut reference to our close relations with the Soviet Union for its part in supporting us in the battle to which we were destined.

On Thursday, 1 October, the Middle East was to see, in the funeral of Nasser, a spectacle the like of which it had never seen before. Millions thronged the streets and squares of Cairo to cast a last look on the coffin of their leader who had given them his life until the very last.

An atmosphere of gloom and shattering grief descended on the whole of the Arab world. Alexei Kosygin who had attended the funeral conferred with Sadat a number of times. Sadat was keen that these meetings be attended by the largest possible number of Ministers. In the course of these meetings, Kosygin pointed out that there was a feeling now in world capitals that the death of Nasser would leave a great vacuum in Egypt and the Arab world; it was important to dispel this impression by an internal unity that must be made obvious to all. It was imperative that the whole world realized that the new leadership in Egypt would walk in the steps of Nasser. Israel, now that Nasser had died, would be more aggressive towards Egypt. The situation in the whole area was menacing; he referred to the crisis in Jordan as an instance of the difficulties we could be facing in the future. He added that the US would continue to provoke some Arab States against others and exploit any vacuum in the leadership in Egypt to achieve this. In fact, they were now putting it about that the new leadership in Egypt was weak and would be unable to achieve what Nasser had striven for. He asserted that the Soviet Union would continue to honour all the agreements concluded between the two countries, whether in the military, economic or any other field. Marshal Zakharov had discussed the military aspects with General Fawzi, and the Soviet Union would continue to do all in its power to consolidate the Egyptian armed forces. He had requested the late President to work towards ending the presence of most of the Soviet experts, especially in the field of air-defence missiles, and replacing them with Egyptian teams; President Nasser had asked that this be postponed for another six months until Egyptian experts had completed their training. Now, Kosygin said, we feel it is incumbent on the Egyptian side to exert every possible effort to replace Soviets with Egyptians before the commencement of battle. This was in fact equally Nasser's viewpoint, he added. Military and political alertness were decisive in these critical conditions; the US could drive Israel to wage war on Egypt at any moment and consequently the responsibilities borne by the new leadership were colossal.

Sadat replied by saying that we seek peace and an end to bloodshed but that we would not surrender one inch of our land or the Palestinian question. As regards internal unity, this would continue as long as we continued to adhere to the policies laid down by the late President Nasser.

It was obvious that Kosygin and his delegation wanted to be reassured that Egypt would continue to adhere to Nasser's policies and that Egyptian–Soviet relations would not be affected adversely by the death of Nasser – a matter that was the subject of extensive speculation at the time. This concern was not confined to the Soviets but was equally of interest to all the delegations that came to Cairo. Nasser's death was considered by them not only as the death of a president and a popular leader, but as the death of a man who represented an overwhelming national movement that had swept across the whole area, leading to the fall of the ramparts of imperialism one after the other, a movement that polarized the Arab masses everywhere when powers hostile to freedom and independence tried to bring about their downfall. Nasser had faced up to many calamities and trials, to rise above them every time with increased determination, a man who held tenaciously to the rights of his Arab nation and who would emerge finally stronger and more formidable. Doubtless the defeat of June 1967 was the biggest disaster he had to face in his struggle against foreign forces, but he did not for one minute doubt his ability to correct it in the end. Until the last moment of his life he fought a stubborn fight to rebuild Egyptian armed forces from scratch; led the War of Attrition; refused partial solutions, and continued preparations for the day of the restoration of the occupied territories.

Israel and some American circles were gleeful at the death of Nasser. Chaim Bar-Lev, C-in-C of the Israeli army, told students of the military college in Israel, in November 1970, that now Nasser had died the future for Israel was promising. Such an attitude may be understandable in the light of Nasser's refusal to surrender one inch of land to satisfy Israel's appetite for expansion. What is not understandable, however, is that some American circles should share the view that Nasser was a stumbling block in the road to peace, which reveals a deliberate attempt to misunderstand his historical role. Nasser refused a peace that meant surrender, but he had the courage and the ability to seek a durable, just peace. He was the Arab leader who accepted Resolution 242 in spite of its rejection by a number of Arab States and the apprehensions of Arab public opinion over some of its implications. He was also the Arab leader who accepted the Rogers Initiative, in spite of his conviction that the PLO would criticize him for it. In both cases he was convinced of his ability eventually to rally the whole of Arab opinion to his way of thinking.

The real obstacle to peace was in fact Israel, and Israel was encouraged in its intransigent posture by a group of Americans who were in control of the foreign policy of the US and who considered Nasser as the enemy of their country because of his refusal to participate in US military pacts or grant her military bases and influence at the expense of Arab interests. If there was a Soviet presence in the Middle East, it was engineered by that particular team of US politicians. The practical result of Kissinger's policies was the growth of the Soviet presence. Increasing US alignment to Israel, steady and growing arms supplies to it, a determination to lend permanency to its occupation of the Arab territories advocated by Kissinger – these were the direct reasons for the presence of Soviet experts, Soviet pilots and Soviet arms in Egypt in 1970.

Kissinger and others like him could only deal with one particular kind of leader, like the Shah of Iran, whom he described in his book as 'progressive, reformist and one of the close allies of America, a leader who left a deep impression on me'. He went so far as to describe the Shah as 'one of the pillars of stability in a vital and troubled area'. Events that have taken place later specifically in Iran only illustrate how divorced his diagnosis was from reality, as much as when he claimed that Nasser and his foreign policy were an element for instability in the region!

The main shortcoming of Kissinger and other American

politicians of his type was their inability to conceive that their problem was with Arab nationalism, which they could never either grasp or come to terms with, but would hastily denounce as radical and hostile to their interests in the area. For Nasser not to be considered anti-American, he had first to relinquish his faith in Arab nationalism and its principles. Nasser had confronted the Soviet Union in 1959 for the same reason. At the time, Khrushchev, as well as other Soviet leaders, considered that the concept of Arab nationalism as upheld and advocated by Nasser was a factor hostile to them and should be replaced by the Marxist concept of the unity of the working class. Nasser rejected this concept and entered into a fierce public debate with the Soviets that led to strained relations for a number of months. Eventually, however, the Soviets became reconciled to the fact that Nasser would never abandon his faith in Arab nationalism. Their American counterparts, however, maintained their rejection of Arab nationalism – until it could be subjugated to their policies and made to work on their behalf. So, while the Soviets resumed dealing with Nasser, accepting this radical difference between them, the US maintained its hostile attitude. It was natural, therefore, that some Americans would feel elated at his death, believing that the main obstacle to peace with Israel was now removed, as Mrs Meir never tired of telling them: peace was impossible as long as Nasser stayed. The question was: to what extent did subsequent events prove or disprove this assumption, and how far would they move towards peace, now that the main obstacle towards achieving it – in their claim – had been removed, namely Nasser.

9

Struggles inside the United Nations

With the assumption of power by a new president, it was important he should be given a chance to study the situation before taking any decisions. The ninety-day ceasefire would terminate on 7 November, and I had to proceed immediately to the meetings of the new session of the UN General Assembly where I would be asked to give a decision on its renewal. Sadat called for a meeting of the Egyptian Defence Council on 30 September and it recommended renewal for a further period of three months.

My mission was far from easy. The US had accused Egypt of violating the ceasefire and had joined Israel in clamouring for the removal of Egyptian missiles from the Suez Canal front. US ambassadors addressed official memoranda to the capitals to which they were accredited, making the same claim and arguing that nobody should expect peace in the Middle East as long as Israel had no confidence in that peace.

I had no choice but to face this challenge and I chose the UN forum for a rebuttal of the allegations and to submit the documents proving that, in fact, it was Israel and the US that had violated the ceasefire arrangements. This was an exacting task, as I had planned to secure from the General Assembly a resolution in our favour, which would mean that Israel would reject it, and it was expected that the US would join her and exercise pressure on member States. Consequently, my success depended on convincing the Western countries to refrain from supporting the United States.

I began contacts with the world capitals, supplying them with all the relevant data that would prove the validity of Egypt's position. The most powerful arguments I used to expose and denounce the US stand were the messages, statements and declarations made from official US quarters. The pictures and information supplied to us by Soviet satellites were only a confirmation of Israeli violations. Israel, moreover, never denied that she had built new fortifications along the Bar–Lev Line.

One of the TV networks in New York asked me to appear for an interview. I noticed from the questions posed that an attempt was being made to establish the US accusations levelled against Egypt and to maintain that the US had honoured her obligations, which forced me to take out of my pocket the *note-verbale* that had been handed to me by Bergus in Cairo. I read that part which contained the US pledge to refrain from supplying Israel with more military aircraft during the application of the ceasefire. I then referred to recent announcements by the US administration that it would supply Israel with more Phantoms as constituting a flagrant violation of that pledge. (The American pressmen's dismay was no less than that of the diplomats at the United Nations when they read the *note-verbale*.) At press conferences and during my contacts with heads of delegations I would refer to my conversation with Ambassador Richardson, who had headed the US delegation to Nasser's funeral. I would say that it was the government of his country that had volunteered, without a request from our side, to tell us the number of Phantoms and Skyhawks it would deliver to Israel; it had further volunteered, at no request from our side, a pledge to refrain from supplying Israel with further aeroplanes so long as the ceasefire remained effective. The US then backed down on its voluntary pledge and announced it would supply Israel with a further eighteen Phantoms. I would say, further, that we had not violated the ceasefire arrangements, we had not installed new missiles or established new sites in the Suez Canal area. I would inquire why the US had not waited until Jarring's arrival in the area to set out the ceasefire arrangements rather than undertaking this task herself.

I must admit that I was not very happy about causing embarrassment to senior State Department officials, but I was aware that in dealing with the US I was not dealing with one particular person or department but was dealing, in the final analysis, with the American establishment itself, and that if Henry Kissinger, as National Security Adviser, could finally succeed in subverting the Initiative that carried the name of his colleague, then this was the responsibility of the US President, who would allow such contradictions inside his administration.

On 15 October I conferred with William Rogers and he showed me pictures taken by the 'U-2' reconnaissance aeroplanes of our new missile sites along the Canal front. I pointed out smilingly that there was no need for me to see the pictures; they established that the missile sites exist – which we had never denied. 'The difference between us and the US is that while you maintain they are new sites established after the ceasefire, we assert that they are not. Notwithstanding the fact that we have every right to defend ourselves by the establishment of defence missiles on our territory,' I continued, 'you have (as much, if not more, than we) evidence of Israeli violations of the agreement, yet you never refer to that.' I concluded by saying that it would be more to the point to concentrate on the main subject which was that Jarring should be allowed to fulfil his mission.

I have no doubt that Rogers was aware of the weakness in his government's stand, especially among the UN delegations, and was therefore very anxious to dissuade me from raising the issue at the General Assembly, claiming that quiet diplomacy was a better avenue.

I said I had already had three years of that quiet diplomacy – to no avail; my impression was that it was high time the international community was made aware of the true facts of the situation. I told him further that I would contact Jarring the same day to inform him that, unlike Israel, we would continue to deal with him. I finished by assuring him, in the name of President Sadat, that we were still willing to consider any avenue that would lead to a just, comprehensive settlement.

Inside the United Nations was an atmosphere of a diplomatic battle between us and the United States. It was, therefore, of tremendous importance to us as to what kind of resolution we would be able to secure.

When I realized that my consultations with the different groups inside the US had potentially good results, I submitted the case to the UN in its entirety. In order to highlight the bad faith of the Israeli position and the retreat of the US from her early posture, I posed the question to the General Assembly: 'What pretext has Israel in refusing to contact Ambassador Jarring for the implementation of that part relating to Jordan in the US initiative, when Israel has not accused Jordan of violating ceasefire arrangements? Can the US explain her viewpoint with regard to Israel freezing the American initiative in relation to Jordan?' I posed another question to the United States: how could it justify Israel establishing fortifications on our occupied territories and find this acceptable when, at the same time, it sees our fortifying the sites of our air defence, situated 200 kilometres inside our international borders, as an illegal act justifying putting a stop to Jarring's mission and thwarting the four-power talks by withdrawing from it?

The draft resolution was finally put to the vote. Israel termed it 'the Arab resolution' which was a misnomer since the draft was submitted by an Afro-Asian group, while seven of the Arab States rejected it. The resolution was adopted by a large majority. Only fourteen countries voted on the side of the United States and Israel in rejecting the draft. It was the most eloquent answer to Israel's position and the US campaign against us.

The substance of the resolution also had great political significance. The main clauses stipulated the following: condemnation of the continued Israeli occupation of Arab territories since 5 June 1967 (lending thereby a clear interpretation to the fact that withdrawal should be from all occupied Arab territories); the inadmissibility of occupying territories by force and the necessity of relinquishing them; recognition of the rights of the Palestinian people as indispensable for the establishment of a durable and just peace (this goes beyond Resolution 242 which was confined to the liquidation of the effects of armed conflict in June 1967); underlining the necessity of implementing Resolution 242; that the state of war should be terminated; that the ceasefire should be extended for another three-month period; and that the Secretary-General of the UN should submit a report within two months on the activities of Ambassador Jarring in his capacity as special representative, relating to necessary talks for the implementation of the Security Council resolution.

This resolution represented a severe setback to the United States, especially since the Western countries did not join the American stand. The request that the Secretary-General submit a report within two months over the progress of Jarring meant that both Israel and the US would face further international isolation inside the UN.

Since the two months offered to the Secretary-General would end on 5 January 1971, I conferred with him before my departure from New York, to say that Israel would continue to create obstacles in the way of Jarring and would continue to refuse to deal with him. However, in the light of the complete isolation it faced as a result of this resolution, I expected that it would, a few days before 5 January, express its willingness to contact Jarring.

Before my departure for Cairo I conferred again with Rogers. I assured him that we would continue to deal with Ambassador Jarring and that we would adhere to the ceasefire for another three months as stipulated by the General Assembly's resolution. I mentioned that the United States had in the meanwhile a golden opportunity to advance towards peace in the area and that, with a new president in power in Egypt, good relations based on mutual respect could be established. If relations between the US and Nasser had worsened, which led the US to adopt a hostile attitude to Egypt, the US could now, in the light of past experience, work towards establishing confidence and a just peace. Rogers listened attentively to what I said, but I imagine his interest was not great enough to prompt the US administration to use the opportunity to re-build bridges with the Arab world through a serious quest for peace. William Rogers was a man deserving respect. Helped by a team of Middle East experts, he was well aware of the nature and extent of US interests in the area and entertained a real desire to safeguard those interests and to develop them; he did try to achieve a balance between those interests and the just peace demanded by the Arabs. He did think that this was feasible, once the US had succeeded in curbing Israel's compulsion for expansion at the expense of others. On the two occasions I conferred with him I was aware of a change in his tone. The first time, he raised the point of our alleged violation of the ceasefire in order to influence our stand. The second time, however, he was made aware by the General Assembly resolution that the international community was not ready to support Israel in its occupation of our territories. On the other hand the situation changed greatly after the UN resolution. Instead of the diplomatic and political campaign against us, both the US and Israel were on the defensive. The international community had decreed that movement of its missiles by Egypt was not the obstacle to peace; the real obstacle was the delaying and obstructing tactics of Israel.

On my return, I expounded to Sadat my feeling that Rogers

was in an uneasy position since it was unreasonable a man would contradict himself to this extent in such a short period. Rogers was the one who had proposed a three-month ceasefire in his initiative submitted to us in June. Now he was adopting a contradictory stand at the four-power Foreign Ministers' meeting, invited by U Thant to issue a statement for Jarring to resume his mission while extending the ceasefire for another period. Rogers rejected this proposal, demanding that the ceasefire should be permanent, a matter that Israel had always sought after diligently. The result was that, naturally, no statement was issued. I told Sadat I felt that a change had taken place in the American administration's position in order to undermine the Rogers Initiative and that this would render a peaceful settlement more untenable than at any time in the past.

In order to consolidate our political gain after the adoption of the resolution, we had to mend the Eastern Front after the damage inflicted on it during the September events. The opportunity came when General Hafez al-Assad assumed authority in Syria. He arrived in Cairo and on 26 November signed a new military agreement with Egypt. At the same time, we received a message from King Hussein expressing his desire to come to Cairo. Arab countries were still enraged at the confrontation of his forces with the Palestinian resistance in September. Sadat, however, keen as the King to re-establish the Eastern Front, welcomed him to Cairo on 2 December. At the talks that ensued, King Hussein complained of the lack of coordination with the Iraqi forces that were dispatched to his country to confront Israeli aggression; he demanded that such forces should be put under Jordanian command, especially as the Iraqi government was continuing to attack him. Since King Hussein was on his way to the United States to confer with President Nixon, Sadat told him that Egypt still adhered to its political line of rejecting partial solutions; and Egypt was serious in its quest for peace, provided it meant complete Israeli withdrawal from all occupied Arab territories and the restoration of all political rights to the Palestinian people.

King Hussein said that he was equally bound by his commitment to reject partial settlements and that he would transmit the Egyptian point of view, which coincided with the Jordanian view, to President Nixon. On prospects for the near future,

(a) John F. Kennedy and Mahmoud Riad

(b) Mahmoud Riad and Sir Alec Douglas-Home in London. 5 January 1971.

Gamal Abdel Nasser with Mahmoud Riad

Soviet Foreign Minister Andrei Gromyko and his wife welcoming
Mahmoud Riad and the visiting Egyptian party

Mahmoud Riad dining with Henry Kissinger

(a) Mahmoud Riad with King Hussein of Jordan

(b) Mahmoud Riad with King Faisal of Saudi Arabia

(a) Anwar Sadat's first Cabinet

(b) *Left to right:* Anwar Sadat, William Rogers, Joseph Sisco and Mahmoud Riad

(a) Chou En-lai entertains Mahmoud Riad

(b) Mahmoud Riad with Kurt Waldheim

(a) Mahmoud Riad
with Yasser Arafat

(b) Sheikh Zayed,
ruler of the United
Arab Emirates,
with Mahmoud Riad

Sadat said he expected the coming few months to be decisive and that there was a possibility we would confront Israel militarily after the termination of the second ceasefire on 5 February 1971, and consequently he considered the stationing of Iraqi forces in his territory to be of crucial importance although he (King Hussein) might define the zones for their presence. King Hussein said he agreed not to undertake any step in this direction until after consultations with Egypt.

At the end of the talks, King Hussein was careful to state that, even with the success of present efforts to revive and consolidate the Eastern Front, he would like to state that the Eastern Front would not be able to bear alone the liberation of Arab land without Egypt; consequently, he was concerned about knowing Egypt's position in this respect. Sadat reassured him that Egypt would definitely fight to liberate its land and that confrontation with Israel would be in February after we had seen the results of this new extension of the ceasefire although he, Sadat, did not believe that Jarring would make any progress. The meeting resulted in improving relations between Egypt and Jordan. The PLO was in favour of such a step so that King Hussein would relax his suppression of the Palestinians.

The following months saw an escalation of tension between Egypt and the US when the latter announced its intention of supplying Israel with more arms despite Israel's refusal to establish any contact with Jarring. Rogers addressed the Senate on 8 December: 'The military balance has been jeopardized by the heavy deployment of surface-to-air missiles by Egypt in collaboration with the Soviet Union. The funds requested for Israel will be used largely for aircraft and electronic equipment which will help restore the military balance.' The same day the US Secretary of Defence said that $500 million were needed that year for military credit sales to Israel.

This new US offer incensed all the Arab countries; while Egypt had built the missile network to defend the lives of its people, the United States considered this a grave sin and was therefore going to supply Israel with more bombers and electronic equipment to enable it to continue its marauding raids on Egyptian territory. Sadat decided to send a delegation to Moscow comprising Fawzi and myself, headed by Ali Sabry, the Vice-President, to demand more arms from the Soviet Union.

We arrived in Moscow on 20 December and the following morning we had our first meeting with Brezhnev who was accompanied by Podgorny, Kosygin, Gromyko and Marshal Grechko.

Ali Sabry began the talks by referring to the utter failure of the American initiative which Egypt and the Soviets had accepted. He referred to the hardening of the US position with its attempt to impose a permanent ceasefire while doubling its military and economic support to Israel. We therefore felt that it was important to further consolidate our political, economic and military ties with the Soviet Union.

The following day I discussed the political situation, mentioning that the US objective was to expel the Soviet Union from the area and to suppress the powers that refused to submit to Israeli conditions and the establishment of military pacts in the region. I referred to Kissinger's declaration that the Soviet Union should be expelled from the Middle East and that Egypt should not be allowed to gain supremacy in confronting Israel. I added that it was now clear, after the failure of Rogers' initiative, that Israel would not withdraw without a war. I proposed submitting a draft resolution to the Security Council for imposing sanctions on Israel, in spite of the fact that the US would veto such a resolution. 'We have received the support of the international community with the resolution of the General Assembly on 5 November, and it will remain for us to intensify our campaign for the further isolation of Israel in the international arena.' I then projected a new concept, namely that the great powers offer guarantees for peace in the area after the withdrawal of Israel from all the occupied Arab territories. Such guarantees extended by the great powers to the two parties would be a rebuttal to Israeli demands for expansion on the pretext of safeguarding its security. Such guarantees should be further issued through the Security Council and would mean the stationing of great powers' forces, as part of a United Nations international force, in order to stop any aggression by either party against the other.

The Soviets did not take the floor until the third meeting on 25 December, after a number of bilateral meetings between Marshal Grechko and General Fawzi, and between Gromyko and myself. Brezhnev declared: 'Now the world knows that Israel has refused to implement the Security Council resolution and is supported by the United States in this posture, you may ask: what is to be done? We cannot give you an answer. You now possess an army that numbers over 750,000 fighters. What we request is that you study all possibilities in order to choose the best way. We have to prove that it is Israel, with the support of the United States, that is rejecting peace . . . We agree with you about the difficulty of extending the ceasefire for a third term because of domestic considerations. We intend to exert some political efforts before the termination of the period of the present ceasefire. We still have some forty days. The situation may change tomorrow. It is therefore inadvisable to say that it is impossible to extend the ceasefire, especially now that you are projecting a new element relating to the guarantees of peace and the participation of forces from the great powers. We consider your proposal is in itself a peaceful initiative which Israel, who claims to be in need of protection, will find difficult to reject. If we can secure the approval of the United States, Israel, we can assume, will equally agree. If the United States and Israel reject this proposal, then the world will be even more aware of Israeli expansionist plans. We intend to contact both France and Britain over this point.

'We have to strive so that Jarring will resume his mission. We have the support of France in this direction. As to submitting a draft resolution to the Security Council for imposing sanctions on Israel, we have studied this possibility before and we know that the US will veto such a resolution. Now we understand that you may consider a third extension to the ceasefire if a new element is introduced. We believe that you should adopt a flexible policy. You don't have to announce you will resume firing, especially in the light of one Security Council resolution for a ceasefire and another for the withdrawal of Israel. Israel can always claim that the Arabs have refused to implement their part of the resolution.

'We still have some time for political activity. For instance, Mahmoud Riad will pay a visit to France and Britain. For our part, we will contact the US and continue to pressure her. Our advice is that you do not announce what you want to do after 5 February, the date for ending the ceasefire. In any case, you must work to strengthen the Egyptian army and study the use of modern arms and increase the training of your pilots. In this respect, we shall extend to you all possible assistance. As regards an overall military confrontation with Israel, we cannot convey our approval to you. This is a matter that needs proper study until you are assured of success 200 per cent. To fire your artillery is one thing, but an all-out attack is another. Yet you have a huge strong army and excellent arms. Therefore I repeat we cannot tell you what you should do.'

On the question of military cooperation Brezhnev expressed the willingness of the Soviet Union to respond favourably to all our demands relating to help in military production operations, for example, the production of helicopters, aircraft spare parts, 130-mm-calibre guns, heavy mortars and radar apparatus. He also agreed that we could postpone repayment of 350 million roubles over the next four years, and said that more economic help would be extended to us.

We repeated our demand for the supply of the long-range missile-equipped Tu.-16 aircraft. Ali Sabry said that our deterrent capacities would remain weak until we possessed this aircraft. It was obvious that the Soviet leaders had reverted to their belief that we should not initiate large-scale operations for the liberation of the land. Now they were inclined to the view that the ceasefire should be extended and we should resume our political activity, in spite of the fact that Israel had closed all doors in this direction. At the same time, I noticed that, despite this, Brezhnev had dealt with the power of the Egyptian army and mentioned the fact that it now numbered more than 750,000. Clearly, the Soviets favoured a peaceful solution and, if Egypt opted for a military one, they did not want any part in adopting such a decision . . . thus, a decision for war was Egypt's alone.

On the other hand, the US government had announced that it was considering earmarking an additional $500 million to finance sales of military equipment to Israel in 1971, at the top of which would be highly developed aircraft. The significance of this was obvious: the US had decided to extend military support to Israel after it had deserted the Rogers Initiative and the comprehensive settlement. In addition, some Israeli sections, headed by Dayan, were backing a new proposal by which Israel would withdraw to a line thirty to forty kilometres east of the Suez Canal, on condition that Egypt would agree to adopt the measures neces-sary for reopening the Suez Canal to international navigation. Sadat denounced Dayan's proposal at a meeting of the Central

Committee of the Socialist Union on the grounds that it would lend permanency to the ceasefire. Dayan's proposal offered Israel military advantages since it could, with a few forces concentrated in the Sinai passes, continue to control the whole of Sinai. The Israeli government, however, preferred for political reasons to occupy the eastern shores of the Suez Canal.

At the same meeting I spoke about the oil potentialities of the Arab world. I said: 'There are still Arab levers for pressuring the US, since it receives some $2,000 million from the Arab region which are recycled to Israel in the form of aid and arms. We should not stop oil production but should control it in a way that would serve the interests of the oil-producing countries, not those of the United States. The objective would be to bring the US to an awareness that her real interests lie with the Arab countries.'

To put such a project in motion, it was necessary to reach an agreement with the Arab oil-producing countries within the framework of a plan for the total mobilization of Arab resources for a final confrontation with Israel, and to alert the US to the dangers to its interests resulting from its alignment with Israel, and to peace in the region which had become more gloomy in December 1970 than at any time since the cessation of the War of Attrition and the backing down of the US on her pledges to support Jarring's mission.

10

The Year of Decision

The year 1971 was a decisive one; it was considered to be so by William Rogers who wrote to me in January saying: '1971 is a critical year . . . If it is over with no peace achieved, the Middle East will find itself on the road to a continuing and costly conflict.'

Rogers asked me to ensure that Egypt adopt measures that would contribute to peace, and informed me that he had asked Israel to do the same, maintaining that the US itself would play a positive role. When the year ended without peace being achieved, the Middle East did find itself on the road to a continuing and costly conflict. I had hoped, of course, that Rogers' role would have extended to more than gloomy prophecies. All through 1971 Rogers did exert honest efforts for the realization of peace, and if he failed in the end, it must be attributed to Nixon's stopping his support for Rogers' initiative and finally relinquishing him in favour of Kissinger.

I arrived in London on an official visit on 5 January and on my arrival met Sir Alec Douglas-Home, the Foreign Secretary, and Edward Heath, then Prime Minister. I explained that Jarring could overcome Israel's evasiveness by adopting my proposal for the establishment of an international force from among the great powers to safeguard the security of both Israel and the Arab countries. I mentioned that I had the approval of Leonid Brezhnev and the willingness of the Soviet Union to participate in the proposed force. Heath showed interest and began to question me on several points relating to its composition, duties and location. I explained that the Security Council should be the organ to issue a resolution for its formation, that its duties should be combative, not merely observational, and that it would be stationed in the same sites where the UN emergency force was, only on both sides of the frontier line, and that no country should be permitted to terminate its duties except through a Security

Council resolution. I added that it was possible to agree on demilitarized zones on both sides of the border on all fronts with Israel. Our fundamental condition for the formation of this force would be that Israel withdraw to the 4 June 1967 borders on all fronts. It was obvious that the British Prime Minister was now more convinced than at any time in the past of our sincere quest for peace and, together with Douglas-Home, welcomed the idea of an international force that would satisfy Israel's demand for security.

On 6 January, I arrived in Paris and conferred with Maurice Schumann, the Foreign Affairs Minister, and President Georges Pompidou who welcomed the guarantees for peace I had proposed and expressed France's willingness to participate in the proposed international force; they reiterated that France would continue to refuse the supply to Israel of arms as long as it continued to occupy Arab territories. Next, in Rome, I met with Aldo Moro. Italy had become increasingly concerned over the Middle East problem inasmuch as it posed a major problem to the security and stability of the Mediterranean countries, of which Italy is a major European party. Consequently, Aldo Moro welcomed the idea of an international force to maintain peace between the Arabs and Israel.

When I had made sure that there was a congenial atmosphere for projecting the idea, I sent Jarring a letter on 14 January, proposing the establishment of a force composed of the four great powers in the Security Council and demilitarized zones on both sides of the border as the best possible guarantees for the establishment of peace and security for the Arabs and Israel.

Nicolai Podgorny arrived in Cairo on 13 January to attend the celebrations for the completion of the High Dam and to resume the political talks which we had initiated with Brezhnev in Moscow in December. The first meeting took place on 14 January at Qubba Palace with Sadat heading the Egyptian side. We were aware that Podgorny was the Russian diplomat always chosen for uncomfortable roles, so I was therefore apprehensive as to what new points he was going to raise in the meeting. Sadat began the talks by demanding more support for our air defence, reiterating our request for the deterrent arm so that military parity could be established with Israel, conducive to a peaceful settlement. Sadat mentioned that we were considering inviting a

Security Council meeting to consider the Israeli position which, while refusing to abide by Resolution 242, was now in favour of a permanent ceasefire that would lend permanency to its occupation of the Arab territories. Sadat then asked me to explain recent political developments. I referred to the progress we were making at the UN and to the approval given by the Soviet Union, Britain and France to our proposal for peace guarantees, and that the US had communicated its approval to us through its representative in Cairo. Israel, however, had promptly rejected the proposal which once again proved the fallacy of its need for territory to safeguard its security. I added that we might raise the problem again at the Security Council as an exercise in political action. We had to be aware, however, that the US would object to any resolution that did not conform to Israeli wishes, while its objective at present, as had been expounded by Henry Kissinger, was to expel the Soviet Union from the region. In the following meeting, Sadat stated that the ceasefire period would not be extended unless some progress in the political situation was achieved.

Podgorny took the floor to pay tribute to our political activities at the UN and in talks with the UK, France and Italy which had made it clear to the world that Egypt was sincerely concerned about peace, while Israel was not. He deprecated calling the Security Council for a meeting to discuss the problem anew. Not only would the US reject such a motion but, even if the Security Council convened, we should not expect more than a resolution commending the resumption of Jarring's mission and a renewal of the ceasefire. He said it would be advisable for us to consider a renewal of the ceasefire for another period. At that point I realized the uncomfortable nature of the message which Moscow had asked Podgorny to convey to us.

Podgorny continued to comment with notable ill-humour on my remark that the US was striving to oust the Soviet Union from the area, saying that this was not an easy matter and that the Soviet Union had both the power and the plans to foil such attempts. He then became quieter and apologized for the tone he had used but said he felt he should be honest with us; he went on to propose that I proceed to Moscow to consult with Gromyko, for there might be new elements that could be explored and studied, especially if we finally decided to go back to the Security Council.

Sadat said he was disinclined to go to the Security Council. With regard to extending the ceasefire, he said that we would find ourselves, at the end of a further three months, back where we started. The War of Attrition was the strong motive behind the Rogers Initiative. If the US and Israel were even now not convinced of our firm intent to liberate our territories, he doubted if they would ever move, added to the fact that international public opinion would eventually lose interest in the case. Sadat concluded by approving my visit to Moscow to coordinate political action with the Soviet Union.

At the conclusion of the talks, it was obvious that the Soviet Union did not favour a resumption of the War of Attrition or our going to the Security Council, which coincided with the US position as expounded in Rogers' letters to me. Podgorny was furious when I claimed that the removal of the Soviet Union from the area was now the US objective, unaware of how events would develop in the following year, which led to their final departure from Egypt.

With the beginning of 1971, Rogers encouraged Jarring to submit an initiative from his side that would re-activate efforts towards peace. In this context I received three messages from Rogers paving the way for this initiative and informing me that similar contacts were being made with Israel. His first letter reached me on 15 January to maintain that the US would strive to establish a durable and just peace, consistent with Security Council Resolution 242. He was encouraged, he wrote, to see Israel accept indirect negotiations under Jarring. He admitted that he did not expect Egypt to approve all Israeli proposals but said we could submit counter-proposals. His optimism was reflected in his admonition that I should not consider what the Israeli proposals conveyed, but rather what they did not. He concluded by referring to the importance of the resumption of Jarring's mission which led him to advise against inviting the Security Council to convene, commending the courageous stand of the late President Nasser when he accepted the American initiative in June of the previous year.

I had sent Jarring my answer to the Israeli proposals Rogers referred to one day before I received his communication. The Israeli proposal was nothing but a repetition of what it had been saying for years and ignoring, of course, the cardinal point for

establishing peace: total withdrawal from all occupied Arab territories. What was new and worthy of attention, however, was a
demand that attempted to abrogate Egypt's commitment to the
rest of the Arab world. The tenth clause of its proposals read:
'non-participation in hostile alliances and prohibition of the
stationing of troops of other parties which maintain a state of
belligerency against the other [party, i.e. Israel]'. According to
this clause alone, Egypt would have had to withdraw from the
Joint Defence Agreement with the Arab States. In fact, Israel
could consider Egypt's membership of the Arab League itself as a
hostile act. The Israeli objective here was to alienate Egypt from
the other Arab countries, as part and parcel of the partial settlement it had been seeking from the outset.

In answering the Israeli proposals, I referred to the necessity of
implementing Resolution 242, arrangements for guarantees for
peace and the establishment of a force in which the four great
powers would participate.

Rogers wrote to me again on 27 January to commend our
decision not to insist at the present time on inviting the Security
Council to convene while he requested a temporary ceasefire so
that Jarring could proceed with his mission in a suitable
atmosphere.

The UN's Secretary-General had sent me a letter appealing to
the concerned parties to extend the ceasefire. After I had
consulted with Sadat, he decided to respond to the appeal and
announced the extension officially in a speech in the People's
Assembly on 4 February.

Rogers wrote to me again to express his optimism over Jarring's
resumption of his mission and to state that while both Egypt and
Israel had enough military power to ensure their nation's survival, neither had the power to impose its will on the other
through military means. He added: '. . . we believe we can look
forward to the early development of a situation in which not only
can the US play an increasingly helpful role, but the four powers
in concert can begin to make a meaningful contribution on the
question of guarantees'. He mentioned also that in the following
stage Jarring would be able to concentrate on definite points,
namely peace, withdrawal, frontiers and peace guarantees.

To dispel any doubts we might still entertain over the US
position, a third message from Rogers was communicated to me

on 31 January to state that the US had not changed its stand in relation to Israel's withdrawal to Egypt's international frontiers. he added that the US intended to discuss peace guarantees during the four-power meetings when it would ascertain for itself that the talks under Jarring were moving in a constructive way and were not obstructed either by an invitation for the Security Council to convene or by a resumption of hostilities. When Bergus handed me this message, he said that the most important thing at the time was for the Egyptian government to place its confidence in the US for two or three months more. I answered him that we had done that before and there would be no harm in trying it once again.

On 4 February, I went to the People's Assembly to listen to Sadat's speech. While I was reading the text of the speech before its delivery I noticed that after announcing his approval of a thirty-day extension of the ceasefire be began to speak of an initiative from his side. He had written: '. . . Egypt adds to all the efforts exerted for peace a new Egyptian initiative and she considers that abiding by it will be a true criterion for the desire to implement Security Council Resolution 242. We demand that during the ceasefire period a partial withdrawal of the Israeli forces from the east bank of the Suez Canal be effected as a first stage in a timetable which would be drawn up for execution by the Security Council . . . If this is undertaken in the course of the period we have defined, we are ready to start promptly in clearing the Suez Canal and to reopen it to international navigation and the service of world economy . . . We believe that this initiative will help Ambassador Jarring in eliciting agreement on definite measures for the implementation of the Security Council resolution . . .'

Upon Sadat's arrival I approached him to discuss the implications of this initiative. My view was that many countries would assume we had retracted from our insistence on a total withdrawal – a matter which would perplex and confuse those countries that supported us. I also said that Jarring was about to submit definite proposals and it would perhaps be more fruitful to concentrate on these, since they would be undertaken under the banner of the United Nations. However, President Sadat had a different point of view; he believed that this initiative would gain us the support of countries that had been harmed by the

188 The Struggle for Peace in the Middle East

closure of the Canal and that, should Israel reject this initiative, the whole world would stand against it, isolating it completely. It was also his view that we stood to lose nothing by putting forward this initiative, even if it was not implemented or responded to. In his speech he mentioned further that he had written to Nixon, requesting his support in solving the problem, but had received a reply expressive of a position completely aligned to Israel.

By 8 February Jarring had finalized his initiative and submitted it to both Egypt and Israel. The gist of it was that Israel declared its commitment to withdrawal to Egypt's international borders (and equally from the Gaza Strip in order to re-establish the *status quo ante*) in return for an Egyptian pledge to sign a peace agreement with Israel stipulating the termination of the state of belligerency, recognition of Israel's right to exist, recognition of the right of every country to live in peace within secure and recognized borders, cessation of hostile activities from the territory of each country on the territory of the other, refraining from intervention in the internal affairs of each other and safeguarding free navigation in the Tiran Straits, according to arrangements relating to Sharm el-Sheikh which (Jarring explained to me later) meant the stationing of UN forces there for this reason.

My reply contained our consent to pledge the execution of all commitments relating to us in the initiative, including the signing of a peace agreement and other matters consistent with the Security Council resolution in return for total Israeli evacuation. I sent the reply to Jarring on 15 February and handed a copy to Donald Bergus; the latter was elated at our positive response and commented after reading the copy: 'Here are the magic words.' He admitted that our response constituted a colossal step. I said to him: 'You realize now that we have responded favourably to all demands made by Mr Rogers and the American government?' He concurred with this, adding that he was certain that the Israeli response would be equally positive, and that if Israel tried to evade the issue, the US government now had all it needed to pressure Israel into accepting.

Israel, however, rejected Jarring's initiative in its entirety and launched a smear campaign against the UN Secretary-General's special envoy, claiming that he had overstepped his mandate. I called in the great powers' ambassadors and asked them to urge their respective governments to take a positive step. I also called in Bergus and asked him about the position of his government *vis-à-vis* the Israeli attitude. It had become clear to us that both Rogers and the State Department had little say in defining US foreign policy. Reports received during that period all pointed to the fact that the right of decision on foreign affairs matters had been delegated almost completely to Henry Kissinger, the National Security Adviser to the President.

Once again a golden opportunity for peace in the area had been dissipated by the Israeli compulsion for expansion. I was asked by a member of my staff whether Jarring's initiative, which confined itself to the Egyptian front, was not in fact the partial solution we had always rejected. My view was that we were responding to an initiative from a representative of the UN who was charged by the Security Council to undertake the implementation of Resolution 242 which deals with all fronts. The representative of the Secretary-General cannot confine himself to the Egyptian front and claim he has implemented the Security Council resolution; he will have to move to the other fronts and apply the same principles that were applied to the Israeli–Egyptian front.

On 15 February, Tito arrived in Cairo for talks with Sadat. He described the present situation as much worse than a year or even six months ago. During Nixon's recent visit to Belgrade, the US President had concentrated more on the increasing presence of the Soviet fleet in the Mediterranean than on the continued Israeli occupation of Arab land, nor did he offer any ideas for solving the Middle East question.

Tito listened to Sadat's explanation of his 4 February initiative for opening the Suez Canal if Israel would effect a partial withdrawal from Sinai, our acceptance of the Jarring initiative stipulating the signing of a peace agreement with Israel, and our later acceptance of U Thant's appeal for an extension of the ceasefire. Tito then maintained that we should not extend the ceasefire at all, since Israel's political stance had become extremely weak and public opinion had been lending its support to Egypt for some time. He stated more than once that Egypt should choose the proper time to employ its military forces to liberate its territory after all peaceful attempts had been foiled.

Tito was very critical, however, of the opening up of the Suez

Canal in exchange for a partial withdrawal in Sinai, however extensive that was. He said that once this was effected, the world would lose interest in the withdrawal of the Israeli forces from the remaining occupied Arab territories. He said that the US, in its increasing involvement in South East Asia, had a vested interest that stability should be maintained in the Middle East, in which case Egypt should exploit this situation to exert every possible pressure, military or political, at its disposal.

I felt the necessity of resuming contacts with the US government and told Bergus on 22 February that I was anxious to learn the position of the US and what it intended to do in the light of Israel's refusal to withdraw. I added that we had accepted Rogers' advice, approved Jarring's proposals, refrained from raising the issue at the Security Council, and extended the ceasefire. Rogers had further stated that he considered our reply to Jarring as constructive and positive. What now, I asked him.

Bergus answered that his directives boiled down to two points: that Washington considered Egypt's response as a serious step forward and that it had impressed on Israel the necessity of an equally positive answer to Jarring. Four days earlier, in answer to a question put to him by a press man as to whether he was ready to use his powers of persuasion to get the Israelis to accept something along this line (Jarring's), Nixon was very evasive, saying that it was not beneficial to use 'our powers of persuasion' with either Israel, Egypt or Jordan. He said the problem was extremely complicated – which was always the pretext when no action was contemplated.

Bergus came to see me on 1 March to inform me that US efforts with Israel had not succeeded. He told me that the US government would continue in its attempt to change the Israeli reply, that Rogers would like to conduct talks with us for the extension of the ceasefire, and finally that he was going to propose to the four-power meeting a statement that would contain the following points: that they reaffirm their support for Resolution 242 and that the parties should cooperate with and respond positively to the special representative (Dr Jarring), that they agree to continue their preliminary examination of guarantees and that the parties should continue to refrain from firing. Bergus added that his government preferred the avenue of the four-power meetings to the Security Council, that the draft statement of the four powers did not specify any deadline for the termination of the ceasefire and that his government would request that Egypt follow suit so that ample time could be offered for exploring a political settlement.

I asked Bergus to convey to Rogers my opinion that the situation was extremely serious in view of Israel's rejection of peace in favour of expansion, that while its claim was its desire to live in peace with its neighbours (supported by Nixon's adage 'live and let others live'), and while consequently all American projects were concerned with safeguarding this security in return for its withdrawal from the occupied territories, the latest Israeli posture of refusing Jarring's proposals which had been accepted by Egypt was enough to unmask Israeli intentions completely. The least the US could do in a situation of this nature, I concluded, was to withdraw its financial and military aid to Israel. As regards Rogers' proposed four-power statement with its refusal to set a deadline for the ceasefire, I thought it only appropriate to remind him that imposing a three-month deadline was fundamentally an American condition proposed by Rogers himself. I did not see how the US could argue now that such a condition imposed a pressure under which she could not act. I referred to a recent statement by Nixon deploring the instability in the area due to the Soviet presence, to say that this was obviously an attempt to obscure the real issue: Israeli occupation of Arab territories and Israeli raids on civilians which forced us to invite the Soviets to help us, and that the Soviets could not in the final analysis remain against our will.

Sadat left the same day for Moscow on a secret one-day visit. This was his first visit after assuming the presidency. It was the first time that talks at this level would take place without my being there. The reason was easy to come by. In view of the deadlock we had reached, increasing international support and the view of friendly countries that we should move to military action, I was becoming aware of the increasing necessity for military action. I was thinking along these lines when the Soviet Ambassador to Cairo asked to see me. To my surprise and dismay he began talking about the necessity of pursuing our political efforts for a peaceful settlement. I was disturbed by his tone and answered him impatiently: 'You come to me now to speak about a peaceful solution? What have we been doing for the last three years? What was our response to Jarring only a few days ago but a further proof of that? What more do you expect us to do?' The Ambassador tried to intervene, but I continued: 'I don't want to indulge in an argument with you but to communicate to your government that there is dissatisfaction in the army that the military equipment we have already contracted for has not yet been delivered, and we urge you to deliver it as soon as possible.' I sent the minutes of this meeting to Sadat and he countersigned them: 'I approve every word said at that meeting.'

In Moscow, the whole one–day visit was confined to one topic: Sadat went into a long discussion with the Soviet leadership concerning the delivery of the arms needed; he conveyed to the Soviet side that everything I had said was an expression of his views and he requested that they deliver them promptly.

On 4 March, the British Ambassador came to see me and referred to the draft declaration proposed by the US side to the four-power meeting and said that Rogers had made the insertion of the paragraph relating to a permanent ceasefire a condition of its approval by the US and that, if this statement was not issued, Jarring would most likely relinquish his mission.

I answered that to accept no deadline for the ceasefire when Israel had rejected Jarring's proposals meant that we accepted the continuation of Israeli occupation of our territories and those of other Arab countries. If the US had failed to persuade Israel to answer Jarring positively, it was illogical that it should attempt to impose a new concession on us in Israel's favour.

On the following day, 5 March, the Secretary-General of the UN issued a report in which he recorded Egypt's positive stand in relation to Jarring's proposal and Israel's negative response, and appealed to Israel to respond favourably to Ambassador Jarring's initiative. The last extension of the ceasefire ended on 7 March and was not extended by Egypt, which meant that the resumption of military operations depended entirely on Egypt's will.

At a four-power meeting on 11 March Ambassador Malik (the Soviet permanent representative at the UN) while proposing that a statement be issued demanding that Israel respond positively to Jarring's proposals said that the US was obediently carrying out any caprice of Israel, for instance in supporting Israel's demand for an unlimited extension of the ceasefire. He added that the US suffered from a 'fear of Israel or, more specifically, fear of the Zionists'.

It should be admitted, however, that Rogers, in a press conference on 16 March, had dealt with some issues in a way that was in total contradiction of Israel's concepts: he supported Jarring's mission and the concept of international guarantees and expressed the willingness of the US to undertake a suitable and responsible role in the proposed international force. He elaborated on the guarantees by accepting the participation of other countries besides the four powers. He answered directly Israel's allegation that geography was the sole consideration when thinking about security. He said: 'Now, we do not think so . . . Certainly in modern-day world situations, geography is ordinarily not important. The difficulties now involve . . . the question of aquisition of territory which Egypt says is unacceptable, and it is also unacceptable to the Security Council . . . Then there is the question of Israel's security. Anything that does not provide security to Israel is unacceptable to us . . . We think there is a middle ground. The security aspects do not necessarily require acquisition of territory. On the other hand, we recognize that Israel has to be satisfied that its security is guaranteed, and the US is prepared to play a leading role in that guarantee . . .'

Israel unleashed a vehement attack on Rogers, led by its Prime Minister, Mrs Meir, herself who castigated the American Secretary of State in hard-hitting terms which astounded diplomatic circles. However, Nixon, instead of supporting Rogers, abandoned him, thereby killing both Jarring's initiative and the efforts towards peace of his own Secretary of State.

After the failure of Jarring, there remained on the scene only Sadat's initiative. This initiative, however, was the subject of critical speculations from some friendly countries. Lupez Bravo, Foreign Minister of Spain, arrived in Cairo on 9 February. At our first meeting he asked me why we took it upon ourselves to announce a stage in the partial solution in Sinai while telling them that we were seeking a comprehensive settlement with Israel on all Arab fronts. I explained that Sadat was seeking specific steps to be taken within the framework of a comprehensive settlement. When I accompanied him the evening of the following day to Sadat, he raised the same point, at which Sadat chucklingly said: 'You are repeating what Riad here told me before', and assured him that he would never give up on total settlement.

On 26 March, I was again touring some Western capitals. In Rome, Aldo Moro, who was now lending us his total support, said we had done all that was asked of us. At Pisa I met President Tito who happened to be on a visit to Italy and who expressed his dissatisfaction at American shilly-shallying and reiterated that we should concentrate on a comprehensive settlement and veer away from partial solutions; he expressed his despair of reaching a just solution to the Arab cause through peaceful efforts. He mentioned that the non-aligned countries would never forgive us if we forfeited one inch of land. On that visit I became aware that part of Italy's growing interest lay in the adverse effects the continuation of the crisis was having on its economy. Moro told me that in his recent talks with Rogers he had received the impression that Rogers did not approve of Israel's rejection of Jarring's proposals and that the US would adopt a more positive stand towards the implementation of the Security Council resolution. I informed him that we would welcome Italy – a major Mediterranean power – in the UN force for peace guarantees.

I arrived in Paris where I met Jarring on 29 March. Jarring said that after Israel's last position he frankly felt he had nothing more to contribute or add to the efforts he had exerted during recent years and that now he had reached the conclusion that there was absolutely no hope of achieving any progress since Israel's rejection of his proposals meant, in fact, its rejection of its commitments as stipulated in Resolution 242, in spite of Egypt's willingness. Jarring added that he felt great disappointment at the failure of the great powers, headed by the US, not even seriously to attempt to persuade Israel to move earnestly towards peace. . . Consequently, he felt that he had no other choice but to withdraw from his mission and return to his post in Moscow.

In Paris, I was received by President Pompidou, on 1 April. He told me in clear terms that nobody could ask Egypt to render more than it had already done, that it was illogical to expect that any Egyptian would accept giving up his territory to satisfy Israeli expansionist claims, and that nobody had the right to demand this. Concerning Sadat's February initiative, he asked me why it was projected in such a manner as to give the impression that Egypt was inclined to accept a partial solution. I assured him that what Sadat intended was a comprehensive settlement in which the withdrawal of Israel to a distance east of the Suez Canal would be but the first stage. Following this meeting I dispatched a lengthy cable to Sadat, whereupon he undertook to release a statement to the press in order to dispel this misunderstanding, saying that his initiative was tied to a total settlement.

I left Paris with my view of the futility of attempting a peaceful solution reinforced. I met Gaston Thorn, the Foreign Affairs Minister of Luxembourg, an extremely able man, and Josef Lunz, Foreign Minister of Holland, and was made aware of his dilemma: an honest man, he saw that right was on our side but, at the same time, he represented a country which felt great sympathy for the plight of the Jews at the hands of Hitler and, like many other European countries, failed in the process to distinguish between sympathy for the Jews and the intransigent policies of Israel as a State.

I concluded my tour with a visit to Greece, which had always stood by us and had historic ties with Egypt, and from there I flew to Tehran in response to an invitation by the Shah of Iran.

I reported on my tour to Sadat and commented that the document that enjoyed international support at present was Jarring's, and that Israel was trying, with the help of the US, to divert attention away from it and to the proposal for opening the Suez Canal. I also mentioned what Aldo Moro had communicated to me, a piece of information he had received during his last visit to Israel: that there was an Israeli determination to annex the Syrian Golan Heights, the West Bank, Jerusalem and the Gaza Strip, and to demilitarize the greater part of Sinai in case of its restoration to Egypt. I also quoted Zahedi, the Foreign Minister of Iran, who was in close contact with the US administration, as saying that the US was not willing to exert any effective pressure on Israel. I quoted Tito's words that the US objective during this period was merely to gain time and to establish a no-peace no-war situation which would undermine the morale of the people and the armed forces of Egypt and that as Egypt hastened with its military operations so it would be in a better position. The Shah of Iran had told me that it was imperative for Egypt to undertake military action if it wanted to reactivate the situation and that the War of Attrition waged by Egypt all through 1969 and 1970 had cost Israel colossal sacrifices, the extent of which they did not disclose. When I told Sadat that Israel was generating the impression that the February initiative was meant as a partial solution with Egypt which would be confined to an agreement for opening the Suez Canal while Israel would continue to occupy Sinai, he said that he would officially declare his withdrawal of that initiative. When I objected, he reminded me that I had been against it from the outset. While this was true, I said that I did not feel that, now it had been announced at the level of the President of the Republic, it should be withdrawn, although we would have to confirm to the various capitals of the world that it was vitally linked to the comprehensive settlement of the Middle East crisis. The President accepted this interpretation and announced it in his speech on the occasion of Labour Day.

On 15 April, I flew to Moscow for consultations arranged during Podgorny's visit in January. In Moscow I agreed with Gromyko over our joint political action; we agreed that Israel was not going to withdraw, that the US would not exert pressure on it in this direction, that the opening of the Suez Canal should be within the framework of a comprehensive settlement, that there was a necessity for the presence of the concerned parties with Jarring at the four-power meetings in New York (this was originally a proposal from Schumann in order to reactivate the situation), that the four great powers would participate in extending peace guarantees after Israel withdrew to the 4 June borders, that observation posts be established by the UN in Sharm el-Sheikh to supervise free navigation, and that Israel's evacuation to 4 June borders apply to East Jerusalem; we gave total support to all legitimate rights of the Palestinians and finally, in connection with the establishment of a Palestinian State, we recorded King Hussein's pledge in a message to Sadat that we would conduct a referendum among the West Bank inhabitants after liberation to decide their destiny including the right to establish a State of their own.

Meanwhile, Kosygin had sent a message to Nixon on 28 February in the wake of the Israeli rejection of Jarring's initiative. Later, while in Cairo, the Soviet Ambassador handed me a copy of Nixon's reply which argued that it was the Soviet Union's military activity in the region that was responsible for halting any progress. Nixon's message did not contain any constructive elements. Donald Bergus informed me that Rogers would like to visit Egypt within a tour he was planning, to discuss the latest developments.

Rogers arrived on 4 May and began by saying that this was the first time that a US Secretary of State had visited a country with which he had no diplomatic relations, and that this was done to prove his sincere desire to establish a peaceful settlement. He added that in spite of the fact that the peaceful settlement had not yet been achieved, yet there was progress, thanks to the steps taken by the Egyptian government to create a favourable atmosphere, especially in its forthcoming response to Jarring's proposals. He added that the position of the US which now enjoyed the support of a substantial part of the mass media was against substantial regional adjustments: 'We are trying to persuade Israel that her position is not sound. Pressure is a distasteful word in international relations.' He continued that he wanted to make it clear that the US was not asking Egypt to render more than it had already done. He added that Israel had to do something to reactivate the negotiating process but the US did not want a confrontation with Israel. With regard to the proposal by Sadat to reopen the Suez Canal, he referred to the fact that Moshe Dayan had made the same proposal and that Mrs Meir promised to consider it, that while the US might not have a national interest in reopening the Canal (as it would be more advantageous to the Soviet Union), it still favoured such a step since it would offer Jarring a time framework for his mission. However, the US did not consider this an end in itself and it should be phrased in a way that would clarify this meaning. Therefore it was important to make sure that an interim agreement did not hinder the final settlement relating to territories and to the Palestinians. He concluded by saying that the US believed that the present atmosphere was more conducive to a settlement than it had been last year and that the alternative to a settlement was war and destruction.

Sisco intervened to make proposals that he knew beforehand we would not accept. He said that the US had the impression that agreement could be reached in four areas: the opening-up of the Suez Canal and the pull-back of Israel from the Canal front. Here Rogers interrupted, saying that the word to use in this connection was withdrawal, not a pull-back. Sisco continued his list referring to a ceasefire that would be part of the interim agreement, and the fourth point: how to relate the interim agreement to the comprehensive settlement. I answered that I would pose certain questions when we resumed our meeting but at this juncture I had a fundamental observation to make. I recapitulated the talks with the US side that had preceded the adoption of Resolution 242 and that at the time the US had pledged to be fully bound by the resolution. In fact, in 1967 we had done exactly what the US was proposing now and yet that remained unimplemented.

On the following day we resumed our talks and I referred to the three rounds of talks we had had with the US during the preceding year; I concluded: 'After all these years, I would like to consider that your present visit would be decisive in that either we have war or peace in our region. Yesterday you mentioned that war will be destructive, and I agree with you. Last year, upon our meeting in New York, I tried to explain that we were concerned about raising the standard of living in Egypt, which makes us really concerned about peace . . . Yet we are also faced with the threat of an Israeli compulsion for expansion. We needed three years of exploring every avenue for peace to prove to the world at large that Israel's concern was for expansion, not peace. The latest instance was its refusal of Jarring's proposals. An Israeli cabinet minister has declared recently that Eisenhower ordered Ben Gurion to withdraw from the Egyptian territory and he had to abide by this order, but that now Nixon cannot give us such orders. We don't want you to give orders to anybody. This is the duty of the Security Council. We both know, however, that Israel will not withdraw until it is forced to do so. There are two ways: we can undertake this ourselves and we may succeed or fail; or we try this by peaceful means whereby we would have to depend on your cooperation . . . I have here a thirteen-page report relating to American promises and obligations that have not been kept. Yet you speak about "persuading them to move towards peace". We would like to know how many months, how many years, that would need. The situation now boils down to the following: you have tried to persuade them and they have refused. You do not wish to pressure them yet you do not want us to raise the issue at the Security Council. The result is Israel's defiance of everybody, including Jarring and the UN's resolutions.' I went on to point out that with regard to opening the Suez Canal it was not our objective, since it was bound to happen one day. On the economic side we might be losing revenue because of its closure, but Arab support exceeded the Canal revenues. The problem was restoring all our territories; consequently, what we should be discussing was a comprehensive plan for Israeli withdrawal. If Israel was ready to accept Jarring's proposal then we could talk of a solution along two stages: in the first stage Israel would withdraw to a line from al-Arish in the north to Ras Mohammad in the south, while we would undertake to clear the Suez Canal and our forces across the Canal; in the second stage Israel would complete its withdrawal to our international borders and from Gaza according to a timetable for each stage. 'There is another point I have to be crystal clear about: we are not ready to accept the demilitarization of all Sinai, even if Israel accepts the demilitarization of the Negev Desert. Can you persuade Israel to accept Jarring's proposal? And if they refuse, what are you going to do?'

'All we can do,' he answered, 'is to work towards persuading Israel. There is a complicating factor: the Soviet presence. If we close our eyes to this Soviet presence in Egypt you will not get total American support, for if we say we will stop all arms to Israel, people will point to the Soviet presence and their arms supplies to you. This is a fact that we have to face.' Rogers also referred to differences in the US and the Egyptian interpretations of Resolution 242.

When we resumed talks, Rogers was again harping on the Soviet theme: 'You asked me what I could do to implement our declared policy; the answer is that we will do all we can without spoiling the negotiating process. Had there been no Soviet presence in Egypt we could have acted differently. You have asked me whether Israel has a map delineating its borders. We are not aware of the existence of such a map, although we are aware of Israel's broad thoughts on the question of territories – which we are reluctant to voice because you will not easily accept them, and to voice them may complicate matters . . . although an active diplomacy may alter these thoughts in such a way that you could accept them.'

Sisco began to pose what he termed hypothetical questions relating to withdrawal arrangements, most significant of which was whether the Bar-Lev Line of fortification could be left intact, after Israeli withdrawal, and no attempt undertaken to destroy it. (I asked him whether the Israelis intended to re-occupy the

Bar-Lev Line – Rogers answered that these were all interim arrangements and not a final solution, thus implying the possibility of an Israeli return to Bar-Lev.) Sisco continued by wondering whether Egypt could decrease its forces on the west bank of the Suez Canal, and whether we could, as a 'symbolic gesture', agree to an exchange of prisoners of war. On this last point, Rogers said that he would be grateful and appreciative, even if no agreement was reached, if we would at least agree on this matter for it would have a great impact on American public opinion. Egypt had a large number of Israeli prisoners of war in custody as a result of the War of Attrition, including a number of Phantom pilots for whose release Israel had elicited the good offices of many countries in 1970. Sisco added that such a gesture would consolidate our international position and reassert the support we had acquired.

My response was: 'First of all, I have a comment to make on what you mentioned as a difference between us in interpreting Resolution 242. After the adoption of the resolution and in our consultations with you, all through 1967, we were never made aware of such a difference. The basis of our political movement was the restoration of all territories invaded by Israel in June 1967. When I spoke in connection with total withdrawal from Egypt I was anxious to keep my words within the framework of Jarring's note, which stipulated Israel's withdrawal to Egyptian international borders. Your [Rogers'] project of 1969 stated the same in clear terms.' Rogers answered in the affirmative but referred to certain conditions relating to Gaza, the demilitarized zones, and arrangements for Sharm el-Sheikh which would be left for negotiations. I answered that we were aware of that, but fundamentally Israel had to withdraw to 4 June borders. I moved then to the issue of the Soviet presence, expressing the view that we did not consider it a complicating factor, in fact we viewed its acceptance into the international force for safeguarding peace as an element in the settlement and a contribution to a peaceful solution. Indeed, we considered it a good precedent for cooperation between the four great powers for maintaining world peace.

I next said that the interim step would be tied to the final solution based on Resolution 242 which they now claimed we were interpreting differently – giving me the impression that we were moving in a vicious circle.

I referred to Sisco's 'hypothetical questions' by saying that the answers were contained in the paper I had handed to them which contained our ideas on withdrawal arrangements and how they could be conducted in two stages.

When my talks with the US delegation headed by Rogers ended, they conferred with Sadat with no new views injected beyond what had already taken place in the two sessions of negotiations with me. Rogers conveyed to Sadat once again that he would conduct talks with Israel and if something were achieved, especially as regards an interim agreement within the framework of a total solution, perhaps Sisco would return to Cairo.

The views of Rogers in Cairo reflected the weakness of the State Department and the retraction of the US. A year before, it had not raised a difference in the interpretation of Resolution 242 but it did now, and went further to speak of an interim agreement. It considered that the mere mention by Israel of a 'withdrawal' was a noteworthy achievement. In fact, it did not promise anything beyond 'persuading' Israel, while a year earlier it had suspended delivery of Phantoms and Skyhawks in order to pressure Israel.

My interpretation was that while the War of Attrition waged by Egypt had reached its climax in the preceding year and had forced the US into a more serious quest for peace, now, with the prevailing quiet on all fronts, the US felt no urgency, nor even a desire to speak in terms of a comprehensive settlement. The reference by Rogers to the Soviet presence in Egypt as an obstacle to an American effort to establish a comprehensive settlement was evidence of this. Kissinger had already used that logic in an attempt to divert attention from the essential issue to a totally different issue, namely the Soviet presence in Egypt. The fallacy of this logic would be exposed the following year, when the services of Soviet experts and advisers in Egypt were terminated without the US making any progress towards a comprehensive peace.

After Rogers' departure reports started reaching me pointing out that US circles were claiming that Egypt had accepted a permanent ceasefire. Our permanent representative at the UN, el-Kony, cabled me that the permanent representative of France had informed him that the Israelis were asserting that they had received assurances from the US that Egypt would not resume firing after the lapse of the ceasefire period on 7 March and that the US, in its turn, had received these assurances from a prominent Egyptian figure. I took this message to Sadat who denied it and, when I told him of the view of some friendly countries that we should resume military operations, said that it was likely that we would do so in May or June (1971). Again, after four days, I communicated a message to Sadat I had received from the Yugoslav Ambassador in Cairo, to the effect that the US Ambassador at the UN, Christopher Phillips, had informed the Yugoslav representative at the UN that there was an understanding between the US and Egypt that no military operations would take place for at least two months; Sadat commented: 'Let them say that, it is a good cover for us.'

Sisco came to Cairo after the talks Rogers had had with the Israelis. I conferred with him on 9 May, after which he was received by Sadat.

Rogers' visit to Israel was utterly ineffective. He failed to convince Israel to accept a comprehensive solution on all fronts, he failed to persuade Mrs Meir to accept his initiative for withdrawing from Sinai, or for accepting Jarring's proposals for a withdrawal from Sinai, coupled with signing a peace agreement with Egypt.

None of this came as a surprise to me. The real surprise was a proposal by Sisco suggesting that an agreement for opening the Suez Canal should not be related to total withdrawal, which constituted the worst possible proposal that we had ever received since the June War. I promised that we would transmit our views on it after studying it. I called in Bergus on 20 May and handed him a written reply in which I referred to Sisco's proposal as the 'Canal Agreement' for, in fact, that was exactly what it amounted to. The Israeli project as conveyed by Sisco included these pledges: Egypt would open up the Suez Canal for navigation and the passage of Israeli ships according to a partial solution that did not stipulate its withdrawal to our international borders or withdrawal from other occupied Arab territories or the solution of the problem of the legitimate rights of the Palestinian people; it demanded a permanent ceasefire on the Egyptian front and a promise that no Egyptian forces would cross the Canal. Sisco added that he had a feeling that Israel would be ready to withdraw a certain distance away from the Canal but would maintain personnel of the armed forces in civilian clothing along the Bar-Lev Line to defend it. Rogers had mentioned earlier that Israel would maintain the Bar-Lev Line as long as the final solution was still pending. Sisco also informed us that Moshe Dayan preferred there to be joint Israeli–Egyptian arrangements, which meant that he wanted to keep the UN out of the picture.

Israel, I wrote, had transformed a partial solution into a solution that would lead us to a surrender to its dictates which we vehemently refused and reiterated our position as announced by Sadat: that the partial solution should be tied to Israeli evacuation to Egyptian international borders, that the Egyptian forces should cross the Canal and occupy a line east of the Sinai passes, that the ceasefire be fixed for a period of six months during which Jarring would lay down a timetable for the implementation of Resolution 242 on all fronts.

I was aware that the US was pressuring us into retreating to positions much worse than those we faced after the Israeli victory in June 1967. I also became aware that Bergus, during that period, was spreading in diplomatic circles the story that while I was insistent on a comprehensive settlement, Sadat did not object to a partial solution unrelated to a total withdrawal. When I raised this point with Sadat, he called it a mere attempt at agitation.

The same month, the European group began to move cautiously to issue a statement in which it referred to close historical ties binding Europe to the countries of the Middle East and to their mutual interests, invited all the concerned parties to work for the success of Jarring's mission, and affirmed the necessity of a complete implementation of Resolution 242. The novelty of this was that it was the first time since the Second World War that European countries would attempt to adopt a line on foreign policy without previous reference to Washington.

The last devious attempt of the US came from Rogers himself. On 23 May, Bergus called on Mohammed Riad, my *Chef de bureau*, and informed him that he had prepared a paper which he would like to pass to us in a purely personal capacity, claiming that it might help us in drafting a memorandum on Egypt's position on the partial solution and that we might introduce some amendments to it if we wished. The paper was, in fact, an interim agreement for a partial solution by which Israel would withdraw to an undefined line in Sinai, referred to as 'Line A–B', after which Israel would commit itself to withdrawal to a frontier line to be agreed upon in the Peace Agreement with Egypt. The draft was craftily worded inasmuch as it proposed the signing of a partial agreement with Israel under Jarring along the lines adopted in the Armistice Agreement we had signed with Israel in 1949, under Ralph Bunche, which was equally a temporary agreement. The term of the new agreement was to be six months but the UN representative could extend the ceasefire continuously. It did not refer to complete Israeli withdrawal to Egypt's international borders but to a line to be agreed upon by Israel.

I felt dismay and concern at the position of a Secretary of State who, after the failure of his initiative, was now presenting us with an Israeli project which he had previously criticized and rejected and who, because of his unwillingness to present it to us himself, sheltered behind Donald Bergus.

When I announced that the note represented the lowest pitch to which the US position had deteriorated, Washington tried to deny any knowledge of the note, because of the detrimental reactions it had in the Arab world and in various world capitals. When I was asked by Joseph Kraft of the *Washington Post* how I qualified it as an official communication, I answered that I did not assume that the representative of the US in Cairo was working on his own behalf but on behalf, and at the directives of, his government. 'We do not deal with phantoms,' I said, which induced Kraft to refer to it in his press report as the 'Phantom Note'.

Rogers' visit to Cairo aroused Soviet apprehensions. It initiated a change in our approach. While contacts with the US had been channelled through the Soviet Union before, now we were having direct contacts. This came in the wake of US statements relating to the necessity of ousting the Soviet Union from the Middle East. Consequently, as soon as Rogers and Sisco terminated their talks in Cairo, Moscow informed us of their wish to send a delegation to Cairo headed by Nicolai Podgorny. The delegation arrived on 25 May and talks began the following morning. After the first session was over, Podgorny, in a private meeting with Sadat, handed him a copy of a treaty for cooperation and friendship which the Soviet Union would like to conclude with Egypt. Sadat informed me of this, saying that he approved of our signing the treaty so that the Soviets would be assured that no change had occurred in Soviet–Egyptian relations. When the talks were resumed, Sadat referred to the situation and the importance of the coming battle, since hope for a peaceful solution was minute, said that building Egyptian military force was the way to the realization of a peaceful settlement and liberation of the land, and emphasized the need to attack the problem that year. Podgorny reverted to his recurrent theme, saying that avenues for political activity had not yet been totally exhausted, but then admitted that the US position had not changed: not only had bilateral talks with the Soviet Union stopped, the US was also obstructing the four great-power talks and Jarring's activities. Further, the US refused to exert pressure on Israel. Dealing with the question of developing relations between Egypt and the Soviet Union for the consolidation of the Egyptian position, he proposed a meeting between Gromyko and myself to lay the foundations for such a cooperation based, of course, on the draft treaty he had brought and which Sadat had approved. I noticed that the draft treaty was seriously deficient. Previously, in our relations with the Soviet Union we had been receiving arms without there being a friendship treaty; now that we were to approve the conclusion of such a treaty, the absence of any text or reference to a Soviet pledge to supply us with arms necessary for the liberation of our land became noticeable, so I asked Gromyko to introduce a clause which would bind the Soviet Union to consolidate Egyptian defensive power and extend to Egypt all necessary military help. Gromyko had to refer to Podgorny who, in his turn, had to get the approval of his colleagues in Moscow. In the meanwhile I explained to Sadat that the amendments I was requesting, although of a general nature, would nevertheless give the treaty some military content. The treaty was officially signed on 27 May.

King Faisal, who obviously was concerned about the conclusion of the treaty, arrived at the head of a large Saudi delegation. Sadat assured him that the treaty in no way changed Egypt's position.

Harmel, the Belgian Prime Minister and Minister of Foreign Affairs, paid us a visit during that period and spoke of a wave of optimism in Western capitals as a result of US reports that it was on the way to reaching an agreement with Egypt. I showed him 'the phantom draft agreement' to establish that there was no progress in the US position but, in fact, retrogression. I continued that we had faced a similar situation a few days earlier when Schumann, the French Foreign Minister, had informed us that Rogers had communicated to him that Egypt was about to conclude an agreement with Israel for ending the state of belligerency, in return for an Israeli withdrawal of about thirty kilometres in Sinai – which made me dispatch to Schumann all the documents relating to our talks with the US. He was astounded at the US position. When I told Harmel that we were further from peace this year than ever, Harmel said that he was quite convinced of the validity of our position although he was perplexed at the US attitude; that he now realized the futility of concluding an agreement for a limitation of arms in Europe when arms were being stock-piled in the Middle East. If Belgium was striving for security and stability in Europe, he continued, it was well aware that a just and comprehensive peace in the Middle East was an integral part of European security; as long as the Middle East remained a source for threatening security, Europe's success would remain in doubt. An understanding between East and West was direly needed; Western Europe should play a prominent role in establishing peace in the Middle East, the starting point of which could be to work for the implementation of Jarring's paper.

It had been agreed with Podgorny that the exchange of ratification documents of the treaty should take place in Moscow, so I flew there on 29 June for this purpose. On my arrival I met with Gromyko, when I reviewed the latest developments in our contacts in the light of US retractions. I referred to international support and the recent resolution adopted by the African Summit Conference for the withdrawal of Israel from all occupied Arab territories and the establishment of a follow-up Committee composed of the Heads of State. This came after Abba Eban's visit to eight African countries to dissuade them from adopting a unified position against Israel.

Gromyko was in full agreement with my political analysis; he emphasized the necessity of relating all partial agreements to the final comprehensive settlement and setting a timetable for the implementation of each stage of withdrawal.

In my meeting with Brezhnev on 2 July, he was anxious to find out Arab reactions to the treaty. I said that the Arab countries appreciated our position fully. Although King Faisal had had some apprehensions, he had been convinced by our explanations during his recent visit to Cairo. I then argued that, in the absence of viable political solutions, we must move to military action, since we were in danger of losing the support of world public opinion and when resorting to the UN, after all the resolutions it had adopted in our favour, could render our case as ineffectual as the issue of Rhodesia was at the time. Now we wanted the Soviet Union to furnish us with the maximum possible in military help. Brezhnev then said: 'I want you to convey that we are committed to the implementation of the treaty between us, not only in the letter but in its content and spirit. It is true you now have a powerful, well-armed army. The decision to initiate or refrain from military operations is entirely yours, of course. It is my view that such an important issue as peace or war is of such moment that it has to be studied with exceptional care. If a unanimous decision is taken by President Sadat and his government, it should be based on careful analysis and comprehensive study.' He added that he requested President Sadat to continue his political efforts as the international situation could easily change.

It was obvious to me that Brezhnev had reservations about beginning military operations, although he made it clear that it was Egypt's right to go to war, if it so decided. However, if Egypt took this decision he would suggest a joint meeting between the Ministers of Defence, to be followed by a meeting between him and Sadat, so as to avoid the possibility of another setback to Egypt.

When Gromyko accompanied me to the airport, I told him that the army in Egypt was determined to initiate war, but that they were complaining of the shortage of certain kinds of arms and ammunition. Knowledge of this fact made some of the officers suspect that the Soviet Union was not anxious to extend sufficient help. Gromyko said that Brezhnev wanted to be doubly sure that the army would not suffer another setback.

On my way back, I visited a number of East European countries and was assured that their support depended on a complete conviction of the justice of our case, not merely following the

Soviet line. In Belgrade I met Tito who said that while he objected to the passage of Soviet planes over Yugoslav skies to participate in Soviet manoeuvres, he was ready to permit this if the objective was to help Egypt. When I referred to the shortages we were suffering in some kinds of ammunition, he said that an Egyptian military delegation should come to Yugoslavia which manufactured several kinds of ammunition used by Egypt. He reasserted his view that Egypt had no choice now other than military action.

11

Kissinger in Search of a Role

George Bush, then US representative at the UN and now Vice-President in Ronald Reagan's administration, at the four great powers meeting in New York on 13 May defined US policy in the Middle East as the implementation of Security Council resolutions and the support of Jarring's mission; but he went on to advocate the conclusion of the interim agreement for opening the Suez Canal and for Jarring to supervise the conclusion of such an agreement. When Jarring told Bush that he refused this assignment, Bush claimed that his refusal came after a meeting he had had with Gromyko, and asked Malik to clarify this. Jarring, in fact, conceived of his mission as the establishment of peace according to Resolution 242 and not to an interim agreement or a partial settlement unrelated to it. His refusal to abide by US instructions was in fact a confirmation of his impartiality.

On 27 July at another meeting of the four great powers, Bush said that the US had the impression that both Egypt and Israel were desirous of concluding an interim agreement for opening the Suez Canal, that Sisco would proceed to the area for consultations on this matter and that the US would exert every effort so that it could be put into effect. Sisco failed to persuade Israel to accept a second stage for the evacuation of its forces after the interim agreement. In fact, all he could get from Israel was a withdrawal of seven to ten kilometres east of the Suez Canal so that the Canal would remain within range of its artillery. He therefore did not stop over in Cairo to inform us of the results of his visit but left this assignment to Bergus who on 22 August called on Mohammed Riad to inform him that Sisco had discussed, in three meetings with Israeli leaders, some of the principal points relating to the interim agreement, such as the relationship between it and the comprehensive settlement, Israel's navigation through the Canal, how the Canal would be serviced, an Egyptian presence east of the Canal, the extent of Israeli withdrawal, the means to supervise the implementation of the agreement and the nature of the ceasefire. Bergus added that Sisco did not submit official American proposals and that the US government felt, in view of obstacles still encountered, that it had not, as yet, reached the stage whereby it could enter into talks or discussions with Egypt for the conclusion of an agreement.

After I reported Bergus' message to him, Sadat despaired of the US position. When I was informed by Rogers that 1971 was a year of decision, Sadat reiterated this expression in his statements, convinced that the US was going to exert a real effort towards peace. However, he was soon to come up against an American retraction of its previous overtures coupled with a doubling of its arms supplies to Israel, when he announced to the People's Assembly that he proposed to open up the Suez Canal to prove Egypt's goodwill in seeking peace and to facilitate international navigation; yet if this was misunderstood as a quest for partial or separate solutions, we would not have reopened it, but would have flattened it. Meanwhile, Kissinger had succeeded in freezing US moves by obstructing Rogers' initiative and efforts.

In view of these developments, I felt a need to reassess the political situation, so I invited a number of Egyptian ambassadors to the major capitals to participate in this study. Among them were Dr Murad Ghalib, Ambassador to Moscow, Dr Mohammed Hassan al-Zayat, permanent representative to the UN (both of whom were to succeed me in my post), Hafez Ismail, Minister of State for Foreign Affairs, who was later to become President Sadat's adviser for national security, and Dr Ashraf Ghorbal, now Egyptian Ambassador in Washington. Our deliberations concluded that there was no hope of reaching a just and comprehensive solution for peace and that there was no other alternative but to resort to military action.

I had always maintained, in discussions with Nasser and General Fawzi, that the first stage in a military operation should be to reach and seize the passes in Sinai, which action would stir up the world's leaders into a serious quest for peace. From a military point of view, our control of the passes would put us in such a strong offensive and defensive situation as to allow our air force to use airports in the Suez Canal area, offering it a longer range than it had had in the past. Israel, on the other hand, would have nothing but the Sinai desert to fall back on, in the event of the Egyptian forces launching an attack from the passes, and this would force Israel, if it decided to hold to positions in an open desert, to use the whole of its army to stop the Egyptian army undertaking military operations in the direction of the frontier line, a situation which Israel could sustain neither militarily nor economically. It would further be left without forces sufficient to defend itself against possible attacks from the Syrian and Jordanian armies along the Eastern Front. The Israeli economy could not endure, for an extended period, the loss of large numbers of men joining the army.

At that time I happened to read a report prepared by General Ahmed Ismail, Chief of Intelligence (who later became Minister of War) in which he advocated a reactivation of the War of Attrition. I managed to convince him that while that was valid at a certain period, it was no longer, since Israel had exploited the ceasefire to consolidate the Bar-Lev Line of fortifications which would render our artillery fire against it less effective than in the past, while Israel could respond by raiding our heartland; in the present circumstances, only a major military success could re-activate the situation politically. To be more certain I contacted General Mohammed Sadek, the Minister of War; he objected strongly to a War of Attrition and maintained that our military operation should have as its objective the liberation of the whole of Sinai.

Sir Alec Douglas-Home, the British Foreign Secretary, arrived in Cairo at my invitation. During his talks with me he asserted the necessity of Israeli withdrawal to Egyptian international borders and said that Britain would participate in the arrangements for peace guarantees within the framework of the UN. I then left for New York to attend the General Assembly session and paid a return visit to Rogers in Washington. Rogers invited me to a business luncheon that was attended by Sisco. During our conversation he injected a new tone and I could not figure out then whether it was deliberate or a slip of the tongue. He said that President Sadat accepted the interim agreement and the partial settlement and that it was I who rejected them and insisted on a comprehensive settlement. I resented his remark as an improper attempt to intervene between Sadat and myself. I answered calmly, however, by referring him to an official statement made by Sadat on 16 September to the effect that he would accept a first stage in Israeli withdrawal only within the framework of a total withdrawal from Arab territories. I said that I assumed he already had knowledge of this statement. The statement, in fact, also maintained that the US had indulged in deceit and double-dealing by claiming that her contacts with us were still going on (which was not true) and that we accepted the partial solution (which was equally a misrepresentation of the situation). I felt that Rogers' words were discourteous to Sadat, since he was attributing to Sadat views opposite to his public statements. Sisco said heatedly: 'We want to make a hero of President Sadat.'

I maintained my calm and answered him: 'Mr Sisco, Sadat would not accept your making a hero of him; he will be quite satisfied instead to regain the occupied Arab territories.'

My impression was that Rogers was anxious, as a last attempt, to gain a point in his own favour by maintaining that his successful contacts did continue. I had made a statement the preceding day on TV, saying that no contact between us and the US had taken place for two months and twenty days, during which period the US had not informed us how it visualized the partial Israeli withdrawal taking place and how it could be related to the comprehensive settlement. I also said that Rogers had informed me, during his latest visit to Cairo, that he could not ask us for anything beyond what we had already done for the cause of peace and that he was disappointed in Israel's stance.

Senator Fulbright, Chairman of the Foreign Relations Committee of the Senate, had just submitted a project for a settlement to the Middle East problem, including the withdrawal of Israel from the Arab territories, the termination of the state of belligerency, the stationing of UN forces on both sides of the frontiers, the signing of a treaty between the US and Israel in which the US would guarantee Israeli frontiers prior to 5 June 1967, and the settlement of the Palestinian refugee problem. Israel, naturally, rejected this project while I conveyed to him, during a meeting the same day, that we were ready to accept it. He told me, however, that I should not depend on the Senate for its approval, only on his support. Fulbright was upset. He disclosed to me that the Senate had refused to earmark federal funds for social development projects in the State he represented, while Israel managed to induce the Senate to offer aid for similar projects in Israel.

My next appointment was with Kissinger but he said nothing of consequence during our meeting. A few days later, however, I was surprised to receive a message conveyed through one of Rockefeller's aides that Kissinger would like to meet me secretly in New York. Consequently, together with my wife, I received an invitation from Mr and Mrs David Rockefeller on 7 October for a dinner which was attended by Kissinger. After dinner, Kissinger and I moved to the study for talks. The moment we were alone, Kissinger asked me to keep this meeting secret since he wanted to talk to me away from the red tape of the State Department; he said that nobody would know of this meeting except President Nixon.

This was not an encouraging beginning. The only time in the past when I had come across a similar situation was with a newly independent, developing nation and, of course, I could not conceive that a major power like the US would resort to such behaviour. In fact I began to wonder whose words I should accept: those of the Secretary of State or of the Adviser on National Security, and how could any nation maintain confidence in the consistency of the policies of the US with such rivalry within the administration itself over decision making in international affairs.

Kissinger said that he had been careful to steer away from the Arab–Israeli question because of the fact that he was himself a Jew which could give the impression that he would favour Israel, that he was appreciative of our position towards the territories occupied by Israel, and that he had read my speech of the day before to the UN General Assembly and would like to study the problem of which he knew little so as to ensure his success when he intervened and so that he would not expose President Nixon to a failure in election year. Kissinger added that if he found himself unable to do anything or was uncertain of success he would tell me this in all frankness. I referred to the smear campaign alleging that there were divergent views between me and President Sadat regarding the kind of settlement we were seeking and stated that, while I was not concerned at such a campaign, my concern was over US–Egyptian relations which badly needed the building of bridges of confidence. I added that, unless we arrived at a comprehensive settlement for a durable peace, I was convinced we would be inviting a series of wars, and that supplying Israel with quantities of highly sophisticated US arms, far from imbuing a sense of security conducive to peace (the theory advocated by Kissinger himself), was in fact an invitation for fresh aggression against its neighbouring countries. If it was a question of security, I said, we had proposed solid guarantees for the security of the two sides. There was also the possibility of a limitation on arms in the area as part of the peace guarantees. So far as the US was concerned, I concluded, Sadat was anxious to build good relations with her – but not at the expense of liberating our territories. Kissinger asked me about the interim agreement relating to the opening of the Suez Canal and I explained to him the reasons for our rejection of it if it was separated from the essential issue. He replied that he understood this, then went on to project a strange theory which I could not accept: he said that if he was in our place he would not insist on the withdrawal of Israel in the first stage of this agreement for a substantial distance, for in that case the withdrawal line would turn into a permanent line. As regards tying the interim agreement to the comprehensive settlement, Kissinger thought it would be difficult. He would favour the duration of the interim agreement being one year rather than six months, in view of it being election year. He next asked me whether we were willing to conclude an agreement with Israel alone, without waiting for similar agreements to be signed with Syria and Jordan. I replied that a durable peace necessitated that agreements should be concluded with all concerned Arab countries, although this did not mean they should all be signed on the same day.

I left Kissinger with a sour taste in my mouth. To claim that he had not studied the issue was not truthful. It was equally obvious that he had adopted the Israeli position – concentrating on an interim agreement separate from the final solution, the necessity to separate Egypt from the other Arab countries in the final settlement and insisting that we should not demand a substantial withdrawal.

The following day Rogers repeated a proposal he had made to the General Assembly two days earlier, that Sisco should act as mediator in Israeli–Egyptian negotiations towards an interim agreement to open the Suez Canal which would be operative for a certain period, after which Israeli forces would withdraw to a line agreed upon (not Egypt's international borders). I asked Rogers: 'If, for argument's sake, we accept your proposal and Israel, after the first stage, refuses to withdraw, what should we do then?' He answered with amazing simplicity: 'In that case you can do what you like!'

On 9 October Jarring, referring to the present deadlock, said to Mohammed Riad: 'For the last four years I have felt that your Minister, Mahmoud Riad, was exaggerating when he talked about Israel's expansionist schemes and US alignment to Israel. Now I realize how true everything he told me was. The US does not want me to proceed with my mission, especially after I refused to undertake the interim agreement – unrelated, as it was, to the comprehensive settlement.'

With the deadlock that all political efforts reached in 1971, there was a necessity to reassess the situation so Sadat left for Moscow on 11 October and asked me to join him there. I left New York for Moscow and when I met him I mentioned that there was a feeling prevalent among the UN delegations that there was an Israeli–American rigidity, specifically due to Israel's conviction that Egypt lacked the will to fight and that Soviet policy preferred not resorting to force to liberate our territories. The following day, 12 October, we met with the Soviet leaders. Sadat referred to the US position and said that he welcomed Nixon's message of 6 July in which he asserted that the US would adopt a definite position, but then contacts between the US and Egypt had ceased until they were resumed with Foreign Minister Riad during his recent visit to the US, without Washington as yet defining its position as it had earlier promised.

When the ceasefire deadline ended on 7 March, he went on, the Soviet advice was that we continue our peaceful efforts, which we did against our better judgement. We had received Rogers in Cairo who had maintained that Egypt had done all it could and had listened to Sadat's proposition for a two-stage withdrawal. After that there was a complete *volte-face* on the part of the US. In their latest contact four days ago, Rogers had proposed to Riad that both Egypt and Israel send representatives to negotiate with Sisco for opening the Suez Canal and a limited withdrawal in Sinai, unrelated to the final solution. The question now was, what to do next.

The Soviet side, as was its custom, began to pose questions: What was the Saudi position? What was the position of the other Arab countries? Sadat assured them of Saudi support, and explained the extent of support extended by other Arab countries. Brezhnev wanted to hear from me the results of my latest contacts in the US, which I summarized to the meeting. At the conclusion of the session, Sadat said that at present Egypt felt the need to reopen the issue by a limited military operation; consequently he would request the Soviet Union to establish military parity between Egypt and Israel.

At the second session, Sadat concentrated on the shortage of some arms, which had led the armed forces in Egypt to raise questions about the reasons the Soviet Union had for failing to supply them. At the following meeting Brezhnev began to hint at US attempts to spoil relations between Egypt and the Soviet Union. He said: 'We have agreed that Resolution 242 will be the basis for resolving the problem. We are not against a staged-out settlement but that every stage should serve the interests of Egypt and not be a response to US–Israeli dictates, and that these stages should finally not include any measure that would obstruct the total implementation of the Security Council resolution for total withdrawal from other Arab territories. We find in the latest US proposals a wicked attempt to sow differences between Egypt and the other countries that use the Suez Canal.' Turning to the military situation, he said: 'We have heard we have not supplied you militarily with all your demands. This may be true, since the military never cease making demands. Yet the Egyptian army is at present a strong army with an air defence that Socialist countries of the Warsaw Pact do not possess. During the attrition war, especially in its last phase, Egyptian air defence succeeded in shooting down fourteen Israeli Phantoms. We therefore do not subscribe to any statement belittling your military capabilities. The question, however, as was posed today, is whether or not the Egyptian army is capable of undertaking major operations to liberate Sinai. I will ask Marshal Grechko to give his views on this.'

Grechko said: 'There are three factors that define the capability of any army: the number and quantity of its arms, the quality of the arms it possesses and, finally, its morale. I would like to point out that you have superiority over Israel in the number of your soldiers and in its arms.' He went on to read from a paper in front of him, drawing comparisons between the power of Israel and the combined power of Egypt and Syria. He indicated an Arab superiority of two to one in numbers and quantity of arms, especially in tanks, artillery and air-defence missiles. As regards aircraft, he indicated that they were not so decisive, but that the Arabs maintained a superiority in the number of aircraft of almost two to one. The US Phantom, he indicated, can carry seven tons of bombs but, when it does, its speed is limited to 900 kilometres an hour. The Vietnam experiment proved the possibility of shooting down a Phantom carrying its full load by a MiG, consequently the US pilot was forced to release his load before he reached his target so that he could gain more speed if intercepted by a Vietnamese MiG. With regard to naval arms, Egypt had an overwhelming superiority over Israel. In engineering equipment, Egypt had sufficient to erect nine bridges over the Suez Canal. Egypt had recently received all apparatus needed for opening gaps in the minefields, also electronic jamming battalions.

General Sadek, while confirming the figures in general terms given by Grechko, raised some points relating to the inefficiency of some of the arms supplied as compared to their US counterpart, especially the Soviet tank 34 and the short range of the MiG compared with the Mirage or the Phantom.

Brezhnev then said that in view of the figures given by Marshal Grechko, it was obvious that we had gone a long way in consolidating the Egyptian army, and consequently he did not approve of the claim that Egypt was not on a par with the Israeli army. He was concerned about what he had heard then of the weakness of the Egyptian forces because if such talk spread among army personnel, the army would never be in a position to fight, however many arms it received. Army men should be convinced that skill in the use of arms was the secret of success. However, he felt it was the Soviet Union's duty to make good any shortages. 'In any case,' he continued, 'you should pursue your political efforts and continue the contacts with Nixon. While I do not subscribe to the feeling of despair in the contacts that are going on at present, I would like to emphasize the necessity of the Arab countries standing as one if they are to regain their rights. In our coming meeting with Nixon we will discuss both Vietnam and the Middle East. The important thing, in the meanwhile, is to maintain your steadfastness and not make concessions.' He added that Egypt now had 9,500 Soviet military experts to train the Egyptian forces, but it was still essential to have a complete plan for civil defence in which the whole populace would participate.

He then announced the decision to supply Egypt with arms which, he said, would have a decisive effect on what was going on. 'You will be supplied with long-range Tu. aeroplanes, equipped with rockets. I request, however, that you do not refer to it as a deterrent and do not disclose in any way the fact that we have supplied you with them. You will also be supplied in the year 1971/2 with 100 MiG-21s and Sokhois, in addition to a MiG-23 squadron which will reach you in the second half of next year. You will also be supplied with a 180-millimetre artillery regiment with a range of 42 kilometres in addition to 240-millimetre mortars. You will also receive more crossing equipment, including three new bridges, and more apparatus for opening gaps.' The size of the deal agreed by the Soviet Union and announced by Brezhnev was colossal and of a value that amounted to $288 million.

The Soviet position had never been more clear or outright than in this visit. They had advised a continuation of our political efforts; a unity of Arab action without reference to progressive or reactionary governments while US policy resisted all attempts at Arab unity and worked against countries that it considered 'radical', like Egypt and Syria; they counselled us not to make any further concessions; and finally, what was of greatest moment and significance, the assessment of Marshal Grechko of the military situation. At the same time they refrained from sharing in the responsibility of a decision for war which demanded, in their view, that Egypt have the will to fight. I felt, after listening to Grechko's report, that our decision in favour of war should not be delayed any further, and I said as much to Sadat on our way back to Egypt.

A few days after our return to Cairo, Tito arrived on 20 October for a one-day visit, on his way to the US for talks with Nixon. In our talks with him, he mentioned that he would be in Washington on the following Tuesday (26 October) and was anxious to become acquainted with our views before that meeting. He added that when he had talked with Nixon during his recent visit to Belgrade, the main topic had been his concern over the Soviet presence both in Egypt and in the area in general. As a solution, Tito advised Nixon to exert pressure on Israel to withdraw from the occupied territories. Nixon answered that he could not. Tito said: 'Then you must expect an increasing Soviet presence in Egypt and the whole area, since Israel was directly responsible for this presence.'

Sadat answered that American anxiety over the Soviet presence had also been conveyed to him by Rogers, who had insinuated that any Soviet presence should be removed from Egypt and the area as a condition of a comprehensive settlement. Sadat had answered him that the presence of the Soviet fleet in the Mediterranean was not Egypt's concern since the US also had a fleet there. Egypt offered the Soviets facilities in Egyptian ports in return for their support but they did not maintain bases. 'I mentioned to Rogers,' he continued, 'that we have Soviet military units attached to SAM-3 missiles but these are not stationed along the front but in the heartland of Egypt, to offset Israeli raids on our industrial establishments and civilian population. Once a peaceful settlement is established, all Soviet units in Egypt will be withdrawn.'

Sadat went on to say that he had received a message from Washington on 6 July asserting that the US henceforth would not confine its role to that of postman but would submit a working paper to the two sides. The message next posed a number of questions. ' "Did the Soviet–Egyptian treaty impose any restriction on Egypt's political movement?" My answer, of course, was in the negative. Another question was: "Is Egypt ready to resume diplomatic relations with the US after the first stage of Israeli withdrawal?" I answered: yes. A third question concerned the situation after the first stage of a settlement with Egypt: "Will the Soviet units withdraw from Egypt?" I answered that they would withdraw as soon as we were assured of a solution. The US emissary answered that in the light of these answers the US government would work for the materialization of the initiative. On 4 February, I declared for opening the Canal. Sisco subsequently visited Israel and conducted talks there, but he did not contact us thereafter, and no working paper was presented, while the US was spreading the news that an agreement was about to be concluded with us, which was not true. I therefore announced in a public speech on 16 September that the US had retracted on its promise. Finally, before my departure for Moscow, the Americans contacted me in Cairo and Riad in New York to offer the conclusion of an agreement for opening the Suez Canal, unrelated to the problem of Israeli aggression and the total solution.' Tito then advised strongly against any partition of the solution and never to allow Israel to enjoy the fruits of its aggression. Before he concluded, he referred to a talk he had had with Brezhnev in which the Soviet leader said the Soviets had been reluctant at first to send experts to Egypt, but had finally to agree in view of Egypt's pressing need to rebuild its armed forces. The combat units were dispatched at Nasser's insistence to offset Israeli air raids deep into Egypt and that, while the US was making a big issue of the Soviet presence Brezhnev was expressing his readiness to withdraw all Soviet units and experts from Egypt the moment a settlement materialized, and that included Israel's withdrawal. Tito added that Brezhnev had informed him of this with the knowledge that he would relay it to Nixon. And so, while Rogers announced during his visit to Cairo that the Soviet presence prevented the US from making a serious move towards peace, this argument was invalidated by the Soviet offer – yet we failed to notice any US reaction.

On 20 November Sadat delivered a speech to the People's Assembly in which he welcomed the support received from the Soviet Union and said that the US had three objectives in the area: the ousting of the Soviet Union, the isolation of Egypt from the rest of the Arab world and the liquidation of the Socialist experiment in Egypt. He added that we could not accept the no–peace no–war situation indefinitely and that we would make our decision in the proper time, the proper circumstances and in the proper way.

On 5 November four African Presidents, Leopold Senghor of Senegal, Ahmado Ahigo of the Cameroons, Yacob Juan of Nigeria and Joseph Mobutu of Zaire, arrived in Cairo as representatives of a committee of ten African presidents established by the most recent African Summit which had met at Addis Ababa on 22 June to intercede for a total Israeli withdrawal from the occupied Arab territories and in support of Jarring's mission. The four expressed complete conviction in the strength and justice of our position. When Sadat told them we would raise the issue again at the UN General Assembly at the end of November, they requested that this be postponed until December, since they were to visit Israel, and Sadat agreed. The four Presidents then proceeded to Israel, had talks with Golda Meir and returned to Cairo once again on 23 November, with a clear picture of Israeli expansionist schemes and colonialist policies. From that time, they have lent total support to all UN or non-aligned resolutions condemning Israel.

I was in New York on 27 November to raise the issue once again at the General Assembly. My speech was a comprehensive review of Israeli violations and aggressions in the area, its persistent rejection of all peaceful solutions, and the role of the US in supporting Israeli occupation of Arab territories. The Israeli representative took the floor promptly after me to comment on my speech by saying that Egypt wanted to persuade the UN to adopt a resolution unacceptable to Israel in order to use it as a pretext for war. This was a correct assumption on his part.

The resolution, unlike the one of the previous year, had the support of West European countries and was passed by a majority of seventy-nine votes, while thirty-six countries abstained, among them seven who felt that it did not denounce Israel sufficiently. The countries who voted against it were six Central American countries plus Israel. The US, in view of the overwhelming support of West European countries, could not help but abstain, using the argument that the resolution was unbalanced. Its position was the subject of severe criticism since the resolution in fact projected all its previous stands. The resolution which was adopted on 13 December represented a far-reaching political defeat for Israel, which became completely isolated in the international arena, and a severe blow to the US which lost its leading role even among its allies in Western Europe. It was equally an international document, giving licence to Egypt to move militarily to liberate its territories. The text of the resolution expressed concern 'at the continuation of Israel's occupation of the Arab territories since 5 June 1967', reaffirmed 'that the acquisition of territories by force is inadmissible and that, consequently, territories thus occupied must be restored . . .', and demanded finally the 'withdrawal of Israeli armed forces from territories occupied in the recent conflict'.

After the adoption of the resolution, Rogers contacted me from Washington to urge a resumption of talks with Jarring and said that he had conveyed the same message to Abba Eban. It was obvious, however, that Jarring could not proceed before securing a positive answer from Israel to his proposals of 8 February. Jarring had informed us accordingly before proceeding to Moscow. Consequently Rogers' communication was of a purely formal nature.

Israel, of course, continued to reject the General Assembly resolution to respond favourably to Jarring. The Soviets, meanwhile, informed the US in November of their approval for a final settlement that would be undertaken in two stages, the first stage to include Egypt opening up the Suez Canal for a substantial withdrawal of Israeli forces, and the second, Israeli withdrawal to 4 June positions on all Arab fronts in return for peace guarantees. The USSR had further expressed their readiness to withdraw all their experts and military advisers from Egypt the moment a comprehensive peaceful settlement was achieved. The Soviets informed us of this step on their part to convince us that their moves for a settlement were continuing. The US ignored the Soviet proposal. It was approaching an election year in which Nixon was anxious to win Jewish votes

On my return to Cairo I mentioned at a press conference that the rejection by Israel of General Assembly resolutions left us no option but the liberation of all Arab territories occupied by force.

I briefed Sadat on the results of my recent talks with Rogers, that there was no progress towards peace, that Mrs Meir had managed to secure a promise from Nixon for more Phantoms, and that with the approach of an election year we should expect further support for Israel and responses to its demands, while there was speculation that Rogers' role had been terminated completely.

And so the situation early in 1972 was such that Sadat felt that all the hopes he had pinned a year before on the US were crumbling. He charged me to proceed to the Arab Gulf countries to urge their immediate response to some economic demands and to the People's Republic of China to confer with Chou En-lai. However, while in the Arab Emirates I received a cable from him to return, as he had decided to form a new government. I returned and was appointed adviser to the President on foreign affairs. I stayed in this post for only six uneventful months.

12

Sadat Evicts the Soviet Experts

Although Nixon won the 1968 election without the Jewish vote, he was anxious during his election campaign for a second term to win the American Jews to his side and consequently issued directives to the State Department to freeze all its efforts and initiatives in the Middle East, and on 2 February concluded a note of understanding with Israel, promising to supply it with forty-two Phantoms and eighty-two Skyhawks. The seriousness of this deal lay in the fact that it came at a time when a total lull had ruled the Arab fronts for almost a year and a half. More serious still was an American pledge, contained in the same note, that the US would not undertake any new political initiatives in the Middle East without prior discussion with Israel.

With this unprecedented pledge, the US position in the Middle East became a hostage to Israeli policy and the US forfeited its freedom of movement. Only then did Israel accept a new US proposal for proximity talks with Egypt under the supervision of Sisco which excluded Jarring and the Soviet Union. When Sadat rejected the talks being confined to the Suez Canal, all serious attempts towards peace ceased. And so Nixon did not offer to resolve the Arab–Israeli conflict, confining himself to projecting the strife as a US–Soviet confrontation and ignoring the Soviet pledge to withdraw their personnel once a satisfactory settlement was obtained. Nixon must have had elections on his mind when, in an address to Congress on 9 February, he launched a vehement attack on the Soviet Union. He said: 'The Soviet Union's effort to use the Arab–Israeli conflict to perpetuate and expand its own military position in Egypt has been a matter of concern to the US. The Soviet Union has taken advantage of Egypt's increasing dependence on Soviet military supplies to gain the use of naval and air facilities in Egypt. This has serious implications for the stability of the balance of power regionally and globally. We hope the Soviet Union understands that it can serve this interest [of avoiding a major conflict in the Middle East] best by restraint in its arms supply, refraining from the use of the dispute to enhance its military position . . .'

The Chinese government, in the meanwhile, intimated that it expected my visit in February, although I was no longer Foreign Minister; however, the visit was postponed until March when Nixon announced that he would visit China in the second half of February.

I arrived in Peking on 22 March, and was received with much fanfare. At the airport, besides the leaders of the country, there were thousands of young men and women cheering and carrying the flags of the two countries. This was, in fact, owing to the close relations that bound the Chinese leaders, especially Chou En-lai, to Nasser since their first meeting at Bandung in 1955. Chou En-lai had visited Egypt twice before the Israeli aggression and was aware of the influence Nasser enjoyed in the non-aligned countries, the Arab world and Africa, and used to listen attentively to my explanation of conditions in Africa. When the Israeli aggression took place in June 1967, China stood staunchly at our side and extended military and economic assistance and when, during the Cultural Revolution, China withdrew its ambassadors from nearly all capitals of the world, Cairo remained the only capital where it maintained an ambassador.

My visit was the first attempt to explore new possibilities of Chinese support. I was mainly concerned about military support and, although China was in no position to supply us with modern aircraft, it could supply us with various ammunition and other kinds of arms which China was manufacturing locally.

I explained to Chou En-lai the political situation and our sense of futility after seeking for just and peaceful solutions, which left us with the only alternative, war. I told him that huge military aid by the US to Israel made our military needs increase proportionately, especially for those types of arms which were necessary for the success of our military operation. We did not need military superiority over Israel, only military parity. The snag was, however, the type of aircraft the Soviets were supplying us with. He asked me whether the Soviets had supplied us with MiG-23s. I shook my head, saying that they had another, more developed aircraft, namely the MiG-25 which was used in Egypt exclusively by Soviet pilots for reconnaissance purposes over Israeli positions in Sinai, and that this aircraft had proved its superiority to the Phantom. I explained to him the size and nature of the US arms supplies to Israel which were aimed at preventing Egypt from attempting to liberate its territories; Soviet arms, despite the fact that they had considerably raised our military power, did not compare with US arms supplies to Israel, forcing us to rely on our own potentialities, especially if we succeeded in coordinating with both Syria and Libya during the battle.

Chou En-lai asked me what I expected from the forthcoming talks between Nixon and Brezhnev in Moscow in May. I replied that there was a fundamental understanding to prevent a military confrontation between the two in our region. At the same time the US had declared that it would not exert any pressure on Israel, especially during the present election year. However, we did not expect the Soviets to sell the Arabs to the United States, for they would thereby endanger their presence and influence in the whole of the Arab world. Consequently, we entertained no hope of Nixon and Brezhnev reaching a solution to the Middle East crisis during that meeting.

Chou En-lai also inquired about the recent internal troubles in Egypt (he was referring to the university students' demonstrations) and I answered that there was a great feeling of frustration over the continuation of Israeli occupation of our territories without our being able to confront it militarily. Symptoms of impatience were strongest and most vocal among university students.

Chou En-lai said: 'Both the US and the Soviet Union are trying to control the Middle East area. The best way you can confront this is by a further consolidation of Arab and Palestinian action so that neither the two powers nor either one of them could tear the Arab world apart and sow seeds of friction among its countries. When Nixon was here we felt that he was strongly aligned to Israel and that he would not undertake any change in his policy *vis-à-vis* direct negotiation from the vantage point of Arab weakness which, of course, will allow Israel to dictate its conditions on Egypt and the Arabs in general. We believe that your confrontation with Israel does not depend solely on the quantities or types of arms that each side possesses. In fact, if you are going to wait until a military parity between you and Israel prevails, this may mean that Israeli occupation of Sinai, the Golan and the West Bank will continue for many years. We were in favour of the War of Attrition you waged against Israel. I do not think that you had parity with Israel at the time, but in the end you were able to force the US to come out with ideas for a comprehensive settlement. Now you are negotiating in an atmosphere of complete passivity on the war front, waiting for new US efforts and new Soviet arms. This is not a situation in your favour. The forthcoming talks between Nixon and Brezhnev will be a bargaining process between the two powers, although I personally doubt that the Soviet Union will cede their interests in the Middle East, yet the Middle East crisis will be related to other problems in Asia and Europe which may weaken Soviet support for the Arab countries. The restoration of territories occupied by Israel will not be accomplished except by military force; any other avenue will entail concessions at the expense of your national independence; therefore do not depend for military action on the Soviet Union. Our experience in China proves this, nor are you without your own experiences in this direction. Since we do not conceive the possibility of the emergence of one Arab country in your area, which would be the ideal arrangement to resist Israeli–US invasion, we feel that unity of Arab action will be a greater help to you than depending on Soviet assistance. The Soviets have been supplying you with military assistance for the last five years, yet they tell you now that the aircraft you need are not available, at a time when they have amassed at our borders a million soldiers equipped with missiles and long-range aircraft which they should have supplied to you to liberate your territories and to the Vietnamese people to resist US imperialism.' He referred once again to the forthcoming Nixon–Brezhnev talks, mentioning that the Soviets might, while bargaining with the Americans, concede some of their positions as they had done over the Berlin problem at the expense of the German Democratic Republic. China would continue to stand by Egypt and to support her, and he expressed willingness to extend all possible military assistance, although China did not produce all the arms that we needed, and suggested that a military delegation from one country visit the other to study this matter in detail.

The following day at a dinner party given by the Egyptian

Ambassador in my honour, Chou En-lai made a speech in which he said that no victory could be achieved at the negotiating table unless it had first been achieved by fighters in the field of war, and that only military victory can force the enemy to withdraw.

The Chinese position on the Middle East issue was that a mistake had been committed originally, namely the establishment of the State of Israel, and that the Palestinians were the only people entitled to establish a State on their own land. Consequently China had rejected Resolution 242 and, when they joined the UN, consistently refused to subscribe to any resolution that referred to it.

When I returned to Cairo, relations with the Soviet Union had grown strained because of delay in the delivery of certain arms that had already been contracted for during Sadat's visit in October 1971. Sadat was further incensed when he suggested paying a visit to Moscow that same month (December), to be told that the visit could take place on 1 February. Sadat proceeded to Moscow on the date suggested by the Soviets in order to impress on them that the situation in the area did not allow for any delay and to demand that the Soviet Union promptly deliver the arms already contracted for. Brezhnev promised to do so and stated that the 100 MiG-21s would reach Egypt before the end of 1972. He also promised the delivery of twenty bombers Tu.2 and 200 tanks 62, and stated that measures would be taken to manufacture the MiG MF completely in Egypt in 1979. Brezhnev referred to his forthcoming talks with Nixon in May and promised that he would try then to reach a decisive solution.

One month after that visit, the Soviet Ambassador in Cairo communicated a message to Sadat from the Soviet leaders, inviting him to Moscow again on 27 April. The reason, as stated by the Ambassador, was to consult over all the details relating to a peaceful solution before the arrival of Nixon. Sadat accepted the invitation and told the Soviet side that the acceptable solution was the one previously handed to Rogers during his visit to Cairo, emphasizing the necessity of relating the first stage (which included the opening up of the Suez Canal) to the final stage, Israeli withdrawal from all Sinai. He also confirmed three points: the non-acceptability of any US proposal for a limitation of arms until after the resolution of the crisis, no concessions with regard to the 4 June 1967 borderlines and finally the non-acceptability of the no-war no-peace condition.

Brezhnev said that the Soviet Union would strive to reach an agreement with Nixon but it was of the opinion that Nixon could not exert pressure on Israel in an election year. It would be better therefore to reach an agreement with him which would not be implemented before 1973, after his re-election. An arrangement of this sort demanded that we facilitate this undertaking by refraining from military operations.

Sadat, who had been amazed at his sudden invitation to Moscow, was now aware that its purpose was to dissuade him from initiating hostilities before the end of 1972. He agreed to this, but demanded that he be supplied with all Egypt's needs in arms and ammunition before the end of October of the same year so that he would be in a better military position when Nixon was re-elected in November.

Sadat returned to Cairo on 10 May following his longest visit to the Soviet Union. On 14 May Marshal Grechko arrived with contracts for the arms agreed upon: 200 Tanks 62, sixteen Sokhoi 17, eight SAM-3 battalions and all the required ammunition. Half of this was to be delivered during 1972, the rest during 1973. This was a hopeful gesture by the Soviet Union and encouraged Sadat to decorate Grechko and his aides. In the course of all these contacts, the Soviet Union still maintained that attention should be given to a peaceful settlement and military action be postponed until the end of 1972, hoping that some progress would be achieved, while Egypt was convinced that no such progress would be forthcoming, either then or after the re-election of Nixon. The Soviet Union, on the other hand, possessed no leverage to pressure Nixon into changing his policy. As a matter of fact, before his arrival in Moscow, Nixon sought to acquire greater negotiating power by paying a visit to Peking in February, establishing with China a rapprochement which was greatly disturbing to the Soviet Union. He was also keen to display US military power during his visit by concentrated overkill raids in Vietnam and by mining the waters of Haifung port, to prevent the entry of Soviet ships. This last measure was a direct blow at the Soviet Union and many observers expected the Soviet Union to postpone the visit. The Soviet Union, which had few if any winning cards, welcomed the visit of Nixon in the hope that détente would, in the long run, be more beneficial to its interests. As regards the Middle East, they felt that an understanding at the Summit would constitute a recognition by the US that the Soviet Union had interests in the area.

During the meeting the two parties agreed over eight principles which were drawn up by Gromyko and Kissinger as a basis for a solution to the Middle East issue. These were that the settlement should be comprehensive, although it could be implemented in stages; that the Israeli forces withdraw from territories (using the English version of the Security Council resolution) occupied in 1967; that any border changes should be with the consent of the concerned parties; that security guarantees might include demilitarized zones and the presence of UN forces in Sharm el-Sheikh with international guarantees in which both the US and the Soviet Union would participate; the termination of the state of belligerency, free navigation in international waters, recognition of the independence of all countries of the area including Israel, and finally the problem of refugees.

On 29 May, a joint statement was released which contained a number of principles the two parties subscribed to, including their support of Resolution 242 and Jarring's mission. The communiqué also mentioned that a resolution of the Arab–Israeli conflict would lead to a military relaxation in the area.

When I received this statement I could discover no new elements in the principles announced; they were either a repetition of clauses in Resolution 242 or proposals we had previously agreed to – and some we had proposed ourselves, for instance, international guarantees. Israel, however, considered the results of the meeting to be in its favour inasmuch as they did not stipulate explicitly that withdrawal should be to 4 June positions, and consequently we were once again at the same position we had been in for five years: principles that are accepted but differences in the interpretation of certain words they contain.

On 6 June, the Soviet Ambassador in Cairo handed a letter from Moscow to President Sadat about the summit meeting, the gist of which was that the position of the US had not changed. Sadat, however, was more anxious to receive the dates of delivery of arms promised for 1972, so he sent General Sadek, his Minister of War, to Moscow on 8 June; he was assured by Marshal Grechko that Egypt would receive all the arms it needed for winning the battle. On the other hand, Brezhnev told him that Israel was putting forward unacceptable solutions and that

Moscow would not reach an agreement with Washington at the expense of Egypt.

Upon his return, Sadek conveyed his impression that the Soviet Union was trying to keep things under control and would not agree to any Egyptian military action until November 1972, and that it would continue to delay the delivery of arms, in the hope of reaching a peaceful solution in the meantime.

Sadat waited for a message from the Soviet Union over the arms promised and the dates of their arrival to no avail, until he decided in the first week of July to terminate the work of Soviet experts in Egypt, and informed the Minister of War accordingly on 8 July. The Soviet Ambassador requested a meeting with Sadat which was fixed for the following day. The Ambassador conveyed Moscow's reply to Sadat's communication; but it dealt exclusively with the political situation without touching on what Sadat was most anxious to learn, namely arms deliveries. Sadat then informed the Ambassador of his decision to terminate the work of Soviet experts and to put Soviet military units under the command of the Egyptian army; if this was not acceptable to the Soviet Union, they could also leave Egypt before 17 July.

The Ambassador was taken aback. At first, he had the impression that the matter was open to debate, then he realized that the decision was final and that he was being asked to convey it to Moscow and to put it into effect. In order to soften the effect of the decision, Sadat sent the Prime Minister, Aziz Sidky, to Moscow with a suggestion that a joint communiqué be issued, expressing Egyptian gratitude to the Soviet Union on the occasion of the termination of the work of its experts in Egypt; but Brezhnev refused to subscribe to such a statement and said that Egypt could handle this situation in any way it saw fit, but alone.

One of the expected consequences of this resolution was the creation of tension in Egyptian–Soviet relations, since the ousting of Soviet experts was a US objective overtly declared by Kissinger since 1970 and referred to by Rogers in his talks in Cairo in 1971. The removal of the Soviet experts in such an abrupt manner constituted as great a political defeat to the Soviet Union as it was a political gain to the US. It was inevitable that, as a result, we should expect a further delay in Soviet military supplies and in payment facilities which we used to receive in the past. The military loss lay in the withdrawal of Soviet military units which extended support to Egyptian air defence in the heartland of Egypt, added to 100 Soviet pilots who flew the MiGs, a number of new missile battalions, and those who manned the sophisticated electronic equipment which the Soviets considered of a highly secret nature and consequently did not deliver to the Egyptian army. There were also the MiG-25s which were flown by Soviet pilots and performed reconnaissance flights over Israeli positions in Sinai. All these military units, which numbered over 6,000, together with 2,000 experts (8,000 personnel, not counting their families) did withdraw – a matter which definitely left a serious gap in our air defence and our military power.

In my own assessment, the factors that contributed to this decision were Soviet procrastination on one side and US extravagance in promises made to Sadat. The Soviets were apprehensive of our resorting to military action, although they were quite convinced that the US would never move towards complete implementation of Resolution 242. Yet they were anxious to avoid any possibility of a confrontation with the US in the area. Talks with Nixon in May drove the Soviet Union into the field of international bargaining where issues other than the Middle East were of a more pressing nature to the Soviets. Though there was unanimity over the impossibility of Moscow forgoing its support to the Arab countries' right to restore their occupied territories, yet delay in helping them to accomplish this end, after five years of occupation, represented to Cairo a kind of backing down on this undertaking. Nothing would have dispelled this misapprehension except the immediate delivery of the arms needed and a timetable for their delivery.

The absence of a prior understanding between Egypt and the US over the termination of the Soviet presence made the US disregard this serious decision on the part of Sadat and in the process ignore all previous statements made by its administration. There was misapprehension in the minds of many political observers that once the Soviet presence was terminated, Nixon would move promptly towards a just and peaceful settlement. The fact was that the US turned its back on Egypt as if the measure adopted was of no concern to it. (A friend of mine asked Kissinger, after he was relieved of his job as Secretary of State, about the negative attitude of the US to Sadat's ousting of the Soviets. Kissinger answered that his negative attitude was the only logical one in the circumstances; there was no morality in politics and it was not the job of the US to volunteer to pay for something that was given to it gratis.) Egypt failed to reap any political gains, while it forfeited military advantages it had possessed.

This decision was undertaken in the middle of an election year, during which Nixon was seeking the Jewish vote; and this militated against the possibility of our gaining political advantage from the US administration.

There is equally an aspect of this situation which I have to touch upon in the light of my past experience of the Soviet scene and Soviet thinking. I believe that the Soviets, after being informed of Sadat's decision on 8 July, reached a definite posture before the arrival of the Egyptian Prime Minister. It should be recalled that when Nasser informed the Soviets of his approval of Rogers' initiative in 1970, they objected to Egypt going along with an American move. It was obvious, later, that their objection was to the form and not the essence: the form reflected on their being a major power, but in essence they approved Nasser's acceptance because it confirmed their preference for a peaceful solution. When the Egyptian Prime Minister arrived in Moscow, their dissatisfaction was over the manner in which they had been expelled from Egypt. As regards the matter itself, I feel, deep in their heart they must have welcomed it, as witness the speed with which it was implemented, leaving the country before the deadline fixed by Sadat. The reason was that Nasser had succeeded, throughout the preceding few years, in convincing them to participate with combative units and pilots. Nasser, however, saw that such an involvement in the Egyptian hinterland would allow Egyptian pilots to undertake offensive operations over the front. It also meant to him that the weight of the Soviet Union was on his side. The Soviets, on the other hand, were hopeful that their mere military presence would constitute a pressure on both Israel and the US to accept a peaceful solution, which was not achieved but, instead, led to an escalation of the US position. The Soviets were in fact very reluctant to maintain their military presence, once the war was going to erupt, with all the obligations it would entail on their pilots and air-defence units. They therefore felt relieved when Sadat released them from these obligations. That, in my opinion, is the reason why the Soviet Union continued, after the departure of its experts and units, to support Egypt militarily – in fact, it supplied Egypt with more developed arms than were made available earlier, and continued to do so after the October War of 1973.

I stayed in my job as political affairs adviser to the President for six months when Sadat conveyed to me that he would like to nominate me for the post of Secretary-General of the Arab League, in view of my long years of work in the Arab field and the many personal contacts I had with nearly all Arab leaders and because of the need for Arab coordination of policies.

The Arab League Council met on 1 June, when I was elected Secretary-General of the League. When I met Sadat, on 11 June, he informed me that he would continue to prepare for the battle and expected me to exert efforts within the Arab League to achieve a maximum of support and Arab solidarity.

The first problem I was faced with in my new post was the escalating tension in relations between the PLO and the Lebanese authorities. The agreement concluded in 1969 between the two parties under my supervision was exposed to violations from both sides, endangering the solidarity of the Eastern Front. I proceeded to Beirut on 28 June, and conferred with President Faranjia. His complaint was directed towards the presence of armed Palestinian elements in Beirut and other Lebanese cities, endangering internal security. The fact that some Palestinian groups were undertaking guerrilla operations against Israel from Lebanese territories exposed Lebanese villages and towns to Israeli reprisals, and Lebanon was in no position to confront these Israeli attacks. He therefore demanded that the Palestinian resistance movement consider the circumstances of Lebanon and refrain from endangering its internal security or giving Israel any justification for waging reprisal attacks.

When I met Yasser Arafat, Chairman of the PLO, he assured me that the Palestinian commandos did not fire from inside Lebanese territory, but infiltrated into Israel from all positions, so that both Israel and the rest of the world would be aware that the Palestinians would continue their struggle until they regained their right to establish their own State.

Despite these conflicting attitudes, I managed to bring the two parties together on the understanding that the Cairo Agreement should be maintained and respected. I knew, however, that troubles would arise once more and that this problem would not be solved until the Palestinian question itself was solved.

The situation relating to the Eastern Front was extremely vulnerable. The Palestinian resistance movement was still at odds with King Hussein. Syria, which supported the Palestinians, was in conflict with both Jordan and Lebanon. In order to increase the rate of Jewish immigration, Israel had decided that it was in need of 400 million cubic metres of water by 1980, and started casting greedy eyes on the River Litani in South Lebanon. Consequently my constant cry in Lebanon and other Arab States was that Israel would try in the near future to control South Lebanon.

On 1 July, I toured the Arab countries of the Maghreb, with the objective of studying their contribution to the coming battle. I heard grave doubts raised over Egypt's seriousness in under-taking any major military operation to liberate its occupied terri-tories. They referred to the many Egyptian statements, including Sadat's about 1971 being the decisive year. In the meanwhile Washington was spreading rumours about a political agreement being under discussion with Egypt which, although untrue, created confusion and raised doubts in Arab capitals.

I proceeded to Arab capitals where I would reassure them that the battle was approaching, and that every Arab country should participate in consolidating mainly the Eastern Front, empha-sizing that participation should not be arbitrary or casual, but organized. My tour led me to the conviction that efforts should be exerted to organize Arab action, and the importance of con-tinuous consultations among the Heads of Arab States so that every one of them would feel a personal share in making deci-sions. Consequently, when the Arab League convened on 1 September, I proposed the formation of a committee comprising Ministers of Foreign Affairs and Defence to work out a plan for joint Arab action. The Committee met in Kuwait on 15 November when it was decided that a meeting of Arab Chiefs of Staff should take place in Cairo on 12 December, to decide on the military assistance that each Arab country could offer to the forthcoming battle. At the meeting of Arab Chiefs of Staff, both Saudi Arabia and Kuwait pledged that each would offer a squadron of Lightning aeroplanes (a British fighter-bomber with a longer range than the MiG); Libya agreed to supply Egypt with two squadrons of Mirage aeroplanes. It was also agreed to establish an Arab industry for military production. A study from the Military Assistant Secretary of the Arab League surmised that the capital sum needed for the Arab industry for military production would range from £400 million to £1,200 million, according to the targets to be decided upon. This project was finally to materialize with joint capital from Egypt, Saudi Arabia, Kuwait and Qatar.

A meeting of the Arab Defence Council in Cairo at the end of January 1973, comprising Ministers of Foreign Affairs and Defence, had succeeded in deepening the sense of collective responsibility in all Arab countries. Such a total mobilization of efforts necessitated the settlement of inter-Arab differences. It was also decided that operations should be conducted along three fronts: the Northern Front with Syrian forces, the Eastern Front with the Jordanian army and the Western Front with the Egyptian Army. Any other Arab forces could join any of these three fronts. All the fronts would operate under a supreme commander, General Ahmed Ismail, the Egyptian Minister of War. In addition to previous commitments by Saudi Arabia and Libya, Iraq pledged five squadrons of MiG-17s, MiG-21s, Hawker Hunters and Tu.16s. Algeria pledged four squadrons of MiG-17s and MiG-21s, Morocco a squadron of F.5s. So the Arab countries had promised to supply both Egypt and Syria with a total of fourteen squadrons, plus armoured and mechanized divisions, a level of support that had not been achieved before. Saudi Arabia, the Emirates and Libya each pledged a squadron in 1974.

A resolution was issued by the Arab Defence Council charging that General Ahmed Ismail should follow up the implementation of these resolutions. I had to attend to the irritating problems of inter-Arab differences that arose every now and then and try to contain them promptly, together with the perpetual task of settling old differences.

In May 1973, the confrontation between the Palestinian resistance and the Lebanese army flared up again. I was in Lebanon for four days, in round-the-clock meetings with leaders of the two sides; I then proceeded to Damascus for a meeting with President al-Assad who shared my concern for containing any conflict that could obstruct military preparations for the battle against Israel. I did not leave Beirut until we had succeeded in drawing up complementary agreements to the Cairo Agreement, with which we managed to contain the crisis for the time being.

All through that period I kept in close touch with Sadat, in order to liaise between Cairo and the other Arab capitals. On 26 May, while flying with him to Cairo from a meeting of the African Summit in Addis Ababa I mentioned that a continuation of political discord between Egypt and Syria on one side and King Hussein on the other would hinder the required coordination. The differences at the time were caused by a project of King Hussein, for the establishment of a united kingdom, comprising Jordan and the West Bank after its liberation, which was adamantly rejected by both the PLO and most other Arab countries. Sadat was determined to make use of all available Arab force, most specifically Syria and Jordan. I proceeded to Damascus and had a meeting with Assad on 31 May. I found in him a strong resolution for resuming the war. I therefore concentrated on the necessity of making use of the Jordanian army in the forthcoming battle, mentioning that it should not rest only on the Egyptian and Syrian forces but that Jordan should participate in it. The problem, however, lay in the necessity of putting an end to the media campaigns against King Hussein, so as to reach a state of cooperation between the two countries. Assad said that time would be needed to create the proper atmosphere for a restoration of normal relations.

The following day I flew to Amman and repeated to King Hussein the importance of his armed forces in the forthcoming battle. The memories of the June 1967 War, when he had entered the battle with little preparation, lack of coordination and with faulty information, finally to lose the West Bank, remained with him. When I explained to him the drastic changes that had taken place since then, he expressed his complete willingness to participate in the battle which should, however, be preceded by a meeting of the Heads of State of the three countries.

Since I was aware that this would take time, I said I could convey to him right away the views of both Sadat and Assad, who were both anxious that his forces should participate. I then proceeded to make a limited demand from King Hussein. I mentioned that I did not know the specific date of the battle, but, whenever it did start, there was a danger that the Israeli forces might encircle the southern Syrian front by moving across Jordanian territories. In this case, could the Jordanian forces be deployed in a manner that would prevent such a possibility? King Hussein readily agreed, saying that this was his obligation anyway, whether there was prior coordination or not. In fact, when the war broke out on 6 October, he accomplished this promptly and moved Jordanian units to Syria to join in the fighting.

In the first half of 1973, preparations in both Cairo and Damascus for the coming battle had reached their most active and, in spite of the secrecy that enveloped them, it was difficult to hide them completely, in view of their magnitude. Yet the CIA had abandoned the possibility of either Egypt or Syria waging a war after the long period of ceasefire and Sadat's decision to terminate the role of the Soviet experts. It had assumed that the net result of the decision was that Egypt had given up thoughts of a war with Israel, and the Soviet Union, in its turn, had given up arming Egypt.

The main US concern was the evaporation of the danger of a confrontation between the two superpowers in the Middle East. In his report to Congress on 3 May 1973, Nixon said: 'The danger of an inadvertent great-power confrontation over the Middle East was reduced by the Moscow Summit, and also by a decision by the Government of Egypt in July to request the withdrawal of most Soviet military personnel from Egypt.'

Simultaneously with war preparations, Sadat was making contacts with the US in a last attempt to avoid war. Nixon referred to these contacts in his report to Congress, mentioning that all through the latter part of 1971 and 1972 the US continued to conduct indirect talks between Egypt and Israel for an interim agreement but without success. What he did not refer to was that, through 1973, there were secret contacts going on between Hafez Ismail, Sadat's National Security Adviser, and Kissinger who proposed that the final agreement would include the recognition of Egyptian sovereignty over Sinai on condition that Israel maintained posts in Sinai for long periods under the title of security arrangements. Egypt rejected this condition and insisted on a total withdrawal from Arab territories. Kissinger then proposed a postponement of talks until after the Israeli elections which were to take place in October 1973. This implied that every time there was an election in either the US or Israel, the issue would have to remain pending, which in practical terms meant it could, as far as the US was concerned, remain pending for ever . . . a state of affairs that must have contributed to Sadat's final decision to enter the war.

After Hafez Ismail returned to Cairo, Golda Meir paid a visit to Washington which guardedly proposed the withdrawal of Israeli forces from Egypt. When Mrs Meir refused, the US administration accepted this placidly. Mrs Meir then asked for a new arms deal to be delivered promptly. Nixon, who at the time was in the turmoil of the Watergate scandal and had rendered himself a hostage to Israeli pressure in the process, readily agreed.

Cairo was incensed at the cheap way Kissinger was deceiving us. He denied the arms deal to Hafez Ismail after news of it reached the American press, to be rebuffed within a few days by the Israeli Foreign Minister who confirmed the news officially. In a speech on 1 May, Sadat mentioned that the peaceful settlement proposed by the US through Hafez Ismail was nothing but a mirage and an attempt to mislead and delude us, and that the US was now in such a position that it would toe Israel's line, whatever it demanded. He also referred to the statement of the Israeli Foreign Minister, that the objective of the latest US arms deal was to deter the Arabs and scare them, by saying that now he was acting in the equal capacity of Foreign Minister of the United States, as he took it upon himself to explain its policy to the world.

In May there was another meeting between Hafez Ismail and Kissinger in Paris which equally led to no result but was probably motivated by Kissinger's desire to prove to Moscow, on the eve of the second summit meeting between Brezhnev and Nixon, that the US was in control of the situation.

Hafez Ismail, under instructions from Sadat, tried to get a clear picture of the role the US was ready to play, and whether it would continue to act as Israel's advocate or adopt a neutral role of mediation; what would be its position if Egypt, as had happened in the past, accepted an American project which would later be rejected by Israel; and finally, why the US continued to flood Israel with arms, at a time when it was conducting contacts for a peace settlement. Ismail, of course, did not get one clear answer from Nixon while Kissinger continued his gamesmanship, offering nothing but evasive answers. In his June meeting with Nixon, Brezhnev also failed to persuade him to accept the necessity of an Israeli withdrawal from the Arab territories so that peace could be established in the area.

Egypt, meanwhile, in its quest of mobilizing world public opinion before waging war, in April requested the Secretary-General of the UN to prepare a comprehensive report reviewing all the efforts exerted by the UN over the situation in the Middle East since 1967, in the light of which the issue could be debated by the Security Council. The report was submitted on 18 May, and the Security Council convened at Egypt's request on 6 June to study it. It was a detailed review of Israel's repeated and continuous attempts to obstruct the implementation of Resolution 242. The representative of Tanzania spoke on behalf of the Organization of African Unity, warning that the Organization was going to adopt political and economic measures against Israel if it continued its aggressive policy (this warning was put into effect after the October War, when most African countries severed relations with Israel). The Chinese representative compared Israel's concept of secure borders with Hitler's *Lebensraum* theory.

When the Council resumed its meetings after the termination of the two-power Summit Meeting in the second half of July, the US representative tried to persuade Dr Zayat, the Egyptian Foreign Minister, to discontinue the debate and be satisfied with what had already been said. Sadat, however, was determined to continue the debate and submit a resolution, although he was aware that the US would veto it.

A draft resolution was submitted on 25 July denouncing Israel in the strongest terms for its continued occupation of Arab territories, expressing the Council's anxiety over the non-cooperation of Israel with the special representative of the Secretary-General of the UN, and affirming that a peaceful solution could only be achieved on the basis of respect for national sovereignty, territorial integrity and the rights of all countries and the legitimate rights and aspirations of the Palestinian people.

The US was the only country to vote against the draft resolution, consequently vetoing it. All the rest, including Western countries and the Latin American countries, approved it.

In his 23 June speech Sadat termed the US policy chicanery; he declared that Egyptian policy rested on three bases: Egyptian self-power, the extensive Arab potentialities and Soviet political and military support.

That year also saw the beginnings of the energy crisis to which the Arab countries held the key, as well as the important role the currency surplus of the Arab oil-producing countries could play in the world economy – two new factors that, well used, could contribute to Arab power.

Egyptian relations with the Soviet Union were meanwhile in a state of paralysis. Yet the visit of the Egyptian Prime Minister to Moscow in October 1972, and that of the Minister of War in March 1973, had led to a relaxation of tension and consequently to the signing of a new agreement by which the Soviet Union would supply arms to Egypt, including three types that Egypt had not received before: a squadron of MiG-23s, a missile brigade T17R, and SAM-6 missiles, in addition to armoured cars of a new type, artillery and anti-tank rockets. The Soviets further promised to return the MiG-25s to Egypt, as well as the sophisticated electronic units. In fact, when Hafez Ismail visited Moscow in July, Brezhnev assured him of continued Soviet support and said that détente with the US would never be at the expense of their support for the Arab issue.

Relations with the Soviet Union began to improve as a result of the renewal of the agreement extending facilities to its fleet in the Mediterranean and the supply of new arms to Egypt.

At the beginning of August, Egypt was completely ready for battle and Sadat, in a final attempt to urge the US to take a step forward, gave an interview to *Newsweek*, in which he mentioned that the battle was approaching. Neither Israel nor the US took that statement seriously. Israel had deluded itself into believing that the Egyptian leadership had lost the will to fight, and would announce to its visitors that Israel could lick the Egyptian army within forty-eight hours.

The US, on the other hand, with Kissinger in full control of foreign policy, felt absolutely no urgency to move, especially since their greatest aspiration – driving the Soviets out of Egypt – had been accomplished without either commitment from their side or a prior agreement with them.

On the Arab front, agreement between Egypt and Syria was complete. The Egyptian Minister of War paid a visit to a number of Arab capitals and in Damascus reviewed the last arrangements for the battle. Sadat also paid a visit to both King Faisal and President Assad in August.

I was inclined to issue invitations to an Arab summit meeting, to finalize Arab coordination and participation in the battle; but fear of a leak concerning details relating to the war made both Egypt and Syria decide against such a meeting. There was, however, a Summit Meeting of the confrontation States (Egypt, Syria and Jordan) on 10 September in Cairo, during which the resumption of diplomatic relations between Egypt and Jordan was decided upon. This meeting occurred three weeks before the battle, and therefore it was impossible to acquaint Jordan with the war plan at this stage, but the meeting had the effect of getting Jordan to extend all assistance to Syria, once the war started.

When the Arab League Council met in the second week of September, an atmosphere of complete understanding, and an awareness of the political challenges the Arab countries had to face up to, prevailed. It was decided that we continue our meetings and deliberations during the General Assembly meeting in New York.

At the Arab Foreign Ministers' first meeting in New York, we received an invitation for 25 September for lunch from Kissinger, newly-appointed Secretary of State. Some Arab Ministers felt that there should be a unanimous decision to decline his invitation as an expression of our dissatisfaction at the American position, but it was finally agreed that this was a matter that should be left for each country to decide upon. Five Ministers declined, namely those of Algeria, Syria, Iraq and South Yemen, and thirteen attended. After the meal, Kissinger delivered a speech reiterating some of the points he was fond of raising with us: that his Judaism did not influence his political decisions, that the US was seriously seeking peace, and warning that he could not perform miracles. Then he chose to speak sarcastically of Resolution 242: that it was not clear – it was rather obscure – full of adjectives and ambiguity. In my speech of reply I stated that this resolution had not come down to us from Mars so that we could differ over its interpretation: it was worded by people who were still alive, and that when I participated in drafting it, its implications were clear to me and to everybody else inasmuch as it stipulated Israeli withdrawal from all occupied Arab territories for a durable peace. If Israel interpreted it differently, that was because expansion rather than peace was the overriding factor to it. Its obduracy rested on US support and encouragement, militarily and politically. I concluded by warning that after six years of a futile quest for a peaceful settlement, we must expect the renewal of war at any time.

13

The October War

The war began when I was in New York, together with Arab Foreign Ministers, for the UN session. Dr Zayat, the Egyptian Foreign Minister, telephoned me around ten in the morning of 6 October, New York time, to inform me that Egyptian forces had crossed the Suez Canal.

I recalled my last visit to the advanced positions of our forces west of the Suez Canal in 1971. I could see then the Israeli positions on the other side and the sandy mounds erected by Israel which were later to be raised to a height of twenty metres to protects its forces from the fire of Egyptian forces and to constitute an obstacle against the tanks. I also saw the pipes protruding through the sandy mounds to jet out large quantities of napalm, and capable of turning the Canal into an inferno. I remembered also the words of General Mohammed Fawzi before the erection of the mounds and the napalm pipes: that the General Command had estimated that losses in the Egyptian armed forces crossing the Canal might amount to 20,000 soldiers. After that visit, I had a talk with General Mohammed Sadek, who replaced Fawzi as Minister of War, on how we were going to tackle these barricades; he said we had tried opening gaps in them by hitting them with a special kind of rocket, but without much success. We had also experimented with special forces trying to demolish mockups of the mounds with bulldozers; while this was feasible, it proved a very hard and expensive operation. I learned, later, that a young Egyptian engineer had suggested powerful pumps that would use the Canal waters to blast open gaps in the mounds, a procedure that had been used successfully in preparing certain sites for building the Aswan High Dam. Powerful pumps were subsequently purchased from Britain and Germany and experiments conducted with them that proved successful. This remarkable idea helped in achieving both speed and surprise in crossing the Canal while reducing our losses greatly. When I realized that our losses in the crossing operation did not exceed 280 men, this showed to me a high degree of skill and training in a highly complicated military operation. As regards the napalm pipes, our forces succeeded in cementing their openings before the attack.

The real glory of the October War was the remarkable performances both of Syria in the Golan and of Egypt in Sinai, which were both undertaken at the same time and with a high degree of proficiency. In fact this was the first time Israel was to face a real war on two Arab fronts simultaneously.

The following day Dr Zayat informed me that our forces had achieved the crossing of the Canal and the destruction of the Bar-Lev Line of fortifications with complete success and that our forces were in control of the east bank of Sinai and were advancing inside it. In a little while, a number of Arab Foreign Ministers came to see me and inquire as to the next step. I replied confidently that our forces would be moving to occupy the passes. I had in mind Plan 200, the broad outlines of which had been laid in 1968 and which was based on the assumption that crossing the Canal was not an objective in itself – it was a mere water barrier that should be overcome to achieve the first objective, namely the occupation of the Sinai passes. This plan was created under the supervision of General Fawzi. General Sadek, who replaced him in 1971, informed me that some commanders had proposed that the Egyptian forces stop their advance after crossing the Canal and that he had rejected this idea on the basis that it failed to achieve a political gain of any substance, but primarily – from a military point of view – because it could subject our forces to successful counter-attacks from the Israeli side. I therefore could not conceive, by any stretch of the imagination, that Marshal Ahmed Ismail who succeeded General Sadek in October 1972 would attempt a drastic change in the plan which had been operative since 1968 and was being continuously developed as we received more arms and for which the army, since 1968, used to train twice a year through manoeuvres. There were also manoeuvres at the level of commanders, without the deployment of forces. By 1973, the army had attained a high degree of fighting skill that would have enabled it to achieve the objectives of this plan easily. Consequently I began to feel anxiety and bewilderment when time passed after our initial dazzling success without any news of further progress. Two days had passed, enough for us to consolidate our new positions east of the Canal, and to proceed to exploit our success for the achievement of a real political and military objective. I was even more disturbed when news came of the failure of an Israeli counter-attack on 8 and 9 October, when Israel sustained the loss of 250 tanks, yet our forces still failed to move further in the direction of the passes. Only then did I become aware that the Egyptian Military Command was satisfied with its successful crossing operation and had decided to establish defensive positions along the narrow strip of land it had acquired on the Canal stretching no further than ten kilometres. This meant that our forces were deployed in open defensive positions along a line that stretched for 170 kilometres.

When I heard on 16 October that a number of Israeli tanks had broken through the Egyptian defensive line and had crossed the Canal in the Defresoir area, a number of Arab Ministers of Foreign Affairs were greatly disturbed by the news so I had to assure them that such a breakthrough had no military value, that it was expected by the Egyptian Command; and I reminded them of a similar situation in the Second World War when the German army achieved a breakthrough in the US front in the Ardennes and how it was completely destroyed by the US forces. It was not only a knowledge of the principles of war that demanded maintaining a large reserve as a safeguard against possible and expected counter-attacks but, more important, it was awareness of the Egyptian military plan that had for years made provision for such an eventuality. I recalled a conversation I had had with General Fawzi at the end of 1970, when I asked him if we had taken into consideration the advice of President Tito for the formation of a large reserve force. General Fawzi assured me that we had and that it was composed of three mechanical divisions, besides the strategic reserve force, composed of two armoured divisions and capable of tackling any Israeli counter-attack. Furthermore, in March 1971 manoeuvres were mounted in which all army forces participated, under the command of General Fawzi. The manoeuvres which continued for fourteen days were attended by General Okinov, the chief Soviet military expert, and about 100 of his aides who were attached as observers to all the participating army units. The manoeuvre, based on Plan 200, was staged along

the Damietta branch of the River Nile. The forces stationed west
of the Nile branch represented the enemy while General Okinov
and a group of his aides undertook the role of the enemy
Command and confronted the Egyptian Command with unexpected situations from the Israeli side, to examine how the
Egyptian Command would tackle them. Five infantry divisions,
100,000 soldiers, crossed the Damietta branch, by erecting heavy
bridges, and successfully established five bridgeheads in preparation for an advance towards the passes. General Fawzi told me
that at that juncture General Okinov burst in to inform him that
an Israeli armoured brigade had staged a counter-attack and
succeeded in breaking through the Egyptian lines and had
crossed the Canal at the Defresoir zone, while another Israeli
armoured brigade had managed a crossing at Kantara. Fawzi
then instructed the forces that had crossed the Canal to consolidate their positions and to dispatch fighting elements forward
and sideways to obstruct the advance of the enemy. At the same
time he issued orders to two mechanized divisions from the
reserve to engage the enemy and drive his forces east, and to a
third mechanized division to consolidate the duties of the other
two divisions and then to follow up on the success of crossing the
Canal by reaching and seizing the passes. On the fourth day, the
Egyptian forces succeeded in controlling the passes. Fawzi then
proceeded to order the two armoured divisions to advance east of
the passes to engage the enemy tanks and destroy them with the
support of the mechanized divisions which were now replaced by
three infantry divisions occupying the passes. By the end of
twelve days, our forces had successfully liberated the whole of
Sinai. After the success of the manoeuvre, Okinov could not
contain his excitement and fervently congratulated Fawzi.
Okinov's excitement was so obvious that Fawzi asked him, the
following day, what was the reason. He answered that the
Soviets had received information from inside Israel concerning
the existence of a plan termed *Gazelle* which was originally
aimed at destroying the missile wall that Egypt had successfully
erected in August–September 1970. In the course of this operation, the Israeli forces would be flown by helicopter to land
behind Egyptian missile battalions west of the Canal and engage
them in battle, while Israeli aircraft would destroy the missile
sites. Later, however, when the Israeli Command realized that

Egyptian special forces had been stationed to defend the missile sites, Israel replaced this plan with another, still bearing the same name, but which took into consideration the possibility of an Egyptian success in crossing the Canal and had the objective of launching an Israeli counter-attack for a breakthrough of Egyptian lines at the Defresoir and Kantara zones and the establishment of a bridgehead west of the Canal to obstruct the Egyptian offensive and eventually destroy Egyptian forces west of the Canal. Okinov conceived that the best way to off-set the Israeli plan was to stage a manoeuvre to see how the Egyptian Command would handle such an eventuality and when it did so successfully, he could not contain his satisfaction.

Fawzi informed me that after that event in March 1971, he had allocated two mechanized divisions to face possible breakthroughs in Defresoir and Kantara. They were trained on their mission in actual battle conditions several times, to such an extent that one of their commanders, who had later to face the Israeli counter-attack in Defresoir, communicated to Fawzi that his soldiers recognized now every bush in their advance to repel the Israeli attack.

This was the information I had when I assured the Arab Foreign Ministers not to be concerned about the Israeli breakthrough. What I was not aware of at the time, however, was that orders had been issued by the Egyptian Command for engaging our reserve in the battle along the east bank of the Canal; thus we were left without enough reserve forces to face any Israeli counter-attacks.

I had arranged with the Ministers of Foreign Affairs that our meetings during that critical period should be on a daily basis, and we agreed that our discussions with representatives of the major powers in the Security Council should be based on the following foundations: that the objective of the October War was to reactivate the issue politically; that the entry of both Egypt and Syria in the war after more than six years of Israeli occupation gave ample proof that the Arab countries would not accept the *fait accompli* that Israel wanted to impose; that a ceasefire advocated by the US unconnected to a withdrawal by Israel from all occupied Arab territories as a condition for peace was in favour of Israel. Consequently there was Arab unanimity that the ceasefire should be tied to a solution that would impose a complete withdrawal on Israel.

Nixon, meanwhile, had decided to throw all the weight of the US into the battle on the side of Israel; an air bridge was established to supply Israel with thousands of tons of arms – a decision which created a new and serious dimension in the situation. The US administration argued that Israel was going through a critical military situation and her very existence was in danger. This was not true. After the initial shock, Israel was able to amass her forces along the Egyptian front in Sinai and in Golan, and to stop any further progress of the Egyptian forces beyond the bridgehead established east of the Canal, while it managed to recapture the positions it had lost in the Golan to the Syrian forces in the early days of the battle. Israel's existence was not in jeopardy: in fact, Israel was able, in spite of its huge losses early in the battle, to inflict equally huge losses on both Egyptian and Syrian tanks later.

The real reason for a US intervention on this colossal scale was the refusal of both Egypt and Syria to accept a ceasefire. The war had changed into one of attrition which, had it continued for a longer period, would have exhausted the Israeli forces and could have led to the restoration of the Soviet presence. Therefore, the US intervened to bring an end to the battle in Israel's favour.

At a meeting of the Arab Foreign Ministers in New York we had agreed that a delegation comprising the Foreign Ministers of Saudi Arabia, Kuwait, Algeria and Morocco would meet Nixon to dissuade him from antagonizing the Arabs further, and to present him with a note demanding Israel's withdrawal from all occupied Arab territories, respect for the rights of the Palestinian people so that peace could be established and a demand that the US refrain from abetting Israeli aggression. The meeting was fixed for 17 October.

Nixon, at this time, was living under a shadow. His deputy, Spiro Agnew, had resigned a few days earlier on account of a financial scandal, while Nixon's involvement in the Watergate affair was becoming more obvious. I was inclined to accept the assumption that at the time he was concerned only with his personal plight, to the exclusion of everything else.

President Sadat had meanwhile announced on 16 October, one day prior to the meeting of the four Arab Foreign Ministers with Nixon, that the US was supplying Israel with arms that would enable it to continue controlling the occupied Arab territories;

and he severely criticized this American position while expressing his desire for peace, expounding a project for peace by which
Egypt would accept Security Council and General Assembly
resolutions and agree to a ceasefire if Israel would withdraw to
the line of 5 June 1967 under the supervision of the UN, that
Egypt was ready to attend a peace conference at the UN immediately after the withdrawal, and that he was willing to open
up the Suez Canal and clear it for international navigation.

On their return, the Arab Foreign Ministers informed me that
they had conferred with Kissinger before meeting Nixon. The
former told them that, when the fighting began, the US had
proposed an immediate ceasefire and a return of the warring
parties to the line of 6 October and added that the calculations of
the Pentagon and the CIA had asserted that the Arabs would
receive a crushing defeat, equal to their defeat in 1967, but that
these calculations had been disproved. He attempted to convince
the Arab Foreign Ministers that an acceptance of the ceasefire was
for the protection of Arab countries and in their best interests.

When they met with Nixon, Saudi Minister Omar el-Sakkaf
proceeded to explain, in his quiet manner, the Arab point of view
and their desire to establish a just peace; he called upon Nixon to
work for the withdrawal of Israel.

Nixon said that the US was anxious to maintain good relations
with the Arab countries; then, commenting on US arms supplies
to Israel, he said that they were far less than had been demanded
by Israeli protagonists in Congress, and he promised he would
work for the realization of a just peace in the interests of all the
parties involved. He added that he would not be swayed by
domestic considerations (referring to the Jewish lobby) and that
Kissinger, although a Jew, was working on behalf of the US and
peace. He then went on to repeat what Kissinger had told them
earlier: that US military experts had informed him that Israel
would win the war in no time, but that it was later revealed that
the Arabs had succeeded in achieving much more than was
anticipated. In fact, he believed that the Arabs themselves had not
expected such a success. Nixon then said that if Israel's existence
was endangered, the US would intervene to protect it and he
proposed an acceptance of a ceasefire on the condition that
Resolution 242 be implemented, which he would personally
undertake and see that Israeli forces withdrew. However, he

failed to mention whether withdrawal would be to the 5 June 1967 lines.

The four Foreign Ministers met again with Kissinger, who said that an Israeli withdrawal to the lines of 5 June 1967 constituted a danger to Israel. When the Arab Ministers demanded the solution of the Palestine question by the establishment of a Palestinian State, he said that such a solution would lead to the undoing of Israel or Jordan and that he categorically refused it. In that, of course, he was adopting the Israeli position.

When the Moroccan Foreign Minister, Ben Hima, asked him about the US attitude if Israel were to continue its aggression against the Arab countries after a ceasefire, Kissinger answered that in such a case the US would refrain from extending aid to Israel and opined that Israel would then be unable to continue the war for longer than six days.

In fact, Israel continued its attacks after the ceasefire on 22 October and the US, far from honouring its promise, continued to supply Israel with arms.

Bouteflika, the Algerian Foreign Minister, commented in these meetings that he did not conceive of any change in the US position in aligning itself to Israel and that the war had led to a change only in its approach, and not in its policy. He asked Kissinger about his views on the peace project announced by Sadat the preceding day, and Kissinger answered: 'We differ from Sadat on some points, although there are some constructive points in what he announced. We do not consider Sadat, however, as our enemy.'

Sheikh Sabah, the Kuwaiti Foreign Minister, posed this question to Kissinger: 'How can you claim that you work for peace while you supply Israel with these colossal quantities of arms to enable it to continue its aggression against the Arabs? We have seen a part of these supplies on TV.'

Kissinger had no answer beyond stating that the US wanted to re-establish an arms balance.

At the conclusion of the meeting Kissinger said that he would be going for a ten-day visit to China and that on his return he would concentrate on the Middle East question. Thus it was obvious that Kissinger wanted to bide his time until the result of the battle was known and Israel was supplied with tremendous quantities of arms including the most recent and sophisticated

US missiles. When he said that the matter needed some four weeks before things would materialize, he was implicitly expressing his hope that, within that period of time, Israel would be able to bring her counter-attack to a successful conclusion, which would put the Arabs again at a disadvantage and Israel would be able to dictate its terms. In fact, Bouteflika told me that the impression he took away from the meeting was that Nixon was almost asking them to convince Kissinger of their point of view, that Kissinger had the upper hand in formulating US policy in the Middle East and it would therefore be categorically in favour of Israeli interests.

What was more emphatic in manifesting Arab solidarity in the battle was that, the same day Arab Foreign Ministers conferred with Nixon in Washington, Arab Ministers of Petroleum met in Kuwait, and decided to decrease oil production by five per cent every month until Israel withdrew from all occupied Arab territories.

In the meanwhile I was following the news about the gap Israel had opened in the Defresoir, expecting to hear at any time that our mechanized divisions, trained for meeting any counter-attack, had moved. Instead, Israel announced that it had succeeded in establishing a bridgehead west of the Canal and that its armoured forces were moving in large numbers to the west bank of the Canal. I began to feel that the situation was changing in favour of Israel, after sustaining losses in the first four days of battle that exceeded 450 tanks, while its losses in aircraft on both the Egyptian and Syrian fronts were very high.

On the Syrian front, however, Syrian forces were able to stop the Israeli counter-attack with the help of Iraqi and Jordanian forces.

The US participated directly in the war when its reconnaissance aircraft SR 71 began photographing Egyptian and Syrian positions on Israel's behalf. Studying these pictures, Israel became aware that the armoured reserve forces had crossed the Canal on 14 October to participate in a battle in which Egypt lost 250 tanks and which gave Israel the opportunity to launch its counter-attack and break through our lines in the Defresoir on 16 October. The Egyptian Command announced that day that the Israeli forces that had crossed the Canal amounted to a mere seven tanks; it was not made aware of the real size of the Israeli armoured forces west of the Canal until their number surpassed that of Egyptian forces remaining on the west bank which was rendered vulnerable to Israeli attacks which were receiving the full support of the Israeli air force, as a result of the destruction of a number of Egyptian missile sites. The Israeli forces continued their southward march towards the town of Suez in order to occupy it, but met with failure.

Kosygin arrived in Cairo on 16 October to discuss the military situation and the possibility of Egypt agreeing to a ceasefire before the military situation turned against Egypt's interests. Sadat refused a ceasefire and communicated to Kosygin his project for peace.

I was meeting some Arab Foreign Ministers when, on 19 October, Nixon asked the Congress to approve arms supplies to Israel to the tune of $2,200 million, by far the biggest figure credited by the US for military aid to Israel.

The Arab response came immediately from King Faisal; he announced an embargo on oil shipments to both the US and Holland and stated that he would henceforth decrease his country's oil production by ten per cent every month. Other Arab oil-producing countries followed suit and Bahrein abrogated its agreement with the US for special facilities in Bahrein port. Arab support was not confined to the mere use of oil as a lever; the oil-producing countries extended substantial financial aid, while the Arab countries dispatched part of their forces to the war fronts. During the battle, Arab countries had extended military support to both Egypt and Syria. In Moscow Boumedienne paid $200 million for tanks that he demanded should be delivered promptly to both Syria and Egypt. During and after the October War, Arab military support to Egypt was as follows: on the Egyptian front: three squadrons of MiGs and Sokhois from Algeria, two squadrons of Mirages from Libya, a squadron of Hawker Hunters from Iraq; one armoured brigade from Algeria, another from Libya, an infantry brigade from Morocco and another from Sudan, an infantry battalion from Kuwait and another from Tunisia. Support on the Syrian front was as follows: three Iraqi MiG-21 squadrons and one of MiG-17s; an Iraqi armoured division, an Iraqi infantry division, one Jordanian armoured brigade and a Moroccan armoured brigade.

However, the military situation deteriorated further. On 20

October, Sadat began to witness the delivery of US tanks in large numbers at al-Arish airport, to be unloaded immediately by the Israelis and moved with all haste to the battlefield against Egypt. There were now five Israeli armoured brigades west of the Canal as against three Egyptian armoured brigades. Finally Sadat decided to accept the ceasefire and he informed the Soviet Union accordingly. He cabled Assad of Syria that he had to accept the ceasefire because he could not also fight the US, which would lead to the destruction of the Egyptian forces. He informed him that he had communicated this decision to the Sovet Union, on condition that both the Soviet Union and the US guarantee Israel's withdrawal and the initiation of a peace conference within the framework of the UN to agree on a settlement of the issue according to a Soviet offer made by Kosygin during his visit to Cairo. Assad answered, requesting that Sadat reconsider his decision in light of the capacity of the Egyptian army to destroy the Israeli forces that had crossed the Canal, in the same way that Syria was able to arrest their advance and prepare for a counter-attack.

On 20 October, Kissinger flew to Moscow in response to an urgent invitation from Brezhnev. As a consequence of the deterioration of the military situation along the Egyptian front, Brezhnev was unable to enforce the Arab demands; the best he could achieve was an agreement for a ceasefire, while demanding that all concerned parties should implement Resolution 242 and the US and the Soviet Union would jointly chair the peace talks. The Security Council met on 22 October and adopted Resolution 338, inviting all parties to observe a ceasefire and implement Resolution 242.

Egypt declared her acceptance of the resolution and the ceasefire. I contacted Dr Zayat to find out whether Israel would abide by the ceasefire. He told me what I had both feared and expected: a cable from Cairo informed him that Israel would not observe the ceasefire and was still advancing towards Suez to occupy it.

On 22 October, Zayat called for an extraordinary meeting of the Security Council. The Council reiterated its previous resolution and demanded that the warring parties withdraw to their positions of 22 October. It also decided to send observers to supervise the ceasefire between Egypt and Israel. But Israel paid no heed, continuing its military operations and cutting the road leading to Suez City, despite its failure to occupy Suez, thereby preventing reinforcements and supplies reaching the forces of the Third Army stationed east of the Canal. Sadat made an appeal to both the US and the Soviet Union, requesting they dispatch their forces to drive Israel back to the ceasefire line of 22 October. The US promptly rejected the appeal since it neither wanted a return by Israel to the line of 22 October nor desired to see Soviet forces in the area. In view of the deterioration of the military situation and the continued Israeli operations, Brezhnev sent a message to Nixon on 24 October, demanding that the two powers jointly put Resolution 338 into effect, and in the case of a US refusal, the Soviet Union felt under an obligation to adopt the necessary steps unilaterally.

Nixon's administration at the time was undergoing great convulsions over the Watergate affair with the resignation of Attorney-General Richardson who refused to abide by Nixon's instruction not to reveal evidence of the President's involvement; Nixon wanted to project the image of a strong man who refuses to bow to pressure; he shocked the world and his allies in Western Europe by declaring a state of extreme emergency in the US army on 25 October which meant a state of nuclear alertness in all US bases in the US and Europe. I had a chance later to witness the adverse effect this decision had on European countries which were shown that the US had no qualms over exposing their security to danger withour prior consultations with them.

Dr Zayat again resorted to the Security Council on 25 October, asking it to force Israel to abide by the ceasefire. The Council adopted Resolution 340, reiterating its previous decision and deciding on the formation of a United Nations Emergency Force from amongst the non-permanent member countries of the Security Council, which started arriving in Cairo on 27 October and helped finally in establishing a ceasefire after Israel succeeded in encircling Suez and cutting lines of supply to the Third Army.

I then decided to return to Cairo and, upon my arrival, conferred with Hafez Ismail, the President's Adviser on National Security, who summarized the military situation by saying that there was negligence in relation to the gap, as the initial information relayed tended to belittle its importance and danger; and that, on the basis of this inaccurate information, orders were issued by the Command in Cairo that were equally lacking. When the magnitude and speed of the Israeli breakthrough became apparent, the Command was in disarray as it did not have at its disposal enough reserve forces to tackle the large number of Israeli tanks that had crossed to the west bank of the Canal as a result of the 21st and 4th divisions, which belonged to the reserve, crossing to the east bank of the Canal. He also stated that some of the Egyptian missiles had been removed safely and no casualties were sustained among the missile crews whose training took long months. When I inquired about foreign support received during that period and whether they had not been sufficient to tackle the breakthrough, he said that the Soviet Union had sent three armoured brigades, Algeria two with their crews, Libya one and Yugoslavia another and Morocco had promised one – altogether eight brigades, more than 800 tanks.

I commented by saying that I was amazed that the Command should ignore one of the basic principles of war, namely the necessity of maintaining reserve forces. I referred to a statement made by the Commander of the Israeli front to the effect that when the reconnaissance flights (undertaken by the US air force) showed that three Egyptian reserve divisions had crossed the Canal, he immediately realized there was a gap without defence in the Egyptian line and he decided to break through it. I was shocked to learn further that there was no commander at the front and suggested that one be appointed immediately to correct this flagrant omission. I said that the absence of such a commander was the reason we had failed to exploit our initial success in crossing the Canal with speed and almost without casualties and later failing to advance with all speed to the passes, to exploit the dismal failure of the Israeli counter-attack.

Hafez Ismail also informed me that the US had supplied Israel with immense quantities of tanks and aeroplanes and with highly sophisticated missiles like the Shrike and television bombs and anti-tank rockets that could be launched by helicopters.

I commented on the situation as I conceived it: that the US was not abiding by its promise to force Israel to withdraw to the 22 October line, which conformed with its position all along, which meant in turn that we should adopt a more cautious approach in dealing with it, especially since our acceptance of a United Nations Emergency Force meant a new freezing of the situation;

that I expected that the following step by Kissinger would be in the direction of weakening the Arab position and the Arabs' capacity to exert pressure on the US, especially via a number of factors that could create Arab dissension, among which was the absence of a prior agreement between Egypt and Syria for accepting the ceasefire. There were also conflicting views between King Hussein and the PLO over the establishment of the Palestinian State. Arab forces dispatched to the fronts could not be kept there for any length of time. The financial support now extended by the Arab countries to Egypt and Syria would diminish as time went by. Arab oil-producing countries would find it difficult to continue decreasing their oil production monthly for a long time because of the international pressures that would be exerted on them, especially by the US. In short, my concept of the situation at that time was that our accepting a ceasefire at a time of military hazard had led us once again to a state of no-peace no-war, which meant that the target we were hoping to achieve by the war–reactivating the political situation–had failed.

The conclusion I had come to was to invite an Arab summit meeting in order to intensify Arab mobilization, safeguard the great solidarity that had emerged, and face up to the type of manoeuvres that I expected Kissinger to resort to.

For its part, Egypt had drafted a peace project for a staged withdrawal, by which Israel would withdraw to the 22 October line and an exchange of prisoners of war would take place in the first stage; in the second stage, Israel would withdraw to positions east of the passes, UN forces would be stationed between the Egyptian and Israeli forces, the Egyptian blockade on Bab el-Mandab at the entrance of the Red Sea would be lifted, and the clearing of the Suez Canal would begin; the last stage would include final Israeli withdrawal to Egyptian international borders and the application of a similar scheme for Syria; a peace conference would be convened during the stage of the disengagement of the forces.

By that time Sadat had appointed a new Foreign Affairs Minister, Ismail Fahmy, and charged him with transmitting this project to both Nixon and Kissinger. Nixon repeated that he had already spoken to the four Arab Foreign Ministers about his determination to solve the problem justly and without any domestic pressures; while Kissinger expressed willingness to support the project without the necessity of the US actually adopting it, which meant that Israel had first to accept it – and Kissinger knew only too well that it would not.

On his return, Ismail Fahmy told me that Golda Meir had been in Washington at the same time for talks and that she had refused a withdrawal to the lines of 22 October, at the same time demanding that Egypt lift its blockade on Bab el-Mandab if it wanted permission for the passage of food supplies to the Third Army, east of the Canal. Ismail Fahmy departed from Washington without receiving any definite promise from Nixon, other than that Kissinger would be visiting Egypt and some Arab countries, and an agreement on the resumption of diplomatic relations between Egypt and the US immediately after Israel withdrew to its 22 October positions. It was also agreed that representatives of Egypt and Israel would meet under the supervision of the UN at Kilometre 101 on the Suez road, to discuss necessary arrangements for the disengagement of the forces of the two countries.

On 12 November I received an invitation from Assad of Syria for discussions in Damascus. Sadat had already conferred with him in the course of a quick visit to Saudi Arabia and Kuwait at the beginning of that month. In Damascus I conferred with Assad who was confident and not in the least disturbed over the military situation on the Syrian front. He explained to me that Syria had continued its attack on Israeli positions, while Israel was resorting to concentrated air strikes on the Syrian forces, destroying 1,200 tanks, seventy per cent of which were replaced by the Soviet Union while Syrian losses in anti-aircraft rockets were also replaced as were her losses in MiGs. Meanwhile, the Israeli forces sustained drastic losses, especially when Israel directed the brunt of its attack against the Syrian front, hurling its tanks through the gap it managed to open and reaching a village called Sa'sa'. There the Syrian forces had succeeded in arresting their advance. When Syria lost most of its tanks it refused to give up but continued the fighting and employed its artillery and air force with such efficiency as finally to arrest the Israeli advance. Israel had lost her best pilots in the first days of the battle, as was evidenced in the weakness of later air raids. SAM-3 missiles had proved their efficacy and MiG-21s successfully managed to engage the US Phantoms employed by Israel. He went on to say that Syria was preparing a counter-attack on 21 October, to

destroy the Israeli pocket after completely encircling it and after
Syria had observed that Israeli air sorties had decreased from
1,000 a day to about 250, and it had noticed that the same thing
was happening over the Egyptian front.

The Iraqi forces had requested that the counter-attack be postponed for forty-eight hours, in order to complete their tank
emplacements, when, he said, Syria was surprised to hear of the
decision for a ceasefire. When he learned of Sadat's desire to
accept an immediate ceasefire, Assad suggested to the Egyptian
Command that they use their two mechanized divisions in the
reserve to close the gap on the west bank of the Canal. However,
when he met Sadat in Kuwait after the ceasefire, he was informed
by Sadat that all Egypt had at the time were two brigades and not
two mechanized divisions. 'The agreement between Sadat and
myself before the war laid out that Egypt should occupy the Sinai
passes and not stop ten kilometres east of the Canal. The
Egyptian Command may have tried to correct this mistake on 14
October when it threw in its reserve from west of the Canal, but
by then the opportunity was over, after eight complete days of
Egyptian successes, crossing the Canal, and after Israel had
managed to shake off its sense of shock.' There was also little
coordination between the Egyptian and Syrian commands.
Assad added that the size of the Egyptian army that crossed the
Canal was 100,000 soldiers, so where was the rest of the
Egyptian army? Assad had little information on the proposed
peace conference.

I felt extremely disturbed after this talk for, in the last analysis,
our success, at that juncture and in the future, would depend on
complete confidence and coordination between Egypt and Syria.
If this was to be dissipated, then the US and Israel would have
achieved a greater success than they ever did on the battlefield. I
expressed to Assad my conviction of the extreme importance
of maintaining Arab solidarity, at the heart of which stood
Egyptian–Syrian coordination, and proposed an Arab summit
meeting for this purpose in Algiers, in response to an invitation
by Boumedienne, around the end of that month (November),
after Kissinger would have concluded his tour of the Arab capitals and the African Foreign Ministers their meeting. Assad
agreed, and it was also agreed that it should be preceded by an
Arab Foreign Ministers' meeting on 24 November.

Upon my return to Cairo I reported to Sadat Assad's feelings and his complaint over the lack of coordination between Syria and Egypt, which would have direct effects on the battle which had not yet ended, in spite of the ceasefire.

A few days before my departure for Algiers, Sadat contacted me on 19 November, to inform me that he expected general support and backing from the meeting, while the oil embargo should continue as a lever for pressure. I told him that there were rumours being spread by Israeli circles that he, Sadat, had told Kissinger during his visit to Cairo that Egypt would tackle the Arab oil embargo; therefore it would be convenient if, in his meeting with Arab Heads of State at the Summit, he could dispel such rumours. When I told him that the Soviet Ambassador would be meeting me within a few minutes at his own request, Sadat commented that the Soviets might have extended large quantities of arms and equipment to Egypt, but they had not, as yet, replaced all our losses in aircraft, and they should do so speedily.

When the Soviet Ambassador arrived I told him that I would like to hear the Soviet Union's assessment of the latest developments. He said that the gap Israel had succeeded in opening in the Egyptian front and its establishment of a pocket had in fact done away with the success Egypt had achieved in the first ten days of the war. Egypt should insist on the implementation of the Security Council resolution demanding the return of Israel to 22 October lines. Any argument either by Israel or by Kissinger about the difficulty of defining this line was invalid, since both the US and the Soviet Union had detailed pictures of the positions of Egypt and Israel on 22 October. The Soviet Ambassador added that Kissinger was claiming that the withdrawal of Israel to 22 October positions would require the US to exert tremendous pressure on Israel, which it would rather resort to after Israel's withdrawal to the east of the Canal. If Egypt were to accept this logic, it would lead to a weakening of its positions, for Kissinger was anxious to keep the lines of communications of the Third Army within the grip of the Israeli forces in the coming stage of negotiation, while withdrawal to the 22 October lines would put the Israeli pocket at the mercy of the Egyptian army. The peace project Egypt had proclaimed, he continued, was far below Egypt's previous demands, which included withdrawal from all

Arab territories. Anyway, Egypt should not place much confidence in American promises, unless they were accompanied by effective guarantees for their implementation in order that 'your past experiences with the United States be not repeated'. He commented that Egypt, and the Arabs in general, could have made better use of the Soviet Union, had they consulted with it before the beginning of the battle.

As regards arms supplies, he mentioned that the Soviet Union had extended to Egypt more than 400 tanks 62, in addition to large supplies of SAM-7s. It had also responded to all Egypt's requests in relation to reconnaissance pictures of Israeli positions. As regards Egypt's demands for MiG-23 aeroplanes, these would be delivered the following month. In short, he said, the Soviet Union had supplied Egypt with arms to the value of $1 billion. I asked him if it was true that the Soviet Union was demanding that Egypt pay for its purchases beforehand and in hard currency. He denied this vigorously.

I said that there was an Egyptian complaint that the Soviet Union had not replaced the arms losses. 'There are some quarters in Egypt,' he answered, 'which do not give consideration to the fact that the Soviet Union has suddenly found itself asked for tremendous immediate deliveries on both the Egyptian and Syrian fronts. We have done this within the limits of our capacity. Syrian losses in tanks exceeded one thousand, and they had to be replaced immediately at the same time as we also had to replace Egyptian losses. We were less fortunate with the aeroplane replacements, since those in storage were not sufficient to supply the needs of the two fronts immediately.'

I said that it was important in these critical circumstances that the Soviet Union extend support to both Egypt and Syria as promptly as possible, in order to foil Kissinger's plans on behalf of Israel, adding that I could understand the Soviet leaders' anger at the way their experts had been ousted from Egypt. He interrupted: 'No . . . It was not anger at the time, merely a feeling of disappointment.' I continued that the time was ripe for restoring strong relations between Egypt and the Soviet Union, that supplying Egypt with its arms needs would contribute to the negotiating power of Egypt.

I went on to dwell on the military and political situation, saying that Brezhnev used to impress on us the importance of achieving a measure of Arab unity of action; this had materialized but could not be sustained for long if the present situation continued. Brezhnev also used to remind us of the importance of using oil as a basic complementary arm in exerting pressure. This materialized spontaneously, but again its success and effectiveness could not continue for long. The other important factor was that Kissinger kept saying in Arab capitals that any settlement to be achieved at present would be to the credit of the US while he was in fact sowing the seeds of dissent, while we were hopeful that the approaching Arab Summit Meeting would offset such attempts. The Soviet Ambassador remarked that he was equally hopeful that the resolutions of the Summit Meeting would refer to the friendly stand of the Soviet Union during the battle.

The same day I met Marshal Ahmed Ismail and relayed to him Sadat's directive for a report on the Egyptian military situation for submission to the Arab Summit Meeting. I then referred to the error that had been committed by throwing the reserve forces into the attack instead of keeping them back to perform their original task, namely to safeguard the front against any counter-attacks. I felt that speedy measures should be taken at once to establish a large reserve, and that we should also correct another serious error by appointing an overall commander to the front who could not be directed from Cairo, pointing out that, had there been a commander at the front then, he could have handled the gap at once.

Ismail answered that he personally was the commander of the front and that unfortunately a change in the local command had taken place on the very day the gap was opened. He had ordered an armoured brigade to move against it but the local commander had underestimated what was going on and claimed that it was an Israeli patrol that he could handle with the forces he already had at his disposal. When we realized the size of the Israeli forces that had crossed the Canal, Ismail gave orders for a mechanized brigade to engage the Israeli forces, but it failed.

I conveyed to him Assad's complaint over the conflicting information he was receiving concerning the situation on the Egyptian front and the real size of its reserve forces. Ismail answered that he had an armoured division to defend Cairo. He added that the Egyptian forces were now encircling the Israeli pocket and could completely annihilate it, and that he was only waiting for replacements for losses in aeroplanes, anti-tank rockets and anti-aircraft rockets.

Meanwhile, negotiations between Egypt and Israel through Kissinger had started to reach an agreement when Israel managed to close all roads to the Third Army and control its lines of supply. This was the trump card that Israel was using to impose its demands and which Kissinger was using to pressure Egypt. Kissinger had submitted to Egypt and Israel six points stipulating that both Egypt and Israel strictly adhere to the ceasefire imposed by the Security Council; that the two parties discuss the withdrawal to 22 October positions within the framework of a disengagement of forces under the supervision of the United Nations; that the city of Suez receive supplies of food, water and medicine and that all injured civilians in Suez be removed; that no obstacles should be raised against the arrival of non-military supplies to the east bank of the Canal; that Israeli observation posts on the Suez–Cairo road be replaced by UN observation posts while, at the end of the road, Israeli officers join the UN forces in supervising supplies of a non-military nature reaching the Canal; and that as soon as the UN took over observation posts along the Cairo–Suez road, all prisoners of war including the injured be exchanged.

On 9 November, Egypt approved these points, followed by Israel; Kissinger informed the UN accordingly and the negotiations at Kilometre 101 began. Israel was mainly interested in the exchange of prisoners, and at the same time would intercept the passage of food and medical supplies, pour out plasma needed for the injured civilians in Suez and prevent the passage of gasoline and kerosene under the pretext that they were strategic supplies. In fact Israeli Phantoms attacked Egyptian positions on 9 November.

Meanwhile, Kissinger managed to secure Egypt's approval for the resumption of diplomatic relations with the US, which the American administration had striven to achieve all through the previous five years. The exchange of the prisoners of war began on 16 November and Egypt fulfilled all its obligations. Israel, however, refused to withdraw to 22 October lines after long hours of negotiations which forced Anzio Silasivo, the Commander of the UN forces, to postpone the talks for an indefinite period. Kissinger had therefore backed down on his basic pledge for an Israeli withdrawal to the 22 October lines, while Israel continued its siege of the Third Army.

I arrived in Algiers on 22 November and conferred with Boumedienne who referred to a statement by Sadat that his hopes for an honourable and peaceful settlement which would restore all occupied Arab territories and the rights of the Palestinian people had now reached fifty per cent. I replied that under the prevailing circumstances mine did not exceed one per cent. The fundamental issue at present was to remove the Israeli pocket, since negotiating while it was still there would not enable us to achieve any serious progress towards a comprehensive settlement. Consequently, the first duty of the summit meeting should be to increase the arming of both Egypt and Syria and, since the Soviet Union remained our only source of arms, we should strive to improve our relations with it.

During his recent visit to the USSR in October, Boumedienne had noticed the waning of Soviet–Egyptian relations, in fact a complete lack of confidence. Brezhnev, however, was insistent that both Egypt and Syria should lose no time in accepting the ceasefire, as time might be running against Egypt and if it procrastinated the situation could deteriorate, and he had informed Sadat accordingly. Boumedienne answered him that he was in Moscow to purchase arms and that such advice should be passed on direct to the warring parties.

I also met with King Faisal; he considered the Soviet Union a godless country and had no confidence in it or in arguments that the Soviet Union was the only source of arms available to us, so relations with it should be ameliorated. I touched on the oil embargo and suggested the details of this operation be left to the Arab oil-producing countries to handle according to their own discretion and that no resolutions should be adopted in this respect by the Summit. During this meeting, King Faisal expressed with complete clarity his willingness to put all Saudi potentialities at the disposal of the battle and said that oil was entirely linked with the restoration of Arab rights in regaining the territory and upholding Palestinian demands. On the political level, most countries of the world, including US allies and Western Europe, had become convinced of the erroneous assessments on which the US based its policy in the Middle East. On the economic level, the oil embargo alerted the West in general to the dangerous and explosive nature of the strife in the Middle East. On the military side, the high level of skill and proficiency shown by the Egyptian and Syrian troops had destroyed the myth of Israeli invincibility. These were all elements in our favour which I felt we should continue to project while Kissinger was trying to dissipate and belittle us.

The Arab Summit Meeting convened on 26 November. I reported on the political situation in a closed session, mentioning that the October War had disproved Israeli claims relating to secure borders based on geographical considerations. I also referred to the fact that whatever success we had managed to achieve was based on the power of Arab solidarity between Egypt and Syria, which led to the use of oil as an auxiliary arm in the battle. I emphasized that the objectives of Israel had not changed and that they continued to deny the Palestinians their national rights and to hold tenaciously to occupied Arab territories, and that Israel had expansionist schemes for the Litani River in southern Lebanon. Arab alertness and unity were the only instruments for foiling Israel's schemes. I concluded by summing up the factors that could help us to regain our rights: the people's determination, our vigilant and competent military forces, Arab solidarity, oil, and cooperation with friendly countries.

Both Sadat and Assad gave detailed reviews of the war. While Sadat maintained that the entry of the US with all its military weight on the side of Israel forced him into accepting a ceasefire, Assad asserted that a unity of Arab confrontation countries was still capable of restoring Arab rights and he urged a continuation of the struggle. Other Heads of State emphasized the need for solidarity and, since the representation of Palestine was an important issue to be discussed by the Summit, Talhouni, representing King Hussein, declared that after the liberation of the West Bank, his country was pledged to conduct a referendum by which its inhabitants would have to decide whether to remain in unity with Jordan, become federated with Jordan or achieve complete independence. Yasser Arafat demanded that the PLO be recognized as the sole representative of the Palestinian people.

At a meeting to discuss military support to both Egypt and Syria, the general feeling among members of the Summit Meeting was that the resolutions of the Arab Defence Council were still operative and that further consolidation should be left to bilateral agreements, to avoid publicity. On the political level, the Heads of State affirmed the necessity of liberating all the occupied Arab territories, including Jerusalem, and the restoration of all national rights to the Palestinian people, according to the decisions of the PLO. They also decided that oil should continue to be used as an arm in the battle in accordance with the resolutions of the Arab Petroleum Ministers' meeting. There was also agreement to a proposal which I submitted for establishing a fund to extend aid to development projects of the African countries with a capital of $125 million. The meeting paid tribute to the EEC statement of 6 November and requested that the European countries stop arming Israel and lift their arms embargo on the Arab countries. The Heads of State also adopted a resolution alerting the US to the fact that its policy of alignment to Israel would affect its interests in the region adversely.

In order to emphasize the wish of the Arab countries for the establishment of a just peace, the Heads of State issued a statement at the conclusion of the meeting which declared their willingness to participate in achieving a peace based on two basic principles: the withdrawal of Israel from all Arab territories, including Jerusalem, and the restoration to the Palestinian people of their national rights.

Before my departure I met Boumedienne and he told me that he had talked to Sadat about the necessity of improving relations with the Soviet Union; that while Sadat agreed with him, he felt no desire to take any step in this direction at the present time. Boumedienne also told me that Algeria was ready to finance more arms deals for both Egypt and Syria if this was needed, as long as they insisted on a comprehensive settlement and were not misled by Kissinger into agreeing to limited withdrawals. On my way back to Cairo I was preoccupied with the next steps we should take. It was clear to me that despite the extent of the problem, Arab potentialities were sufficient to tackle it and that the Arab countries would not hesitate to render every conceivable assistance, once the war began again. The key to the situation now was how to maintain this solidarity and achieve complete understanding and mutual confidence between Egypt and Syria and so deepen their commitment to complete Israeli withdrawal.

14

Peace According to Kissinger

Upon my return to Cairo, I requested General Saaddine el-Shazli, Chief of Staff of the Egyptian Army and Military Assistant Secretary to the Arab League, to meet me on 2 December, to consider the implementation of the military resolutions adopted at the Summit Meeting in Algiers. The conversation turned to the October War and I asked the reason why the Egyptian forces, after their sweeping victory in crossing the Canal, did not advance to the Sinai passes. General Shazli answered that the target had been defined as merely crossing the Canal, as it was believed that an advance to the passes would far surpass available military capabilities. I argued that, even if that assumption had prevailed before the battle, new elements had emerged during the battle which should have imposed a change to an immediate advance to occupy the passes. Among these elements were the absence of large Israeli forces on the Sinai front, the attack which had taken the Israeli forces completely by surprise, and finally the fact that Israel considered Golan to be of a higher military priority because of its proximity to northern Israel with its densely populated settlements and towns, so Israel directed its striking forces against the Syrian front. Furthermore, in the first days of the battle on the Egyptian front, a new element had appeared in the efficacy of Egyptian anti-aircraft weapons which managed to inflict large losses on the Israeli air force and in the surprise element of using anti-tank rockets by Egyptian advanced forces, which succeeded in destroying 250 Israeli tanks in Sinai within a period of forty-eight hours.

He said that what happened to Israel in the first days of the fighting had happened to us on 14 October when we lost 250 tanks in the same way, by anti-tank rockets. 'How can we fall into such deadly error,' I exclaimed, 'when we should have changed the tactics of our confrontation so as to spare our tanks inevitable destruction?'

I then inquired about our failure to tackle the Israeli break-through in Defresoir. Shazli answered that the Egyptian Command was highly centralized and that this led to its ignorance of what was happening in the first few hours, so it was unable to take prompt action. With regard to the breakthrough, the Command had not been aware of what was happening until after the lapse of valuable time, during which Israel was able to establish a bridgehead and obtain a firm footing west of the Suez Canal. There were not enough reserve forces to correct the situation, he added. The standing reserve forces had been sent to Sinai. There was only one armoured brigade, and this could not tackle the situation alone. Furthermore, Egypt had lost 120 aircraft which had not as yet been completely replaced. With regard to tanks, Egypt had received enough to enable it to form six new armoured brigades. Beside replacements for lost aeroplanes, Egypt was in dire need of anti-tank rockets and anti-aircraft SAM-6 and -7 missiles. Shazli added that the Israeli pocket could easily be destroyed if these arms were made available, and if the Command were more decentralized. He went on to explain the situation relating to the Israeli pocket, saying that it was composed of three armoured brigades and two mechanized brigades; that the furthest point the Israeli forces had managed to reach west of the Canal was Kilometre 101 on the Cairo–Suez road, and that the average width of the gap was twenty kilometres.

I told Shazli that, if he would prepare a list of arms requirements, we would contact Arab countries, especially Saudi Arabia, Kuwait and the Emirates, in order to purchase them as they had agreed. Also, Boumedienne had volunteered to purchase more arms for both Egypt and Syria if they so requested.

On 7 December I entertained the Soviet Ambassador. He expressed satisfaction at the statement issued by the Summit Meeting concerning Arab appreciation for the support received from the Soviet Union and the Socialist countries.

I asked the Ambassador to convey to Brezhnev the Arab desire prevailing during the Summit meeting at Algiers to improve relations with the Soviet Union and the common feeling that prompt Soviet assistance to both Egypt and Syria and supplying them with the required arms would strengthen their negotiating power, otherwise we could revert to another period of no-peace and no-war which might, if it lasted any length of time, see the emergence of Arab differences and the cessation of the use of oil as a lever for pressure. The supply of arms would not be a financial burden to the Soviet Union, since the Arab countries would pay for the purchase of these arms. However, it was important in my view that the deal should not be put forward as a commercial transaction but should have the character of a political move. I told him what arms were required, according to Shazli, mentioning that time was an extremely important factor. I then moved to the promises that Kissinger had been making, during his contacts with Arab countries, concerning the US determination to achieve a comprehensive settlement – promises that he could not fulfil.

The Soviet Ambassador answered that the problem that faced the Soviet Union at the time was Sadat's lack of confidence in everything that the Soviet leaders did or said. The Soviet Union, he added, continued to extend military assistance to Egypt. Within days, new anti-aircraft missiles and anti-tank rockets would reach Alexandria, and other requirements made by General Ahmed Ismail had been conveyed to Moscow. The Soviet Union was also anxious to extend political support, but was often surprised at moves and events that could weaken their negotiating power with the US, as when Egypt's peace project was communicated to Moscow after it had been announced by Washington. As regards the October war, the Soviet experts' view was that the Egyptian target should have been clearly defined and should have been to proceed with alacrity to occupy the passes, and Egypt had the military power to achieve this end.

This point relating to the passes was of crucial significance to me and I was constantly discussing it with concerned parties. On 10 December, I met General Talaat Hassan, in charge of the Unified Command of the Arab League, who confirmed that the Egyptian forces should have advanced to the passes immediately after crossing the Canal, especially in view of the fact that most of the Israeli tank crews were absent on a holiday, which meant that there was practically no Israeli resistance. He asserted that the surprise was more of a political than of a military nature. Egyptian military movements in preparation for battle were of such a size and extent that they could not be concealed: the roads leading to the front were overcrowded with tanks and armoured cars. Israel, however, refused to believe that Egypt would resort to war.

Like many others, Talaat Hassan was of the opinion that there should have been an advance command of the Egyptian fighting forces. He said that the biggest mistake committed by the military command was in allowing the Egyptian reserve forces to cross the Canal and engage in the fighting which led to the Israeli success of opening the gap west of the Canal.

Political efforts continued in several directions. On 11 December Assad paid a quick visit to Sadat to agree on a unified attitude towards the peace conference mooted by Kissinger. On 23 October, Syria had announced her acceptance of Resolution 338 for a ceasefire on the basis of the complete Israeli withdrawal from Arab territories.

On 13 December, I had talked to the new Egyptian Foreign Minister, Ismail Fahmy, prior to Kissinger's arrival in Cairo that same day, and I learnt from him that he had been informed earlier by Kissinger that the withdrawal of Israel to the east of the Canal was now almost decided upon. Sadat also received encouraging letters from Nixon, and a wave of optimism spread in Cairo circles.

When I mentioned to Ismail Fahmy that several groups were expecting Nixon to submit his resignation within a few months, he said he had been told by Kissinger that Nixon's successor, Gerald Ford, would continue to keep him as his Secretary of State.

I told Fahmy that I had found a consensus among the military that the destruction of the Israeli pocket was, from the military point of view, feasible and we should deal with it so that Egypt would not be negotiating from a position of weakness. Israel would not willingly accept withdrawal east of the passes in Sinai and I had great misgivings that it would try, in the course of negotiations, to drag Egypt into a bilateral agreement with Israel and would abandon Syria thereby.

On 13 December, the French Ambassador notified me that France felt there should not be any delay in convening the peace conference in Geneva and, unless a clear, explicit agreement was reached within three months, no agreement would be reached after that. He also expressed his regret that Western Europe was excluded by the US from attending the proposed conference. Information had reached him which assessed Israeli losses west of the Canal at over ten persons a day, as a result of attrition engagements by the Egyptian forces. He also asked my views over the initiation of a Euro-Arab dialogue (which had been advocated by the French Foreign Minister and favourably responded to by me) and how I envisaged such a dialogue developing.

I answered that it was essential to know, first, how ready Europe was for such a dialogue that would, of necessity, touch on political and economic issues. I added that, for my part, I would contact the Arab countries to find out how ready they were to enter a serious dialogue at this level. We finally agreed to convene a preparatory meeting between the two sides in the spring of 1974, which did in fact take place, marking the beginnings of a fruitful dialogue that is still proceeding.

When I met the Soviet Ambassador on 17 December, I inquired about the Soviets' next step; he informed me he had received a message for Sadat that some of Egypt's arms requirements would be dispatched and that the Soviet Union was facing certain problems which made the delivery of all Egyptian requirements at the speed demanded difficult. On the arms to be delivered, he mentioned twelve MiG-23s, anti-aircraft missiles and anti-tank rockets. He assured me that another large consignment would be delivered to Egypt in February 1974, including the tanks 62 requested by Egypt.

Kissinger paid a visit to Damascus on 15 December, after securing Sadat's approval for attending the proposed peace conference in Geneva. When he asked whether Syria would attend, Assad told him that, unless the objective of the conference was made clear from the beginning (that it rested on achieving Israeli withdrawal from all occupied Arab territories), Syria did not see any point in attending. Kissinger subsequently failed to secure Syria's agreement to attend the conference.

When Sadat found out Syria's position, he sent his Foreign Minister to Damascus on 17 December in an attempt to persuade Assad to change his decision. Assad informed Fahmy that Kissinger had conveyed the impression that, whereas agreement had been reached for a disengagement on the Egyptian front, there were still obstacles to reaching a similar agreement on the Syrian front. When Kissinger had arrived in Damascus on 15 December, he reiterated the same view but added that disengagement on the Syrian front could be debated at Geneva. Kissinger further asked that Syria supply him with a list of Israeli prisoners of war, which he promised not to hand over to Israel until after he had made sure of its willingness to undertake a partial withdrawal on the Syrian front. Naturally, Assad refused this request. Kissinger informed Assad that he had agreed with Sadat 'on everything', meaning that agreement had been secured on all future measures. At the same time, there was a prior firm understanding between him and Sadat that the Egyptian–Syrian positions should be unified and that partial withdrawal by Israeli forces from both the Egyptian and the Syrian fronts would be announced at the same time in Geneva. After what Assad heard about differentiating between withdrawals on the two fronts and that disengagement on the Egyptian front would be announced independently, he could not agree to Syria's participation in the Geneva conference. Assad concluded that if the Egyptian–Syrian alliance was allowed to fall now, it would not be restored for a long time to come. Obviously Assad had the impression that Egypt had not informed him of all the agreements concluded with Kissinger. Kissinger, on the other hand, had played his role craftily in provoking ill-feeling between Syria and Egypt in this critical period by his double-dealing and innuendoes. While he informed Sadat that a disengagement on the Syrian front would be achieved simultaneously with the Egyptian disengagement, he informed Assad that there were still obstacles to be overcome before achieving a disengagement on his front. He also hinted to Assad that agreement with Sadat encompassed 'everything' and was 'complete', insinuating that it touched upon issues Assad was not aware of and could only guess at.

On 17 December, Syria announced its refusal to attend the Geneva Conference and stated that contacts with Kissinger had assured it that the conference would not achieve the Arab objectives relating to Israeli withdrawal from the Arab territories or establishing Palestinian rights. I became aware then that public dissension between Syria and Egypt had begun and that the reason was the decoys Kissinger was using, not least of which was the Peace Conference that did not achieve any peace. I hastened to warn Fahmy against Egypt going alone or with only Jordan to Geneva, as this would initiate an Egyptian–Syrian disagreement that could spread to other Arab countries. I was convinced that Egypt should bide her time and show more concern in coordinating with Syria, and that the conference should be postponed. In the absence of Syria, there would hardly be a peace conference – or peace, for that matter. Postponement was not difficult: the conference was to meet on 18 December, to be postponed to 21 December because of domestic differences in Israel. It was therefore possible to postpone it for yet another period until a basis of understanding could be reached that would allow Syria to attend.

When I learned that the Soviet Union had agreed on the meeting and on participating in it despite Syria's absence, I felt that its participation was not in Syria's interests. I was later to discover that Assad was incensed by the Soviet decision. Kissinger did succeed in sowing seeds of distrust for a while between Syria and the Soviet Union.

Fahmy informed me that Sadat had decided Egypt would participate in the conference, despite Syria's absence.

The Egyptian delegation left for Geneva, anticipating that partial Israeli withdrawal on the Egyptian front would be announced there. The conference was attended by Israel, Egypt and Jordan at the invitation of both the US and the USSR and under the formal supervision of the UN Secretary-General. The conference adjourned the following day without achieving any results. A statement was issued to the effect that a military committee had been set up to discuss disengagement between the forces on the Sinai front only. The committee failed to reach an agreement and the Egyptian delegation returned to Cairo on 28 December.

The failure of the conference was paralleled by a flagging in inter-Arab relations. Syria had informed the Arab countries that the Egyptian–Syrian alliance had crumbled, in view of Egypt's solitary action and Syria's own suspicions that Sadat was moving towards a bilateral solution. Meanwhile, Sadat was irked by Israeli obduracy, especially since he had attended Geneva despite Syria's refusal to do so, and he began to speak publicly of the feasibility of destroying the Israeli pocket.

In the meanwhile, the Military Command in Egypt had re-gained its confidence after the ceasefire and began amassing the forces necessary to destroy the Israeli pocket. Egypt was simul-taneously able to compensate for most of its losses in tanks. It had received six armoured brigades and a reasonable number of anti-tank rockets and anti-aircraft missiles at the time. It had also received a number of SAM-3 missiles. The military plan for destroying the pocket was drawn up and a commander for this operation appointed after it became evident that the operation could not be conducted from Cairo. From a military point of view, the situation of the Israeli forces west of the Canal was extremely fragile. They had trapped themselves in a pocket ninety kilometres long and an average of twenty kilometres wide, encircled by the Egyptian forces on every side except in the Defresoir zone which had a width of only seven kilometres. Once that gap was closed, the Israeli forces would be completely besieged.

General Gamasy came to my office to take the vow as the new Military Assistant Secretary-General of the Arab League after Sadat had appointed him Chief of Staff of the Egyptian forces to succeed General Shazli. He told me that day that the destruction of the Israeli pocket was completely feasible from the purely military point of view. He was weighing every word carefully and I was aware that he was one of the most efficient commanders of the Egyptian army. The Israeli military forces that crossed to the west of the Canal had tried very hard to occupy the cities of Ismailia and Suez, but had failed in face of ferocious popular resistance; consequently they were restricted within the pocket. Israel was unable to supply them with reinforcements while the Egyptian forces besieging them were getting stronger every day. When Sadat said that the Israeli forces were in a trap, this was a valid description of the situation. The Israeli army, for the first time in its military history, was forced, together with its 600 tanks, to take defensive positions, while Egypt had amassed around the pocket about 1,000 tanks, not to mention its superiority in anti-tank weapons and in artillery. The Israeli pocket was within reach of Egyptian air bases. More important was the morale of the Israeli forces, who increasingly felt themselves to be in a real trap, exposed to daily casualties in small, separate engagements. According to UN releases, the Egyptian forces had performed 213 operations, of which 133 took place in the first half of January 1974, causing the death of 187 Israeli soldiers and the destruction of forty-one tanks and eleven aeroplanes.

On 24 December, Sadat approved the military plan for destroying the Israeli pocket, keeping to himself the decision as to the date of its execution. Doing away with the pocket would release the Third Army forces east of the Canal, for the weak point in the Egyptian situation was the position of the Third Army and Israel's control of its lines of supply. Egyptian military thinking was in favour of a speedy and total liquidation of the Israeli pocket, otherwise the Third Army's lines of supply would be completely cut.

When Kissinger met with Sadat in Aswan on 11 January, he was naturally aware of these facts and was therefore anxious to achieve an immediate disengagement. The agreement was reached in record time, in less than a week, while on the Golan front it dragged on for six months. Assad tried to persuade Sadat to postpone announcing the agreement on the Egyptian front until a similar agreement was reached on the Syrian front, but Sadat was of the opinion that it should be announced on the date decided upon, while efforts would be continued for a disengagement on the Syrian front. While announcing the disengagement agreement, Sadat revealed that Kissinger had told him that if Egypt attempted liquidating the Israeli pocket, the US would feel under an obligation to come to the help of Israel, since it could never allow US arms (supplied to Israel) to be defeated by Soviet arms (supplied to Egypt). This was an empty threat, meant to affect the Egyptian decision to liquidate the Israeli pocket. The justification was equally invalid. The US was already fighting against Soviet and Chinese weaponry in Vietnam and was forced to withdraw its forces under the pressure of Vietnamese resistance. It is equally doubtful that Kissinger would have wavered from his support for Israel had Egypt been fighting with British instead of Soviet weapons. The US, on the other hand, could not involve itself in a direct way against Egypt because of international considerations which would pose a serious threat to its interests in the Arab area. Egypt could also, in such a hypothetical situation, invite in the Soviet forces, a large part of which had moved at that time to the south of the Soviet Union. Brezhnev had already warned that Soviet forces might be deployed to force Israel to abide by Resolution 242 and had invited the US to join in such an operation. The US would not have ventured into a military confrontation with the Soviet Union in these conditions: its relations with its Western allies had deteriorated enough through its support for Israel, especially when it declared a nuclear alert and withdrew the Atlantic Pact's stored arms for dispatch to Israel without consulting with the members of the Pact. There was also the increasing shortage of Arab oil, the brunt of which began to be felt by the US and its allies. The US was scarcely in a position to provoke the Arab oil-producing countries into further punitive measures.

On 17 January, Sadat announced that the agreement stipulated the withdrawal of Israel from west of the Canal; that forces on both the Israeli and Egyptian fronts would be reduced; that there would be demilitarized zones between the two lines with a UN forces' presence. He also announced that he had promised Kissinger that the US would be treated like the European countries as regards Arab oil: the boycott on oil supplies to the US would be lifted after the execution of the disengagement agreement on the Egyptian front. With this promise to Kissinger, on 31 January Nixon hastened to declare the possibility of the resumption of supplies of Arab oil to the US. The Arab oil-producing countries felt that this could not be until a partial withdrawal had been effected on the Syrian front. On 6 February, Kissinger reacted by saying that he had been given 'every reason to think that if such steps were realized, the Arab boycott would be removed. If now pressure tactics are continued, it can only be construed as blackmail, and will affect how we conduct our diplomacy.' . . . Another meaningless threat. In fact, the White House official spokesman declared on 19 February that 'the President had warned me against using the word blackmail'.

While Kissinger was claiming that the action taken on the Egyptian front was a step in the direction of a final solution, Dayan declared on 18 January that the disengagement on the Egyptian front was based on his November 1971 proposal for opening the Suez Canal for navigation. His point of view at the time was that the passes represented a better line of fortifications for the Israeli forces than the Suez Canal, especially after Egypt had succeeded in building its missile wall along the Canal. Golda Meir was more explicit when she stated on 22 January that Israel had not accepted any commitments that went beyond the disengagement agreement on the Egyptian front, while Egypt had undertaken not to obstruct Israeli navigation at Bab el-Mandab.

In the meantime, relations between Egypt and the Soviet Union were suffering great strain. The Soviet leaders were convinced that Egypt had decided to exclude them from the negotiating process, so they decided to stop their arms supplies to Egypt. The Egyptian Foreign Minister left for Moscow after the disengagement agreement in an attempt to mend the rift. After his return, a number of Socialist countries' ambassadors came to inform me that the visit had failed to change Soviet convictions that Egypt had put all its confidence in the US, under the misapprehension that it had changed its position, while alienating its real friends who had for many years extended economic, political and military support to enable Egypt to reach a comprehensive settlement.

Sadat issued invitations to a mini-summit meeting in Cairo, comprising King Faisal, Assad, Boumedienne and himself, to lift the oil boycott on the US. Assad suggested the meeting be convened in Algiers since his presence in Cairo might be construed as approval of the separate agreement concluded between Egypt and Israel. The meeting took place in Algiers from 12 to 14 February; it was decided that the meeting of the Petroleum Ministers scheduled for February be postponed. Assad objected strongly to the resumption of oil shipments to the US. The Heads of State decided that the Foreign Ministers of Saudi Arabia and Egypt should proceed to Paris to meet with Pompidou, then to Washington to urge Nixon for a disengagement on the Golan so that oil supplies could be resumed to the US, and that this should be followed by working towards achieving a comprehensive settlement.

I proceeded to Lahore to attend the Islamic Conference on 22 February, where I had a chance to meet with Arab Heads of State. Sadat asked me to postpone to September the Arab summit meeting scheduled for April when disengagement on the Syrian front, together with the resumption of oil supplies to the US, would have been achieved. Boumedienne and Assad were in favour of holding the summit meeting on time: Boumedienne deplored the friction between Egypt and Syria which might lead to a polarization throughout the whole Arab nation; Assad told me how dismayed and disappointed he was when, after cooperating with Sadat fully and faithfully, he heard him announce disengagement on the Egyptian front, letting Syria down despite their agreement that disengagement should take place on the two fronts simultaneously and that then they would attend the

Geneva Conference together after Kissinger fulfilled his promise to Sadat of an Israeli–Syrian disengagement. When Kissinger told him that disengagement on the Syrian front was not feasible at the present time, he refused to attend the Conference and had expected Egypt to follow suit. Assad also referred to the question of the exchange of prisoners of war, which Sadat approved – while believing that it should have been postponed until after the final settlement. Assad continued that we would be ill advised to forgo whatever levers of pressure remained available to us in return for evasive and obscure promises made by Kissinger who was adamantly refusing to offer assurances that Israeli withdrawal would be from all occupied Arab territories. If Sadat had apprehensions about exposing our differences at the summit meeting, Assad said he would like to assure him that he would not discuss them except with him personally or within the framework of a mini-summit, similar to the one convened recently in Algiers. With regard to oil, he said we had agreed at one time not to resume oil shipments to the US until after Israeli withdrawal from all occupied Arab territories had been achieved; then we had agreed that we would do it after the disengagement of forces on both the Syrian and Egyptian fronts. Now Sadat wanted us to do so after a disengagement on only the Egyptian front. He concluded that the differences with Sadat were not over principles but over the means for achieving those principles. He maintained that we should move gradually and patiently and not give up for nothing what we had in our hands. The Syrian–Egyptian alliance should continue, whatever happened, and we should never allow Kissinger to undermine it.

King Faisal said that he did not object to resuming oil shipments to the US – but only after it fulfilled its pledge of disengagement on the Syrian front.

After the return of Arab Heads of State, Kissinger began another shuttle between Syria and Israel but he could not reach an agreement because Israel insisted on continuing to occupy the Syrian town of Kuneitra.

Gromyko arrived in Cairo to confer with Sadat on 2 March, one day after the resumption of diplomatic relations between Egypt and the US. He summarized for me the causes of the mistrust that had developed into basic differences: that the Soviet Union felt that the resumption of complete diplomatic relations with the US before reaching a comprehensive settlement was not only weakening Egypt's position but also that of the Soviet Union in her support for Arab demands. Gromyko went on to compare this position and the position adopted by the Socialist countries when they severed diplomatic relations with Israel as a result of its invasion of the Arab countries in 1967. I was made aware of the Soviet dilemma over what policy to adopt towards an Egypt which was moving fast towards establishing close relations with the US and away from the Soviet Union, which would weaken the role it could play. At the same time, the Soviet Union could not turn its back completely on Egypt after all it had invested in political, economic and military support. The only road left open was to continue its relationship with Egypt while keeping a close eye on future developments. The Soviet role, reduced to the formality of co-chairing the Geneva Conference, had rendered it incapable of influencing events in Egypt.

Meanwhile the Arab Petroleum Ministers who had met on 13 March in Libya decided to meet again in Vienna where, on 18 March, they decided to lift the oil boycott on the US, although both Libya and Syria rejected the resolution. This was a remarkable achievement for the US: Nixon had emphatically demanded that this measure be adopted so as not to give the impression that the US was responding to Arab pressures in its quest for a disengagement agreement on the Syrian front.

Kissinger was again shuttling between Syria and Israel in April and May. The situation in Syria as expounded to me on 6 May by Assad in Damascus was that the tension in relations with the Soviet Union caused by a slackening in arms supplies and the attendance of the Soviet Union at the Geneva Conference had disappeared with prompt deliveries of arms and postponement of due payments. Assad had refused to conclude a friendship treaty with the Soviet Union because, in his own words, friendship is not established through agreements but through cooperation and mutual interests. He had equally refused any Soviet presence for operating SAM-3 missiles – a situation which was later changed when Syria found itself facing the Israeli forces alone. Assad had urged the Soviets to improve relations with Sadat, although he did not approve of Sadat publicizing his differences with them at the same time as he was developing close relations with the US. He concluded by saying that Sadat had left him no option but to continue negotiations until he reached a disengagement agreement.

Syria continued its negotiations with Kissinger, applying pressure to achieve the most favourable results possible, until it succeeded in concluding a disengagement agreement on the Golan front on 31 May. The American mass media projected Kissinger's success in exaggerated terms and there was optimism in the world capitals over the assumption that Kissinger was moving towards a comprehensive solution by adopting a new policy which he termed 'step-by-step', and by constant shuttling between the capitals of the countries concerned. My own assessment of the situation was that for the first six months of 1974 Kissinger, for all his dramatic shuttling between capitals, had achieved nothing more than securing a new ceasefire at lines that were far from the 5 June 1967 lines. Had he wanted, he would have moved directly to a comprehensive solution but now that this opportunity was lost, the US would be unable to achieve further meaningful steps towards a comprehensive peace since Israel was growing more powerful and more obdurate, thanks to US manoeuvres. Direct negotiations, which the US had advocated, proved a dismal failure at the Kilometre 101 negotiations, so the US had to revert to our plan for an intermediate party in Kissinger's shuttles.

The following step, after securing a ceasefire and a disengagement, was to meet in Geneva at a peace conference. However, the UN Secretary-General, Kurt Waldheim, informed me on 16 June that there were differences of opinion among the concerned parties over the date for convening the conference. While Israel, supported by the US, felt that it should not be convened before September since it needed time to consider the next step, in Syria's opinion it should be convened immediately. The Soviet Union concurred in this, feeling that the momentum for peace should be maintained. Egypt preferred to wait until after the meeting of the Arab Summit in September, so as to give the Arab countries time to agree on future steps. Jordan demanded that a disengagement agreement on the Jordanian front be reached first, with Israel withdrawing some eight to ten kilometres from the River Jordan. Israel refused the Jordanian proposal, adhering to Allon's project which advocated the continued occupation of positions along the River Jordan in any future settlement. In spite of King Hussein's repeated efforts with Washington, he failed to enlist US support. In September 1970, Kissinger had declared that he considered Jordan a friendly country; when differences had arisen between Jordan and Syria, the US threatened to intervene militarily on the side of Jordan. Now, however, when the differences were between Jordan and Israel, the US unhesitatingly took the side of Israel. There were further contradictions in US policy: while it maintained that there should be a connection between Jordan and the West Bank (in order to prevent the emergence of a Palestinian State), it refused to tell the Israelis to withdraw ten kilometres, to give some validity to such a claim.

I told Waldheim that I was aware of an optimistic note in Western capitals which was not justified by events. He replied that the Western mass media were claiming that the final solution would be achieved by the end of the year 1974, and that this disturbed him, since he was aware that a final solution was still far off; what had been achieved so far was very limited in its scope and effect.

During the African Summit at Mogadishu, Boumedienne expressed to me his apprehensions at the unstudied rapprochement between Egypt and the US which was paving the way for its control of the whole area. He noted that American policy at present was to rob us of all levers of pressure and sources of strength at a time when estrangement between Egypt and the Soviet Union prevailed and relations were deteriorating. He felt that unless an attempt to correct this situation was made, we would have to face the most harmful consequences. He did not object to improving relations with the US within the framework of our common interests, but he objected strongly to a deliberate attempt to alienate the Soviet Union after all the support it had extended in the past. (Boumedienne was referring to Sadat's statements in April in which he had criticized the Soviet Union publicly and mentioned that Kissinger was contacting both Egypt and Israel for a new agreement that would achieve a further Israeli limited withdrawal in Sinai.)

In June Nixon paid a visit to the Middle East, bringing along with him a couple of hundred aides and mass media representatives. Nixon's domestic problems as a result of Watergate had reached their crisis-point at this time. During his visit he announced that the US was committed to realizing compre-

hensive peace in the Middle East. In his joint communiqué with
Sadat, it was asserted that a durable and just peace rested on the
total implementation of Resolution 242 and should take into
consideration the legitimate interests of the Palestinian people.
At the end of June Nixon conferred with Brezhnev, after which
they issued a joint communiqué reiterating the same principles.
Nixon's visit to the Middle East was his last attempt to win
sufficient support at home to keep his post. He failed and had to
step down and announce his resignation on 8 August. Gerald
Ford succeeded him, declaring that he would pursue efforts for
peace in the Middle East; he kept Kissinger as his Secretary of
State.

The Arab Summit Meeting to be held in September in Rabat
was approaching and, despite differences between Egypt and
Syria, the two countries tried not to widen the rift. As a result
of deteriorating Soviet–Egyptian relations Moscow decided to
postpone the ministerial committees that were to meet in
Moscow in preparation for a summit meeting between the
leaders of the two countries. The Arab Summit had to reach
agreement over Arab relations with the two superpowers, at a
period when the confrontation between them began to reflect
itself in Arab interrelations. At this time I was actively seeking to
consolidate Arab–European and Arab–African relations. I therefore flew to Paris on 31 August where, together with Sheikh
Sabah, the Foreign Minister of Kuwait, I conferred with Jean
Sauvagnargues, the French Foreign Minister, discussing the
Euro–Arab dialogue and the measures that were needed to put it
in motion.

The representation of the Palestinians at the peace conference
was one of the subjects that required prior agreement among the
Arab countries before the Arab Summit began, so a meeting was
convened in Cairo on 2 September, comprising the Foreign
Ministers of Egypt and Syria and the PLO representative. It was
agreed that the PLO was the sole representative of the Palestinian
people; Jordan promptly issued a statement announcing that if
the Summit Meeting adopted this measure, Jordan would consider itself as having no direct involvement in the Palestinian
question.

In my political report delivered at the Rabat Summit on 26
October, I observed that the only lesson Israel had gained from

the October War was to build its military power further to deny the Arabs their rights and to consolidate its occupation of their territories; that the basic political tenet of the US in the Middle East remained full support for Israel. The plan of action for safeguarding the security of the Arab world involved maintaining Arab political unity, increasing the military power of the confrontation States, military coordination between the Arab countries, support for the PLO, the establishment of an Arab base for military industries, and economic cooperation. I also advocated strengthening Afro–Arab relations through the establishment of economic foundations and a fund for technical assistance to African countries.

King Hussein repeated Jordan's objection concerning the issue of Palestinian representation. Yasser Arafat referred to an Algeria Summit resolution which recognized the PLO as the legitimate representatives of the Palestinian people and stated that the present Summit should be bound by it. Sadam Hussein of Iraq said that the October War, both in its military and in its economic and oil aspects, had won us more support as evidenced by the fact that 105 countries had voted at the UN for the presence of the PLO in the world community. Boumedienne said that the October War had had two results: it had proved both the fighting capacity of the Arabs and that the Arabs, for the first time, were no longer being viewed as a group of separate countries, but as an interrelated area bound by many ties. He said that Arab trusteeship over the Palestinians had to be lifted and the sons of Palestine allowed to bear their historical responsibilities, and that this should happen within the following two years at most.

Assad said the impression being given by the debate was that we already had the West Bank in our hands and all we had to decide now was who to hand it to, Jordan or the PLO. The October War had not turned conditions decisively in our favour; it had, however, put us on the proper road and we had to continue on it, relying on our human, military and economic resources, and not allowing the enemy to create friction among us. The great danger was to think that, due to the efforts we had exerted, the US had become our friend and would now abandon Israel. US activities after the October War were proof of this. Kissinger was anxious that the timing of the two disengagement agreements should differ. Had the two disengagement agreements been concluded at the same time, our mutual interests, Egypt's and Syria's, would have been better served. What Kissinger was trying was to sow seeds of disunity between Egypt and Syria. Although he had failed so far, he would try again and again. If it was not true that Kissinger was trying to fragment the Arab world, then he should refrain from negotiating with each Arab country separately. When the United States claimed that the West Bank should remain with King Hussein, it was because it was anxious to obliterate the Palestinian case and the Palestinian people.

Sadat proposed the establishment of a Palestinian government in exile and said they should take every inch of land offered to the Palestinians, whether by Kissinger or by the Devil. He continued that we should ignore all attempts to divide us and continue on the road defined at the Algiers meeting: not to forsake one inch of land, no bargaining over our rights, and to uphold Palestinian rights and self-determination.

The meeting decided to earmark $2,350 million for support to Egypt, Syria, Jordan and the PLO. Saudi Arabia offered to contribute $400 million, Kuwait $400 million, the Emirates $300 million, Qatar $150 million, Iraq $100 million, Bahrein $4 million and Oman $15 million – a total of $1,370 millions. Other countries were willing to contribute, but were not able to commit themselves before referring to the relevant authorities in their respective countries. These were Algeria, Tunisia, Morocco and Libya. Other resolutions included the holding of an Arab–African summit conference, increasing the capital of the Arab Bank for Economic Development in Africa, the consolidation of the Arab Fund for Africa, the establishment of an Arab fund for technical assistance to African countries and a beginning to the Euro–Arab dialogue.

While the Rabat Summit in 1969 had been a failure, this one achieved great success. There was consensus on the importance of continuing the battle, refusal to accept partial or isolated solutions offered by Kissinger, the necessity of supporting the PLO as a symbol of the vitality of the Palestinian cause and the Palestinian people, and assurances to both Egypt and Syria that the whole Arab world stood by them militarily and economically so they could act from the vantage-point of strength. An aura of optimism spread throughout the Arab capitals over the success of the meeting, together with a feeling that the following step would be either a comprehensive settlement at Geneva or a return to the battle.

I was next to attend the General Assembly meeting of the UN with a view to raising the Palestinian issue in November. The Arab countries submitted a draft resolution which stipulated that the Palestinian people were the main party to the issue and that an invitation should be extended to the PLO, as the representative of the Palestinian people, to participate in the deliberations of the General Assembly. Israel and the US voted against, while 105 countries voted in favour, a sweeping and unprecedented success, and so on 13 November Yasser Arafat stood at the rostrum of the General Assembly for the first time. Arafat's speech turned into a resounding demonstration inside the UN building, at which most delegates of the countries of the world participated, denouncing Israeli occupation and hailing Palestinian rights.

On 22 November, the General Assembly adopted a resolution upholding the right of the Palestinian people to self-determination, independence and national sovereignty. Eighty-nine countries voted in favour and only eight, including Israel and the US, voted against it. The same day another resolution, inviting the PLO to attend UN meetings as an observer, was approved by a majority of ninety-three votes.

Reaction in Israel was virulent. Rabin, the Israeli Prime Minister, declared that Israel would communicate with the PLO only on the battlefield.

15

Opportunities Lost for a Comprehensive Peace

The image of Kissinger constantly shuttling between the capitals of the region was superimposed over the action in the form of a heroic drama that was not without its pathetic and occasionally its comic aspects – a drama written, produced and played by Kissinger himself. The role he was anxious to project was that of the great peace-maker; in fact, he was sowing the seeds of discord and friction everywhere he went, deliberately aborting opportunities for a real peace. The first opportunity for peace came at the start of the October War when the US refrained from inviting the concerned parties to a peace conference, concentrating instead on arming Israel to the teeth in an attempt to turn the war in its favour. The second opportunity was lost when Nixon visited the region in June 1974, at which time the US could have exploited the visit and the favourable political atmosphere in the area that accompanied it to move towards the establishment of constructive relations that could have led to a comprehensive peace. Soon after came the meeting between Nixon and Brezhnev and their joint communiqué asserting their agreement on a durable and just settlement based on Resolution 242 and taking into consideration the legitimate interests of all the peoples of the region, including the Palestinians. Nixon, however, failed to adopt any step towards the realization of these pledges. When he resigned in August in favour of Ford, the situation was hardly likely to change. Ford's experience in international affairs was limited and Kissinger maintained his supremacy in decision making so far as the Middle East issue was concerned. He continued his devious step-by-step policy which in practical terms was confined to those steps which Israel permitted.

Consequently when Kissinger promised King Hussein to

undertake a disengagement agreement on the lines of the previous agreements concluded with Egypt and Syria, he was
unable to put it into effect after Israel had rejected it. He subsequently directed his efforts, during his visits to the Arab capitals, to attempts to dissuade them from acknowledging the PLO
as the sole legitimate representative of the people of Palestine at
the Rabat Summit. My comment at the time was that Kissinger
wanted the Arabs to pay for Israel's obduracy. Now and for the
next few years he was anxious to achieve partial settlements and
steered away from the comprehensive settlement.

While Ford was conferring with Brezhnev on 23 November
1974 at Vladivostok, tension prevailed in the region as a result of
the heavy air strikes launched by Israel on the south of Lebanon
and on Palestinian refugee camps; consequently the Middle East
figured prominently in their debate. Their joint communiqué
spoke of the necessity of taking into consideration the legitimate
interests of the peoples of the area, including the Palestinians, and
referred to the necessity of convening the peace conference. The
two parties failed, however, to agree on the date of the conference; the Soviets insisted that it be convened as soon as possible, while the American side was anxious to delay it as long as
possible in response to Israel which was apprehensive of the
Soviets co-chairing the conference and of the UN presence,
however formal it might be, lest this lead to an insistence that it
implement Resolution 242.

The ink had hardly dried on this clear statement advocating a
comprehensive settlement before Kissinger was actively seeking
a new partial agreement between Egypt and Israel, which he had
already discussed with Allon, the Israeli Foreign Minister, in
Washington on 16 December.

Assad had assessed this step accurately as an attempt to obstruct the realization of a comprehensive peace and to alienate the
Arabs from each other. Rabin, the Prime Minister of Israel, gave
further evidence of this when, in December 1974, he declared
that the objective of Israel was to cut Syria off from Egypt. The
Soviet Union joined Syria in opposing the partial agreement,
with the result that Egyptian–Syrian relations declined and
Soviet–Egyptian relations witnessed a further deterioration,
which led Brezhnev to postpone his proposed visit to Egypt in
January 1975.

I invited the Foreign Ministers of Egypt, Syria and Jordan and the head of the Political Department of the PLO to a meeting at the seat of the Arab League, in an attempt to bring a degree of coordination to the confrontation countries, specifically between Jordan and the PLO and in accordance with the decision by the last Summit Conference. We were supposed to follow up this meeting, yet the role played by Kissinger at the time led to a further deterioration of inter-Arab relations and thus put an end to the meetings of the representatives of the four Arab countries. Consequently, in an attempt by the Soviet Union to contribute to the solution, Gromyko came on a visit to Syria and Egypt in February 1975. In Damascus, a joint communiqué was issued which recommended the convening of the Geneva Peace Conference at the end of February and the participation of the PLO. In Cairo no similar agreement could be reached as the Egyptian government felt that efforts should be exerted first to pave the way for its success and refused to issue a joint communiqué. This showed the extent of the breach between the two countries. However, the Soviet Union, desirous of continuing its relations with Egypt, sent a squadron of MiG-23s which had been contracted for before the October War. Kissinger came to Cairo on 12 February to pursue his attempts to obtain a partial agreement between Egypt and Israel and on the following day visited Damascus, but could achieve no progress.

Violent statements were made in Arab capitals denouncing the US policy and stating that the failure to achieve peace might lead to a renewal of the armed struggle which would, of necessity, call for imposing a new oil boycott. In a statement in December 1974, Kissinger warned that the US would employ force against the oil-producing countries. In answer to a press question as to whether it was moral to gain control of other countries' raw material, Ford said that all wars in the past had been motivated by such a desire. This threat created such a furore in the Arab world that Ahmed el-Soueidi, Foreign Minister of the Emirates, stated that the oil-producing countries would blow up their oilfields if the US attempted to gain control of them, while King Faisal stated that he refused to believe that a sane government would drag the world into such a destructive situation.

During his visit to Cairo on 12 February, Kissinger submitted a project for a new, very limited withdrawal of Israel in Sinai in return for Egypt terminating the state of belligerency. Egypt, of course, refused. The mere continuation of talks over a partial agreement had so incensed Syria and the PLO that the Egyptian Foreign Minister asked me to postpone the Arab Summit Meeting scheduled for June 1975 in Somalia, for fear that Arab differences would lead to its failure.

The PLO issued a statement on 25 February denouncing US projects for a partial agreement with Egypt which bartered a part of occupied Arab territory for the entire national issue, struck at the Palestinian revolution and stabbed the Arab liberation movement 'step by step'. The statement accused Kissinger of trying to undermine Arab solidarity and partition the Arab case.

Anxious over Arab solidarity, I paid a visit to King Faisal at Riyadh on 25 February. He had just completed his tour of Damascus, Cairo and Amman, in which he tried to contain the rift among the three countries. He assured me that he would exert every effort to contain the growing differences and said that Ford had given him assurances to work for the termination of the Israeli occupation of Arab territories. Soon after, while he was still full of faith in the future and the role to which he was destined, I received the news that Faisal had been shot dead; this was indeed a great loss for the Arab world and led to rumours that foreign quarters were behind his murder.

During March I was in Lebanon to try to intercede between the Lebanese authorities and the PLO in a situation that was becoming explosive because of daily reprisals. Talking to Arafat, I pointed out to him that Egypt remained the mainstay in seeking a solution to the Palestinian problem and that the PLO should strive to maintain good relations with it and that, when differences in points of view arose over the approach to be adopted, he would be well advised to meet Sadat and work out their differences. He replied that the statement issued by the PLO had been directed against the policy of the US and that they considered it convenient to issue it before Kissinger's return to the area. He added that naturally he could not object to Israeli withdrawal to the Sinai passes which the Egyptian Foreign Minister had communicated to them, but that they were fearful of a political agreement that would succeed in removing Egypt from the confrontation with Israel before the establishment of a total peace. He added that he was certain there would be no disengagement of forces on the West Bank, contrary to what Sadat, quoting Kissinger, had told him. This being the case, the Palestinian question would be frozen until after the 1977 presidential elections in the US, which in turn would contribute to the Palestinian problems in Lebanon. Certain Lebanese elements were irked by a Palestinian presence in Lebanon, and an Israeli withdrawal of some ten kilometres in the West Bank would not only reactivate the issue but would offer a hope that it was approaching solution. In the event of Israel withdrawing any distance on the West Bank, the Arab League could administer the liberated area until elections were conducted.

In Damascus I emphasized to Assad the necessity of continuing strong relations between Egypt and Syria, and he agreed that this was the position to which he adhered firmly. The differences had started the very first days of the October War when the Egyptian forces maintained defensive positions immediately after crossing the Canal, when the plan agreed upon between the two countries had been that the Egyptian forces should reach the passes and beyond if possible, to enable Syria to liberate the Golan and pose a threat to north Israel. We entered the war together, he added, and should have continued to move together. Instead, he had to face the situation whereby Egypt took decisions without consulting Syria. The proposed new agreement in Sinai, which offered limited Israeli withdrawal in exchange for an Egyptian pledge not to engage in military operations against Israel and to open the Suez Canal to Israeli commodities, once agreed upon, would create great tensions in inter-Arab relations, he said.

Assad told me that Kissinger, during one of his visits to Damascus in the time of Ford's presidency, was advocating a step-by-step movement towards a solution without binding the US to a comprehensive settlement. Assad reminded him that Nixon had pledged a comprehensive solution to be applied in stages and that this contradicted what Kissinger was now saying. Kissinger tried to cast doubt on the veracity of this statement; when Assad asked for the minutes of his meeting with Nixon, Kissinger remarked hastily that this was the policy of the former administration, but now he was expressing the policy of the new administration. Assad commented: 'How can we therefore trust any statement made by a responsible American, even if he is the President of the United States?'

In Amman, King Hussein told me that he was not unhappy about the Rabat resolution for recognizing the PLO as the sole legitimate representative of the Palestinian people, since it had put the whole weight of responsibility on the PLO; but he was not satisfied that this resolution would serve the best interests of the Palestinians. A propos the October War, he said that although he had not been consulted on the war plan, he had extended every possible military assistance to Syria.

Kissinger arrived at the area in March and spent seventeen days moving between Egypt and Israel and some other Arab capitals in an attempt to conclude the second agreement between Egypt and Israel. Israel was offering a limited withdrawal in exchange for a separate agreement with Egypt which was not dependent upon agreements with other Arab parties, that Egypt would agree on the passage of Israeli commodities in the Suez Canal, freedom of movement of personnel between Egypt and Israel, the termination of the economic boycott and the state of war and the establishment of a buffer zone between the armed forces of the two parties. Sadat refused to end the state of war unless Israel would concede that her withdrawal would be from all Sinai. Kissinger returned to Washington after Israel refused to give up any of its conditions.

The US felt that it was losing its grip in the area because of Israeli obduracy which would force the Arabs into closing ranks again, thus paving the way to restoration of a Soviet presence. It was ironic that Kissinger's failure to conclude a new agreement between Egypt and Israel, far from harming the Arab position, failed to serve the best interests of Israel. Kissinger expressed deep bitterness at the Israeli attitude.

Ford was equally enraged and declared that the US would have to reassess its Middle East policy; he called together a large number of prominent politicians, among them Dean Rusk, George Ball, Cyrus Vance, Robert McNamara, Peter Paterson, John McCloy, Averell Harriman and William Scranton, and told them to agree on recommendations on US Middle Eastern policy. George Ball had criticized Kissinger's step-by-step policy on the grounds that it was sure to lead to failure; it would be more beneficial if the US moved towards a comprehensive settlement. Most of the others maintained that a Geneva peace conference be convened for a comprehensive peace. Before the end of April,

Ford declared that there were three options before the United States: issuing invitations to a peace conference in Geneva after urging Israel to withdraw from all occupied Arab territories, in exchange for an offer of strong guarantees for the security of Israel; the achievement of a total settlement between Egypt and Israel; and the resumption of a step-by-step diplomacy.

Israel was enraged and succeeded in enlisting its supporters in the Senate; a message carrying the signatures of seventy-six senators urged Ford to respond to Israeli economic and military requirements. In face of this campaign, Ford, who had temporarily frozen new aid to Israel, felt unable to exert any pressure on Israel to attend the peace conference and had to go back to the step-by-step policy which, although widely acknowledged to be a failure, was the only policy acceptable to Israel. Kissinger's failure to conclude a partial agreement between Egypt and Israel led to an improvement in inter-Arab relations that became obvious when the Arab League Council met on 24 March and the Egyptian Foreign Minister announced Kissinger's failure.

I was in Beirut again on 13 April after a group of ten Falangists machine-gunned a bus carrying Palestinians, which led to the death of twenty-nine of them. This led to an escalation of the situation in Lebanon. Armed fighting in Lebanon began to take on the dimensions of a virtual civil war and posed a new problem to the Arab world; it had a particularly unfavourable effect on Syria and the distribution of its military forces, large contingents of which had to be deployed on its frontiers with Lebanon. On the other hand, Israel revealed its desire to control the River Litani's waters and exploited this situation to annex South Lebanon and pose a military threat to the western front of Syria. I managed to get the two parties to agree to a ceasefire, which was announced on 16 March. I then left Lebanon, certain that the situation would soon explode again. On 17 April, I informed Sadat of the situation in Lebanon and expressed my fear that it could develop in such a way as to affect the Eastern Front unfavourably; that immediate action was called for demanding coordination between Egypt, Syria and Saudi Arabia. The following day, Sadat informed me he would be going to Saudi Arabia on 20 April at the invitation of King Khalid, and that he would meet Assad there. They would discuss the Arab situation and the conditions in Lebanon. A joint communiqué which the

Egyptian and Syrian Presidents signed was issued after their meeting in Riyadh; it asserted the necessity of establishing close cooperation between the two countries and stressed that progress on any front should be part and parcel of a comprehensive progress on all the Arab fronts with Israel.

I was in Damascus again on 1 May, where I met Assad to acquaint myself with his expectations over the Geneva conference on 2 May. He told me that he did not pin great hopes on the conference reaching positive results. This was a view which Sadat had communicated to me earlier.

The Syrian Foreign Minister informed me that Brezhnev was not anxious that this peace conference should convene at once; first, he preferred to come to some understanding with Ford in a summit meeting which was being considered at the time.

Assad referred to attempts that were being made to establish a bloc between the Gulf countries and Iran, to safeguard the security of the Gulf area; he expressed his misgivings about a military or regional alliance outside the general Arab framework which would adversely affect the main issue, confronting Israel.

On 10 May I met Ziad Barre, the President of Somalia, in Cairo. He informed me that King Khalid's objection to holding the Arab Summit in Mogadishu was owing to information he had received that Somalia was moving towards Communism and that it had given military bases to the Soviet Union. He asked the King to attend the Summit, then to tour the country in order to find out for himself that there were no Soviet bases. Sadat, he continued, had shown him a map which had been handed to him by the US and which showed Soviet naval bases. Ziad Barre assured him that his government was building a naval port and an airport in Berbera and reiterated that there were no Soviet bases. I asked him about the photographs distributed by the US to Arab capitals showing a missile in Berbera port. I was amazed when he said that it was in fact the minaret of a mosque.

In the meantime I received a communication from Sudan requesting a postponement of the Arab summit meeting, which received the approval of most Arab countries. At this time the Arab countries were concerned over reports relating to the security of the Gulf countries, not within the context of US threats, but from a hypothetical Soviet threat. This was, in fact, an attempt to derail the Arabs from the real issue at stake. I was of the opinion that Arab security was integrated and that if there was a potential threat to any Arab zone, it was the real threat of Israel, which imposed on us the need to keep our forces fully mobilized.

Sheikh Sabah, the Kuwaiti Foreign Minister, arrived in Cairo on 20 June. It was his view that Kuwait did not approve of entering a military alliance with Iran, but it was willing to consider cooperation in other fields. I visited Iran on 5 July to explore relations. Before my departure the Iraqi Ambassador had come to convey to me that his government believed that cooperation with Iran could take place in economic and other similar fields. With regard to security matters, his government was at present studying ways and means of safeguarding navigation in the Gulf waters, but did not advocate concluding a military pact. (I was three hours late arriving in Tehran as the pilot of the special flight that was to take me there misunderstood Tehran for Zahran and flew there instead. The Iranian Foreign Minister and Arab Ambassadors who were expecting me at Tehran airport assumed that the flight had been lost.)

On 6 July I met the Shah of Iran. He reminded me of our conversation of four years ago when I had told him that we would restore our territories by force and how nobody at the time took such talk seriously, least of all the Israelis. He told me that Iran would stand by the Arabs and that he felt that the PLO should establish a government in exile. He complained of the activities of some extremist Palestinian elements that were harming the Palestinian cause and stability in neighbouring countries. (He was referring to reports that some Iranian elements were being trained in sabotage activities in Palestinian camps.) When I referred to Arab–Iranian relations, especially as concerned Gulf countries, and the importance of developing such relations, the Shah commented that the security of the Gulf was the concern of all its countries, that he was not concerned with imposing a definite form of cooperation but rejected the presence of foreign navies or the establishment of foreign bases in the Gulf. He added that Iran would undertake the measures it saw fit for safeguarding the security of the Gulf.

In May, Sadat visited Kuwait, Jordan and Syria and declared in the course of this tour that ninety per cent of the trump cards were in the hands of the US. He then flew to Salzburg to meet

Ford on 1 June, to stress once more to him the importance of Israeli withdrawal to the 5 June 1967 borders and to ask Ford to announce this publicly. Ford declined, reiterating an evasive promise that the US would strive to achieve this.

After the reassessment by the US of its position in the Middle East, Ford believed that a return to the step-by-step policy was the safest approach for his administration, in view of the pressure brought by the supporters of Israel in the Senate. He proposed to Sadat a partial agreement with Israel. Sadat did not object, but he refused to end belligerency in return for the partial withdrawal of Israeli forces. Kissinger arrived in Cairo on 20 August and, by the end of August, had reached an agreement which the two parties approved and signed in Geneva on 4 September. The agreement stipulated: a limited Israeli withdrawal east of the passes in return for a pledge by Egypt that Middle East strife would not be resolved by armed force or the threat of it and its agreement to the free passage of non-military commodities to and from Israel across the Suez Canal and the continuation of the work of the UN forces. It also stipulated that this agreement would continue to be operative until another to replace it was concluded. Israel also made the condition of extensive US military and economic aid to it.

The US accordingly signed three agreements with Israel for colossal military aid that included F-16 aircraft and Pershing missiles, and tremendous economic and oil supplies. The US also pledged not to recognize the PLO or to enter into negotiations with it before its acceptance of Security Council Resolutions 242 and 338, that it should coordinate its policy in the Geneva Conference with Israel and that the US agreed that negotiations with Arab countries would be on a bilateral basis.

The Agreement was announced on 4 September. Demonstrations swept Syria and some Arab capitals denouncing it, as it was denounced by both Syria and the PLO, while the Soviet Union refrained from attending the sitting at Geneva where the Agreement was signed. The US declared that the Agreement was a new step in the direction of a comprehensive solution. However, its clauses and the US pledge not to recognize the PLO or enter into negotiations with it unless it accepted Resolutions 242 and 338 were, in fact, a negation of a comprehensive settlement. It was in fact degrading of the US to impose this condition for it was America's UN representative Goldberg who had insisted in 1967 that Resolution 242 should be restricted to the settlement of the 1967 dispute and not deal with the political aspect of the Palestinian question. For the US to insist that the PLO accept Resolution 242 was not only a condition void of significance, it was a deliberate attempt to place obstacles in the way of a solution to the Palestinian question.

As soon as the Agreement was initialled, Assad sent messages to all Arab Heads of State denouncing it. The Syrian Ambassador in Cairo came to tell me that his government rejected the Agreement. An Egyptian signature agreeing not to resort to war, in spite of the occupation of most of Sinai and other Arab territories, and Egypt's actual termination of the state of belligerency, allowing the passage of Israeli commodities in the Suez Canal, meant that Israel could now concentrate its military forces against the other Arab fronts. Moreover, his government viewed the Agreement as in total contradiction to Arab summit resolutions and conducive to the fragmentation of the Arab front. Assad visited Moscow on 9 October to request military support, since Syria was now facing Israel alone, after the Egyptian withdrawal from the battle. A joint communiqué issued by both Assad and King Hussein on 11 December maintained that the Agreement had created a breach in Arab relations and that it did not represent any Arab gain but only served the enemy. The point of view of the PLO was that the termination of the state of war with Israel and lifting the economic boycott on it would affect the Palestinian cause adversely.

Saudi Arabia, aware that its role in maintaining Arab solidarity debarred it from levelling criticisms against any Arab party, directed its censure on the US. However, on 2 September Kissinger paid a visit to King Khalid to assure him that the US would now attempt a new agreement in Golan as well as trying to reach a solution to the Palestinian problem and putting an end to all the problems that existed between Israel and the Arab countries. On 29 September, Prince Saud al-Faisal, Foreign Minister of Saudi Arabia, said on American TV that US pledges for reaching a peace would be barren, in view of its substantial arms shipments to Israel, while at the same time it rejected dealing with the Palestinians. He expressed deep concern over the supplying of Israel with Pershing missiles that have a range of

500 miles and can be equipped with nuclear warheads.

At the end of October Sadat paid a visit to the US where he delivered a speech to a combined gathering of the Senate and Congress. He stated that the Palestine question remained the crux of the Middle East strife and demanded that the US lend its support to the Palestinian right to a national home; he also expressed anxiety over US arms shipments to Israel.

On 10 November 1975, a group of non-aligned countries succeeded in getting the approval of the UN General Assembly to a resolution stipulating that Zionism was a form of racism and racial discrimination. The rection of Israel to this resolution was virulent, especially since some speakers equated Zionism with Hitler's fascism. At about this time Sadat was delivering a speech in the People's Assembly in which he announced the abrogation of the friendship treaty between Egypt and the Soviet Union on the grounds that the Soviet Union had not respected its treaty obligations to supply Egypt with arms and spare parts. Although this decision was expected to have some effect on US policy, the fact that it coincided with a presidential campaign robbed it of any possible benefit in this direction. In fact, as usually happens in such circumstances, the campaign saw the two candidates, Ford and Carter, trying to outbid each other in order to win over the Jewish vote.

A deterioration in the situation in Lebanon demanded an inter-Arab action to save Lebanon. An understanding between Egypt and Syria was an essential factor in this direction. Consequently, the Foreign Ministers of Saudi Arabia and Kuwait agreed with Assad on 9 May to a meeting between the Prime Ministers of Egypt and Syria in Riyadh on 28 May, which Sadat approved when they met him the same day. For my part, I issued invitations to the Arab League to meet on 8 June to study the situation in Lebanon. I had received a message from the President of Lebanon, Faranjia, that the entry of Syrian forces into Lebanon had been at the request of the Lebanese authorities, in order to restore security to Lebanon. He accused the PLO of violating the Cairo Agreement. The Council of the Arab League decided to order a ceasefire and to establish an Arab peace force, under the supervision of the Secretary-General of the Arab League, which should be dispatched immediately to replace the Syrian forces. A committee, composed of myself and the Foreign Minister of

Bahrein, was also to proceed immediately to Lebanon. I left for Damascus, where I met with Assad who approved joint Arab action and welcomed participation in solving the Lebanese problem if the Arab countries so wished. The following day I impressed on Yasser Arafat the necessity of improving relations with Syria, which was able to extend protection to the Palestinians against any attempts to halt their resistance.

There was a difference of opinion over the jurisdiction of the Arab security force. President Faranjia insisted that the Syrian forces remain and signed a statement rejecting the Arab security force. At one of our meetings he said that the Arab peacekeeping force would not be able to perform its duties and that what was needed was a deterrent Arab force to impose peace. A preparatory meeting was convened in Riyadh, comprising the Heads of State of Saudi Arabia, Egypt, Syria, Kuwait, Lebanon and the chairman of the PLO; it decided to transform the Arab security force into a deterrent force with jurisdiction to impose a ceasefire, maintain security and remove all armed manifestations and collect heavy arms under the command of the President of Lebanon.

The Summit Meeting was held in Cairo on 25 October. I told the meeting that Israel was the only party benefiting from the strife in Lebanon. Assad spoke of the return of good relations with Egypt. Sadat said that Israel was committing a miscalculation when it assumed it could re-export defeatism to the Arab nation. The Summit endorsed the Riyadh resolution that a deterrent force be sent to Lebanon; this was the first of its kind in the history of the Arab League.

To follow up the success this meeting had in restoring Arab resolution for solidarity, I mentioned to Assad the need to further consolidate Egyptian–Syrian relations through constant contacts.

I met with King Hussein in Amman on 9 November; he was happy at the restoration of good relations between Jordan and Egypt. While I was with him, Assad telephoned and communicated to him my proposal for constant contacts between the Heads of the three countries, to maintain an Egyptian–Syrian–Jordanian coordination.

Assad arrived in Cairo on 18 December at Sadat's invitation, and the two agreed on the establishment of a unified political command for the two countries; they also demanded that the peace conference at Geneva meet no later than March 1977.

Meanwhile, Jimmy Carter had won the US presidential election and emerged on the world scene, projecting the image of a man who adheres to principles and upholds human rights. In fact, the solution to the Palestinian problem did not demand more than the application of those values that Carter was expounding. An added cause for optimism was the termination of Kissinger's control over US foreign policy and his replacement by Cyrus Vance, who was known to be a man of integrity.

I was convinced that we were in need of the type of cooperation that had emerged with the Egyptian–Syrian joint political command, which would help us in the next hard stage of negotiations at Geneva. With the beginning of the year 1977, I would ask myself continuously whether we could really maintain a unity of Arab action, or whether this unity would disappear at the first sign of differing points of view.

16

Sadat's Visit to Jerusalem

Carter assumed the presidency of the US in January 1977, bringing with him new ideas and a new working team, and injecting thereby fresh hope in the Arab capitals that the US would seek a more constructive approach than that of Kissinger. In February Carter announced the need to move speedily to a comprehensive settlement. The road was not quite paved for such an achievement, however, because of the many obstacles that Kissinger had laid in the road to any solution that might prove unacceptable to Israel. There was the US pledge in February 1972 not to undertake any initiative without prior discussion with Israel and, later, the pledge in September 1975 to refrain from recognizing or negotiating with the PLO before its approval of Resolution 242, irrelevant as it was to the Palestinian question. There was also a pledge that the US would veto at the Security Council any resolution that did not conform to Israel's interests. There were also pledges made to the Arab side; but Israel had the weight of the powerful pro-Jewish lobby that always managed to force the US administration to retract on such pledges. Moreover, Kissinger had actively worked to supply Israel with such colossal quantities of arms that the Israeli army managed to double its size by the beginning of 1977, while its air force, according to Israeli statements, increased by thirty per cent, and acquired the most recent and highly sophisticated aeroplane in the world, the F-15. It also managed to increase its number of tanks by more than fifty per cent; with the most recent US tanks, artillery force was doubled and was furnished with long-range, more developed cannon, and infantry brigades were transformed into mechanized brigades. Israel had received all its requirements in armoured carriers, which increased by some seven hundred per cent. With this enormous military superiority, Israel felt more secure in clinging to the occupied territories.

With Egypt signing the Sinai partial agreement in September 1975 and its pledge not to use force, the Eastern Front was facing a serious imbalance in military force in favour of Israel.

Economic aid also increased after the October 1973 War. In 1974, it reached $2,200 million, to increase further in the following years, when it reached, with other American sources of aid, some $3½ billion a year, which meant a yearly bonus of $1,000 to every individual in Israel from the US.

The military power of the Arab States, on the other hand, declined after 1973, when the Soviet Union ceased supplying Egypt with arms. On the political level, Arab solidarity, which was the mainstay of Arab power, and the pressure we could exert by withholding oil supplies, had equally become infirm. The declaration of a unified political leadership between Egypt and Syria, which Sudan later joined, revived hopes for a return of Arab solidarity, but I felt that more than a mere declaration to repair bridges of confidence between the two countries should be attempted, to avoid differences in the future.

Meanwhile, Carter began his moves in February, by sending Cyrus Vance, the new Secretary of State, on a tour of Egypt, Syria, Jordan, Saudi Arabia and Israel. The reason for this prompt action by the new administration was that it already had at its disposal a study called the 'Brookings Report', which was drafted in late 1975 by a number of Middle Eastern experts including Brzezinski, the National Security Adviser to Carter. The study outlined a comprehensive solution which could not be achieved without a phased withdrawal by Israel from the territories it occupied in June 1967, with such modifications as were mutually acceptable and the establishment of peaceful relations also in stages, together with the right of the Palestinians to self-determination which meant either an independent State or a federation with Jordan, on condition that the Palestinians accepted the sovereignty and integrity of Israel. It also stipulated the presence of peace guarantees. Vance's talks during his tour were based on the conclusions of this report. Vance recognized Arab unanimity on the importance of PLO participation in order to reach a comprehensive settlement. Assad maintained that there should be one Arab delegation which would speak on behalf of all the Arabs, and he reiterated this same point to Carter when he met him in Geneva on 9 May. Israel, however, informed

Vance that it rejected both a unified Arab delegation and the presence of representatives of the PLO. Carter proposed the participation of Palestinians who were non-members of the PLO. He also said that the Arab side could participate with one delegation at the first sitting of the conference and thereafter split into committees on a geographical basis; this meant a return to several Arab delegations at Geneva.

The representation of Palestine at the Conference was an essential matter that could not easily be by-passed. At the UN in 1947, the Palestinian people had been represented by a delegation which demanded independence and the termination of the British mandate, at a time when the representation of the Jewish Agency was controversial. The PLO was sanctioned to speak on behalf of the Palestinians in the UN General Assembly, its commissions and specialized agencies. To deny it participation at the Geneva Conference was to ignore a fundamental condition for peace.

Carter adopted an approach which was different from that of the two preceding presidents. Not only did he conduct talks himself, he also projected his views to the American people in an attempt to win public opinion to his support. He made a statement to the press on 9 March, while Rabin was on a visit to Washington, to the effect that Israel should withdraw to the 5 June 1967 borders although there might have to be some minor adjustments, but that remained to be negotiated. He also cast doubts on the validity of Israel's concept that its borders should rest on geographic considerations; when Israel refused the establishment of a demilitarized zone on its territories, he stated that the demilitarized zone 'might very well be a line that is fairly broad, say twenty kilometres or more, where demilitarization is guaranteed on both sides'. Some days later, he stated that the Palestinians should have a homeland of their own.

These statements raised Israeli anxiety, especially when Carter abrogated the decision made by Nixon to give Israel priority in arms supplies over NATO members. Faced with Israeli fury over these statements, he tried in later statements to appease its demand for secure borders outside the international borders by saying that defensive borders might or might not conform to legal borders and that it was possible to grant Israel defensive facilities outside the permanent recognized borders. Sadat retorted, during his visit to Washington in April, that no country should have more than its international borders.

Begin had just taken over the premiership of Israel; he was the leader of the extremist faction which rejected the establishment of a Palestinian State and the return of Israel to 5 June 1967 borders, and declared that Israel had liberated Judaea and Samaria (the West Bank), making it clear that he considered them to be part and parcel of Israel.

The State Department issued a statement that, in consideration of Arab acceptance of peace with Israel, Israel should withdraw from the occupied territories on all fronts and agree to the formation of a Palestinian homeland.

Carter invited Sadat to visit Washington in April and, during the talks, touched on the problem of Palestine, maintaining that to establish peace it was necessary to seek a solution to the problem.

When Carter met Assad in Geneva on 9 May, Assad stressed the absolute necessity for the establishment of a Palestinian State in the West Bank and Gaza, and told him that Syria would condone any ties to be established between the new State and Jordan, in accordance with the wishes of the two parties.

Begin visited Washington in July, and Israel mobilized its supporters to exert the most extreme pressure on Carter to agree to Israel's schemes and to respond to its economic demands. Immediately upon his return to Israel, he announced the establishment of three new settlements in the West Bank, thereby throwing down a challenge to the US administration which had declared that the establishment of settlements in the occupied territories was contrary to international law and constituted an obstacle to peace.

I visited London in July and met with the Foreign Secretary, Dr David Owen, to convey to him my impression that the time was opportune for the European community to move towards cooperation with the US administration for the establishment of peace. He answered that they were in touch with Washington and were convinced of Carter's goodwill in this direction. He then sprang on me the question: what would the situation be if Carter failed. I answered that we had to consider such an eventuality in historical perspective, and that the problem started in 1947 when the General Assembly decided to establish the State of Israel in a part of Palestine. In the thirty years that had elapsed since this act, four wars had taken place. The problem could continue for another thirty years and with it similar strife until peace is achieved, so we would be well advised to try to accomplish it now and thereby save ourselves and the world all the inevitable sacrifices and ordeals of a war.

The following day I met a number of Members of Parliament, among whom was Walter Dennis who was also an expert on the Middle East question. He had met Brzezinski two weeks earlier; he conveyed to me his impression that, in fact, the US administration was serious in trying to achieve a peaceful settlement but that in view of the obstacles raised by Israel it might be forced, instead of moving directly to a comprehensive solution, to adopt a more circuitous route which would need a longer time. He sensed that the US needed the aid of the Arabs who should be trying to influence events. In explanation of this point, he said Israeli military superiority over Egypt was increasing and this put the Arab side into a weaker bargaining position, and Egypt should therefore try to repair this situation. Syria was receiving arms from the Soviet Union and he did not feel that Washington was irked by this. He also referred to the fact that the Arab countries possessed oil revenues and a currency surplus that could, if used properly, lend weight to the Arab negotiator. From the talks I had in London, I felt that the information available to official circles was that Carter would not pressure Israel by freezing arms supplies and that the Arabs should depend more on themselves and their sources of power instead of shouldering the US with the whole responsibility for finding a solution to the problem.

In August Yasser Arafat showed me a working paper transmitted to him by the US administration for his comments. It contained a proposal that the PLO declare its approval of Resolution 242 and, if it so wished, could refer in this declaration to the fact that it did not tackle the Palestine question in a satisfactory manner. With his colleagues, Arafat had suggested that the approval should be tied to the national rights of the Palestinian people, the right to establish a State of their own, and the repatriation of refugees according to UN resolutions, but that the US had rejected this formula. I inquired about the *quid pro quo* the US would offer if the PLO approved Resolution 242 according to the suggested US formula. He answered that in such a case the US would express its willingness to conduct a dialogue with the PLO. I inquired if that was an edict for entering heaven, and added: 'Suppose the dialogue began and ended, as we should expect, in achieving nothing, the result would be that the PLO had approved the resolution which did not treat the Palestine issue and would imply its recognition of Israel at a time when Israel rejected any recognition of either the PLO or the establishment of a Palestinian State.' Arafat mentioned that there was a proposal being considered by some Arab capitals to get the Security Council to issue a new resolution which would amend Resolution 242 and would deal with the Palestine question. I rejected this idea, remarking that at that time we were in a weak position both militarily and politically and that this could reflect on the type of resolution that would be passed, inasmuch as it might not be in favour of the Palestine question and even might be weaker than the present resolution. I also asked him what Arab interest would be served by a new resolution. 'We have 242 which tackles the Israeli aggression of 1967 and demands Israeli withdrawal from the occupied Arab territories, and we have a resolution from the General Assembly in 1947, which demands the establishment of a Palestinian State.' The US, I concluded, could not go on ignoring the case of a whole people, the Palestinian people; the time would come when it would have to recognize its representatives and its right to a State of its own.

Vance paid a second visit to the area in August in an attempt to expedite the convening of the Geneva Conference. On his return, a State Department spokesman declared that the US supported the participation of the PLO in the peace talks at Geneva, if it declared its acceptance of Resolution 242. This was tantamount to an admission by the US that the PLO was the representative of the Palestinian people. The implication did not escape Israel, and Begin vehemently attacked the statement which could usher in a dialogue between the US and the PLO.

On 1 October, a joint US–Soviet communiqué was issued inviting all parties to the conflict, including the representatives of the Palestinian people, to attend the conference and emphasizing the necessity of solving the Palestine problem in a way that would safeguard the legitimate rights of the Palestinian people. The new factor in the communiqué was the reference to Palestinian *rights*; the previous administration had confined itself to reference to Palestinian *interests*. The communiqué was welcomed by the Arab countries and the PLO, as well as by France, several other European countries and by countries of the Third World.

On 4 October, Carter went further in an address to the UN General Assembly, saying that 'the legitimate rights of the Palestinians must be recognized'. Israel's outrage knew no bounds. Begin challenged the joint communiqué, declaring that all the Palestinian territories were part and parcel of Israel, and proceeded to begin building more settlements. Carter's reaction was to retract and on 5 October he allowed a joint US–Israeli communiqué to be issued during Dayan's visit to Washington which claimed that the acceptance of the US–Soviet communiqué was not a prior condition for attending the Geneva Conference.

The situation turned into an exercise in political frivolity. In its joint communiqué with the US, the Soviet Union had not insisted on pinpointing the PLO as the representative of the Palestinian people, in exchange for US recognition of the legitimate rights of the Palestinian people. However, when the US in the subsequent communiqué granted the right to reject these same legitimate rights, it rendered its written agreement with the Soviets of no consequence or value whatsoever.

While Israel succeeded in invalidating a document which had been agreed upon by the two superpowers, the Soviet Union expressed dismay at US impotence and the world capitals were astounded at the amount of American subservience to Israeli pressure. Further evidence of this was soon to emerge when, on 28 October, the US refrained from voting on a General Assembly resolution denouncing the establishment of Israeli settlements, while 131 countries voted in its favour.

In fact Carter told a delegation of the Jewish Congressmen at the time: 'I'd rather commit political suicide than hurt Israel.'

In view of this negative posture by the US, I invited the Arab Foreign Ministers who were in New York at the time for the General Assembly meeting to a meeting at which we decided that there were grave difficulties facing the Geneva Conference and agreed to convene the Arab League Council in Tunis on 12 November to consider issuing invitations to an Arab summit.

There was, however, one positive aspect in the policy of the US administration. Its approach did exclude partial or separate agreements – which were Kissinger's speciality – and was anxious to move towards the meeting in Geneva. This in itself meant that the US position had greatly improved over the last four years. However, it needed a demonstration of concerted effort by the Arab countries to lend support to the US, to force Israel into moving towards a comprehensive peace. I felt that an Arab summit conference could achieve this.

On 9 November, a few days before my departure to Tunis, I was invited to attend a speech by Sadat at the People's Assembly. Sitting beside me was Yasser Arafat. Sadat spoke of Egypt's willingness to attend the Geneva Conference for the sake of peace and despite the problems raised by Israel which related to formalities in order to obstruct the convening of the conference. He then added: 'I am willing to go to Geneva, nay, to the end of the world. In fact I know that Israel will be astounded when I say that I am ready to go to their very home, to the Knesset, to debate with them.' We took these words to be an exaggerated form of challenge. The most that Israel aspired to was to negotiate with an Arab country in a foreign capital, e.g. Geneva. At that time, the Arab countries considered a visit by a foreigner in authority to Jerusalem as a hostile act, which made a US Minister who was on a visit to Israel a few weeks earlier decline a visit to that city. The Arab boycott regulations barred any foreigner coming from Israel to land in Arab territory. Therefore it did not occur either to Arafat or to myself, when we shook hands with Sadat after he had delivered his speech, even to inquire as to the significance of that statement.

In Tunis, to my surprise, I was asked by the Syrian Foreign Minister how serious that statement was. It was just a casual remark, I said, for how can you imagine that such a thing could happen? His doubts remained until we were joined by the Egytian Foreign Minister who asserted that the statement was meant to reaffirm Egypt's desire for peace. Any lingering doubts disappeared when the Egyptian Foreign Minister helped in drafting a resolution affirming the unity of Arab action, exposing Israel's attempts to partition Arab struggles, and lending support to the PLO. The Council also decided that an Arab summit would meet on 15 February 1978.

It became obvious, however, that while the Egyptian Foreign Minister was subscribing to these resolutions which were expressive of the strength of Arab solidarity, and they were being adopted unanimously, contacts between Egypt and Israel were being conducted through Washington to arrange for Sadat's visit to Jerusalem. An invitation from Begin arrived on 17 November and an official spokesman announced that Sadat had accepted the invitation and would proceed to Israel on 19 November, in accordance with the letter received from Carter that was attached to Begin's invitation.

Before his departure for Jerusalem, Sadat paid a visit to Damascus where he tried to convince Assad of the validity of the visit. Assad, however, pointed to the violent Arab reaction that he would have to face. Sadat said that even if such a reaction took place, it would disappear within three months, for within that period the Arab–Israeli strife would have been resolved, since Israel would be at a loss to find an argument to justify its continued occupation of Arab lands.

The Egyptian Foreign Minister, Ismail Fahmy, to whom the visit came as a surprise, resigned. I learned later that Sadat did discuss the possibility of the visit with him earlier. He argued against it and, when Sadat did not respond, he left with the impression that the President had changed his mind. The Minister of State for Foreign Affairs, Mohammed Riad, who was completely unaware of such a visit, declined to join the delegation that accompanied Sadat to Israel, and resigned.

The world watched the visit and the emotional reception given to Sadat on its TV screens with mixed emotions. In Israel there was overwhelming joy for nobody there would believe that this was the President of Egypt visiting Israel and advocating a permanent peace at a time when Israel continued to occupy Arab territories. Other world capitals were startled at this audacious step and hailed it as a great achievement in establishing peace between the Arabs and Israel. In Arab capitals, however, people watched the scene on their TVs with a mixture of incredulity and deep grief. How could this happen? Egypt, who, for the last thirty years, had upheld enmity for Zionism and Israel to the Arab nation through its leaders and mass media and had demanded that Arab countries adhere to its boycott. How *could* this happen?

Syria denounced the visit, which it considered a violation of all previous Arab agreements, and its unified political leadership with Egypt collapsed. Iraq proposed an Arab mini-summit composed of the presidents of Algeria, Syria, Libya and South Yemen and the PLO to form a rejection front against Sadat's initiative.

In a speech to the People's Assembly on 26 November, Sadat asserted, however, that the visit had not resulted in relinquishing any legal or historical right of the Arab nation, including our title to Arab Jerusalem; and he added that Egypt had no intention of concluding a separate agreement with Israel. He denied that it even meant a separate agreement with Israel; he said that Zionist pressure groups in some countries (he was referring to the US) had been neutralized while others had been polarized, and that everybody would come to realize the dimensions of this change in a few weeks. He also declared that, as a result of his visit, a large number of Israelis in authority had become convinced that the Arabs would not accept any settlement that did not include both the liberation of the Arab territories occupied since June 1967 and the establishment of a Palestinian State.

Sadat, who expected that his visit to Jerusalem would force Israeli leaders to move towards peace and that the US would urge Israel to undertake a similarly audacious move, invited representatives from Egypt, Syria, Jordan, Lebanon, the PLO, Israel, the US and the USSR, and the Secretary-General of the UN, to a meeting in Cairo in December. The Arab countries and the Soviet Union refused to attend. The meeting, with Egypt and Israel and representatives from the US and the UN, failed to achieve any political results.

An Arab mini-summit was convened in Libya comprising the presidents of Libya, Syria, Algeria and South Yemen, with Yasser Arafat and an Iraqi Minister; they decided to freeze their diplomatic relations with Egypt. The Egyptian reaction was to sever its diplomatic relations with these countries. Arab differences exploded and Egypt's isolation in the Arab world began.

Begin arrived in Ismailia on 24 December with a 'peace project' which was in fact a separate agreement with Egypt; attached to it was another agreement for self-rule in the West Bank and Gaza which sanctioned continued Israeli occupation of those areas. At the press conference held on 26 December, Begin declared that Security Council Resolution 242 did not impose a total Israeli withdrawal from the occupied Arab territories. The meeting ended without achieving anything beside the formation of two committees: one political, at the level of the Ministers of Foreign

Affairs in the two countries, and the other military, at the level of the Ministers of Defence. The possibility of a Geneva conference was therefore completely undermined.

Sadat's position was, however, rendered precarious. His visit to Jerusalem had not been, as he expected, a short cut to peace. Arab public opinion began to turn away from Egypt and to raise an accusing finger at the new US administration for the deterioration in the situation and its failure to act against continued Israeli obduracy. There were even Arab accusations that it was in fact the Carter administration that was trying to sow the seeds of friction among the Arabs. The US tried to deny these accusations in a number of Arab capitals. Herman Elits, the US Ambassador, came to see me on 8 December to affirm that the US was not in any way involved in Sadat's visit to Jerusalem. He also confirmed that Sadat had not consulted with the US before he issued invitations for the Cairo meeting. Elits explained that the position of his government was to give support to Sadat's initiative, but at the same time it saw the importance of a comprehensive peace and felt that separate agreements between Egypt and Israel would only lead to a continuation of the Arab–Israeli conflict. I supported the US position in seeking a comprehensive settlement, and pointed out that this demanded that peace guarantees should be extended to all parties, not only to Israel.

When Elits referred to Arab differences that stood in the way of US efforts to achieve a comprehensive peace, I explained that confidence between Egypt and Syria had completely evaporated, that Assad was quite convinced that Sadat was seeking a separate agreement, despite his statements to the contrary, and Syria also believed that the US was playing a prominent part in this direction. I pointed out that Vance was scheduled to visit Syria shortly; he would be rendering a valuable contribution if he could give evidence to Assad that there would be no separate arrangement.

Elits asked what would happen if Egypt and Israel concluded an agreement, even if the US was not in favour of such a step. I answered that disapproval of the visit to Jerusalem was not confined to Syria; there were other Arab countries that had denounced both the visit and its outcome. In the eventuality of a separate agreement, these countries would be joined by the rest of the Arab world. 'You also have to be aware of the role of the Soviet Union which has persistently rejected partial solutions and would consequently feel under an obligation to continue to arm Syria – or any other Arab country that so requested it. Consequently the no-peace no-war condition will prevail, breeding more radical tendencies and a state of increasing unrest, which might lure Israel into undertaking military operations against Syria and the PLO, when the Soviet Union would not remain a bystander after losing its presence in Egypt.' I concluded that this whole train of possible actions and reactions, which might well have adverse effects on US interests, could be avoided if Carter would implement moves along the lines of a comprehensive settlement as he had proposed, which would make provision for safeguarding the security of both Israel and the Arab countries.

King Hussein arrived in Cairo the same day. He had had a meeting with Assad a few days earlier and told me that Assad was extremely enraged, as he was quite convinced that what Sadat was seeking–in collusion with the US–was a separate settlement, and that any meeting, under the guise of either Geneva or Cairo, would equally be an attempt to mask a bilateral agreement. The Syrians were not happy about Hussein's present attempt to contain the rift for they believed that it would come to nothing. Sadat, with whom he had had a meeting that afternoon, assured him that he was seeking a comprehensive solution. King Hussein told me that he would be going on to Saudi Arabia to confer with King Khalid, and I mentioned that a meeting of the Heads of State of the confrontation countries, at the invitation of Saudi Arabia, might save the deteriorating situation at that time. At a meeting with the US Ambassador in the middle of December after Vance's visit to the area he told me that Assad had communicated to Vance that Syria was willing to attend the Geneva Conference at the appropriate time and after the political imbalance, caused by Sadat's visit to Jerusalem, had been corrected.

The joint Egyptian–Israeli Political Committee convened in Jerusalem on 17 January, attended by the Ministers of Foreign Affairs of the two countries. The Israeli side announced its determination to continue the occupation of all Palestinian territories. Begin, meanwhile, had waged a counter-campaign to dissipate the effects of Sadat's visit on world public opinion and, particularly, Israeli public opinion. He employed abusive words in his comments on a statement by the new Egyptian Foreign Minister,

Mohammed Kamel, which called on Israel to withdraw, and arrogantly told the Egyptian pressmen that Israel did not need Egyptian recognition for their right to exist but recognition of their right to their territories – meaning Palestinian territories.

When Sadat became aware of the failure of the Political Committee to achieve the admission by Israel that it would forgo its demands in the West Bank and Gaza he ordered his Foreign Minister to return to Cairo on 19 January. Begin then began to harp on the theme of Israel's security which he maintained would not be safeguarded by the visit of the Egyptian President to Jerusalem but by its military superiority and by preventing the establishment of a Palestinian State.

All Arab hopes pinned on the goodwill of the US President crumbled when Israel began a large-scale invasion of the south of Lebanon on 16 March, in which it employed over 30,000 of its military forces and occupied territories in South Lebanon. The US had assured many Arab capitals that it would not allow Israeli aggression against Lebanon. The Security Council met and passed a resolution demanding the withdrawal of Israel from the Lebanese territories and instructed the international forces established by the Council to undertake the responsibility for security in South Lebanon. The US, which had subscribed to this resolution and was careful to have it passed before Begin's visit to Washington, was once again unable to persuade Israel to allow UN forces to reach the borders of Lebanon, and so they were unable to cross the River Litani. The US administration advised the Lebanese President to dispatch a battalion to South Lebanon as symbol of its sovereignty. The Lebanese authorities were in the process of following the American advice when the US Ambassador in Beirut telephoned Fouad Boutros, the Lebanese Foreign Minister, after midnight to ask him to stop the battalion, as Israel objected to having a Lebanese battalion stationed in the south of Lebanon!

Washington was being rebuffed at every turn. Not only did it fail to persuade Israel not to attack Lebanon; it also failed to implement the Security Council resolution to which it had subscribed, and finally it failed to follow through a suggestion it itself had made, namely stationing a Lebanese battalion in a part of Lebanese territory.

At a meeting of Arab Foreign Affairs Ministers I was invited to on 27 March, to consider the Israeli invasion of Lebanon, the Egyptian Foreign Minister said that the Egyptian initiative should not be viewed as a failure until after its results had become obvious. It had gained the support of world public opinion and had led to a deep rift between the US government and Begin; in fact differences were spreading within Israel itself. I summed up the situation to the Foreign Ministers in the following terms: Sadat's visit to Israel had resulted in a serious breach in inter-Arab relations; the peace offer made by Egypt had been turned down by Israel; Israel's attack on Lebanon was a blow to the peace initiative and to all Arab countries; and it was important, now more than ever, to re-establish unity of Arab action through an Arab summit meeting. At the suggestion of the Kuwaiti Foreign Minister, Sheikh Sabah, a committee was established under the chairmanship of Numeiri, President of Sudan, with the Foreign Affairs Ministers of Saudi Arabia, Kuwait, the Emirates, Jordan and North Yemen, and myself as members, to attempt a conciliation preparatory to holding a summit meeting.

I left for Damascus for a meeting with Assad, on 4 April 1978, in an attempt to bridge the widening gap between him and Sadat. Assad mentioned to me that Sadat had told him, during his visit prior to proceeding to Jerusalem, that the problem was not the Israeli occupation of the Arab territories but the psychological barrier that prevented them from releasing their grip on these territories. Assad commented that the visit had surely destroyed the psychological barrier that drove the Arabs to persevere and stand up against Israeli aggression; the visit had also upset the balance of power in favour of Israel, and Egypt had made concessions that Israel never dreamt of, in exchange for nothing.

I pointed out that Sadat had already stated that, should his initiative fail, he would publicly declare this, and that he still adhered to a comprehensive settlement and refused a separate one. I added that it was obvious now that Begin not only rejected Sadat's offer but was also challenging the UN resolutions by establishing new settlements in the occupied territories. I proposed that a meeting of the confrontation Arab States should convene, to face these impending dangers. Assad retorted that no such meeting was feasible until after Sadat had declared the failure of his initiative so that the meeting could be convened with clarity of insight and would be able to lay down a plan of action to which all presidents could subscribe.

I then proceeded to Riyadh to meet King Khalid. At the meeting I got the impression that Saudi Arabia considered Sadat's initiative to have been aborted by Begin's rejection of the peace plan, and that there was an opportunity for the Conciliation Committee to bridge the differences between the Egyptian and Syrian points of view.

I flew to Amman on the following day. King Hussein's point of view was that an Arab summit should convene; he informed me that he had prepared a working paper based on the Rabat Summit resolutions for its study. I supported his proposal and suggested that it should be preceded by a meeting of the con-frontation States to ensure the success of the Arab summit.

When I visited the Arab Gulf countries, there was agreement over trying to establish an Egyptian–Syrian understanding before an Arab summit meeting. On my return to Cairo I con-tacted the Egyptian Foreign Minister and conveyed to him the desire expressed by the Arab countries I had visited for the return to an understanding between Egypt and Syria. He returned my call after a while to say that Sadat supported any effort to establish Arab rapprochement.

On 1 May, Numeiri arrived in Egypt to begin his conciliatory mission. After his initial round of talks with Sadat, I was called to Alexandria where Sadat told me that he responded favourably to the efforts that were being exerted for the re-establishment of Arab solidarity, that he was ready to resume political relations with those Arab countries with whom he had severed relations, and that he agreed to attend an Arab summit meeting at any time and anywhere. He added that he still adhered to a comprehensive settlement, the withdrawal of Israel from the occupied Arab territories, the right of the Palestinian people to self-determi-nation and the establishment of their State, and believed that his initiative had not failed but had succeeded in activating inter-national efforts in the direction of peace and was receiving strong support in all the world capitals. He added that he did not agree to a Sudanese proposal to announce to Egypt that it would cease all contacts with Israel and would channel them through the US; that he was ready, however, to stop such contacts taking place in Cairo prior to the summit meeting; but that they might, if the necessity arose, be continued outside Egypt.

I told Sadat that it was my impression after my last Arab tour that real misgivings existed among those countries that were the object of Israeli threats, especially after the Israeli aggression on Lebanon and the failure of the US to prevent it. Because of those fears, I sensed a genuine desire among the Arab countries to put an end to differences between Arabs and they felt that Egypt could play a leading role in this direction. There should be one clear target for the proposed Arab summit; I could not conceive of a better one than to agree on the implementation of the Rabat resolutions demanding the consolidation of the military and economic strength of the confrontation countries. Sadat commented that any support extended to us by the Arab countries would definitely help our negotiating power at the peace conference.

On 5 May I accompanied Numeiri to Damascus where we conferred with Assad. Numeiri said that Egypt was adhering to a comprehensive solution and that it had frozen the meetings of the Military and Political Committees with Israel but that it could not refuse a request by Israel for a joint meeting, otherwise it would be accused of not desiring to achieve peace. Numeiri proposed the resumption of political relations between Egypt and Syria in preparation for an Arab summit meeting.

Assad outlined Syria's attitude once again: it did not accept the visit to Jerusalem or any of its results. The initiative had failed because of Begin's rejection of Sadat's proposals; it was therefore incumbent upon Sadat to declare the failure of the initiative and to terminate bilateral contacts with Israel, so that inter-Arab cooperation could be established on a clear basis.

In view of the polarized attitudes of Egypt and Syria, it became evident that no Arab meeting could be convened at any level.

Begin declared the necessity of the continuation of Israeli forces in some parts of Sinai under the pretext of safeguarding Israel's security while Dayan declared at the joint Egyptian–Israeli ministerial meeting held at Leeds Castle in England in July that Israel could not withdraw from all Sinai except at a price. The Egyptian–Israeli talks therefore came to an end.

Carter, aware of the dead end which faced Sadat, intervened to salvage what he could. He sent Vance to the area in August to visit Israel and Egypt, and a statement was issued in which Carter invited both Sadat and Begin to meet with him on 5 September at Camp David.

The Egyptian Foreign Minister, Mohammed Kamel, came to see me after Vance's visit to Cairo to assure me that Sadat had reiterated to Vance the importance of a plan for total peace. Vance had told him that the US would have to come out with her project for peace at the opportune time and that Carter would then have to present his ideas on the subject to the American people, to enlist their support against the pressures to which he was exposed from the supporters of Israel within the Senate. Vance added that the features of his scheme were not far from the Arab demands, although they were not exactly a duplicate of them.

After the announcement of a tripartite meeting in September at Camp David, and aware that a general invitation to an Arab summit meeting was futile, I decided to make a quick tour of Arab capitals in August with the objective of urging on the Arab leaders the need to make it clear to Washington that peace could never be attained except through a comprehensive settlement. In Riyadh, prior to my being received by King Khalid on 14 August, Prince Saud informed me that Vance had intimated to them that Carter would work for a comprehensive solution at Camp David that would conform to Arab demands based on Resolution 242, including the withdrawal of Israel on all fronts with minor adjustments along the armistice lines in the West Bank, a prohibition on establishing settlements in the Arab territories, and the right of the Palestinian people to participate in determining their future. Vance also communicated to the Arab capitals he visited that Carter was determined to stick to his plan, even though he was aware that if he maintained this position, his term of office might not be renewed. Then I met King Khalid and Prince Fahd and they told me their point of view was to encourage the US in its efforts to achieve a comprehensive settlement. Saudi Arabia was anxious to lend support to Sadat for the establishment of a comprehensive peace. It undertook to finance an F-15 aircraft deal of fifty planes from the US and, together with Kuwait and the Emirates, pledged to extend financial aid to Egypt to the tune of $2 billion for 1977.

In Damascus the position over a rapprochement with Egypt remained unaltered. In the evening, Yasser Arafat called on me and expressed his deep misgivings over the Camp David meeting since he was convinced that the US was unable to work for the realization of the Palestinian State and feared that this would impose a longer period of struggle on the PLO.

The following day I met King Hussein in Amman; he expressed pessimism over the outcome of the Camp David meeting, saying that it would not lead to a comprehensive settlement. His public statement, while it welcomed the meeting, expressed grave reservations.

On 17 August, I arrived in Baghdad where Sadam Hussein told me that the US was in no position to exert pressure on Israel, and that Sadat's visit to Jerusalem was not a tactical move, but a new main line that should have been preceded by inter-Arab consultations.

In Kuwait the following day, Sheikh Jaber told me that he had declined to respond to Vance's request for Kuwait's support of the Camp David meeting, since he was already convinced of its failure.

At Abu Dhabi, Sheikh Zayed felt, in spite of his misgivings, that all efforts for achieving peace should be given a fair chance.

On my return to Cairo, Camp David was approaching and while Sadat was fully confident that it would end in a comprehensive settlement, most Arab countries believed that it would not.

17

Camp David

I was in constant touch with Mohammed Kamel, the Egyptian Foreign Minister. I tried, during the brief period prior to his departure for Camp David, to acquaint him with as much information as I had about the case. I was aware, however, that he, together with the Egyptian delegation, would face a tough job; Israel was in a far superior bargaining position compared to Egypt. Its forces were still in occupation of most of Sinai, the Golan, the West Bank and Gaza, after the failure of the October 1973 War to liberate the occupied territories. The military balance was tipped because of US aid in Israel's favour. In 1978 the strength of its army had doubled as compared with 1973, while the strength of the Egyptian army had substantially decreased as compared with 1973.

By signing the partial agreement with Israel in 1975, Egypt pledged to refrain from using force against Israel, while agreeing that the partial agreement would remain operative until replaced by another. Consequently Israel felt no danger of a military threat from Egypt or even a resumption of the attrition war. There was also the fact that Israel had a complete plan of minimum and maximum demands that had been laid down by the Zionist establishment in clear-cut terms. Israel had executed the first stage of that plan in 1948 with the establishment of the State; the second stage was carried out in 1967, with the occupation of all Palestinian territories, and was expanded by occupying Sinai and Golan.

The Israeli delegation at Camp David had therefore already achieved the non-negotiable minimum which was the second stage of the Zionist plan, namely the acquisition of the whole of Palestine. The occupation of Arab territories outside Palestine was not dependent exclusively on military superiority but, more

so, on international political factors, and was consequently nego-
tiable. The personality of the negotiator was equally relevant.
Begin had taken over at a period when negotiations were acti-
vated by virtue of Carter's insistence on seeking a comprehensive
settlement. Begin, the leader of Israeli extremism, was a staunch
adherent of Israeli expansion who, prior to the birth of the Israeli
State, had conducted successful terrorist operations against
British mandate forces and extermination massacres against Arab
villages in Palestine; he was therefore, from an Israeli point of
view, the ideal person to insist on the maximum. Sadat's visit to
Jerusalem failed to impress him and appeals for peace made no
impression on him; he arrived at Camp David in the same
extremist frame of mind as when in his early years he butchered
the villagers of Deir Yassin. He persisted in maintaining his
rejection of withdrawal from the Arab territories in return for
peace, stating that Israel would not withdraw from the West
Bank and Gaza, a position that was also voiced by Weizmann, the
Israeli Minister of Defence, who was considered by Cairo to be a
moderate.

In August, after Vance's visit to Israel and the Arab countries,
in the course of which he asserted that Carter would submit a
project for a comprehensive settlement, Begin declared that only
a separate agreement with Egypt could be concluded. On 1
September, *Davar* published a quote from Begin that he had
reached an agreement with Peres, the leader of the opposition in
the Knesset, over five points: Jerusalem was the eternal capital of
Israel, Israel would not return to the frontiers of 1967, the Israeli
army would remain in its positions along the River Jordan and
would continue to be stationed in the West Bank and Gaza.

Begin was further assured that he could veto any project for a
comprehensive peace that might be submitted by Carter, because
of the strength of the Israeli lobby and the restraints introduced
by Kissinger on US Middle Eastern policy. After receiving US
assurances, however, Sadat stated that the US possessed ninety
per cent of the trump cards. What happened at Camp David
proved that the trump cards were really in the hands of Israel.
Sadat, on the other hand, had no trump cards to play at Camp
David. He had forfeited all his capacity to apply pressure in the
negotiations for the disengagement agreement in Sinai in 1974
and the partial agreement in 1975.

Prior to the first agreement, Egypt had been exerting military pressure by way of engaging the Israeli pocket west of the Canal in an attrition war, while Sadat, after receiving large supplies of tanks and arms, was threatening to wipe it out altogether. At the same time he had closed Bab el-Mandab at the entrance to the Red Sea to Israeli navigation. Israel, meanwhile, was assiduously seeking the exchange of prisoners of war, for domestic reasons. The US was demanding an end to the Arab oil boycott and the Suez Canal was still closed to international navigation. Egypt forfeited all these levers for pressure by interceding with the Arab oil-producing countries to lift their oil embargo, re-opening the Suez Canal and allowing the passage of Israeli commodities.

When in 1975 in the partial agreement of Sinai it pledged to refrain from using force and agreed to the stationing of UN forces and US observation posts in Sinai to relay information to Israel on any Egyptian military movements, it had forfeited everything. In fact the position of the Egyptian would-be negotiator became even more fragile when the visit to Jerusalem resulted in the severance of any military cooperation with the Eastern Front and the cutting-off by the Arab oil-producing countries of economic aid and the financing of arms requirements to Egypt. The Soviet Union had, in its turn, ceased its arms supplies to Egypt in response to the measures Sadat adopted against it and his public attacks on the Soviet Union. Egypt therefore lost the support of the Soviet Union which had balanced US support to Israel, as well as its main source of arms, at a time when US arms kept flowing into Israel.

Sadat went to Camp David armed only with the knowledge that the Arab cause was just, in other words that he was in the right, and supported by UN resolutions and favourable world public opinion. In world politics, however, the rudimentary fact is that right without might is untenable. Ever since its 1967 aggression against the Arab countries, Israel had trampled all over UN resolutions, and it gave no heed to world public opinion. As a matter of fact, I did predict as much in a press interview with a Kuwaiti paper when I said: 'Believe Begin when he says that he will not withdraw and believe Carter when he says that he cannot pressure Israel.'

Sadat must have been aware of these factors, but he had reached a position in which he could not decline Carter's invitation to Camp David following a series of failures: the failure of his visit to Jerusalem, which was verified at his meeting with Begin at Ismailia, and, later, the failure of the joint Political Committee both in Jerusalem and at Leeds Castle. Sadat would not announce the failure of his initiative inasmuch as he felt it was well received by Western public opinion. Then came Carter's invitation to salvage the situation, and Sadat accepted it promptly.

Camp David meetings began on 5 September and ended on 17 September with the signing of the 'Framework of Peace' agreement.

Sadat, who refused to believe reports he was given about the power of Zionist pressure in Washington, refrained from adopting a negotiating posture by presenting the maximum in Arab demands, to allow himself leeway for manoeuvre. On the first day of the talks, he submitted a peace project which conformed to a large extent to the ideas conveyed to him by Carter and Vance. The project stipulated the withdrawal of Israel from the Arab territories in exchange for the conclusion of peace treaties between Israel and the Arab countries concerned, complete recognition, termination of the Arab boycott and freedom of navigation in the Suez Canal. As regards Palestine, the project proposed the termination of the Israeli military administration in the West Bank and Gaza with a five-year transitional period, during which Jordan would undertake the administration of the West Bank and Egypt that of Gaza, in cooperation with the representatives of the Palestinian people. Before the termination of the transitional period, the Palestinian people would be allowed to exercise their right of self-determination, including the right to establish a State of their own. With regard to Jerusalem, the Egyptian project proposed the withdrawal of Israel from Arab Jerusalem and the formation of a joint municipal council for the city, with equal numbers of Israelis and Arabs for its administration. The Security Council would guarantee the peace treaties and the borders of the different parties.

According to American sources, Begin followed Sadat's recital of the draft with obvious impatience and distaste. The Israeli Premier turned down Sadat's project as he had previously turned down the project outlined by Sadat in Jerusalem.

With the rejection of the Egyptian project, it was expected that the US would submit its project, about which Vance had informed the Arab capitals. A week passed without movement by the US side in this direction; when Mohammed Kamel urged it to do so, he was told by Elits that unexpected obstacles facing Carter had caused the delay.

The Israeli delegation had brought to Carter's attention the written pledge by the US not to offer initiatives without prior consultation with Israel. This prior consultation was transformed, under Zionist pressure, into prior approval. With the US project equally rejected, nothing remained on the negotiating table but the Israeli position. The US project was amended in such a way as to conform to Israeli demands and, excluding Golan, confined itself to a separate agreement between Egypt and Israel. Israel even went a step further, arrogantly demanding the preservation of its settlements in Sinai.

Sadat perceived at once that he could not meet the Israeli demands; he decided to depart and informed Vance accordingly. Carter met Sadat, having managed to persuade Begin not to insist on the preservation of the Israeli settlements in Sinai; Carter conveyed this to Sadat who, considering he had scored a point, decided to stay on. Begin, by emphasizing the issue of the settlements in Sinai in order to incense the Egyptian delegation, gave the impression that the success of the negotiations depended on that issue. When he conceded it, it therefore looked as if he had made a great concession.

Carter on the other hand, realizing the pointlessness of urging Israel to accept a comprehensive settlement, turned to the weaker party in the negotiations, the Egyptian side, and leaned on it to accept a bilateral agreement with Israel within an ambiguous framework for a solution to the Palestine question, and a more ambiguous promise to work for the completion of the comprehensive solution along stages. Carter, to enhance his popularity and better his chances for re-election, had to conclude the agreement at any price. The price was Palestinian rights – in fact, the issue of peace in the region.

The Egyptian Foreign Minister realized that he could not participate in approving a framework that turned from a total peace agreement to a separate peace agreement between Egypt and Israel. He also resented the presumption that Egypt should speak on behalf of the Palestinian people; consequently, he tendered his resignation while still at Camp David and did not take part in the ceremony of signing the agreement.

Israel had achieved what it wanted at Camp David. What it had attained was a reflection of its military and political power, the failure of Carter to stand up to Zionist pressures, and the lack of any negotiating power on the Egyptian side. Besides the procedural mistake committed by the Egyptian delegation in submitting its peace project on the first day instead of insisting that Carter submit his own so that the initial confrontation would be between Israel and the US, the Egyptian project was in fact a reflection of its weak position. It proposed that the Arab countries sign peace treaties with Israel and extend to it complete recognition and the exchange of relations at all levels in return for the withdrawal of Israel. None of these commitments was imposed by Security Council Resolution 242, and the Egyptian delegation had no mandate to offer them on behalf of the other Arab countries without their prior approval.

As regards the Palestinian issue, the Egyptian delegation had no right to speak on behalf of the Palestinians, just as it had no right to offer proposals that stood in contradiction to UN resolutions relating to the issue, for example the partition resolution stipulating the establishment of two States, one Palestinian and the other Jewish, and the many other resolutions relating to the repatriation of the refugees or offering them compensation.

In spite of the concessions made by the Egyptian delegation in the name of other Arab countries which had not delegated it to speak on their behalf, Israel had rejected everything in the Egyptian project that was connected to a comprehensive settlement and agreed only to sign a peace treaty with Egypt by which it would withdraw to Egypt's international frontiers within a period of three years, in return for Egypt's full recognition of Israel and the establishment of diplomatic, economic and cultural relations between the two countries, the lifting of the economic boycott and free navigation for Israeli ships in the Suez Canal and the Straits of Tiran.

The Egyptian delegation had proposed the establishment of demilitarized zones on both sides of the frontier. Israel, in the Framework Agreement, refused the establishment of demilitarized zones on her side of the border but insisted that this should be applied to almost three-quarters of Sinai, and added that Egypt should not maintain more than one brigade within an area fifty kilometres east of the Suez Canal.

Sadat signed another document relating to the West Bank and Gaza which pretended to tackle all the aspects of the Palestinian issue and the establishment of self-rule, yet this document does not contain one single reference to the withdrawal of Israel from the Palestinian territories and the right of the Palestinians to establish their own independent State. It is therefore, in my view, a document without political or legal validity, for nobody is allowed to speak for the Palestinians except those who represent them, namely the PLO which has been recognized as such by the whole world including the US, which conceded as much when it asked the PLO to approve Resolution 242.

I had assumed that when Carter, upon his assumption of the presidency, was seeking a comprehensive solution and rejecting another armistice agreement, he was aware of the dimensions of the issue. When I read the Framework Agreement, however, I was amazed at his disregard for fundamentals relating to Arab feelings and sensitivities. For instance, reference in the Agreement is made to Jordan and Jordanians fourteen times as if Jordan was one of the States of the US or an Egyptian province, with the assumption that the King of Jordan will hurry to either Washington or Cairo to do their bidding. In fact, the US and the other signatories to the Framework went even further, in defining the role of the UN without bothering to consult with the members of the Security Council, again assuming that the UN was an office of the US administration.

Once again, on one of those rare occasions when the whole of the Egyptian and US delegations met (most of the meetings were conducted among the heads of delegations), Mohammed Kamel, the Egyptian Foreign Minister, made the remark that if the Soviet presence in the region disturbed the US, a comprehensive settlement would put an end to this presence. Carter answered that a US–Egyptian–Israeli agreement would better accomplish this end. Carter was thereby repeating an Israeli concept for the establishment of a military alliance among the three countries that would enable Israel to control the whole region. He should have been aware that military blocs had always been anathema to the Egyptians and other Arab countries, and for him to raise this point in an Israeli context would have been even more repulsive.

On 29 September, Saunders, the deputy Secretary of State, came to see me in New York to explain the advantages of the Framework that had just been signed. He explained that his government realized the impossibility of achieving a comprehensive solution in one stroke and had decided that the best way was to move to a solution of each problem one at a time, meanwhile offering both the Palestinians and Israelis an opportunity for co-existence during the transitional period. He referred to the stipulations of the agreement for ending the Israeli military administration and the establishment of a Palestinian Authority from among the inhabitants of the West Bank and Gaza, and a Palestinian constitutional assembly, and that this would lead to the establishment of a Palestinian government with its own sovereignty after five years (the transitional period), which would convince the Palestinians of the advantages to them of the agreement.

I answered that if circumstances had forced Egypt to sign on its own an agreement which denied it complete sovereignty over part of its own territories, then every Egyptian would feel that the security of Egypt was in danger and that an Israel that attacked Egypt twice, in 1956 and 1967, might be more tempted to do so again in the future. 'It is indeed ironic that Israel, which always clamoured in the past for Arab recognition, when this recognition came from Egypt, failed in the Framework to refer to its borders with Egypt and insisted instead on an article on the freedom of movement of persons and commodities between the two countries' – which meant that trade relations with Egypt were more important than Egyptian recognition of Israeli borders.

Saunders was astonished that the Framework contained no mention of Israeli frontiers and had to look through the document to ascertain the fact for himself. When I referred to contradictions in the Framework over the transitional period relating to Palestinian self-rule, he said that it was a question of 'bad phrasing'. I said that the drafting of Resolution 242 had taken us some two months and that I failed to see the sense of urgency that led to drafting this agreement and signing it within two days.

I reminded him of Carter's speech at the General Assembly in 1977, when he emphasized that the objective should not be the achievement of another armistice agreement after which war could break out again, and to Carter's and Vance's assurances all through 1977 and 1978 relating to the broad outlines of a solution, to say that the framework did not reflect any of these promises and failed to achieve a comprehensive peace, and that consequently we faced the very situation that Carter had warned against, namely the outbreak of renewed hostilities. I added that while I did not approve of the principle of discussing the Palestinian question in the absence of representatives of Palestine, I noticed that the Framework's references to self-rule were couched in ambiguous and elastic terms, and that it allowed the continuation of Israeli occupation of the West Bank and Gaza. In fact, it invited the formation of joint Jordanian–Israeli military patrols to safeguard the security of the borders: the borders here, from the context, have only one meaning: the River Jordan, which meant that the Framework had fallen into a serious trap: the recognition of the River Jordan as the borderline between Israel and Jordan. 'Is that what the US means, and how can it expect the Jordanian forces to participate in safeguarding Israeli occupation of the West Bank?'

In fact the agreement explicitly gave Israel the right to prevent the return of Palestinian refugees who had been expelled by Israel from the West Bank and Gaza in 1967. There are another two million Palestinians in Lebanon, Syria and Jordan who have been expelled since 1948. Without seeking a solution for all these refugees, they will continue to be a source of disruption and unrest.

I added to Saunders: 'In spite of your optimistic interpretation of the article on the West Bank and Gaza, Israel has gone a long way in tying that area to Israel, through the extension of its public services like electricity and transport to the West Bank and Gaza. No inhabitant in the West Bank can dig a well without the permission of the Israeli authorities, under the pretext that Israel owns a share in these subterranean waters. With regard to the future, we must consider that the agreement that has been concluded at Camp David is confined to Egypt. We still have a long way to go and hard efforts to exert to reach a comprehensive settlement. It was US procrastination that led to this situation and which will expose the region to unrest. I have heard from certain diplomatic circles that Israel was trying to convince the US that the Arab reaction of anger will subside shortly. I assure you that the problem goes much deeper. There is a genuine feeling that what has happened poses a threat to the security of the Arab countries, now that the Egyptian army has been excluded from confronting Israel. Israel does not conceal its expansionist schemes either in Lebanon or Jordan, as evidenced by statements made by both Ben Gurion and Begin.'

Saunders, however, assured me that Carter was determined to reach a durable peace and that what had been achieved was a step in the right direction. The US, he said, had successfully prevented Begin from annexing the West Bank and now the Palestinians had the right to establish their own government.

None of this, of course, has taken place in the course of the three years since this conversation took place. In fact, what happened was exactly the opposite, with Israel's hold on the West Bank and Gaza tightening even more and with the establishment of further Israeli settlements.

On the same day I spoke with Saunders, I listened to Vance's address to the UN, in which he said that the Camp David Agreements constituted a framework for a comprehensive peace, and that further efforts would be exerted to achieve the legitimate objectives of the Arabs, while safeguarding the security of Israel.

He referred to Carter's address to the joint session of Congress in which he had said that these agreements dealt with a comprehensive settlement between Israel and all her neighbours, as well as the difficult question of the Palestinian people and the future of the West Bank and the Gaza area. Vance asserted that Carter's position was that peace agreements could be neither just nor durable until they solved the problem on the basis of the legitimate rights of the Palestinian people. He asserted further that it was US policy to consider the building of Israeli settlements an act contrary to the Charter and the peace process. Vance added that the Agreements provided for the termination of Israeli military occupation and for the institution of a self-governing Palestinian authority within a few months, that the Palestinians would participate in all aspects of the negotiations relating to their own future and the final status of the West Bank and Gaza, and that the problem of Palestinian refugees would be solved on the basis of UN resolutions.

I familiarized myself with the statements made by the Israeli leaders, specifically those made by Begin after he signed the Camp David Agreements in which he asserted that Israeli sovereignty would continue on the West Bank and Gaza even after the termination of the five-year transitional period and that Israel would continue to build settlements in the occupied Palestinian territories. I realized that Carter and Begin were talking two completely different languages and that each was interpreting the agreements according to his own leanings. In fact I felt that Vance's address, containing precise details relating to the solution of all pending problems, was nothing more than an idle exercise in wishful thinking, and that Carter and his aides had led themselves into believing that they were really on the road to achieving peace. That was the great act of self-delusion.

When Carter invited Begin and Sadat to meet him at Camp David, he must have known only too well that no comprehensive peace could be achieved without the presence of all the concerned parties whom he had previously invited, together with the Soviet Union, on 1 October 1977. It was natural that Syria, Jordan and the PLO would direct their severe criticism at these Agreements, which had taken place in their absence and which contained concessions they could not accept. The Soviet Union, which had always been a major party to all attempts to establish peace in the area, did not hesitate to express its censure of what had taken place via an address by Gromyko to the UN in which he described the Camp David Agreements as a new measure adopted against the Arabs and an attempt to obstruct the achievement of a just peace, asserting that no durable peace could be established unless the Palestinian people won their right to establish an independent State. The posture of the Soviet Union was not merely one of anger and frustration; it was a political position that no comprehensive peace could be established without Syria and the PLO. Carter ignored the Soviet Union in the negotiations but failed to end its role in the region. In fact it accomplished the opposite, for the Arab countries, like Syria, that rejected the Camp David Agreements addressed themselves to Moscow, asking for more help and aid which led to further Soviet pressure and increased the possibility of a US–Soviet confrontation.

The French Foreign Minister proclaimed at the UN General Assembly the need for a comprehensive solution in accordance with Resolution 242, in which all the concerned parties would participate, and that such a solution should rest on Israeli withdrawal from all the territories occupied in 1967 and the recognition of the right of the Palestinian people to a homeland, and peace guarantees to all the countries of the area. He was speaking on behalf of substantial enlightened sections in Europe, saying that the Camp David Agreements fell far below achieving a total solution.

Before my return to Cairo, I made a point of reiterating my views to Saunders and other personalities I met at that time in two public speeches to the Arab-American Chambers of Commerce in Houston and New York on 6 and 12 October. In my speeches I maintained that the Camp David Agreements would fail to achieve peace in the region. Meanwhile, Sadat announced in a message to the Egyptian people from Washington that what had been reached at Camp David was a comprehensive solution which opened the door to all parties and specifically to the Palestinian people whose long night was nearing its end, and a new dawn was about to come forth with the termination of military rule and withdrawal from the West Bank and Gaza except from those points required for security.

Before his departure from Washington, Begin declared that he had not committed himself to suspending the establishment of new settlements for longer than three months, which was the period mentioned in the Agreements for reaching a peace treaty between Egypt and Israel. Consequently, in October the Israeli government decided to double the number of inhabitants of settlements in the West Bank and Gaza. Begin went a step further and declared his intention to transfer his office and that of the Israeli Foreign Minister to Arab Jerusalem, intending thereby to assert that what had been reached was merely a separate treaty with Egypt. He further asserted that no foreign army, including the Jordanian army, would be allowed into the West Bank and that only the Israeli army would be stationed in it, even after the five-year transitional period.

The Camp David Agreements had far-reaching effects on all the parties concerned. Israel had achieved all its objectives inasmuch as it acquired the approval of both Egypt and the US for the continuation of its occupation of the West Bank and Gaza; it had successfully manoeuvred Egypt, the largest Arab country, out of the Arab confrontation with Israel, and got Egypt to approve the establishing of diplomatic, economic and cultural relations with it.

With regard to Western Europe, reactions varied from lukewarm support to a reserved rejection, as with France.

The PLO issued a political statement denouncing the Agreements; the Palestinian people both within and outside the occupied territories declared a general strike on 20 September while demonstrations swept over the towns and villages of the West Bank and Gaza. The Mayor of Nablus, Bassam al-Shak'a, declared that the Peace Agreements ignored the Palestinian people and would in fact increase tensions in the region. Algeria, Syria, Libya, Democratic South Yemen and the PLO held a summit meeting in Damascus on 20 September to denounce the Agreements in strong terms.

While Arab positions were moving towards a total Arab rejection of the Camp David Agreements, the US was sending its emissaries to Arab capitals to publicize the Agreements. The Soviet Union issued a statement denouncing the Agreements and warning Israel against attacking Syria.

While in New York I met with the Arab Ministers of Foreign Affairs who were unanimous in considering the agreement as of a separate nature; no Arab country was entitled to speak for the Palestinians or make concessions on behalf of the other countries. One of them, however, commented that he would have better appreciated the position of Sadat had he declared that he had failed to achieve a total settlement but had managed to get Israel's approval for withdrawal from Sinai which, after all, represented two-thirds of the occupied Arab territories. He added that he could not, however, accept that Egypt would sign an agreement that dealt with the Palestinian question in the absence of the Palestinians and that Sadat would go on to insist that the agreements he had signed were the bases for a comprehensive settlement.

I received a cable from my office in Cairo informing me that Iraq had issued invitations to an Arab summit meeting in Baghdad, on 1 November, to be preceded by a meeting of Foreign Affairs Ministers on 20 October. Iraq had decided to extend the invitation directly and not through the Arab League, as its Charter stipulated, since this would have meant inviting

Sadat, which Iraq wanted to avoid. Consequently, I considered it inappropriate to attend the Foreign Ministers' meeting preceding the Summit. When I realized, however, that all Arab countries had responded to the invitation, I decided to attend the Summit which was called upon to consider the gravest situation facing the Arab nation since the establishment of the Arab League.

The Arab Summit at Baghdad began with an address by President Al-Bakr of Iraq who chaired the meeting. He said that the Arab countries had agreed on the minimum in Arab demands at the Summit Meetings at Algiers and Rabat. The Camp David Agreements, regardless of our different views of them, stood in flagrant contradiction to that minimum. They had, moreover, been approved by the personal decision of Sadat, without reference to the Arab nation or to the parties to the strife. While we did not dispute the right of every Head of State to act within the framework of his country's sovereignty, yet we could not condone or disregard this act which extended far beyond his country, in which he took it upon himself to terminate a struggle which had been the main concern of the whole Arab nation for thirty years in a long, bitter and costly struggle. Sadat's agreement to establish political, economic and cultural relations with Israel had created a new situation in the region which would change the mode of transaction between him and his Arab brothers. We did not want to isolate Egypt which lies in the heart of every Arab, while its Arab people have contributed generously to the Arab nation and to the Palestinian question. The President of Egypt alone bore the responsibility, it was he who had deserted his nation.

After he had finished, he turned to me and said: 'I give the floor to the Secretary-General.' I felt all eyes on me and could sense what was going on in their minds. Before the meeting, I had heard various delegates wondering whether I, as Secretary-General of the Arab League, would adopt a position different from that of the Egyptian President.

My statement was inspired by my experience of the problem over many years. I said that despite the many plans we had outlined since the beginning of our confrontation with Zionism to withstand its aggressive propensities, our planning had been lacking inasmuch as Israel had succeeded in every invasion it had waged against us. I referred to the plan endorsed by the two Summit Meetings (in Algiers and Rabat) to enhance the military and economic powers of the confrontation countries and which had not been effectively implemented. I referred also to the October 1973 battle, planned jointly by Egypt and Syria, which could have had better results, had the planning been more comprehensive. I continued by saying that as long as Zionism, with its expansionist policies and commitment to the gathering of the Jews of the world into the land of Palestine, remained the moving force in Israel, the Israeli threat to the Arab nation would remain. Israel was implementing its expansionist scheme by stages. It might withdraw, to pounce again as when it withdrew from Sinai after its aggression of 1956, to reoccupy it in 1967. It might sign agreements, to trample over them when it considered the time opportune, as when it signed agreements with four Arab countries in 1949, to violate them when it assaulted Egypt in 1956, Egypt, Syria and Jordan in 1967, and finally with its invasion of South Lebanon. Israel did not pay due respect to international charters, or to its obligations, or to its signature on any document if, at a certain moment, they stood in the way of its compulsion for expansion.

Peace could only be established, I continued, on the basis of a comprehensive settlement which would both fulfil Palestinian aspirations to an independent State of their own on their land, and would guarantee Israeli withdrawal from all occupied Arab territories. The Camp David Agreements did not only fail to provide for this peace but equally fell short of achieving this objective.

King Hussein proposed that the meeting end by outlining a plan for the building of Arab self-power on all levels so as to swing the present power balance in favour of the Arabs. Such a plan, he said, would be a long-term one which would begin with the establishment of an obstructive bulkhead around the territories which Israeli aggression had not yet reached. The Arab action plan demanded the total mobilization of all Arab resources and capabilities. There was no way to face aggression with half the force required. Either we succeed or we fail, there was no midway point between the two.

I met with Sheikh Zayed, the Head of the Emirates, that day and he said he would be conferring with a number of Heads of State soon; he felt that the meeting should come out with some positive results and asked me my views on how to achieve this. I repeated to him what I had already conveyed to some other

Heads of State that day: it was not enough to denounce the Camp David Agreements, though such a denunciation was important in order to underline to the US the Arab countries' rejection of the great change its policy had undergone when it accepted a separate agreement and ignored the Palestinian rights, after Carter had proclaimed his insistence on a comprehensive settlement and on the Palestinians' right to a homeland. Due emphasis should have been given to the Rabat resolutions which had demanded the consolidation of the defensive and economic capabilities of the confrontation countries and all other Arab countries, and that those resolutions should be implemented. At the same time, it was important not to be led into attempting to isolate Egypt from the other Arab countries. It would be fruitful, therefore, for a delegation of some Heads of State to meet with Sadat and discuss the Camp David Agreements with him, to question him as to how they could achieve a comprehensive peace. I proposed that the delegation be headed by King Hussein, in view of his detailed knowledge of the problem and of what went on in the West Bank. He had also posed the US a number of questions relating to the more obscure points in the Agreements. The delegation should comprise Sheikh Jaber, Prince of Kuwait, Sheikh Zayed, Head of the Emirates, and Prince Fahd, Crown Prince of Saudi Arabia, all representing countries that had exerted innumerable efforts to maintain and defend Arab solidarity.

A number of Heads of State questioned the practicality of such a dialogue and wondered whether there was a possibility Sadat would change his attitude and refrain from signing the peace treaty. I answered that I did not believe that Sadat would rescind what he had agreed to at Camp David. I added, however, that we were facing one of two alternatives: either a complete alienation between Egypt and the Arab countries which would adversely affect both Egypt and the Arab countries, or an attempt to reduce the harm already done, through a dialogue which might help Sadat to cling more tenaciously to the comprehensive solution he had advocated early on at Camp David.

On the morning of 4 November, a meeting confined to heads of delegations and the Secretary-General of the Arab League took place to discuss the role of the delegation. The majority view was that no dialogue was relevant after the signing of Camp David, and consequently it was decided that a delegation, headed by the

Lebanese Prime Minister and comprising ministers from the Emirates, Iraq and Syria, would appeal to Sadat to revoke Camp David.

On the evening of the same day Sadat was addressing the People's Assembly; he remarked that he had heard in news bulletins that the Baghdad Meeting, without prior consultation, had sent a delegation to meet him and that it was already on its way to Cairo but that he would not receive it. The delegation, consequently, returned to Baghdad the same day without performing its mission.

The Meeting at Baghdad therefore turned to the painful decision, whether to suspend Egypt's membership of the Arab League and transfer the Arab League's seat from Cairo. During private conversations I was able to sense the perplexity of some and the grief and anguish of others. One delegate expressed himself in the following terms: Egypt's leading role in the Arab world was of far greater dimension than that of the Soviet Union among the Eastern bloc or the US in the Western world for, while the two superpowers maintained their leadership in their respective worlds by virtue of their military power, Egypt achieved her leadership in the Arab world by virtue of a common heritage and her great cultural and political contributions both in the past and during the present century. Her revolution against British imperialism in 1919 and the leading role of Nasser against foreign control had inspired the Arab countries and had offered an example and lent impetus to countries of the Third World that were struggling for their independence.

From my side, I tried to keep open a line of communication between Egypt and the rest of the Arab countries by proposing that, while every Arab country had the right to express its views on Camp David in any manner it saw fit, by either freezing or severing its relations with Egypt, Egypt's membership of the Arab League should be maintained, although League meetings could take place outside Cairo, as had happened within the Organization of African Unity which was meeting at the time away from its headquarters at Addis Ababa. I strived hard to maintain this relationship, for nothing was more painful to me than the severance of Egypt from the body of the Arab nation, representing the final dissolution of all the efforts of my political career to uphold unity of Arab action.

After long deliberations the Meeting issued a number of

resolutions, the most heartaching of which was the suspension of Egypt's membership in the Arab League and the transfer of the seat of the Arab League. The resolution also declared Camp David to be in contradiction to the resolutions of the Arab Summits in Algiers and Rabat and judged that the Agreements concluded at Camp David did not lead to the just peace sought by the Arab nation; consequently they were rejected and so were all their political, economic and legal consequences. Moreover, the Summit decided to extend financial support over a period of ten years to Syria, Jordan and the PLO to the tune of $3,500 million: Syria to receive $1,850 million, Jordan $1,250 million and the PLO $250 million. $150 million were also earmarked for the support of Palestinian perseverance in the occupied territories. It was hoped that such financial support by the Arab oil-producing countries for the Eastern Front would correct the imbalance of power caused by Egypt leaving the confrontation with Israel.

The resolutions adopted at the Baghdad Summit stipulated adherence to the Palestinian issue inasmuch as it represented the core of the Arab–Israeli conflict, and no party had the right to concede this basic commitment. The peace sought by the Arabs rested on the total liberation of all territories occupied by Israel since 1967, including Jerusalem; and a pledge was given to restore the national rights of the Palestinian people, including the establishment of a Palestinian State under the leadership of the PLO.

The Heads of State invited Egypt to forgo the Camp David Agreements and to refrain from signing a peace treaty with Israel. Once Egypt responded to this invitation, it would be invited to return to its natural position in the unified Arab ranks, whereupon it would be the duty of the other Arab countries to resume support for it and shoulder its financial burdens within the framework decided by the Baghdad Summit for the consolidation of the confrontation countries. However, once Egypt signed the peace treaty with Israel, not only would its membership in the Arab League be suspended and the seat of the Arab League be transferred from Cairo, but also the Arab Ministers of Foreign Affairs would meet in Baghdad to adopt the measures necessary to safeguard the interests of the Arab nation in all fields, including the application of boycott measures against Egyptian companies, institutions and persons who dealt directly or indirectly with Israel.

On 2 February 1979 the second Camp David talks began between Moshe Dayan and Dr Mustapha Khalil, the Egyptian Prime Minister, and with Vance present, in order to reach the final draft of the Treaty.

Carter arrived in Cairo on 8 March and addressed the People's Assembly; he promised a comprehensive settlement and honouring the rights of the Palestinian people, but he failed to get the Israelis to accept either and, on his way back, he stopped at Cairo airport to speak about the necessity of defining the basic elements in the Peace Treaty between Egypt and Israel.

Sadat left for Washington and signed the Peace Treaty with the Israeli Prime Minister on 26 March. It conformed to the principles stipulated in the Camp David Framework for Peace. However, the Israeli side managed to introduce a new principle in Article Six which practically cancelled Egypt's Arab commitments through its membership of the Arab League and the Arab Joint Defence Agreement. When the Egyptian delegation tried to correct this by inserting an interpretation in the appendix of the Treaty that would reconcile her contradictory obligations, the result was only a re-statement of Article Six which read 'the Parties undertake to fulfil in good faith their obligations under this Treaty, without regard to action or inaction of any other Party and independently of any instrument external to this Treaty' which, in practical terms, meant that if either Jordan or Syria was attacked by Israel, Egypt would have no right to extend support or assistance to either. The content of this particular item had been conveyed by Israel to Egypt through Jarring as early as 1971.

On the same day that witnessed the signing of the Peace Treaty by Egypt and Israel, the US signed a 'US–Israel Memorandum of Agreement', which included the US undertaking, in the case of a violation or threat of violation of the Treaty of Peace (assumed in the context of this memorandum to be against Israel), 'such remedial measures as it deems appropriate, which may include diplomatic, economic and military measures'. The following item elaborated on the nature of these measures in the words: 'The United States will provide support it deems appropriate for proper actions taken by Israel in response to such demonstrated violations of the Treaty of Peace.' In fact, the US will 'be prepared to consider, on an urgent basis, such measures as the strengthening of the United States' presence in the area, the providing of emergency supplies to Israel and the exercise of maritime rights in order to put an end to the violation'. There was even more: 'The United States will oppose and, if necessary, vote against any action or resolution in the United Nations, which in its judgement adversely affects the Treaty of Peace', and finally the US will endeavour to be responsive to the military and economic assistance requirements of Israel. The US further pledged that it would not only refuse to supply weapons to parties that could use them against Israel but would not supply or authorize the transfer of such weapons from third parties for use in an armed attack against Israel.

All these obligations that the US undertook on behalf of Israel came as an unpleasant surprise to Sadat, whose Prime Minister was handed a copy by the US Ambassador the day previous to its signing without prior consultations with Egypt. In view of the seriousness of these hostile pledges, the Prime Minister of Egypt promptly dispatched a message to Vance before the Memorandum could be signed, communicating Egypt's dismay and grave concern over the contents of the Memorandum. While Egypt had accepted that the role of the US was that of a complete partner in the Peace Treaty, by virtue of this document the US had assumed the role of arbiter in determining whether there has been a violation or threat of violation, despite the presence of an article in the Treaty that provided for the settlement of disputes, which was nullified by the present US pledge to Israel. The Prime Minister wrote in addition: 'You have given Israel a commitment to take such remedial measures and to provide appropriate support for proper actions taken by Israel in response to violations of the Treaty. We consider such a commitment exceedingly dangerous as it binds the United States to acquiesce in action taken by Israel, however arbitrary, under the pretext that certain violations have taken place.' The letter concluded that Egypt believed the Memorandum to be detrimental to the peace process and did not consider itself bound by it.

The Egyptian Prime Minister sent another letter the following day, maintaining that the Memorandum would affect the whole process of peace and stability in the area adversely and he therefore rejected it for the following reasons: the contents of the Memorandum were based on alleged accusations against Egypt and provided for certain measures to be taken against her in the hypothetical case of violation, the determination of which was largely left to Israel; the US was supposed to be a partner in a tripartite effort to achieve peace, not to support the allegations of one side against the other or to assume that Egypt was the side liable to violate its obligations; the Memorandum could be construed as an eventual alliance between the US and Israel against Egypt. It offered the US rights that were neither mentioned nor negotiated with Egypt, and empowered the US to impose punitive measures, which raised doubts about future relations and could affect the situation in the whole region; and it gave the US the right to impose a military presence in the region for reasons agreed between Israel and the US. This was a matter Egypt could not accept; in fact, it cast grave doubts concerning the real intention of the US since it could be accused of collaborating with Israel to create such circumstances as would lead to an American military presence in the area, a matter which would certainly have serious implications, especially on stability in the whole area, and could lead to other alliances to counter this one.

This military alliance that emerged between the US and Israel represented the apex of the success of Israeli diplomacy. The US was now not merely involved in safeguarding the security of Israel; it was posing threats to Egypt's security at a time when Egypt lacked any guarantees in this direction. It also became obvious that the Peace Treaty had become the context for imposing a US military presence in the area and imposing restrictions on the sale of weapons to the Arab countries.

The harsh terms in which the two letters from Egypt were couched were expressive of the degree of Egypt's disappointment in the US position which had descended to the level of duplicity and double-dealing. The Memorandum was explicit in projecting the policy that is being applied in the region at present which, while it continues to support Israel militarily and economically, works towards extending its military presence.

Egypt's rejection of the document did not stand in the way of its implementation, however. Isolated both in the Arab world and internationally, Egypt was unable to oppose this Israeli–US military alliance. On 26 March Sadat and Begin signed a document entitled 'The Complementary Agreement on the Establishment of the Palestinian Self-Governing Authority With Full

Autonomy in the West Bank and Gaza Strip,' in which they invited Jordan to participate in negotiations for the implement-ation of the provisions relating to the West Bank and Gaza in the Framework for Peace signed at Camp David. In the event of Jordan deciding not to do so, the negotiations would be held by Israel and Egypt.

Jordan did refuse and consequently Egypt undertook to con-duct these negotiations alone, in spite of the categorical rejection by the Arab countries and the PLO, who reiterated that Egypt had absolutely no right to speak on behalf of the Palestinian people and was not empowered in its Treaty to accept the con-tinuation of Israeli occupation of the Palestinian territories.

After the Baghdad Summit I had decided to resign from my post as Secretary-General of the Arab League. Relations between Egypt and the Arab countries had collapsed, which rendered my commitment to promoting unity of Arab action no longer ten-able. I transmitted my letter of resignation to the Arab heads of State on 22 March 1979. In it I referred to the great pride I had taken in serving a cause I believed in all my life, long years before it became my sole responsibility as Secretary-General of the Arab League, namely Arab unity. Although I was aware that achieve-ment of this goal was not near at hand, at least a minimum of unity of Arab action should be achievable at all times. I had exerted every effort to maintain this minimum, but recent deve-lopments had rendered even that tiny amount unattainable; con-sequently I was unable to continue the mission I believed in and had tried to the best of my ability to achieve, and would request that my job be considered terminated as from the end of March 1979. When the Arab League Council met at Mogadishu on 24 March, I informed it of my resignation.

The Arab Ministers of Foreign Affairs and Ministers of Economy met in Baghdad on 27 March to decide upon the immediate withdrawal of Arab ambassadors from Egypt and to recommend the severance of political and diplomatic relations with Egypt within a month. They also reiterated the resolution for suspending Egypt's membership of the Arab League and the temporary transfer of its seat to Tunis. On the economic level, they decided that all loans or economic aid to the Egyptian government would cease and that boycott regulations would be applied to Egyptian companies dealing with Israel.

I was still at my office in the Arab League when I received these resolutions. It was a tragic day which I could never, in my wildest dreams, have imagined possible. I began to visualize the train of events that led to that sad day when the Arab countries announced the termination of Egypt's leading role and the Israeli flag was hoisted in Cairo, while Arab flags were taken down, when the question posed itself: why did Sadat finally agree to sign this separate treaty with Israel?

The answer has already been implied in the chain of events I have related. Sadat had forfeited all his levers for exerting pressure at the time of the Disengagement Agreement, and later during the Partial Agreement for Sinai. He decided thereafter to visit Jerusalem under the assumption that the visit, of itself, would convince Israel to give up all its demands which he conceived as motivated by concern for its security, what he termed its 'psychological barrier'; this barrier would disappear once he talked to the people of Israel from the rostrum of the Knesset, offering them Egypt's acceptance and an eternal peace.

When Israel persisted in rejecting his proposals for a comprehensive peace, he clung to Carter's bountiful promises, declaring that the US held ninety per cent of the trump cards, but ignoring the stark fact that the balance of power had turned decisively in favour of Israel. In the period between his acceptance of the ceasefire and his signing of the Treaty with Israel, Israel managed to acquire sweeping military superiority and to persuade the US to accept restraints on its Middle Eastern policies. Meanwhile, Egypt's relations with the Arab countries and the Soviet Union declined, leaving it with little, if anything, to fall back on.

When Sadat went to Camp David and submitted his project for peace – which was almost in conformity with US views on the subject – he felt certain that Carter would stand by him, only to discover to his dismay that Carter had no alternative but to go along with Israel's insistence of a separate treaty, with a promise to strive to complete it with future settlements on the other Arab fronts.

Sadat then had a choice of two courses: to declare his rejection and return to Cairo empty-handed after he had burnt his bridges with the Arab countries and the Soviet Union, the source of his arms and his political and economic support, or to sign whatever he could get. Consequently, he signed the Framework for Peace,

then the Peace Treaty with Israel. By the time he became acquainted with the terms of the Memorandum of Understanding
between the US and Israel and came to realize the extent of perfidy
and double-dealing it contained, he had reached the end of a road
of no-return. He protested and rejected it, but neither his protest
nor his rejection availed him anything or could change the new
map of relations between the countries of the region that had
already been masterminded by both the US and Israel. Egypt,
who had led the Arabs, had been the protagonist for the aspirations
of the Arab nation, had supported the liberation causes of the
Third World, had confronted the military alliances and refused the
establishment of military bases, was not isolated within its borders
while the US was busily working to establish its military presence
there. With the exit of Egypt, the largest Arab country, from the
consortium of nations that confronted Israeli ambitions, Israel was
posing new threats and dangers by almost daily incursions into
South Lebanon, threatening to attack Syria and casting greedy eyes
on the Arab Gulf area with its oil riches.

The inevitable conclusion must be that what had been achieved
was not a step towards peace, but towards further instability and
unrest and an invitation for renewed hostilities.

I therefore feel that this book, which set out to put on record
the development of the Arab–Israeli conflict and the Arab quest
for peace, has not ended. There are further chapters, still un-
written and still to be unfolded in time, of further events, clashes
and wars. Israel will not refrain, now that it has reached the
height of its military power, from continuing its policy of
threats, blackmail and expansion; the US will strive to establish
further its political and military control over the region.

It is probably high time that we realsed that the solution we beg
at the doors of the countries of the world is in fact in our own
hands, in the development of our own self-power and in the
closing of our ranks and that we ourselves hold the keys to the
solution; otherwise we will continue to wander in the labyrinth
of US–Israeli manoeuvres.

I am hopeful that this book will offer the younger generation
of Arabs a lesson, for they are our hope to resume the struggle for
a real and durable peace, a peace in which Israel will give up the
Arab territories under its control and will accept co-existence
with an independent State of Palestine.

Index